C000097589

THE
Frank Sinatra
FILM GUIDE

Daniel O'Brien

© Daniel O'Brien 1998

All rights reserved. No part of this publication
may be reproduced, in any form or by any
means, without permission from the publisher

Printed and bound in Great Britain by
Butler & Tanner Ltd, Frome and London
for the publishers
BT Batsford
583 Fulham Road
London
SW6 5BY

ISBN 0 7134 8418 7

A catalogue record for this book is available
from the British Library

Designed by DW Design Ltd, London

Acknowledgements

Grateful thanks to Jeremy Front, Anne Jackson,
Burt Kennedy, Gary Kramer, Mark Lonsdale, Ben
O'Brien, David O'Leary, Richard Reynolds, Tony
Sloman and Bud Yorkin. Thanks also to the people
at TLA Video, Philadelphia and Portswood Library,
Southampton.

Illustrations: Stills from *Step Lively*, *Double
Dynamite*, *Not as a Stranger* and *Pal Joey* courtesy
of Gary Kramer and Jerry Ohlinger. Tony
Bill/Nancy Sinatra *Marriage on the Rocks* still sup-
plied by Flashbacks. All other illustrations supplied
by the British Film Institute Stills, Posters and
Designs department. All photographs originally
issued as publicity material by copyright holders
RKO (*Higher and Higher*, *Step Lively*, *The Miracle
of the Bells*, *Double Dynamite*); MGM (*Anchors
Aweigh*, *It Happened in Brooklyn*, *The Kissing
Bandit*, *Take Me Out to the Ball Game*, *On the
Town*, *The Tender Trap*, *High Society*, *Some Came
Running*, *Never So Few*, *Dirty Dingus Magee*);
Universal (*Meet Danny Wilson*); Columbia (*From
Here to Eternity*, *Pal Joey*, *The Devil at 4 O'Clock*);
United Artists (*Suddenly*, *Not as a Stranger*, *The
Man With the Golden Arm*, *Johnny Concho*, *The
Pride and the Passion*, *Kings Go Forth*, *A Hole in
the Head*, *Sergeants 3*, *The Manchurian Candidate*);
Warner (*Young at Heart*, *Ocean's 11*, *4 for Texas*,
Robin and the 7 Hoods, *None But the Brave*,
Marriage on the Rocks, *The Naked Runner*);
Samuel Goldwyn (*Guys and Dolls*); Paramount (*The
Joker is Wild*, *Come Blow Your Horn*, *Assault on a
Queen*); Twentieth Century-Fox (*Can Can*, *Von
Ryan's Express*, *Tony Rome*, *The Detective*, *Lady in
Cement*); Filmways (*The First Deadly Sin*).

Contents

INTRODUCTION

Why has Sinatra not developed the professional pride in his movies that he takes in his recordings?
Pauline Kael

I made some pretty good pictures... and I tried a few things that turned out to be mistakes...
Frank Sinatra

Frank Sinatra is one of the cinema's great enigmas. Throughout the strange and murky history of motion pictures, few major stars have enjoyed as uneasy a relationship with the film industry, both as popular art form and profit-driven production line. The man variously known as The Voice, The Boss, Chairman of the Board, The Pope and several less flattering epithets appeared in 56 feature-length films, yet for many he barely qualifies as a film star of the first rank and some would argue that Sinatra never really earned his movie spurs at all. From his co-starring debut in the wafer-thin RKO musical *Higher and Higher* (1943) to his belated comeback/farewell performance in the downbeat policier *The First Deadly Sin* (1980), there is a near constant question mark hanging over Sinatra's big-screen career. Why should a phenomenally successful singer - regarded by even his detractors as probably the number one popular entertainer of the twentieth century - take valuable time out from recording and live performances to work in a medium he frequently confessed to finding tedious and frustrating on largely mediocre projects. True, it took a cannily chosen supporting role in *From Here to Eternity* (1953) to relaunch Sinatra's utterly moribund career during the early 1950s, yet in comparison to his renewed singing success, first with Capitol Records, then on his own Reprise label, his second coming as a film star proved a bumpy ride, with only *The Man With the Golden Arm* (1955) and *The Manchurian Candidate* (1962) enjoying widespread acclaim. Three hits out of 44 starring roles is a poor average, reflecting only too clearly the popular

perception of Sinatra's film work as a secondary, largely uninspired spin-off from his far more considerable musical career. Daughter Nancy describes her father as 'a phenomenon of life, a force of nature', but how many self-respecting phenomena seek out guest roles in *Cannonball Run II*?

This take on Sinatra the film star is, however, utterly bogus, a piece of self-perpetuating mythology bearing as much relation to the facts as the contrasting depictions of Sinatra the man as either flawed saint or whimsically beneficent monster. Leaving aside his numerous and largely negligible cameo/guest appearances, Frank Sinatra's body of film work is as varied, impressive and rewarding as that of any other top Hollywood star, including Sinatra's two 'golden age' heroes - and friends - Humphrey Bogart and Spencer Tracy. Progressing from the amiable, awkward, girl-shy dreamer of his early musicals to the beat-up, world-weary law enforcer of his last major work, Sinatra at his best brought charisma, presence and unquestionable acting ability to the screen, not to mention an unsurpassed singing voice. It is undeniable that he had at least his share of disappointments, compromises and outright flops. Anyone passing a Sunday afternoon sitting through *Can Can* (1960), *4 for Texas* (1963) or *Marriage on the Rocks* (1965) would be fully justified in wondering why Sinatra bothered to show up for filming. Sinatra's apathetic performances in these films suggest he felt the same way. His behaviour, both on set and on location, at times left a great deal to be desired, whether as a result of temperament or power-play, often suggesting an emotional development largely arrested during early adolescence. Even in a better mood, Sinatra's tendency to treat his more lightweight vehicles as a chance for a good time with his buddies yielded unremarkable results, with laziness and self-indulgence emerging triumphant. But to damn a star for his failures and ignore the successes is neither illuminating nor fair. The Humphrey Bogart revered as a supreme movie icon is the hard-boiled/soft-hearted anti-hero of *The Maltese Falcon*, *Casablanca*, *The Big Sleep* and *The African Queen*, not the uneasy, miscast leading man of *Passage to Marseilles*,

The Two Mrs Carrolls, *Tokyo Joe* or *The Left Hand of God*. Similarly, the Frank Sinatra to watch and admire is not to be found in asinine musicals or dumb comedies but in *Suddenly* (1954), as a psychotic hired killer; *Young at Heart* (1954), as a failed composer with an apparent death wish; *Some Came Running* (1958), as a war veteran and burned-out writer, or *The Detective* (1968), as an ageing, unhappy cop faced with the failure of both his marriage and his career. In these and numerous other roles, Sinatra carved himself a niche in cinema history that amounts to far more than prancing about in a sailor suit for MGM, picking up an admittedly undeserved Academy Award for *Eternity*, and playing crooks, cowboys and gangsters with his Clan friends. If there is an element of wastage or disappointment to his film career, it is one endemic to the entire Hollywood machine, both during and after the studio system era. Movies have always been a percentage game and Sinatra scored better than most.

First glimpsed on the big screen as early as 1935 (in black-face), Frank Sinatra began his movie career proper in his capacity as *the* hottest new singing star of 1942 and probably the first teenage idol ever. Having wowed a 5,000-strong audience during his first solo stage appearance at New York's Paramount Theatre, Sinatra rapidly became too big a phenomenon for Hollywood to ignore. The initial response was cautious, however, indicating some wariness on the part of studio bosses as to what exactly Sinatra could do in a film and how long audiences would pay to see him do it. Three recent bit appearances as a straight singer - two as part of the Tommy Dorsey Band, one as a solo artist - revealed little more than a potent light baritone voice, pleasantly unremarkable boy-next-door looks and an impressive talent for injecting lyrics with a real sense of feeling. Fine for singing spots but hardly surefire leading man material. A further drawback to Sinatra as a screen property was the nature of his pre-existing audience, largely teenage girls, which virtually guaranteed him a fairly brief shelf-life as a top attraction. Adolescents have a way of growing up and moving on and the next generation always finds new heroes of its own. There

was the possibility that Sinatra might catch on with the wider film-going public but this involved a serious gamble on untested talent that few were prepared to make, especially given the mutterings from older generation spokesmen that Sinatra was a bad influence on the nation's youth, contributing to the growing rate of truancy and delinquency.

So it came to pass that second-division outfit RKO decided to take a chance on Sinatra and put him in two speedily shot musical comedies, *Higher and Higher* and *Step Lively* (1944), in the hope of exploiting his popularity while it was at a peak. Deservedly mediocre box-office receipts revealed a slight flaw in RKO's cynical game plan, and it was Sinatra's still-flourishing record sales and sell-out concerts rather than any new-found movie appeal that prompted MGM to first request the singer on a loan-out basis and then buy out his contract altogether. Studio boss Louis Mayer was also a sucker for Sinatra's rendition of the *Showboat* standard 'Ol' Man River', a factor which helped keep the singer in Mayer's favour until the end of the decade.

Dressed up in a dark blue sailor suit, teamed with Gene Kelly and photographed in gaudy Technicolor, Sinatra's MGM starring debut in *Anchors Aweigh* (1945) brought him his first movie hit, plus a highly lucrative contract with the studio guaranteeing $1.5 million over a five-year period. The film itself was a cumbersome series of flimsily linked - and highly variable - set pieces which came to life only when Sinatra sang or Kelly danced, though sadly not together, neither able to match the other's level of ability in their respective fields. From this high point, Sinatra's Hollywood career took an almost immediate downturn, gradual but inexorable. Rapidly acquiring a reputation for being late on set, then throwing star tantrums once he'd actually turned up, Sinatra's after-hours behaviour soon became a far more considerable headache for his bosses. Rumours of extra-marital liaisons with MGM starlets Marilyn Maxwell and Lana Turner filled the gossip columns. Right-wing newspapers attacked Sinatra for his too-liberal politics - accusing him of communist sympathies - and alleged Mafia connections. All this could have amounted to

Anchors Aweigh. Sinatra crowds Gene Kelly and Kathryn Grayson.

naught had Sinatra continued to draw the cinema crowds, but of his eight starring vehicles released during the 1940s, only two - *Anchors Aweigh* and *On the Town* (1949) - were hits, while a ninth, the dreary RKO comedy *Double Dynamite*, was shelved for nearly three years. Having gambled a considerable amount of time, money, patience and damage limitation on Sinatra, MGM found that their investment simply wasn't paying off.

Sinatra's fall from grace at MGM offers an intriguing chicken/egg situation: did he falter at the box-office because the studio placed him in sub-standard vehicles - *The Kissing Bandit* (1948) being the most notorious - or did MGM give Sinatra second-rate material because they rapidly discovered that without Gene Kelly at his side audiences just didn't want to know. Certainly, the overall quality of Sinatra's first decade in movies is not terribly inspiring: largely fatuous musicals whose occasional bursts of imagination or energy fail to compensate for

absurd plot lines and indifferent handling. After the crunch year of 1947, which saw Sinatra losing his teen following to young pretenders Eddie Fisher, Frankie Laine, Johnnie Ray and Tony Martin, and being threatened with prosecution over a public punch-up with journalist Lee Mortimer, not even the critical and commercial success of *On the Town* could save him. In any event, the return of the men in sailor suits proved to be almost entirely Gene Kelly's show, a triumph for the film's co-star, co-choreographer and co-director which left Sinatra largely reduced to a support act. Arguably the most interesting of Sinatra's 1940s efforts is the RKO production *The Miracle of the Bells* (1947), a bizarre necrophiliac fantasy featuring the star's first straight(ish) dramatic performance as the beatific Father Paul, the Catholic priest who knows all. Having taken his amiable but shy boy/sailor/bandit-next-door persona about as far as it could go, Sinatra needed some sort of a break.

Critics mocked, audiences stayed away in greater numbers than ever and MGM hurriedly shoved Sinatra back into musicals, hoping to erase his first half-decent acting role from the public consciousness.

Sinatra's longevity as a film presence is in many ways deceptive. While his on-screen career covers nearly half a century, he enjoyed barely 15 years as a steady box-office draw, from his much hyped comeback in *Eternity* - surely one of the most impressive resurrections in the history of popular culture - to his last 1960s hit with the cheerfully cynical private eye mystery *Lady in Cement* (1968). During this period he made the most of his opportunities, appearing in thrillers, musical dramas, medical soap operas, musical romances, intense character dramas, westerns, epics, war films, satirical comedy, caper movies, disaster movies, comedy westerns and broad comedies of manners. Not all of these took the public fancy, and there were a couple of dodgy patches during the 1960s when Sinatra appeared to be selecting projects to test his fans' loyalty - *Assault on a Queen*, for example. Grilled at the time, he protested that the good scripts simply weren't there; other accounts suggest that he simply wasn't looking for them.

The emphasis placed on *Eternity* in any account of Sinatra's film career can be similarly misleading. While valuable beyond all measure for relaunching him as both a bankable star and a serious dramatic actor, the film is by no means Sinatra's best, nor his own performance as downtrodden yet unbreakable GI Angelo Maggio among his strongest. Sinatra's instinctive grasp of the character plus extensive on-the-job coaching from co-star Montgomery Clift combined to produce a highly competent supporting performance, yet he has scant screen-time and the film itself, while astutely cast and well-crafted, is a superficial, sanitised and ultimately rather sour reduction of the original James Jones bestseller. Academy Award hype aside, there is a stronger case for pointing to Sinatra's subsequent film, *Suddenly*, as the real beginning of his acting renaissance, his chillingly unsympathetic portrayal of a would-be presidential assassin drawing some deserved praise but little audience response. Sinatra himself cited his career

Meet Danny Wilson – a garishly fictionalised biopic of Sinatra

doldrums-era performance in the self-exploiting musical drama *Meet Danny Wilson* (1951) as his real acting debut, but neither script nor direction gave him enough to make a convincing case. Throughout the remainder of the 1950s, Sinatra could be relied upon to deliver an effective star performance even if the overall film proved to be flawed, as with *Kings Go Forth* (1958), or downright terrible, as with *Not as a Stranger* (1955). His much maligned and mocked performance as a Spanish guerrilla leader in the underrated Napoleonic drama *The Pride and the Passion* (1957) is by no means the embarrassment of reputation and stands, at the very least, as an honourable failure. It wasn't until the 1960s and *Can Can* that a discernible element of indifference, not to say outright boredom, began to creep into some of Sinatra's lesser work. The party atmosphere of the Clan films tended to undermine the discipline necessary to effective movie-making and Sinatra's lack of affinity for brash comedy became all too evident in films such as *Come Blow Your Horn* (1963) and *Marriage on the Rocks*. Long-standing rumours that Sinatra just didn't care about his films anymore took on gradually more force and following the back-on-track tough guy trilogy that culminated in *Lady in Cement*, the by now veteran actor would star in only two more movies, the misfiring comedy western *Dirty Dingus Magee* (1970) - a film so little regarded not even its director possesses a copy - and the honourable last bow *The First Deadly Sin*, a commercial and critical disappointment.

The case against Sinatra the film star has tended to focus on the accusation of wasted talent rather than no talent at all. An Academy Award and a further nomination - for *Golden Arm* - are difficult to dismiss, even if one regards the whole Oscar industry as an upmarket cattle show or incestuous pat-on-the-back. Over the years, numerous friends and colleagues of Sinatra publicly expressed the feeling that if only he would make the effort and take his film career with appropriate seriousness, he could be one of the best, if not the new King of Hollywood. Bogart, who numbered Sinatra among his very few close actor friends, felt the singer lacked the maturity and dedication necessary to translate his raw talent into a first rate movie career. Billy Wilder, a self-professed devotee of both the artist and the man, claimed he could never risk hiring Sinatra for a film, fearing all the while that the latter would simply lose interest and sneak off with his latest girlfriend: 'I'm afraid he would run after the first take.' Stanley Kramer, producer-director on the troubled productions of *Not as a Stranger* and *The Pride and the Passion*, put it more bluntly: 'If Sinatra really prepared for a role, researched it, he'd be the greatest actor in the world.' Even Shirley MacLaine, who got an early career break opposite Sinatra in *Some Came Running*, lamented her co-star's dislike of rehearsals and multiple takes: 'He feels polishing might make him stagnant'. MacLaine also put forward the theory that some deep-rooted fear of failure held Sinatra back from giving his best to most performances, providing him with the handy get-out clause that, should his work be criticised, he could

always riposte with the claim that he hadn't really been trying. This holds some water in the case of films such as *Can Can* - which co-stars MacLaine at her most teeth-grindingly shrill - or *Sergeants 3*, but evaporates with a film like *The Manchurian Candidate*, a hugely controversial project that only made it to the screen thanks to Sinatra's determination.

Sinatra's notorious impatience with the process of film-making - manifested as early as *Step Lively* - certainly caused serious friction on a number of his films. Directors, co-stars and technicians who did not share his enthusiasm or flair for fast, spontaneous work rapidly found themselves at odds with the man. In one of the more famous Sinatra incidents, the star allegedly stopped work mid-take during the production of *Young at Heart* and demanded that the film's Academy Award-winning director of photography be replaced with a cameraman who could work faster. How much this attitude was due to an irreconcilable clash of legitimate working methods and how much sheer impatience and laziness on Sinatra's part is difficult to determine. Several of his later films have an over-casual, under-written and under-rehearsed feel, indicating a star anxious to be elsewhere once an acceptable take was in the can. It is undeniably the case that a number of Sinatra films - *Meet Danny Wilson*, *The Pride and the Passion*, *The Naked Runner* (1967) - were never completed as intended owing to their star's refusal to shoot all the required scenes (largely a result of location boredom or private-life angst). On the other hand, the justly famous cold-turkey sequence in *Golden Arm* was filmed in one take with no prior rehearsal and remains one of Sinatra's most impressive scenes. As a rule, if the material was good and the director, cast and crew sympathetic to Sinatra's approach, the results could be outstanding.

Another potential stumbling block for Sinatra's claim to screen greatness is his comparative dearth of credits with the more acclaimed Hollywood film-makers. Leaving aside his late 1940s work with the then brand new creative team of Gene Kelly and Stanley Donen, Sinatra starred or co-starred under the direction of Fred Zinnemann (*Eternity*); Joseph L. Mankiewicz (*Guys and*

Sinatra in The Man With the Golden Arm –
desperate to kick his heroin addiction

Dolls); Otto Preminger (*Golden Arm*); Vincente Minnelli
(*Some Came Running*); Frank Capra (*A Hole in the
Head*); John Frankenheimer (*The Manchurian
Candidate*) and Robert Aldrich (*4 for Texas*). Even from
these seven collaborations, only the films with Preminger,
Minnelli and Frankenheimer are truly first rate. *Eternity*
is highly polished schlock; *Guys and Dolls* is an over-
produced, overblown mishmash of a musical with only
one effective scene; *Hole* is a pleasant but curiously
underwhelming comedy and *Texas* is unspeakable.
Stanley Kramer and John Sturges could also be included
in this modest pantheon, especially given their successful
work with Sinatra - Sturges on the war drama *Never So
Few* (1959), but with quantity comes also a drop in
quality. Kramer, famed for his liberal dramas of social
conscience and responsibility, usually merited points for

effort rather than achievement and Sturges' well-earned
reputation as a top action director plummeted after the
early 1960s. In any event, all this really tells us is that
powerful stars and powerful directors do not always
make for compatible bedfellows. Nor can Sinatra be
singled out as the one reason several of these films failed.
Zinnemann was an art-house director badly in need of a
commercial hit when he worked with the star, Capra a
faded talent in noticeable decline, and both Mankiewicz
and Aldrich were attempting to tackle genres for which
they had no affinity whatsoever.

Of more interest is the fact that, despite his activities
as a film producer from the mid-1950s, Sinatra
assembled relatively few regular film collaborators from
any field over the years. This is in marked contrast to his
singing career, where he enjoyed long and fruitful

partnerships with lyricist Sammy Cahn, composers Jule Styne and Jimmy Van Heusen and conductor-arrangers Axel Stordahl, Nelson Riddle, Gordon Jenkins and Billy May, all of whom were recruited for Sinatra movies with varying success. A glance through the star's film credits offers up producer Howard Koch (six Sinatra movies), director Gordon Douglas (five) plus cameramen William H. Daniels (eleven) and Joseph Biroc (five). With regard to Sinatra's fellow actors, apart from the MGM-dictated partnership with Gene Kelly, it's basically just his fellow Clansman Peter Lawford (four); Dean Martin (seven); Sammy Davis Jr (three) and Joey Bishop (two), plus honorary Clan 'mascot' MacLaine (two and a half), tough-guy character actors Richard Conte (four) and Henry Silva (four) and fresh-faced juvenile Tony Bill (three). Cynical observers would claim that the brisk turnover of Sinatra co-workers is just one more reflection of his reputation for on-set moodiness and unpredictability. Alternatively, it can be reasonably argued that, despite the numerous Sinatra-controlled film

Directing **None But the Brave?**

production companies - Kent, Essex, SinCap, Dorchester, SAM, Artanis, Sinatra Enterprises, the star never felt a pressing need to become a one-man film factory. Lucrative movie deals, notably with United Artists during the 1950s and Warner Brothers during the 1960s, gave Sinatra a level of control, both financial and creative, he evidently felt to be sufficient.

Of course, there is one substantial skeleton in Sinatra's movie-making closet. His 1960 attempt to take more hands-on artistic control over his work, turning director with the controversial project *The Execution of Private Slovik*, resulted in one of the most humiliating fiascos of Sinatra's entire career, with the film abandoned and Sinatra's position as untouchable superstar badly shaken. His one subsequent film as director, the flawed but intriguing anti-war drama *None But the Brave* (1965) showed him to be up to the task but lacking the necessary commitment and passion for further work as a producer-director-star. If there is one genuine might-have-been element to the star's film career, it's Sinatra the auteur, despite considerable assistance on *Brave* from regular collaborator Gordon Douglas.

One final point worth making with regard to Sinatra's position as a legitimate film star is the way he transcended the standard downward-spiral career pattern of the popular singer turned film performer. Bing Crosby, Sinatra's inspiration, rival and friend, enjoyed a lengthy sojourn in movies which largely boils down to the little-remembered *Rhythm* series of the 1930s/40s; the popular, if less than classic *Road* films with Bob Hope and Dorothy Lamour, and his first two appearances as a jovial priest in *Going My Way* and *The Bells of St Mary's*. True, he also played a more dramatic role, an alcoholic ex-singer, in *The Country Girl*, but the film itself is mediocre and Crosby failed to pursue this new direction. Sinatra buddy Dean Martin, freed from the shackles of Jerry Lewis, notched up impressive starring performances in *The Young Lions*, *Some Came Running*, *Rio Bravo*, *Bells Are Ringing* and *Kiss Me Stupid* but spent too much of his movie career in lacklustre westerns, feeble comedies - several at Sinatra's invitation - and the dreary Matt Helm spy spoofs. Elvis Presley,

The Detective – exploiting the new tolerance and appetite for graphic violence.

having displayed real star power in *Jailhouse Rock* and *King Creole*, found his promising film career fatally compromised with a slew of lighter-than-air musical fluff. Barbra Streisand, the one singer-actor since Sinatra to achieve real long-term Hollywood power and substantial film roles, has largely scuppered her movie career via bloated egotism and meagre output, making each new Streisand production an 'event' to be revered by her fans and spat on by her detractors. Even in his most arduous and valued performances for *Golden Arm* and *Manchurian Candidate*, Frank Sinatra was never a show-off star. Indeed, his most enduring movie persona is that of the heroic loser, the tough-tender man of integrity who values honour and true friendship above material success and social standing. Time and again he loses the woman he loves - or thinks he loves - whether to his best friend or comrade-in-arms (*Anchors Aweigh, It Happened in Brooklyn, Meet Danny Wilson, The Pride and the Passion, Kings Go Forth*), an ex-husband (*Tony Rome*), an ex-boyfriend's bullet (*Some Came Running*), terminal illness (*The First Deadly Sin*) or his own moral choice (*The Devil at 4 O'Clock, The Detective*). He throws away years of loyal service to a hallowed institution when he realises that continued success is dependent on him embracing a corrupt or unjust system (*Never So Few, The Detective, The First Deadly Sin*). Sinatra also has a strong track record of dying in his films - at a rate few contemporary stars would consider wise - in ways tragic (*From Here to Eternity*), heroic (*The Pride and the Passion, The Devil at 4 O'Clock, Von Ryan's Express*) and much deserved (*Suddenly*). The fresh-faced gimmick co-star of *Higher and Higher* became both a charismatic leading man and an actor determined to test his powers and risk his star image. What more could be asked?

1

Teen Rage

1943-1944

HIGHER AND HIGHER 1943

It's for you. Name of Sinatra.
Mickey the maid

On 30 December 1942 Francis Albert Sinatra made his debut as a solo performer at New York's Paramount Theatre. Having paid his dues with stints among the ranks of Major Edward Bowes and his *Original Amateur Hour* artistes, the Harry James Orchestra and the Tommy Dorsey Band, the 27-year-old Italian-American from Hoboken, New Jersey, stood before a 5,000-strong audience and delivered a knock-out performance. On 12 August 1943, Sinatra arrived at Pasadena Station, California to be greeted by 5,000 teenage fans as he made his way to Hollywood and the beginning of his film career as a fully fledged leading man. Stopping one station short of Los Angeles to avoid the expected throng, he found his plan backfiring, ending up trapped at the station for two hours while police cleared the crowds. A traumatic experience, perhaps, yet clear evidence that the fans who'd swooned over 'All Or Nothing At All' were just drooling in anticipation of their idol's new movie magic.

The box of tricks for this particular spellbinder came courtesy of the RKO Pictures Corporation, smallest of the major Hollywood studios and probably the least financially stable. The parent company, Radio-Keith-Orpheum, had bitten the dust in 1933 and its surviving subsidiary often looked like going the same way. Sinatra's solo guest appearance in the surprise-hit Columbia musical *Reveille with Beverly* (1942, see Appendix 1) had demonstrated his potential as a box-office draw and RKO needed all the audience pullers it could get its hands on. Negotiating through his appointed agents GAC (General Artists Corporation), a minor league version of MCA (Music Corporation of America), Sinatra signed a seven year deal with the studio which paid $25,000 for his first picture, with a cumulative 100 percent pay rise for each subsequent film, and allowed him one non-RKO film on loan-out per year. Sinatra later claimed that he'd never expected his first films for RKO to amount to much, and he was quite right. Devised by press agent cum manager George Evans as a shrewd form of portfolio diversification, the new film deal might at least broaden Sinatra's fan base, shifting a few more records and concert tickets.

Loosely based on a flop Broadway musical written

Higher and Higher - Sinatra marvels at Milly the Maid's (Michèle Morgan) transformation.

by the half famous team of Gladys Hurlbut and Joshua Logan, with one song contributed by the highly respected Richard Rodgers-Lorenz Hart duo, *Higher and Higher* hardly offered the most dazzling showcase for young Sinatra. For starters, he had no say in the songwriters, or songs, used for the film and had to be content with recruiting arranger Axel Stordahl - a fellow Dorsey veteran - as his one off-camera artistic decision. Aware of the original show's limitations, the studio requested an extra song, 'I Couldn't Sleep a Wink Last Night', for Sinatra from composer Jimmy McHugh and lyricist Harold Adamson, and hired writers William Bowers and Howard Harris to provide additional dialogue. Most of the latter duo's energy appears to have been spent devising feeble Sinatra in-jokes and the end result still smacks of utter mediocrity. The

non-Sinatra songs, including the Richard Rodgers-Lorenz Hart number 'Disgustingly Rich', are instantly forgettable and the choreography ploddingly unimaginative. The token storyline is flimsy to the point of non-existence, involving a group of enterprising servants attempting to restore their bankrupt employer's fortunes by passing one of the maids off as his marriage-hungry daughter. Indeed, one of the oddest aspects of the film is its failure to actually incorporate Sinatra into the plot. Appearing as a fictional version of himself, he is little more than a guest star, third-billed above the title with an 'and' to prefix his name. This is a pretty accurate listing as *Higher and Higher* is a film with a story, characters and Frank Sinatra singing a bit. Those of a more charitable disposition may attempt to make a case for it as a subversive satire on bourgeois pretensions and greed - not to mention socialist-style business enterprise - but a questionable subtext or two without an interesting surface isn't much of an attraction. Indeed, the idea of a meek young woman being manipulated into a loveless marriage to bail out her co-workers and useless boss is rather cold-blooded.

The production set-up for *Higher and Higher* was very much of the 'B' variety, using modest standing studio sets, crude back projection and no location work. Producer-director Tim Whelan had been a protégé of comedy star Harold Lloyd before departing for England in 1928 and directing several films for UK mogul Alexander Korda, notably *Q Planes* (1939) and approximately 20 percent of *The Thief of Bagdad* (1940). Returning to the United States in 1940, Whelan found his career experiencing a marked downslide - from *Thief of Bagdad* to *The Mad Doctor* (1941). Now an RKO regular, Whelan had recently worked as both producer and director on the studio's musical comedy *Seven Days' Leave* (1942), with Lucille Ball and Victor Mature, doing a competent enough job to be entrusted with the Sinatra assignment. *Seven Days' Leave* belongs in the category of cheery mediocrity and *Higher* represented no great improvement. The direction is unimaginative, often static, with much use of medium shots, and Whelan allows his cast to overplay, emphasising the material's stage origins with little concession to the film medium. Unlike his director, cameraman Robert De Grasse had worked on a number of 'A' list RKO productions - *Stage Door*, *Bachelor Mother*, *Kitty Foyle* - and would photograph all four of Sinatra's feature films for the studio.

Filming began in mid-August 1943, lasting eight weeks. Sinatra's top-billed co-stars were the decidedly odd-couple combination of French actress Michèle Morgan and comedian Jack Haley, who'd already attained his career peak as Tin Man in *The Wizard of Oz* (1939). Morgan had first come to international attention looking soulful in a beret and raincoat in Marcel Carne's *Quai des Brumes* (1938). Impressed by Morgan's performance in the latter, top American agent Charles Feldman arranged a contract with RKO. The studio had little idea what to do with her, first buying the rights to the Eric Ambler thriller *Journey Into Fear* as a career-launching showcase for Morgan, then giving her role to Dolores del Rio. If *Higher and Higher* was intended as some kind of consolation prize, Morgan must have been mightily unimpressed. Badly miscast as Milly the dowdy scullery maid, she handles her flat dialogue with commendable professionalism most of the time, but the character's supposedly touching innocence borders on the dim-witted and the result is embarrassing (her singing isn't great either). The outcome of her apparently unrequited love for valet Mike O'Brien (Haley) is predictable from frame one and the clothes and hairstyle provided for Morgan's scenes posing as a high society debutante do her no favours. The more assured supporting cast included former Ziegfeld star Leon Errol, an implausibly rubber-faced Australian comic with an amusing walk and a severe drink problem. His role as dissolute yet loveable drunkard Mr Drake probably required little in the way of major acting. Sinatra was given a tentative love interest in the form of starlet Barbara Hale, and musical/comedy back-up from Victor Borge, Mel Torme and Dooley Wilson, who'd played it again in *Casablanca* the previous year.

As for Sinatra himself, the novice actor is really the best thing in *Higher and Higher*, despite RKO's nervous,

self-conscious treatment of him. Approximately 25 minutes into the film, there is a knock on the front door of Drake's residence. Drake's junior maid Mickey (Marcy McGuire) answers and in the doorway stands Sinatra. He delivers his first ever line of dialogue: 'Good morning. My name is Frank Sinatra' and the lovestruck maid faints into his arms. He has that effect. Dressed in a casual yet smart jacket, with bow tie, slicked-back hair and flowers for Milly, this 'Frank Sinatra' is a wholesome, clean-cut version designed for easy public consumption (no hot temper, shady friends or rampant extra-marital libido here). Sensibly underplaying his lines, Sinatra projects a pleasant manner, his appealing ordinariness underlined by his slight build, prominent ears, pointy chin, large lower lip and generously sized nose - not a million miles away from the sad-monkey looks of Fred Astaire or Stan Laurel. His only connection to the plot at this point is that close neighbour Sinatra often waves to Milly from across the courtyard and is concerned about not seeing her for the past few days. He then launches into 'I Couldn't Sleep...', accompanied by Dooley Wilson on piano and a disembodied orchestra in the background. The song is nothing special, but Sinatra gives the lyrics an emotional warmth that puts the surrounding film to shame. The fact that the feelings conveyed are strictly platonic is an unusual touch that enhances rather than weakens the effect. Confident vocally, Sinatra appears just a little awkward physically, betraying his lack of acting experience. He seems unsure what to do with his hands, often clasping them together, and exiting from his last shot of the scene with Morgan, he glances into the camera just as they move out of frame. Following this five-minute appearance, Sinatra gets to sing three more songs. Dressed in a tuxedo, he delivers 'The Music Stopped' at the Butlers Ball, also participating in a modest dance with Morgan and Hale. Reverting to jacket and bow tie, he then duets with Mickey the maid - a feistier version of the young Judy Garland - on 'I Saw You First', which includes the interesting lyric 'Think you could ever stand a crooner?' Sinatra failed to show fan McGuire the same consideration off-camera, the actress becoming upset over her idol's detached manner and preoccupation with his other business interests. Song number four, 'A Lovely Way to Spend an Evening', is partly sung to tune of Tchaikovsky's Pathetique Symphony, which presumably was someone's idea of class. Aside from his half-baked romance with Hale - little more than an underwritten plot contrivance to tidy up loose ends - Sinatra's only real purpose in the story is to serve as Milly's friend, confidante and moral guide. In his longest scene, towards the end of the film, he dispenses words of wisdom: 'I think that marriage is an institution that no family can do without', convincing her that a loveless marriage for money is just not right.

As for the Sinatra in-jokes, the cast deliver them with all the verve and panache they deserve. Following Sinatra's first appearance, Drake stumbles downstairs, complaining to his assistant about the noise:

DRAKE: Sandy, who was that singing down here? Bing Crosby?
SANDY: Bing bang Sinatra.
DRAKE: Well, he'll never get anyplace.

This less than side-splitting exchange was either an accompaniment to or hurried replacement for the script's original Sinatra-Crosby joke, which involved a cameo appearance from the man himself. During a street scene, Sinatra and Crosby would ride past each other on bicycles, stop, dismount, stick out their tongues, then ride on to much audience hilarity. A long-time fan of Crosby, Sinatra met the champion crooner for the first time in September 1943, during production on *Higher and Higher*. Alas, Crosby couldn't make the shooting dates - either that or he cost too much - and all that remains of the idea is Sinatra riding a bicycle with an unlit pipe clenched in his teeth, demonstrating admirable co-ordination but little comic effect. At least Crosby could sing with a pipe in his mouth. Having exhausted their Crosby-related repertoire, the writers appeared to lose what little enthusiasm they had. Following another Sinatra entrance, Milly turns to Mike:

Higher and Higher - Going Dutch. Matchmaker Sinatra offers encouragement to Marcy McGuire and Mel Torme.

MILLY: You remember Mr...
MIKE: Yes, yes, we've heard that name before.

Last and probably least, when Barbara Hale expresses a romantic interest in Sinatra, her allegedly English maid ripostes with: 'He looks just like someone I heard on the radio.' This is the kind of film where the most impressive artistic touches are the opening and closing titles. *Higher and Higher* begins with the credits ascending into a cloud filled sky - white clouds, of course, this is a feel-good movie. It's a little literal-minded, to be sure, but that's a minor quibble. At the conclusion, the newly united Milly and Mike waltz off into the same sky. Sinatra then appears, floating in the air while he sings a reprise of 'The Music Stopped', and growing to giant size. The notion of teenage idol as celestial being is an intriguing one. Pity there's nothing quite so interesting in the actual movie.

With filming completed, Sinatra returned east to New Jersey, the contract for his next RKO movie already signed and the production scheduled to begin in December. The studio's decision not to wait for the box-office returns on their first Sinatra opus before launching into a second could be taken as a sign of RKO's confidence in their new star. Alternatively, they were desperate to milk his youthful following before it evaporated. Carefully timed to catch the Christmas market - if ever a film needed audience goodwill this was it - *Higher* was released on 18 December 1943 in the bigger American cities, with a general release in January 1944. While denied the top spot on the credit roll, Sinatra was the major focus for the film's publicity drive. Disregarding his three previous feature appearances, RKO promoted their film as Sinatra's screen debut. Posters announced THE SINATRA SHOW, along with the understated legend:

'The voice that's THRILLING THE WORLD teamed with a half dozen popular top-flight comedians in a glittering, glorious musical show - chock full of romance with haunting whistleable songs, dances, laughs!'

Sinatra also got the biggest picture on the advertising, his beaming face dominating the bottom right-hand corner of the posters. Reviews were mixed, with a curious west/east coast pro/anti split. The *Hollywood Citizen News* declared: 'He portrays himself so naturally that you catch yourself thinking, "He can act, too".' The *Hollywood Reporter* took a similar line: 'People who have never understood his appeal to swooning fans...will have no trouble in buying the guy they meet on the screen here.' The *New York Herald-Tribune* offered a more balanced view of the new star's screen 'debut', pronouncing that Sinatra 'does his stint remarkably well for a comparative novice. His ugly, bony face photographs well; his voice registers agreeably enough... and he handles himself easily.' Influential *New York Times* critic Bosley Crowther was unimpressed, making the rather obvious comment that 'Frankie is no Gable or Barrymore' and dismissing the overall film as 'a slapdash setting for the incredibly unctuous renderings of the Voice. He is graciously permitted to warble and ooze out what passes for charm.' According to columnist and friend Earl Wilson, Sinatra was genuinely taken aback by the harsher critical jibes, quite possibly feeling that such a modest production hardly merited such heavy artillery. Of all the reviews, the verdict from the *Los Angeles Times* proved the most prescient in the light of Sinatra's subsequent film career: 'The crooner certainly doesn't fulfil the cinema's traditional idea of a romantic figure, which may be a break for him eventually. He...appears more at ease than we expected, and should find a place as a film personality with careful choice of subjects.'

As expected, the bobby-sox crowd turned up in reasonable droves - with accompanying sales of sheet music and magazine covers - but the wider cinema-going public proved largely indifferent, resulting in disappointing box-office. By way of compensation, the specially penned 'I Couldn't Sleep a Wink Last Night' received a 1944 Academy Award nomination. Despite the unspectacular domestic receipts, not to mention Sinatra's relative obscurity overseas, *Higher and Higher* was given a fairly rapid British release in May 1944, when it met with overwhelming apathy. Describing Sinatra as 'America's new pin-up crooner', critic Dilys Powell proceeded with a genteel hatchet job largely at the expense of the star's looks: 'Mr Sinatra is a young man with a triangular, knobby face, high cheekbones, a rather pronounced jaw-line and a voice with the quality of slightly worn velveteen.' Sinatra would not be a big box-office draw in Britain until his *Eternity* comeback. His next movie for the studio would be a musical version of a Broadway hit which had already generated one flop for RKO and showed every sign of producing another.

Step Lively -   Sinatra expresses his approval of Gloria De Haven's acceptably small hat (opposite page).

STEP LIVELY 1944

*Voice like that and the guy wants
to be a playwright.*

Gordon Miller, bankrupt impressario

It all began with Zeppo Marx. Three decades on, Sinatra would marry Zeppo's ex-wife, Barbara Marx nee Blakely. For the time being, he contented himself with starring in a reworked version of an RKO property negotiated by Zeppo as a vehicle for his older, funnier brothers. *Room Service*, a frantic John Murray-Allan Boretz farce set in the world of down-at-heel show people, had been a huge success on Broadway after premiering in the summer of 1937. Ever in need of a hit, RKO made a deal with producer George Abbott to obtain the film rights for $255,000, a record amount at the time. Feeling that the material could be ideal for showcasing the Marx trio in a more mainstream comedy, Zeppo Marx approached the studio with his idea. Released in late September 1938, the Marx Brothers *Room Service* flopped to the net sum of $340,000. Having blown over $500,000 on the production, an understandably aggrieved RKO felt they hadn't got great value for money on the deal. Barely five years later they decided to revamp the property Sinatra-style in an attempt to recoup the original investment. Nice try but no cigarillo. After a bright start, *Step Lively* lapses into treadmill routine, despite the unusual sight of

bearded chorus boys spouting water from their turbans.

The musical remake began life under the more sedate title of *Manhattan Serenade*. Most of the production team on *Higher and Higher* were retained, with one notable addition. Having made two films in a row with dual responsibilities, Tim Whelan happily surrendered the producer slot to Robert Fellows, a former Warner employee. Appreciating that top-billed Sinatra could not yet carry a film on his own, RKO assembled a solid supporting cast, even approaching MGM to borrow two of the larger studio's second rank stars. Bland leading man George Murphy was cast in the Groucho Marx role of a wheeler-dealer theatrical producer who persuades naive aspiring playwright Sinatra to participate in his new show. Gloria De Haven, recruited as Sinatra's love interest, was one of the numerous MGM starlets who never quite made it. For a touch of suave sophistication, RKO hired Adolphe Menjou, star of *The Front Page* (1931) and *A Star is Born* (1937); for gruff comedy relief the studio looked to Eugene Pallette, best remembered for his sword-wielding, mutton-guzzling Friar Tuck in *The Adventures of Robin Hood* (1938). Casting by numbers, to be sure, but quality numbers. Way down the cast list, budding starlet Dorothy Malone was given a brief, unbilled bit part as a hotel switchboard operator, her scant lines amounting to little more than 'Calls for Mr Miller'. A decade on, she would be reunited with Sinatra as a fully-fledged star in *Young at Heart*, her naturally dark hair turned aggressive blonde via the miracle of peroxide.

Of his co-stars, Sinatra got on best with De Haven, nicknaming her 'The Comb' after her habit of near-constant hair preening. Not cutting-edge wit, perhaps, but a good-natured spin on his own tag as 'The Voice'. He probably had less to say to hardline Republicans Murphy and Menjou, close friends and regular golfing partners. Raised as a devout Democrat by his politically active mother Natalie 'Dolly' Sinatra, the star was never slow to parade his ideological beliefs. Sinatra's public support for Franklin Roosevelt's 1944 re-election campaign attracted a lot of flack from the right-wing press, who claimed that frivolous showbiz celebrities had

no place on political platforms. Hollywood tended to agree, feeling that politically outspoken stars risked alienating at least half their potential adult audience.

Having been landed with a score over which he had no say for *Higher and Higher*, Sinatra now got the chance to select his own musical collaborators. First choice was lyricist Sammy Cahn, a friend and colleague from the Dorsey days who would go on to write for Sinatra for the rest the his career - '...whenever Frank needs a lyric you can bet I'm there.' Since 1942, Cahn had regularly teamed up with composer Jule Styne and the duo agreed to provide the four modest showstoppers that would serve as *Step Lively*'s major selling point: 'Come Out, Come Out, Wherever You Are', 'As Long As There's Music'. 'Where Does Love Begin?' and 'Some Other Time'. While hardly a milestone in screen musical history, the songs are agreeably catchy, even if 'As Long...' sounds rather similar to *Higher and Higher*'s 'The Music Stopped'. The mildly incestuous-sounding 'Where Does Love Begin?' includes the memorable lyric 'A kiss from my sister doesn't bring on a blister', which is better than anything in *Anchors Aweigh*. Cahn shared a Sunset Towers apartment with Axel Stordahl, back on board as Sinatra's arranger, and the star himself lived only two floors below them for a while.

Step Lively also witnessed the first recorded star tantrum of Sinatra's movie career. During the *Higher* shoot, he had been too preoccupied with the challenge of playing 'himself' on-camera and the sheer novelty of film-making to have much time for arguments. One film on and he felt ready to flex a few star muscles. Ironically, the object of his discontent rested on the head of his good friend 'The Comb'. Sinatra refused to shoot one scene with De Haven after taking a strong dislike to her large hat, walking off the set with the announcement that he'd return once the offending item was changed. Always sensitive about his comparatively modest stature - 5ft 9" on a good day - Sinatra already regarded his co-star as dangerously tall and the hat was just too much to take. Wardrobe produced an acceptably squat substitute and filming resumed.

The only other Sinatra-related slowdown during

production resulted directly from the star magic RKO was determined to exploit. After a few days of shooting, the studio had to declare *Step Lively* a closed set, as far too many RKO secretaries were deserting their desks to watch Sinatra at work. Always appreciative of his fans, the star was happy to sign autographs and chat with his admirers between takes. His employers were less happy about the conversations Sinatra held with visiting journalists. Interviewed on set, Sinatra was recklessly open about his problems with the film business: 'I like making movies, though sometimes it nearly drives me crazy to wait...for years I have been used to rapid work - radio and bands. Out here, I have to sit and wait between scenes.' In this brief press quote lies the key to one of Sinatra's biggest hang-ups as a movie star: he hadn't learned and would never really learn to deal with the slow pace, endless delays and necessary repetition involved in the process. Film-making practicalities aside, the star also had strong reservations about the quality of his second RKO vehicle. According to Earl Wilson, Sinatra was not at all happy with the film during shooting and regularly confided his feelings to De Haven between shots. Just how much this lack of enthusiasm affected Sinatra's performance in the finished film is open to question. It has been claimed that he is noticeably bored-looking in several scenes, yet his occasional flatness of expression could just as readily be attributed to lack of acting experience and inadequate direction from Whelan. First seen in a dark suit and tie, his typewriter under one arm, Sinatra plays the naive yet determined Glen in a slightly twitchy fashion, appearing eager and nervous in about equal measure. He delivers his lines without much flair but the dialogue is fairly mediocre anyway.

In fairness, *Step Lively* is by and large an improvement on its predecessor. Whelan directs with a little more pace, the script is passable and the convoluted plot at least gives the cast some material to work with, notably Walter Slezak as the amusingly named hotel manager Mr Gribble, ('They're not human beings. They're actors'.) Opening the film with a long tracking shot of a hotel bellboy doing his rounds, Whelan also throws in a reflection shot and an overhead dolly, hinting at a visual flair barely suggested in *Higher and Higher*. The ballroom set piece 'Some Other Time' ends with a Busby Berkeley-style overhead shot of Sinatra and De Haven decoratively arranged on the floor, flanked by a quartet of chorus girls. For the climactic 'As Long as There's Music'/'Some Other Time' reprise/medley, the stars appear in dazzling white against a jet black background. Both stylish and economical. Sadly, the decent musical sequences are not matched by the linking plot segments, despite the latter's pedigree Broadway origins. The manic pace, constant rushing about and rapid-fire dialogue fail to disguise the overall second-hand feel to the film. Both Murphy and Menjou overact, the former's shifty-hustler character quickly becoming tiresome. Hiding 22 impoverished actors in his penthouse suite, Miller should come across a loveable rogue, but Murphy only manages the latter element. The film ends with Sinatra, De Haven and Murphy announcing 'That's All!' direct to camera, which is both crass and a direct steal from the Warner Bros 'Merrie Melodies' cartoons.

Nervous acting aside, Sinatra is fairly well incorporated into the *Step Lively* storyline. Unable to generate much interest in his social-conscience drama 'God's Speed'. Glen is fortunately blessed with a magical singing voice, which the script is at pains to promote: 'If that guy was the Pied Piper of Hamlyn there wouldn't be a dame left in town.' Loosely based on the character played by Harpo Marx in *Room Service*, Glen's biggest dramatic moment is the faked suicide-deathbed scene that allows Miller to get his new show rolling while the hotel inspector's attention is diverted. Looking a little lost beneath the bed covers, Sinatra at least manages to convey his character's discomfort. Aside from playing his first 'proper' character, Sinatra also enjoyed his first screen kiss, a full-blooded if not overly passionate clinch with De Haven, playing Miller's neglected girlfriend Christine. Colliding in the hotel lobby – 'Your typewriter's open' – their subsequent relationship is utterly without surprises, the happy outcome laboriously hindered by Miller's scheming. Sinatra's kiss-free 'romance' with Barbara Hale

in *Higher and Higher* had been an utter non-event, perhaps indicative of concern on RKO's part that Sinatra fans would react unfavourably to their idol being pawed and smooched by another woman. Doubtless bracing themselves for a storm of adolescent rage, the studio executives threw caution to the wind and allowed their star full lip-contact. Blessed with blonde hair, pleasant looks and more than passable vocal talents, De Haven makes an effective screen partner for Sinatra, memorably singing 'Come Out, Come Out Wherever You Are' while luxuriating in an on-stage bubble bath. Described by journalist E.J. Kahn Jnr as an 'unprecedented bit of eroticism', the smooch was big enough news to warrant a four-page spread in *Look* magazine. Sinatra also got to snog Anne Jeffreys, cast as predatory budding starlet Jean Abbot, though their faces disappear from view just before the crucial moment. Besides, Glen doesn't fancy her anyway.

Hoping to draw the summer crowds, RKO released *Step Lively* on 27 June 1944. Reviewers, underwhelmed by the film itself, predicted more lust-struck teenage masses. As *Time* magazine put it with just a hint of indecency: 'Sinatra's name on the marquee is sufficient to guarantee lipsticky posters on the outside, moaning galleryites within.' For all the lipstick stains and moaning, the film proved another commercial letdown. The kids still showed up but they didn't bring anyone else with them. Sinatra had another five years to run on his RKO contract and the prospect was becoming less enticing by the day. Two flops in a row could embarrass even the biggest Hollywood star, let alone a novice still largely dependent on his off-screen musical success for continued public interest. By this time, Sinatra had departed CAG for the rather more powerful MCA and his new representatives were not slow to kick-start his apathetic film career. RKO had just borrowed some MGM players; now the favour was to be returned. Taking advantage of the loan-out clause in Sinatra's contract, MCA negotiated a starring role in *Anchors Aweigh*, a lavish A-budget Sailors-in-Hollywood musical that looked a surefire winner.

2

Hello Sailor

1944-1948

ANCHORS AWEIGH 1945

*I was born with a couple of left feet, and it was
Gene and only Gene who got me to dance.*
Frank Sinatra

Gee, I've got a feeling I'm fickle.
Clarence Doolittle

In January 1944, Frank Sinatra appeared at a benefit
concert for The Jewish Home for the Aged, Los
Angeles. The undoubted highlight of his performance
was a show-stopping rendition of 'Ol' Man River'. In
the audience sat MGM boss Louis B. Mayer who,
according to Nancy Sinatra, was moved to tears by
her father's rendition and determined there and then
to sign Frank Sinatra for his studio. Sinatra had been
on the MGM payroll once before, singing with the
Dorsey band in the Eleanor Powell comedy *Ship
Ahoy* (1942, see Appendix 1), though chances are
Mayer never bothered to look at the film. He would
have to wait a little while now that Sinatra was hot
but, as a rule, what Mayer wanted he got.

Sinatra's disappointing start in movies had not
affected his off-screen musical career and he was still
enjoying sell-out performances at such New York hot
spots as the Paramount Theater and La Bomba
nightclub. MGM came calling and Sinatra signed his
loan-out deal with the studio in February 1944. Instead
of the $25,000 paid by RKO, his starting salary at
MGM was $130,000 per film. Impressed by his new star
power, Sinatra knew full well that the deal also offered a
few drawbacks. If the studio bought up his RKO
contract in its entirety, he would have no say in the
scripts he was allocated, and should he refuse to make a
film, the much-dreaded suspension clause would come
into effect until the rejected project had finished
production. That said, the dressing rooms were better
than the ones at RKO and Sinatra was permitted the
luxury of a telephone, normally forbidden on the
grounds that any ringing noise could be heard on set
and ruin a take. The star later described the MGM star
treatment as 'like a womb'; offering comfort, security
and no real responsibility at all. A downside to being at
the studio with 'More stars than there are in the heavens'
was the sudden perspective afforded Sinatra regarding

Anchors Aweigh – Dancing fools. The Gene Kelly masterclass.

his own talents as a film performer. The golden voice that had sufficed at RKO was no longer quite enough and the singing star later admitted to suffering feelings of inferiority and embarrassment among the likes of Judy Garland and Spencer Tracy. Nevertheless, this was the big chance and it might never come around again. What RKO had promised, MGM was delivering: genuine A-1 film stardom.

For all its major failings, *Anchors Aweigh* is an impressively canny piece of merchandise. Cashing in on the immense surge of American patriotism as World War II drew to a victorious close, the film centres on two decorated sailors enjoying a few days' leave in Hollywood, which naturally emerges as a wonderful place where dreams really do come true. There is also a token gesture towards the United States government's then current South American 'good neighbours' policy, with plenty of friendly Mexicans and several scenes set in Los Angeles' Latin quarter. The negligible story consists of four easy-to-follow plotlines: both men, one shy, one libidinous, find romance; an aspiring singing-star gets her big break thanks to Spanish maestro Jose Iturbi (who can't act); a navy-mad orphan - eight-year-old Dean Stockwell - gets to wear the uniform and hang about with sailors. Songs and a few dances are injected at regular intervals. Most important of all, everyone is nice: the navy, the police, the film people, Iturbi, Stockwell's classmates; even Tom Cat, briefly seen offering Jerry Mouse cheese in a cartoon sequence. A blend of ingredients that could hardly miss.

MGM's high expectations for the production were reflected in the budget. At $2 million, *Anchors Aweigh* would be the studio's most expensive musical to date. Not inclined to take any unnecessary risks with such a lavish project, Mayer placed it in the safe hands of Joe Pasternak, who had an impressive track record as MGM's most successful musical producer. This enviable run would later be broken by *The Kissing Bandit*; for the time being Pasternak had no reason to regard his new star as any kind of liability. While Pasternak had not been overly impressed by either of Sinatra's RKO films, he liked the idea of casting him in *Anchors* and

informed the singer that he'd be just perfect for the role of a awkward, girl-shy nerd. Pasternak's assistant feared his boss had rather overplayed the ideal casting angle at the first meeting - which their new star attended with an eight-strong entourage - yet Sinatra called the next day to say yes.

For the director's chair, Pasternak selected George Sidney, a regular collaborator he rated as one of the best in the business. Screenplay duties went to Isobel Lennart, who later subjected Sinatra to *It Happened in Brooklyn* and *The Kissing Bandit*.

Sinatra's co-stars for *Anchors Aweigh* were of the up-and-coming variety rather than established big names. Second-billed Kathryn Grayson had been recruited as a replacement for wholesome singing star Deanna Durbin after the latter defected to Universal. Her 'big break' in Pasternak's mediocre all-star flagwaver *Thousands Cheer* (1943) typified the studio's casual treatment of their new property. Blessed with dark hair and a rather doll-like face, complete with large mouth and upturned nose, Grayson's somewhat precious demeanour in *Anchors* is not terribly appealing, though the script is as much to blame as the performer. Her singing voice, employing a quavering, scale-travelling style, is certainly an acquired taste and hasn't aged well.

Grayson's romantic interest in *Thousands Cheer* was a newcomer named Gene Kelly, who'd scored a personal triumph on Broadway as the anti-hero lead of the 'adult' Rodgers-Hart musical *Pal Joey* (1940). Arriving in Tinseltown, Kelly was placed under a one-film contract by independent producer David O. Selznick, who rapidly discovered that he didn't own any scripts suited to Kelly's talents and loaned him out to MGM for a starring role opposite Judy Garland in the musical *For Me and My Gal* (1942). Arthur Freed, head of the studio's musical unit, was sufficiently impressed with Kelly's performance to persuade his bosses to buy up the star's contract at a modest $750 a week. Kelly rapidly repaid Freed's faith in him, scoring a big hit on loan-out as both co-star and choreographer for the Columbia production *Cover Girl* (1944), a vehicle for the studio's superstar Rita Hayworth. On the strength of his success with *Cover Girl*, Kelly was permitted to do his own choreography for *Anchors Aweigh*, a decisive factor in rendering at least parts of the film watchable. His acting is a different matter. Cast as an outwardly cocksure yet inwardly sensitive navy wolf, Kelly overplays badly at times, resulting in a character who appears loud, smug, overbearing and irritating.

Despite some differences of opinion during shooting, Sinatra became friendly with Pasternak and also enjoyed good working relationships with Kelly and Grayson. True to MGM form, most of the film would be shot on the studio sound stages, with just one scene filmed on location at the impressively vast Hollywood Bowl. It was here that Sinatra enjoyed his first really serious movie screw-up. For the time being, he was busy finding his dancing feet.

Preparations for Sinatra's first major league film role were extensive. Before shooting commenced on 15 June 1944, he had to endure weeks of dance rehearsal with Gene Kelly, a fairly traumatic experience for the relative novice. Sinatra lost four pounds from his already minimal frame during the first rehearsal alone, subsequently drinking six malted milkshakes a day over two weeks to keep his weight healthy. Both Sinatra and the studio management were fully aware of his limitations as a dancer and the script required just the one routine with Kelly. This still involved eight weeks of rehearsal, seven days a week. Sinatra had already acquired a certain notoriety for his dislike of rehearsing; on this occasion he reluctantly accepted it as an inescapable part of the deal. A man of inordinate patience, Kelly painstakingly taught Sinatra both how to move as a dancer and the particular moves necessary for their routine, enduring his co-star's occasional bouts of ill-temper. Sinatra's lack of ability inevitably placed limitations on what Kelly could do in the number, something readily acknowledged by the singer: 'I couldn't dance exactly like he danced so he danced down to me.' It was surely a compliment when a satisfied Kelly informed Sinatra that he'd progressed from lousy to adequate. The suffering continued during filming, with Sinatra nearly collapsing from physical exhaustion early on in the production. Much to the dismay of his employers, Sinatra took the rest of the day off, an unprecedented act of 'mutiny' that had Louis Mayer himself storming down to the set to demand that Sinatra continue work. The star declined and Kelly, aware that he'd been pushing his reluctant protégé just a little too hard, supported Sinatra's decision. While the star had won his case this time around, his confrontational attitude would always make his relations with MGM a little uneasy. Louis Mayer liked Sinatra personally and marvelled at his gift for singing but as a film star he was quickly placed in the 'difficult' category.

With the choreography in the safe hands of Gene Kelly and his assistant Stanley Donen, Sinatra had the chance to make his own musical contribution with regard to the song department. Pasternak sought his advice regarding the choice of composer for the film, suggesting Jerome Kern, Ira Gershwin or the Rodgers-Hart team as the best candidates. Sinatra begged to differ, announcing that he wanted Cahn and Styne or no-one. Neither had any kind of a reputation in Hollywood and Pasternak insisted on bigger names. This brought out Sinatra's stubborn streak, leading MCA head Lew Wasserman to worry that his client could easily be fired from the production if he didn't back down. Wasserman begged Cahn to assure Sinatra that he wouldn't be offended if he and Styne weren't used on the film, prompting the famous reply 'If you're not there Monday, I'm not there Monday.' Cahn and Styne got the job.

For all the plush MGM surroundings, Sinatra did not find the process of film-making any easier at the bigger studio. Lighting a shot for the Technicolor cameras could often take 45 minutes and he rapidly got bored waiting. Director Sidney quickly picked up on Sinatra's preference for fast work and minimal takes and the two enjoyed a smooth(ish) working relationship. Sidney, who later reunited with Sinatra for *Pal Joey* (1957), always defended the latter's one-take approach, arguing that many Hollywood stars, notably Spencer Tracy and Clark Gable, preferred to work the

Anchors Aweigh – Clarence and his Brooklyn girl (Pamela Britton).

same way, feeling that repeated takes could render a performance stale. Sidney's careful handling of Sinatra was probably his greatest contribution to *Anchors Aweigh*. While the director makes good use of the high budget, getting maximum value from the large, colourful sets with generous use of the camera crane, he brings little in the way of style or flair to the movie. When Sidney does attempt a few 'artsy' touches, we get the string section of an orchestra reflected in Iturbi's piano lid or a low angle of Iturbi's fingers shot through a transparent keyboard. This is straining for effect taken to a new dimension.

Sinatra was also anxious to see his career making/breaking performance as quickly as possible and pestered Pasternak to let him look at the daily rushes (screenings of the previous day's footage). This was against studio policy, largely on the grounds that stars never liked what they saw prior to editing and dubbing, but Sinatra persisted until Pasternak agreed on the condition that the footage was for his eyes only.

With a perverse disregard for promises made and plain good manners, Sinatra turned up for the showing with six friends in tow, much to Pasternak's annoyance. The star responded to his producer's justified wrath with a blunt threat to quit the film if he didn't get his way. True to form, the press picked up on the incident, the only serious Sinatra-Pasternak quarrel during the entire production. There was, however, a lot worse to come.

If *Step Lively* had seen Sinatra discussing movie-making just a little too candidly with the press, *Anchors* witnessed his first fully fledged anti-Hollywood outburst, or so the newspapers claimed. Having already been accused of inflated egotism by some columnists, allegedly refusing to grant interviews unless the request went through his agent, Sinatra found himself relying on his co-stars to rally in his defence. Kelly, Grayson and the rest of the *Anchors* cast put their names to a statement pinned on his dressing room door: 'We, the undersigned and those who know him well, know that Frank's head size is normal and that his hat will continue to fit.' Such good-humoured moral support couldn't help Sinatra out of his next press-related entanglement, nor would it have been appropriate. During location shooting at the Hollywood Bowl, United Press agency reporter Hal Swisher interviewed Jose Iturbi between takes. He also caught a few choice remarks from Sinatra, reported nationwide on 9 October 1944: 'Pictures stink. Most of the people in them do, too. I don't want any more movie acting. Hollywood won't believe I'm through, but they'll find out I mean it.' Sinatra quickly issued a fierce denial of the above, printed in *Daily Variety* two days later: 'Hollywood and the picture people have been good to me... I was downright amazed when they showed me the clipping.' Swisher hotly denied that any of the original statement had been fabricated and Sinatra threatened legal action for libel. Then followed the kind of awkward semi-climbdown that would dog Sinatra on several occasions during his film career. His manager, Al Levy, issued a statement that appeared to amount to a partial admission of guilt, claiming that Sinatra had simply been misunderstood. Talking with the crew on one of the hottest days of the year, a worn-out, heavily sweating Sinatra was asked what he thought about movies now. In jest, he responded with the crude, if accurate reply: 'They stink'. Interviewing Iturbi some distance away, Swisher had mistakenly taken Sinatra's joke as genuine criticism. This still didn't tally with the rather more extensive diatribe reported and MGM executives insisted on a full retraction from Sinatra, who was in no position to argue. Accepting the failure of the rapid response damage-limitation exercise, long-suffering press agent Jack Keller handed Swisher a carefully drafted follow-up statement composed by the studio: 'I think I might have spoken too broadly about quitting pictures and about my feeling toward Hollywood. I'm under a seven-year contract to RKO...and I have one more commitment at Metro...and believe me, I intend to live up to my contractual obligations.' Despite this embarrassment and press reports of his alleged relationship with MGM starlet Marilyn Maxwell, Sinatra patched up his relations with

the studio, obtaining permission to hold a special birthday showing of *Anchors* for five-year-old Nancy Jnr and her friends in Lew Wasserman's private screening room at the MCA building. All the same, his first brush with negative publicity had not been handled well and the obvious lessons were not taken on board, either by Sinatra or MGM. The star couldn't shut up and the studio wouldn't keep the press away from him. As to the truth of Swisher's account, the thought does occur that an already insecure Sinatra, prone to outbursts and cooking in his heavy sailor outfit, could easily have given vent to his Hollywood-related frustrations with little regard for the long-term consequences. Just a few derogatory words regarding movies were all the ammunition his enemies in the press needed.

Sinatra's contribution to *Anchors Aweigh* would have to be ruled a qualified success, even allowing for the fact that he is obliged to play second fiddle to third-billed Gene Kelly for much of the film. Clad in a dark blue suit with white trim, a white hat and even whiter teeth, he looks a little uncomfortable in the opening sequence, where a navy band marches in close formation - making the shape of an anchor, then the letters N A V Y when shot from overhead. Technicolor is not altogether kind to Sinatra's face, emphasising his distinct, lined features without flattering them. Kelly looks altogether smoother, despite a very noticeable scar above the left side of his mouth. Nor does the script give Sinatra much to work with. Saddled with the character name 'Clarence Doolittle', he plays a withdrawn bookworm from Brooklyn, a former assistant choirmaster who drinks milkshakes and has to dial the speaking clock when the other sailors call up their dates. Desperate to learn something about women, Doolittle tags along after best friend and reluctant teacher Joseph Brady (Kelly). When Brady offers him a few handy telephone numbers, Doolittle backs off in fear: 'Oh no, I'd be too scared to use them', a line Sinatra delivers with no conviction at all. Doolittle thinks he has found his ideal woman in movie extra Susan Abbott (Grayson) but it's a cafe waitress (Pamela Britton) from his home town he really loves - 'Last night, when she dropped her soup on me, I should have known', leaving Susan conveniently free for Joe. Not so much a love triangle as an easily resolved love square. If it weren't for the tiresome plot device of having characters repeatedly fail to tell each other what's on their minds, the film could be over in half an hour, instead of dragging on over an absurdly prolonged 140 minutes. Sinatra and Britton do make an appealing romantic couple and it's a pity they don't get more screen time together. Surprisingly, there is only one joke at the expense of Sinatra's lack of bulk. Fleeing from MGM studio guards, he hides behind a harp and they can't see him. This sequence, a shameless piece of self-promotion by the film's producers, does generate one unintended laugh when Sinatra is ejected from the studio gates. A few years later it would happen for real.

The Styne-Cahn numbers occasionally enable Sinatra to raise the level of the film a few notches. He and Kelly duet on 'We Hate to Leave', where the lyrics don't get any classier than: 'But we'll be back before the anchors heave.' Sinatra is better off with the solos 'What Makes the Sun Set?' and 'I Fall in Love Too Easily', yet the confidence, precision and sheer power of his voice are at odds with his supposedly meek character. As *Take Me Out to the Ball Game* and *On the Town* later demonstrated, Sinatra and Kelly could make an effective team but *Anchors* affords only glimpses of this potential. In the film's oddest and most stupid scene, the two friends attempt to persuade Susan's date - whom they wrongly assume is unwelcome - that she is a loose-living Navy slut, complete with her own song: 'She's not so choosy/No, not our Suzy/... You'll get woozy.' Even the dance sequence that caused Sinatra so much rehearsal agony doesn't quite come off. Clearly intended as a no-holds-barred showstopper, the 'I Begged Her' number begins with a little light tap work and ends with Sinatra and Kelly jumping in tandem across a series of camp beds in a servicemen's hostel. The sequence consists of three lengthy takes framed largely in long shot and while Sinatra keeps in time with Kelly pretty well, his hard work fails to disguise the fact that Kelly dances with far more poise, precision and athleticism

than his partner. It could be argued that this blatant disparity in ability matches their respective characters, but this rationalisation doesn't accord with the film-maker's intentions. Besides, Sinatra sings a lot better than Kelly. Appreciating that Sinatra would inevitably cramp Kelly's style during their dance together, Pasternak allowed the latter three solo routines to showcase the full rein of his ability. Sinatra and Grayson had the superior billing but Kelly emerged the true star of the piece, overacting or not. Physical considerations aside, his presence fills the screen in a way Sinatra simply couldn't match at the time. The script put him in Kelly's shadow and there he stayed.

The advertising for *Anchors Aweigh* played on the film's patriotic element, with white stars on the blue title lettering and the stars' names in red, pitching the content with the straightforward legend 'ON WAVES OF SONG, LAUGHTER AND ROMANCE!' The film was released on 15 August 1945, scoring rave reviews and a box-office smash, ending up as the year's number two domestic hit and contributing substantially to MGM's record profit margin for 1945. Influential *Los Angeles Examiner* columnist Louella Parsons led the pack with her short-and-sweet verdict: 'Sock artists, sock tunes and sock dances.' Kelly's easy dominance of the film did not go unnoticed and he received the bulk of the press attention, not to mention an Academy Award nomination for Best Actor. *Anchors Aweigh* also received a sentimental and patently undeserved Best Picture nomination. Merited or not, the huge success of the film propelled Sinatra to the front rank of movie stars. Now all he had to do was stay there without Gene Kelly to back him up.

There is a curious postscript to Sinatra's first hit movie. Sinatra, Kelly and Grayson later participated in a unusual 'revival' of the film, starring in a one-hour radio adaptation of the script broadcast on 29 December 1947 as part of the Lux Radio Theater series. Revisiting his first and so far only hit property at a time when his movie career was in increasingly poor shape cannot have been an entirely enjoyable experience for Sinatra. If it served to remind listeners that they had only recently turned out in droves for The Voice, it also underlined the fact that none of his subsequent films had met with similar success.

IT HAPPENED IN BROOKLYN 1947

There aren't any nice days in Brooklyn.
Anne Fielding

Durante can upstage anybody, me included.
Frank Sinatra

With *Anchors Aweigh* riding high at the box-office, Sinatra's earlier flops were quickly forgotten, MGM ensuring that the new star they'd helped create stayed with them. After three months of hard negotiation, MCA agents Lew Wasserman and Hal Friedman had delivered a highly favourable five-year contract for their client's signature in April 1945. Paying $260,000 a year, the deal altered the standard MGM morals clause and granted the star at least one outside film a year, 16 guest appearances on radio, publishing rights to the music used in alternate films and twelve weeks vacation a year. Deals didn't get much better than that.

Sinatra's first film role under his new contract was a 'guest' appearance in the sentimental - and largely fictional - Jerome Kern biopic *Till the Clouds Roll By* (1946, see Appendix 1). Despite some critical carping about his finale rendition of 'Ol' Man River' being delivered in a spotless white suit, Sinatra felt pleased with his performance and the film proved a big hit. With two successes under his belt, Sinatra doubtless expected his follow-up MGM vehicle to be another large-scale Technicolor musical spectacular. What he got was a small-scale story of a demobbed GI returning home to Brooklyn to find some success as a singer-songwriter but no romance. It would be shot in black and white under the supervision of a second division producer and a second rate director. At least it was a musical.

Exactly why MGM decided to throw Sinatra a film that he could only have taken as a demotion - not to say insult - remains one of life's small mysteries. Perhaps

It Happened in Brooklyn – Sinatra admires Jimmy Durante's culinary skills.

they felt the story of unhappy Brooklyn residents was ill-suited to cheery colour, requiring a more sombre approach. The problems faced by World War Two veterans readjusting to civilian life were well documented. Chances are the studio simply didn't have enough confidence in Sinatra as a solo leading man to give him a big budget movie straight away. It's likely they realised that the success of *Anchors Aweigh* gave a much exaggerated impression of his potential box-office appeal. Back in 1945, Sinatra's teen following was still at a peak, audiences were hungry for any old jingoistic drivel and he had Gene Kelly for a back-up man. If he could make a go of *Brooklyn*, then they would think about a more ambitious follow-up vehicle. The relatively modest production also served as a sobering reflection of Sinatra's waning popularity with the teeny-bop crowd and growing studio concern over the star's often unfavourable publicity. Shortly before *Brooklyn* went into production, Louis Mayer contacted Sinatra's MCA management to express his unhappiness over the latter's frequent bad press. Led by the Hearst-owned newspapers, right-wing columnists were forever firing out accusations of subversive communist sympathies and blatant mob involvement on Sinatra's part. Even his success with the Academy Award-winning pro-tolerance propaganda short *The House I Live In* (1945, see Appendix 3) was used against him as evidence of far-Left inclinations. Proof of any such leanings or dealings was thin on the ground, stories of Sinatra canoodling with Lucky Luciano in Cuba quickly discredited, but the mud stuck nevertheless. There were also a few murmurings over Sinatra's alleged ongoing affair with Lana Turner and his exemption from military service on the grounds of a supposedly damaged eardrum. The star did get some weighty support from prominent media liberals, notably Walter Winchell, Ed Sullivan and Erskine Johnson, and for the time being the public stood by their man, if not his movies.

Undeniably the least lavish of Sinatra's MGM musicals, *It Happened in Brooklyn* is in many ways the most likeable. Indifferently written, routinely handled, variably scored and burdened by a couple of dead-weight co-stars, it beats the odds largely thanks to the inspired teaming of Sinatra with Jimmy Durante, generating a warmth and enthusiasm not always found in the Sinatra-Kelly partnership and never in the Sinatra-Kathryn Grayson union. Critic James Agee expressed the film's major strength very well, attributing to it '...a general kindliness which I enjoyed'. *Brooklyn* is no *On the Town*, to be sure, yet it is a better showcase for Sinatra, who gets to be more than a passive foil for powerhouse Gene Kelly. Producer Jack Cummings, a nephew of Louis Mayer, had worked on *Ship Ahoy* and appeared to be aiming for the same level of achievement here. He later collaborated with Sinatra on *Can Can*. Enough said. Director Richard Whorf was a former actor whose recent change of occupation had yet to yield any great results. While he'd been credited

as the sole auteur of *Till the Clouds Roll By*, most of that film's musical highlights were in fact supervised by others, such as George Sidney for Sinatra's segment. Aided by *Anchors* co-photographer Robert Planck, Whorf's direction is competent but little more. His one ambitious touch, an elaborate crane shot across a garden full of dancing soldiers and up to Sinatra looking from a window, is unfortunately marred by conspicuous camera shadow on the left of the frame. Cahn and Styne were back on board for the songs, and the not too demanding musical numbers were devised and staged by Jack Donohue, who later worked with Sinatra on several television specials before directing two of the star's worst films, *Marriage on the Rocks* and *Assault on a Queen*. The piano solos required for a poor-teenage-musical-genius-in-need-of-scholarship subplot were courtesy of 17-year-old Andre Previn, who later trashed Sinatra's Clan films and married his ex-wife Mia Farrow. While both Donohue and Previn were models of professional behaviour during the production, there was trouble in the Cahn-Styne camp. Cahn's agent Eddie Traubner approached Sinatra between takes one day to inform the star that his client wished to concoct the next Sinatra film score in collaboration with Harry Warren rather than Styne. Unimpressed by this double-dealing, Sinatra claimed he already had an agreement with Styne. Understandably hurt, the latter gave his treacherous collaborator a thorough verbal slapping before agreeing to continue their relationship on a rather more wary footing.

While a rematch with Gene Kelly would have probably helped both men's careers at this stage, Sinatra had to make do with Kathryn Grayson. Isobel Lennart's script virtually repeats their relationship in *Anchors*, with ex-GI Sinatra convinced he is in love with Grayson's frustrated opera singer turned inspirational music teacher. Once again he discovers she really loves his best friend, Peter Lawford's English aristocrat turned jive artist, and yet again he finds he really loves a down-to-earth Brooklyn girl, straight-talking nurse Gloria Grahame. A passably photogenic trill-machine, Grayson gets very little to do in *Brooklyn*.

Her one duet with Sinatra, an aria from Don Giovanni sung in an Italian restaurant, falls flat and a lengthy fantasy sequence where she imagines herself as the star of Delibes' opera *Lakme* is pure filler, five minutes of utterly redundant footage.

Thankfully, *Brooklyn* got a much-needed shot of charisma, humanity and good humour with the casting of veteran comic Jimmy Durante, the man with the million dollar nose (as insured by Lloyds of London). A big fan of the comedian, Louis Mayer liked to rub Durante's proboscis for luck, not that this unconventional form of male bonding worked any great wonders for the latter's film career at MGM, typified by supporting roles in the minor musicals *Two Girls and a Sailor* (1944) and *Music for Millions*. Durante and Sinatra became good friends during the *Brooklyn* production, the latter subsequently entertaining serious plans to star in a biopic of Durante (see Appendix 2). Fourth-billed in the role of school janitor Nick Lombardi, Durante's slightly lonely middle-aged bachelor is afflicted by occasional voice strangulation, a treacherous kitchen cabinet door and a strange fixation on the movie *Goodbye Mr Chips* (1939), by pure coincidence another MGM production. Ever optimistic in the face of all his woes, Nick acts as the living, breathing heart of the film, encouraging the other characters to embrace both their potential and their true emotions. It's corny as hell but Durante makes the whole thing oddly plausible. Even his vision of Brooklyn in wintertime, lovingly describing the freezing mud and slush, lingers in the mind.

The presence of co-star Peter Lawford, though interesting in the light of his subsequent relationship with Sinatra, is rather less impressive. A former child actor in his native England, Lawford had been knocking around Hollywood since 1938, notching up unremarkable appearances in the MGM productions *Mrs Miniver* (1942), *The Picture of Dorian Gray* (1945) and *Son of Lassie* (1945). With many of the studio's top stars away on war service, there was a sudden demand for leading men that allowed even relative nonentities such as Lawford to attain passing star status by default.

The future Kennedy in-law proved an amicable acquaintance and the two got on well during the *Brooklyn* shoot. Aware of his co-star's 'difficult' reputation, Lawford felt that Sinatra was still nervous about film-making but admired the latter's professional behaviour during production, paying careful attention to Whorf's guidance and contributing his own suggestions where appropriate. Others were less charitable. Lawford's own performance doesn't really come together at all, for reasons unconnected with the thin script or his part as shy classical musician Jamie Shellgrove. He carries his relatively imposing height awkwardly, moving with little grace; his manner is nervous, his face weak-looking and his voice prissy.

Brooklyn commenced filming on 14 March 1946 at the MGM studios, moving to New York for location shooting in mid-June. According to trash-queen biographer Kitty Kelley, the production team got an early start on the Brooklyn-shot scenes after Sinatra rowed with Nancy Snr over his affair with MGM starlet Lana Turner. Storming out of his new Los Angeles home, the star declared himself available for work on the east coast. Choreographer Donohue found himself with more work than originally scheduled after Whorf decided at the last minute that the film needed an additional musical number - a reprise of 'Whose Baby Are You?' - and called upon Peter Lawford to perform the honours. Reluctant at first, Lawford allowed himself to be persuaded by his director, submitting to hours of rehearsal with Donohue and friendly advice from dance-king Sinatra. For all his reservations, Lawford performed the routine without a mistake on the first take. To the uninitiated, his jitterbugging looks absurd, if energetic, and his singing voice is abysmal.

Brooklyn has gone down in history as one its star's least happy movie experiences. Lawford's endorsement aside, Sinatra's behaviour during production failed to win him many new friends. Resenting the restrictions and discipline imposed by the MGM regime, he rebelled in various petty ways, often turning up late for both rehearsals and filming and sometimes failing to appear at all. Rumours spread that Sinatra was also leaving the set early without studio permission to meet his radio commitments. The resulting delays inflated a budget intended as relatively small, with the crew frequently ending up on double-time. Confronted over his poor attendance record, Sinatra would claim to be either unwell or just plain tired, excuses that cut little ice with his employers. Inevitably, the filming ran over schedule, with the last scenes not completed until early November. Sinatra's extremely cavalier attitude to his contractual obligations helped create an image of laziness, arrogance and lack of professionalism that he never really shed. Interestingly, second wife-to-be Ava Gardner later claimed that until *Eternity* came his way, Sinatra just didn't regard his film career as a big deal. It's possible Sinatra's behaviour also reflected some resentment at being lumbered with a blatantly second-rate script and production, yet he must surely have realised - or at least been advised by his MCA agents - that thumbing his nose at the studio was not likely to aid his cause. In any event, he escaped serious retribution for the time being. Still reluctant to chastise one of his favourite stars, Mayer allowed Sinatra to escape any major repercussions over his behaviour. Sinatra received a formal notification of improper conduct - little more than a figurative slap on the wrist - but suffered no financial penalty. Once again the newspapers picked up on the rumours, with former Sinatra supporter Louella Parsons claiming in a November 14 article that the star had fallen out with his bosses over not being given the rights to a particular song. Sinatra responded with a telegram to Parsons' office, denying any kind of rift with the studio: '...if you care to make a bet, I'll be glad to take your money that MGM and Frank Sinatra do not part company, permanently or otherwise...'. He was fortunate Parsons didn't take him up on the offer. By Sinatra standards, this was a fairly polite denial but it didn't stop him being voted the year's Least Co-Operative Star by the Hollywood Women's Press Club.

It's a pity that *It Happened in Brooklyn* should be remembered more for Sinatra's questionable behaviour than its own merits, as the film marked his best star performance to date. Sinatra is a far more assured performer this time out, displaying a confidence and charisma largely lacking from even *Anchors Aweigh*. While the opening scenes see him still lumbered with the shy, clumsy persona of *Anchors*, Sinatra works at the part with a little more determination and later gets the chance to open out a bit. His character, former shipping clerk Dannie Webson Miller, is predictably too withdrawn to show off his remarkable singing talent in public at first, though his location-shot musical tribute to Brooklyn Bridge lets the audience know what he can do. Thanks to mentor Durante, Sinatra is soon strutting his stuff at the local music store. Their duet on 'The Song's Gotta Have Heart' is the film's musical highpoint, with some lyrics in Russian (or thereabouts), a highly creditable Durante impression from Sinatra and the inevitable lyric 'You can sing/As good as Bing'. The other songs don't really measure up, though an earlier Sinatra-Durante duet, 'I Believe', at least offers a reasonable Sinatra in-joke, with the star too light to tilt a school seesaw.

Probably the most interesting scene in the film involves Sinatra's new job as the music store's song demonstrator, mainly because it reflected the all-too real concerns over the star's fading popularity. Already worried that his ballad-style of singing is out of favour with the jive-crazy kids, Dannie's fears are confirmed when he is called upon to perform 'The Same Old Dream' for a group of teenagers, among them Sinatra's *Higher and Highe*r co-star Marcy McGuire (whose relatively high billing and surprisingly brief screen-time would suggest her role was largely cut in post-production). The kids don't like what they hear - presumably the audience is supposed to feel differently - and launch into their own jazzed-up fast tempo version. Dannie stands back, arms folded, obviously bemused at this kind of music. He gives the song a second try and this time wins the kids over. Sadly, this would be one occasion where life failed to imitate art.

Brooklyn also boasts one striking missed opportunity. The opening sequence of the film, set in a very Hollywood rural England, involves an encounter between bashful Dannie and feisty nurse Gloria Grahame, who scolds her fellow Brooklyn resident for not acting like a proper native: 'A Brooklyn guy is a friendly guy.' Grahame's offbeat but striking looks complement Sinatra's equally out-of-the-ordinary features very well and their scene together cries out for further encounters in the film. Alas, the nurse is never seen again, though at the somewhat odd climax Dannie realises she was the true woman of his dreams all along and sets off to track her down: 'I bet you the Brooklyn Bridge I find her.' Not a good wager. Despite sharing a credit roll on *Not as a Stranger* a decade later, Sinatra and Grahame never worked on the same set again.

Brooklyn premiered at New York's Capitol Theater on 13 March 1947. Most of the reviews were favourable to the star, with *Newsweek* declaring: 'Sinatra becomes a smoother performer every time out.' *New York Times* critic Bosley Crowther agreed: 'Mr Sinatra turns in a performance of considerable charm. He acts with some ease and dexterity.' *Box Office* predicted another hit for Sinatra, a forecast not born out by largely indifferent audience response. *Brooklyn* proved a serious financial disappointment, losing $138,000 on its domestic release - the box-office gross was only $38 more than the production budget - and generating negligible interest overseas.

The only significant dissenter among the critics was *New York Daily Mirror* entertainment editor Lee Mortimer, whose March 14 review delivered a damning verdict on Sinatra: 'This excellent and well-produced picture... bogs down under the miscast Frank (Lucky) Sinatra, smirking and trying to play a leading man.' Having already attacked the star for his alleged mob connections and labelled his fans 'morons', Mortimer shamelessly abused his position as film critic to rake up the Luciano story once more. Shortly afterwards, there was a confrontation between Sinatra and Mortimer at the top Hollywood nightclub Ciro's, resulting in the star being accused of unprovoked assault. With yet more bad publicity on his hands, a court case looming and Sinatra facing a possible six month jail term, Louis Mayer finally put his foot down, ordering his star to

pay Mortimer $9000 in damages and issue a public apology to get the charges dropped. As a further humiliation, Sinatra was instructed to go before the all-powerful head of the Hearst Press, William Randolph Hearst himself, and grovel. Even the boss of MGM felt intimidated by such a powerful faction and Mayer could simply not afford to have one of his stars suffer continual negative publicity. Sinatra probably felt things couldn't get any worse. Then he received the script for *The Kissing Bandit*.

THE KISSING BANDIT 1948

I've been trying to change my name ever since.
Frank Sinatra

I couldn't stand kissing him because he was so skinny, so scrawny.
Kathryn Grayson

Fatuous title. Risible film. Often derided by its star as the very worst movie of his career, *The Kissing Bandit* should at least have offered Sinatra the chance to regain the box-office footing lost by *It Happened in Brooklyn*. He was back with Joe Pasternak, back in glorious Technicolor - courtesy of ace cameraman Robert Surtees - and miles away from glum modern-day Brooklyn in both time and space. Unfortunately, the time was the 1840s, the place a Spanish-controlled colony and Sinatra was playing a man called Ricardo. While the star later made a reasonable stab at a hot-blooded Latin character for *The Pride and the Passion*, in 1947 he just wasn't ready. Recalling the experience a decade on, Pasternak declared the whole business 'a cataclysm that still jolts my blood pressure when I think of the red ink.' Writer Isobel Lennart had already dealt Sinatra a few questionable roles. Here she and partner-in-crime John Briard Harding came up with the champion. Located in 'old California' - basically *Zorro* territory - the script gave Sinatra the doubtless sought after opportunity to portray a straight-laced Boston business graduate who returns to his home town with the intention of running his late father's tavern. Instead, he forsakes his career in hotel management to follow in the old man's more colourful footsteps as a romantic bandit. Sinatra has seldom looked more dejected.

The already shaky project was further undermined by Pasternak's choice of a first-time director, fellow Hungarian Laslo Benedek, who'd once served as Pasternak's assistant. Inflicting this kind of material on a novice can only be seen as an extreme act of cruelty. Not even Busby Berkeley could have taken on the screenplay's camp absurdities and emerged triumphant. It's likely Benedek only got the job because the established MGM directors weren't exactly queuing up to tackle the film. While Benedek would later enjoy a little Hollywood success under the patronage of Stanley Kramer, directing *Death of a Salesman* (1951) and *The Wild One* (1954), his MGM career began and ended here. It's rumoured Benedek couldn't even handle the *Bandit* production, Pasternak quietly replacing him with *Anchors Aweigh* veteran George Sidney early in the shoot.

The bad news didn't stop there. For the first time since *Higher and Higher*, Sinatra could not depend on the sterling services of Cahn and Styne. The songs for *Bandit* were entrusted to the scratch team of Nacio Herb Brown, Earl Brent and Edward Heyman. A respected talent with tunes such as 'Singin' in the Rain' to his name, Brown's work on *Bandit* is by no means terrible, but horrible casting, wretched writing and inept staging leave the songs stranded in a vacuum. As more than one harsh reviewer suggested, the number entitled 'Siesta' serves not so much as a showstopper as a verdict on the film's effect. Brent had worked on *Anchors* as Kathryn Grayson's vocal arranger and the results are even less inspiring this time around. The unenviable job of dance director went to Stanley Donen, striking out a little from the shadow of mentor Gene Kelly. The most interesting aspect of *Bandit*'s musical credits is the presence of no less than seven arrangers, including Axel Stordahl and Andre Previn. Sadly this appears to reflect not the amount of time and care lavished on the score, rather some production

assistant desperately rounding up available talent in order to get the damn thing finished.

The overall feeling of inescapable doom persisted throughout the production. Having managed to avoid kissing her co-star in their two previous films together, Grayson now found that lip-contact could not be avoided during *Bandit*'s less-than-grand finale. Her apparent revulsion at the idea of intimacy with Sinatra didn't help their on-screen chemistry - already struggling to get off the zero mark - or their off-screen working relationship. While Grayson got to sing 'Love is Where You Find It' during the course of the film, no-one in the minimal audience was persuaded she'd found it with Sinatra. It's probably no coincidence that this third Sinatra-Grayson partnership would also be their last.

Increasingly depressed during the filming, Sinatra received a morale-boosting on-set visit from daughter Nancy. Four decades on, Nancy Jr claimed that she always thought the film 'adorable', which places her in a minority of approximately one. Despite this show of support, Sinatra couldn't rouse himself into anything resembling life on-screen and *Bandit* marks one of the few occasions in his film career where he is quite obviously embarrassed to be there, his period costume fitting about as comfortably as a concrete overcoat. Even his first display of screen violence, punching out love rival Count Belmonte (Carleton Young), is utterly perfunctory. Grayson's performance as Teresa is similarly dead on arrival, the actress sharing her co-star's opinion that they were stuck in probably the worst film of all time. The supporting cast, notably J. Carrol Naish and Broadway star Mildred Natwick, offers better value for money, but there just isn't enough in the foreground to support. Naish's blatantly false nose doesn't help matters. A (very) minor point of interest is the presence of Broadway star Sono Osato, who'd recently scored a hit in *On the Town* as 'Miss Turnstiles'. Cast here as a sultry tavern dancer out to seduce the meek Ricardo, she gets to perform Donen's lively, mildly fetishistic 'Whip Dance' while Sinatra cowers on a kitchen chair, but is otherwise wasted. In the usual Hollywood scheme of things, when MGM decided to film *On the Town*,

The Kissing Bandit – Sinatra and Kathryn Grayson demonstrate the sizzling chemistry that made their screen partnership such a hit. By the end of the decade, 10,000 pesos was about Sinatra's price tag.

Osato's role went to contract player Vera-Ellen. Fate can be a cruel jester.

With all the scheduled scenes completed, the studio executives sat down, looked at the *Bandit* footage and realised they'd got a howling dog on their hands. Seeking a token second opinion, the MGM management elected to hold a sneak preview. The hostile audience response confirmed their fears and the film was declared unreleasable in its existing form. All eyes fell on producer Pasternak to come up with a miracle cure. Denied the time, the budget and his star for any serious reshoots - Sinatra was away on the RKO lot filming *The Miracle of the Bells* - Pasternak suggested adding a little more spectacle to the film, in the form of an additional musical sequence. Choreographer Robert Alton devised

a vaguely Latin-style 'Dance of Fury' and recruited three suitable performers: recent MGM signing Ricardo Montalban, Cyd Charisse and future *On the Town* co-star Ann Miller. As Montalban later remarked in his autobiography, 'It was furious, all right, but not enough to save the picture.' Nevertheless, Pasternak declared himself satisfied with the end result. His optimism failed to infect the rest of the MGM management and *The Kissing Bandit* was ultimately shelved for well over a year before being inflicted on the public, by which time Sinatra's 'comeback' movie, *Take Me Out to the Ball Game*, was already in the can. A canny strategy, if a doomed one. The sales campaign for *Bandit* was as lacklustre as the film. Plugging their shabby wares as 'MGM's big, bold, different Technicolor musical!', the advertising department shamelessly attempted to flog *Bandit* on the strength of Sinatra's one previous MGM hit. Proudly announcing 'THE SINGING STARS OF "ANCHORS AWEIGH" TOGETHER AGAIN!', they conveniently bypassed both *It Happened in Brooklyn* and Sinatra's notable double failure to win Grayson's on-screen heart. The all-new Sinatra-Grayson teaming was described as 'The hilarious misadventures of a timid outlaw and the gorgeous gal whose kisses almost killed him!' The phrase 'dead in the water' springs to mind.

Released on 19 November 1948, *Bandit* received predictably terrible reviews. *New York Herald Tribune* critic Otis L. Guernsey Jr described the film as 'a grand Technicolored vacuum...limp Spanish omelette'. Regarding Sinatra's miserable performance, Bosley Crowther pulled no punches: 'Except for appearing gawky, which seems not very hard for him to do, and singing...rather nicely, he contributes little to the show.' *Los Angeles Mirror* critic Justin Gilbert put it even more bluntly: 'While his songs aren't bad, his acting is.' Audiences were similarly unimpressed and the film proved a resounding flop at the box-office. Pasternak stood by his original verdict on *Bandit* as an 'amusing' picture, which gives Nancy Jnr some company, but conceded that any purpose-built crowd pleaser so utterly rejected could only be regarded as a failure.

The Kissing Bandit –
A neatly coiffeured Sinatra explains the script's deeper meanings to director Laslo Benedek.

Hoping to recoup at least some of their investment, MGM released the film's more bearable songs on a long-playing record, a desperate gesture that met with the sales figures it deserved.

This was a particularly bad time for Sinatra to be appearing in flop movies. MGM's profits had been in a steady decline since 1945 and Mayer was under pressure from Loew's boss Nicholas Schenck to cut any dead weight from the studio payroll. Schenck also felt that the overall quality of MGM's product had fallen off - a legacy from the war years when entertainment-hungry audiences would watch just about anything - and *The Kissing Bandit* hardly refuted this view. Bad public relations, mediocre receipts and a questionable professional attitude made Sinatra an increasingly

doubtful proposition for MGM. Only Mayer's personal faith kept him on board. For the time being.

Fifteen months earlier, Sinatra completed his final scene of *Bandit*, fled the set and gave thanks he had a better role awaiting him. Increasingly sick of musicals, the star badly wanted to try his hand at a dramatic part, something he wouldn't end up treating with thinly veiled contempt. MGM weren't interested in Sinatra's desire for new challenges in his career, arguing that they'd signed him as a singing star and had no intention of expensively indulging his misguided ambitions. A mere five days later in August 1947, Sinatra was back on set at RKO for shooting on *The Miracle of the Bells*.

THE MIRACLE OF THE BELLS 1948

Hollywood to St Michael's. That's rather strange.
Father Paul, priest

I'm not going to release a picture with a dead girl in it and that's final.
Marcus Harris, film producer

Generally dismissed as one of the most embarrassing episodes in Sinatra's career, *The Miracle of the Bells* is a lot more intriguing than its shoddy reputation would suggest. This is not to say it's a particularly good film or that Sinatra's performance is an unappreciated gem of acting. Sinatra, usually fairly realistic in appraising his work, later remarked that *Bells* '... turned out less well than we had hoped'. Religious themes tend to bring out the worst in Hollywood executives and this film is only a partial exception. Overawed by its own subject matter - the spiritual rebirth of a poor mining town, indeed the entire nation, through the self-sacrifice of a saintly former inhabitant - *Bells* is overlong, ponderous, variably scripted, melodramatic to the point of no return, sickly sentimental and in somewhat dubious taste. Seldom has a martyrdom motif - Joan of Arc at the stake - been so heavily hammered home. It is also a fascinating study of obsessive devotion beyond the grave - the heroine spends most of the film in a wooden box - and a cynical attack on petty church politics, the profit-hungry funeral business and the exploitation of impoverished workers. As for Sinatra's acting, he deserves at least half a cigar.

By 1947, Frank Sinatra felt an urgent need to break from the typecasting he'd laboured under since *Higher and Higher*. He didn't like the roles he was getting, he didn't enjoy acting in the films and, *Anchors Aweigh* excepted, audiences didn't seem too keen either. MGM had only a diet of increasingly undernourishing musicals to offer and even here he wasn't being given the best projects available. The time had come for Sinatra to use his loan-out clause and he knew exactly which part he wanted, the humble-yet-wise priest in RKO's forthcoming film version of *The Miracle of the Bells*. He'd read the best-selling Russell Janney novel during a long train journey west and felt that the allegorical tale of a deceased film star, her loyal press agent and the mining-town where the 'miracle' occurs offered a chance for him to show off real acting talent. He would even surrender his top-billing spot, going down to third place for the first time since *Higher*. Aside from the challenge of the role, Sinatra was also aware of how well rival Bing Crosby had done with his two clerical appearances as the saintly Father O'Malley in *Going My Way* (1944) and *The Bells of St Mary's* (1945), picking up a Best Actor Academy Award for the former. MCA agent Lew Wasserman was put on the case and went in hot pursuit of the film's producer, industry veteran Jesse Lasky.

Another factor in Sinatra's decision to pursue the role of a priest was a pressing need to counter his increasingly tarnished public image. The Luciano story was still doing the rounds and MGM were extremely unhappy with the continual muck-raking, which their own publicity department appeared powerless to counter. Neither the studio nor the media were impressed by Sinatra's choice of image-change, and the eventual announcement that his $100,000 fee would be donated to the Catholic Church failed to sway them. Columnist Robert Ruark spoke for the right-wing faction: '...it is elegant press relations - the best, because Sinatra, the mock clergyman, hurriedly wipes out the picture of Sinatra, the thug's chum'. Sinatra

was also decried for taking the part on the grounds of his alleged 'communist' politics. Surely the godless could not be permitted to portray the God-fearing. This potentially harmful pre-production furore did not go unnoticed by nervous RKO executives, though just how seriously they took it is open to question.

Jesse Lasky was currently halfway through a two-movie deal with RKO, the latter co-financing and releasing the films. *Without Reservations* (1946), a Hollywood-set comedy romance starring Claudette Colbert and John Wayne, had proved a hit. For *Miracle of the Bells*, Lasky retained the movie-world element, albeit in a very different context. According to Lasky's ghosted memoirs, the inspiration for hiring Sinatra was entirely his own. With leads Fred MacMurray and Alida Valli already cast, the smaller yet pivotal role of the hometown Polish-American priest remained unfilled and no obvious choice of star offered itself. Entirely unaware of Sinatra's interest in the part, Lasky experienced what he later described as a 'brainstorm' and suggested the singer as ideal offbeat casting. The film's scriptwriters, Ben Hecht and Quentin Reynolds, had widely varying reactions to Lasky's choice. Reynolds, like MGM, the critics and just about everybody else, felt it would be a huge mistake. Hecht, after a period of doubt, conceded that casting Sinatra could be good 'showmanship'. Lasky rated the singer's performance in the finished film as 'perfect', attributing the indifferent box-office to poor word-of-mouth from Sinatra's bobby-soxer fans disappointed at the lack of songs. This version of events should be regarded with a little healthy scepticism. Writing a decade after the events, when Sinatra's second coming as a dramatic actor was at its height, Lasky could be forgiven for granting himself a level of foresight not entirely deserved. Other accounts suggest that Lasky was in fact extremely wary of hiring Sinatra for his film, seeking official sanction from the Catholic authorities before agreeing on a contract. He also had to consider MGM's possible response to him giving Sinatra a role the bigger studio didn't want their troublesome star to play. A cordial rival could rapidly become a vindictive enemy. In the event, MGM's displeasure would be directed entirely at their errant contract player.

While returning to the scene of his early, unsuccessful film exploits could have been viewed as something of a backward step, Sinatra had reason to feel at least a little optimism over his reunion with RKO. This new project was not some tinpot 'B' musical to be churned out at maximum speed. Presold to audiences on the strength of the hit original, *Miracle of the Bells* had class written all over it. Along with Samuel Goldwyn and Cecil B. De Mille, Jesse L. Lasky was one of the original Hollywood pioneers, jointly founding the Famous Players-Lasky studio which later evolved into Paramount.

Despite his slightly reduced circumstances, Lasky assembled a quality team for *Miracle of the Bells*. Director Irving Pichel had made an impressive debut with *The Most Dangerous Game* (1932), though he shared responsibilities with adventure-specialist Ernest Schoedsack, an arrangement repeated for *She* (1935). Aided immeasurably by Robert De Grasse's atmospheric monochrome photography, Pichel's careful direction of *Bells* is quite effective, the measured pace and straight-faced performances papering over a lot of the film's flaws. There is a striking fantasy sequence, where Valli's character imagines herself playing Joan at her trial, which makes imaginative use of light and sound. Speaking of flaws, entrusting the screenplay to Hecht and Reynolds proved a mixed blessing. While boasting such credits as *Scarface* (1932), *Wuthering Heights* (1939) and *Spellbound* (1945), former newspaperman Hecht regarded Hollywood with a very open disdain, bragging that he could knock off most scripts in under two weeks (picking up between $50,000 and $125,000 in the process). Hecht had worked for Lasky back in the mid-1920s when he first arrived in Hollywood but felt no obligation to treat his old employer any differently from the other Hollywood taskmasters. His work on *Bells* is uneven to say the least, the script weighed down by clumsy sentiment and flip dialogue. A lot of the screenplay has something of a first draft feel, overwritten in parts, underwritten in others. These faults were perhaps inevitable, given that Hecht was

working on three other scripts at the same time. Reynolds also contributed to the film as the voice of a radio reporter, so at least he got a little taste of what the cast had to deal with.

Once Sinatra was aboard, his role had to be revised and expanded from the original script. Neither Reynolds nor Hecht were available/willing/competent and the task fell to RKO regular De Witt Bodeen, whose naive-poetic style had been put to good use in the Val Lewton horror films *Cat People* (1942), *The Seventh Victim* (1943) and *The Curse of the Cat People* (1944). Faced with an uphill task, Bodeen emerged with honours about even. Perhaps anxious over leaving his star utterly songless, Lasky decided to grant Sinatra one brief *a cappella* number that could be slotted into the script without disrupting the narrative. Cahn and Styne were called upon and came up with 'Ever Homeward', adapted from a Polish folk song. The main score was composed by fomer Disney employee Leigh Harline and offers an absurdly overwrought, if undeniably effective, blend of heavenly choir and heart-tugging strings.

The main stars of the piece, MacMurray and Valli, were about as likely a combination as Jack Haley and Michèle Morgan in *Higher and Higher*. MacMurray had become established as a solid Paramount star during the 1940s, enjoying his greatest success in *Double Indemnity* (1944). Italian actress Valli was a recent David Selznick signing, bound to a long-term contract, and Selznick was happy to loan his discovery to RKO while he figured out what to do with her. Cast as Polish émigré Olga Treskovna, Valli has little to do in *Bells* except look pious and convince the audience that the budding movie star would rather die of tuberculosis - brought on by her childhood intake of coal dust - than fail to complete her Joan of Arc epic and let down the folks back home. This is pretty much an impossible role and to her credit Valli does capture an ethereal, otherworldly quality that renders Olga's suicide mission a little more plausible. MacMurray's initially affable, down-to-earth agent Bill Dunnigan provides an effective foil. Unable to reveal his true feelings for Olga during her lifetime, he risks everything to enshrine her memory. If *Double Indemnity* depicted the dark side of MacMurray's regular guy persona, *Bells* shows a man veering towards the edge of sanity, refusing to let Olga go into her grave a nobody. Awakened by the bells of Coaltown, Pennsylvannia - bells he's paid to have rung non-stop for three days - Dunnigan's first words are for his lost love: 'Do you like 'em, Olga? They're ringing your name baby. Coast to coast.'

While RKO were still in dubious financial shape, they had enough confidence in their new property to invest a $3 million budget in the project. An entire mock-up church was built on the production's Culver City lot, intended to represent St Michael's, the rundown, sparsely attended miners' church presided over by Sinatra's Father Paul.

During shooting, Sinatra was mistaken for a real priest by the mother of an old friend visiting the set. The lady spoke no English and had never heard of Frank Sinatra, which gave the star something of a head start in the plausibility stakes. More enlightened observers would be quick to cry fraud.

While most of Sinatra's scenes were with MacMurray, he got on better with another member of the cast, character actor Lee J. Cobb. Hired to play tough-tender movie mogul Marcus Harris, Cobb was reunited with Sinatra fifteen years later for the comedy *Come Blow Your Horn*.

Much of *Miracle of the Bells* is devoted to a series of lengthy flashbacks as Dunnigan recalls his friendship with Olga, from her humble beginnings as a lowly - and not very talented - chorus girl to her hospital deathbed the day after Joan of Arc finished shooting. Sinatra first appears half an hour into the film, seated at his study desk, as Dunnigan visits St Michael's for Olga's funeral arrangements. Clad in a cassock that looks at least a size too big, he fails to stand up to greet his visitor, an odd touch that never gets explained. Sinatra seems uneasy for much of the scene, swivelling in his chair in small arcs, clasping his hands and blinking too much. Softspoken most of the time, he evidently had trouble translating his real-life affinity for playing tough into his on-screen performance. Called upon to grow angry with an

avaricious mortician during a 'phone call - 'You're a greedy and stupid man Mr Orloff' - Sinatra sounds strained, his lack of acting experience all too evident. Later scenes exhibit a little more confidence, though Sinatra does have to struggle with some questionable dialogue, notably: 'I never thought of the Apostles as press agents'; 'the sins of the poor are mostly in their poverty' and, re St Michael, 'he fought and defeated Lucifer Prince of Darkness', a line he delivers as if it had just been handed to him. Dwarfed by MacMurray, Sinatra has a largely passive role, serving mainly as the former's confidante and moral guide (swap MacMurray for Michele Morgan and we're almost back in *Higher and Higher* territory). At least he convinces the audience that his priest is a far better man than smug social climber Father Spinsky, who runs St Leo's, the biggest church in town and tries to hijack the publicity surrounding Olga for himself.

The Miracle of the Bells – Frank pious as Father Paul.

As for the 'miracle', on the day of the funeral statues of the Virgin and Child and St Michael turn on their plinths to face Olga's coffin. There is a rational explanation: subsidence underneath St Michael's - the result of extensive mine workings - caused their supporting pillars to move slightly. Dunnigan urges Father Paul to endorse the phenomenon as an act of God, the alternative being to destroy people's new found hope and faith. Here Sinatra comes into his own, delivering a suitably inspirational speech with more conviction than the writing deserves: 'I know what makes a saint and I also know what makes a beautiful human being. Such a one lies now at our feet.' There is probably a subtext here regarding the parallels between religion, showbusiness and plain old con-trickery, but it gets swamped by the final images of born-again churchgoers marching towards St Michael's. At least Father Paul can now afford a new roof.

Aware of the sensitive feelings surrounding their production, Lasky and RKO attempted to devise a suitably tasteful promotional campaign. The result stands as one of the worst posters in movie history. Plugged as Russell Janney's *The Miracle Of The Bells* - to keep that bestseller link in the public's mind - the title lettering is flanked by multiple swinging clappers. On the bottom left of the poster are dreadful renditions of MacMurray and Valli, both of whom appear to have pencilled eyebrows and red-glossed lips. Slightly elevated on the bottom right, his eyes raised in the general direction of heaven, Sinatra looks for all the world like a drag queen in search of his wig. Lipstick, eyelashes, eyeliner, eyebrow pencil, the lot. If the Mob stories about him had been true, at least one Hollywood graphic designer would have been given a new concrete wardrobe.

Released on 27 March 1948, *The Miracle of the Bells* met with the critical equivalent of a damn good kicking. *Time* magazine sneered: 'Frank Sinatra, looking rather flea-bitten as the priest, acts properly humble or perhaps ashamed'. *The New York Times* expressed similar sentiments: 'Frank Sinatra appears frightened speechless (and almost songless) by the task of playing a priest...the

picture is so weighted with mawkish melancholia that it drips all over the screen.' *Cue* magazine summed up with damning terseness: 'The picture can be reasonably described as nauseating.' *Bells* did no better on its British release, when the *Monthly Film Bulletin* declared it 'An offensive exhibition of vulgar insensitivity.' Sinatra's MGM bosses were mightily displeased with the deluge of hostile personal reviews and wasted little time letting the star know about it. In no position to retaliate directly, Sinatra took out his own wrath on RKO, informing Lasky that he would not be attending the film's charity premiere in San Francisco. The fact that he was contractually obliged to do so moved him not a bit. Aware how this would be played on by the already cynical press, Lasky begged Sinatra to reconsider, putting his request on a personal favour basis, and eventually the star relented. The premiere was judged a success, much to Lasky's relief, though he later discovered that a still-spiteful Sinatra had taken more covert sabotage action, running up huge hotel and expenses accounts during his stay in San Francisco and charging them to RKO. The film didn't perform so well on general release. Though not quite the outright flop of reputation, *Miracle of the Bells* enjoyed only fair-to-middling box-office, certainly not enough for the producers - and Sinatra - to be able to turn on the critics and tell them where to put their reviews.

Two months later, on 31 May, Sinatra, MacMurray and Valli performed a truncated version of the *Bells* script for the Lux Radio Theater series, so evidently someone felt it was worth trying to cash in on the film. As with *Anchors* the previous year, Sinatra's repeat performance served as a little-needed reminder that his movie career was in poor shape. The outright flop of *The Kissing Bandit* later on in the year didn't help. According to Earl Wilson, the star was genuinely worried about his future in films. Sinatra took the failure of his first proper acting role particularly badly, becoming increasingly embittered about the whole film industry. Furthermore, he now had to return to MGM, cassock between his legs, and face whatever terrible contractual reprisals they had in mind.

3

Back in Uniform

1948-1950

The Lone Ranger and Frank Sinatra are the
prime instigators of juvenile delinquency in America.
Congress accusation

TAKE ME OUT TO THE BALL GAME 1949

Who's that skinny little runt? Gee he's cute.
Shirley Delwyn

They mocked the bandit. They jeered the priest. With one hit, one disappointment and four outright flops to his name, Sinatra's Hollywood standing in 1948 could best be described as shaky. While his MGM pay-packet for the year totalled an impressive $325,833 - only $40,000 less than top star Bette Davis - his box-office take attracted rather less envy. MGM's response to the Sinatra dilemma was both simple and predictable: a reunion with Gene Kelly, the sooner the better. Recent history had proved beyond all executive doubt that Sinatra just didn't draw the crowds without Kelly at his side. The small matters of poor scripts, second-rank productions and blatant miscasting didn't seem to enter into the studio's calculations. There is a case for arguing that MGM never really knew what to do with Sinatra. The magical voice and undernourished body simply didn't accord with their prerequisites for a leading man

and no-one aside from Sinatra thought - or dared - to suggest that the singer was in need of a different song. However thin the amicable-but-shy movie persona might wear, MGM just couldn't picture an alternative. Bad for them, even worse for Sinatra.

Take Me Out to the Ball Game originated in a disagreement between MGM and Gene Kelly back in the summer of 1946. Showing a distinct lack of imagination, the studio could only envisage any Sinatra-Kelly reunion as another *Anchors Aweigh*-style vehicle. Joe Pasternak had devised a storyline involving two demobbed sailors buying a bombed-out government surplus aircraft carrier for $2000 and turning it into a floating nightclub. Never a great fan of the Garland-Rooney let's-put-on-a-show subgenre, Kelly felt Pasternak's outline amounted to no more than a feeble variation on a tired theme and rejected it out of hand. After a little consultation with more adventurous producer Arthur Freed, he suggested substituting a less formula-bound musical spectacular with a baseball background. Not over-impressed with the skills of MGM's story department, Kelly offered to work on the

Take Me Out to the Ball Game – Betty Garrett, Sinatra, Jules Munshin,
Gene Kelly and Esther Williams. Note the bare studio backdrop.

idea himself, centring on two professional ball players
who spend their winters moonlighting as vaudeville
song-and-dance men. Freed thought the end result
unremarkable but bought the outline for MGM in order
to placate Kelly, who netted a tidy $25,000 for his
efforts. A vaudeville veteran himself, Freed had joined
MGM in 1929 as a lyricist, graduating to associate
producer on *The Wizard of Oz* (1939), then full-fledged
producer on hits such as *Babes in Arms* (1939) and
Meet Me in St Louis (1944). Appreciating Freed's
undeniable talent, Louis Mayer allowed him an enviable
freedom in his choice of musical projects. Freed took
his films a little more seriously than Joe Pasternak,
claiming that he operated a policy of 'integrated'
musical numbers, each burst into song and dance

having a plausible narrative reason. This is a slightly
dubious assertion in the case of *Ball Game*, unless
'plausible' means someone shouting out 'Where did you
get that hat?'

Had Freed's original casting plans worked out, *Ball
Game* would have been very different in tone and style
from the movie eventually released. The film went into
preproduction with the star trio of Sinatra, Kelly and
Judy Garland slated as the leads. The task of
transforming Kelly's outline into a workable screenplay
fell to staff writer George Wells, who'd worked on *Till
the Clouds Roll By*, while the score was entrusted to the
song writing team of Harry Warren and Ralph Blane,
Freed's collaborators on the Mickey Rooney musical
Summer Holiday (1948). Garland's abrupt departure

from the project led to the script being heavily revised and the score totally discarded. The result is generally regarded as little more than a genial, lightweight forerunner of *On the Town*, an accurate if slightly dismissive verdict. Set in 1908, during Theodore Roosevelt's presidency, the story involves World Series champions The Wolves and their consternation at having - shock - a woman as their new owner. Sinatra plays Ryan, Kelly plays O'Brien, Esther Williams plays Katherine Catherine Higgins and the level of wit doesn't get much higher. The title drawings are twee, as is the device of having the star names accompanied by bat strikes and loud cheering, and a subplot involving illegal gambling and an attempt to sabotage the Wolves' last game is utterly perfunctory. For all that, *Ball Game* still offers an enthusiastic cast, fast pacing and a selection of decent songs. Commendably brief at 93 minutes, it certainly puts *Anchors Aweigh* to shame.

For the director's chair, Freed selected his old *Babes in Arms* colleague Busby Berkeley, whose patchy directing career had stalled badly after *For Me and My Gal* and the kitsch classic *The Gang's All Here* (1943). Berkeley had already botched one 'comeback' assignment on *Till the Clouds Roll By*, largely thanks to his chronic alcoholism and manic depression, but Freed remained confident he could guide the battered veteran through an undemanding shoot. It's unclear exactly how far Berkeley's responsibilities on the film extended, Kelly and Stanley Donen allegedly directing much of *Ball Game* after Berkeley dropped out part-way through production under a cover story of 'exhaustion'. Donen later claimed that he and Kelly always wanted to direct the entire film themselves and resented Freed's imposition of the clearly incompetent Berkeley. For the record, the direction of the film shows little sign of creative conflict, making effective use of mobile camera crane shots and bold low angles. The most obviously Berkeley-esque touch is a pool sequence featuring Esther Williams' character softly singing the title anthem while swimming on her back. The pale yellow of her bathing suit and matching cap contrasts nicely with the deep blue of the water. Sinatra's

character is so excited he slides down a large palm tree to be near her. Not quite as Freudian as the giant bananas in *The Gang's All Here* but close.

With Warren and Blane off the film, new songs were commissioned from composer Roger Edens and the lyric-writing team of Betty Comden and Adolph Green. Edens had been with MGM since 1935, working on *The Wizard of Oz*, *Meet Me in St Louis* and *Easter Parade* (1948). Comden and Green were best known for their work on the Leonard Bernstein Broadway hit *On the Town*. MGM held the film rights to the show, even though both Mayer and Freed disliked it, and the lyricists were currently under studio contract. Their work on *Ball Game* is just a notch below the more flamboyant libretto for *On the Town*, memorable yet uninspiring. The dominant, twice-reprised title song was written by Jack Norworth and Albert Von Tilzer, with no input from their rather more famous colleagues.

Two Sinatra tunes appear to have bitten the dust during post-production: 'Last Night When We Were Young' and 'Boys and Girls Like You and Me', the latter regarded by Freed biographer Hugh Fordin as one of Sinatra's finest vocal performances. The 'Boys...' footage surfaced in 1993, finally reaching the paying public via a 'special edition' laserdisc release of *That's Entertainment*. Sinatra's co-stars also suffered a little from the scissor-happy studio executives, the Kelly-Williams duet 'Baby Love' deleted on the grounds that the latter couldn't handle the accompanying choreography.

Resigned to a partial rerun of *Anchors*, Kelly assumed Kathryn Grayson would be his romantic interest in *Ball Game*. Freed had slightly higher ambitions for the film and named Garland as the female lead. With Sinatra, Garland and Berkeley to watch over, Freed was taking on a lot of potential trouble when fate stepped in to ease the burden. Already well on the road to pill-popping, booze-slugging oblivion, Garland was declared unfit to work on a musical. Swimming sensation Esther Williams came into bat as a slightly unlikely substitute, hinting at some studio anxiety over Sinatra and Kelly's drawing power. MGM's top box-office star at the time, Williams had little in the way of musical ability - her singing had to be dubbed - but audiences couldn't get enough of her in the pool. The changeover for *Ball Game* necessitated some extensive rewriting, undertaken by Harry Tugend, whose main task was to give Williams at least one aquatic sequence.

Kelly had intended the showy supporting role of comedy-relief ball player Nat Goldberg for his friend Leo Durocher. Freed chose to cast gangly comedian Jules Munshin, who'd attracted MGM's attention with his star-making performance in the 1946 Broadway hit *Call Me Mister*, subsequently appearing in *Easter Parade*. The second female lead went to contract player Betty Garrett, a multi-talented actress-comedienne-singer-dancer sadly wasted for much of her brief film career. For the small yet memorable role of a gruff Shakespeare-quoting assistant baseball coach, Freed cast character actor Tom Dugan. All three would subsequently appear in *On the Town*, though second time out Munshin wouldn't get to stick a lit cigar under his cap.

With all the various preproduction hassles resolved, *Ball Game* commenced shooting on 28 July 1948. The filming went more or less smoothly, especially by Sinatra's standards, the star even posing for publicity shots with four year old son Frank Jnr. According to co-star Betty Garrett, Sinatra was both amenable and amicable for most of the production, making only token complaints regarding extended rehearsals and multiple takes. He did occasionally lark about on set, wasting filming time, but remained largely sensitive to his co-stars' feelings regarding professional behaviour. Sinatra also used his still-considerable star clout to help out his co-workers. During the filming of a short love scene, he insisted that Garrett be given an unscripted close-up, which stayed in the final edit. Back on the dance floor with Gene Kelly, Sinatra worked hard on the musical routines, confident that his dancing teacher would not push him to do anything beyond his still very limited ability. Garrett was impressed by the results, rating Sinatra a quick learner with a natural grace. As with

Anchors Aweigh, the rehearsals were strenuous and Kelly was taken aback by his co-star's minimal lunches: one bottle of Coca Cola and one standard-size Mars bar.

From the maelstrom of recasting, rewriting and rescoring, not to mention alleged creative clashes, departures and Sinatra's own hijinks, *Take Me Out to the Ball Game* emerged as modest yet class entertainment. Sinatra and Kelly largely reprise their *Anchors* relationship, even down to Ryan being smitten by Higgins before realising that a) he really loves baseball groupie Shirley Delwyn (Garrett) and b) Higgins really loves O'Brien, despite initial mutual loathing. Kelly is the brash woman-chaser with dreams of being a full-time vaudeville star. Sinatra is content to spend his evenings playing checkers, though he's beginning to wonder if he's missing anything (the singer was 32 at the time). A little more hot-tempered than before, Sinatra's lack of muscle is a running joke, as is his milkshake dependency and fear of sexually uninhibited women (which required real acting). Twice he is knocked unconscious by giant-sized opponents and then carried off to safety, once by Kelly, once by Garrett, who appears to have no difficulty supporting his weight. Sinatra's nervous courtship of the statuesque Williams is amusingly unlikely, yet the effect doesn't appear to have been entirely intentional. There is a half-hearted attempt in some shots to disguise their relative heights, but Williams very obviously towers over him as he croons 'She's the Right Girl for Me' to the wrong girl. The romance with Garrett is more plausible, beginning with her chasing Sinatra all over the Sarasota Baseball Park while singing 'It's Fate, Baby, It's Fate'. Though not conventionally beautiful, Garrett has a very appealing screen presence and she works well with Sinatra. Even the dimmest studio executive must have realised that she was the only choice for his love interest in *On the Town*.

Aided by some attractive period detail, the musical numbers in *Ball Game* are pleasant without quite reaching classic status. Sinatra and Kelly are first seen on stage performing the title song, dressed in red pinstripe suits and straw boaters. Staged in four long takes, the sequence involves an athletic tap dance which Sinatra executes with more than adequate ability. Kelly is still way ahead in terms of apparent natural ease but his pupil had moved on since *Anchors*. Unlike much of the plot. Their second duet is 'The Boy Said No', a dubious chronicle of their alleged off-season romantic interludes, including one suicide and one aged eleven. Still, with their wholesome characters and powder-blue baseball outfits, Sinatra and Kelly can't be taken too seriously. The 'comedy' number with Munshin, 'O'Brien to Ryan to Goldberg', is less successful, not least because Sinatra appears to lose his nerve towards the end of the song-and-dance, glancing awkwardly at his partners during the last moves of the routine.

Overall, Sinatra acquits himself well in *Ball Game*, especially given the limitations of his role but the surprise success of the film is one-time bobby-soxer Esther Williams. With her strong features, large eyes and full lips, Williams was made for Technicolor (Sinatra once again does less well by the process, his face looking too shiny in some shots, haggard in others). Though sketchily written, K.C. Higgins emerges as confident, independent and always dignified, even when wearing a huge pink feather hat. She is also pretty hot with a baseball bat, 'accidentally' slugging the leering, sexist, groping O'Brien, and dealing with his later romantic advances by pointing out that he has broken the players' ten o'clock curfew: 'It's going to cost you 50 bucks, baby doll.' Although not called upon for any heavy duty dancing, Williams does participate in the abrupt, out-of-character 'Strictly USA' finale, along with Sinatra, Kelly and Garrett. With all the minimal plot strands tied up, the producers clearly didn't know how to end the film. Sinatra and Kelly appear on stage once more, this time clad in electric blue top hats and jackets with matching red-white striped bow ties. They are then joined by their co-stars for a brief patriotic number that reiterates the final romantic pairings, offers glib tributes to one-time contenders Kathryn Grayson and Judy Garland and drops self-conscious references to Sinatra/Kelly rivals Bing Crosby and Fred Astaire. It's all a bit too much like the Garland-Rooney musicals.

Take Me Out to the Ball Game wrapped on 26 October 1948 at a total cost of $1,725,970.54. After a successful preview held in Encino, California on 16 December, MGM premiered Ball Game in New York and Los Angeles on 10 March 1949, with a general release at the beginning of April. While Sinatra's reviews could not have got much worse after *Kissing Bandit* and *Miracle of the Bells*, the critical response to *Ball Game* proved surprisingly lukewarm. Bosley Crowther felt the ingredients had been overextended, throwing in an appropriate baseball analogy: 'Don't be surprised if you see people getting up for a seventh-inning stretch'. *Time* magazine declared that Sinatra and Co. were once again struggling with inferior material: '...a whirl of songs and dances that are easy to forget'. Audiences were a little more enthusiastic and *Ball Game* grossed $4,344,000 at the American box-office. Not a bad total by Sinatra's recent standards, but very disappointing compared to the usual take for an Esther Williams movie. The difference was enough for the film to be rated a flop by many and there was little chance of the total being boosted by revenue from foreign markets. Baseball pictures were regarded as box-office poison outside America, a concern reflected in the film's title change for British cinemas, where *Take Me Out to the Ball Game* became *Everybody's Cheering*. If MGM had worried that non-natives would find the original unenticing and probably incomprehensible, the new title reflected an optimism not borne out by the public response. For Sinatra, the frustrations and anxieties of his film career were largely unresolved. Having once more played an efficient second fiddle to Gene Kelly, his position at MGM remained much the same. *Ball Game* had arrested the downward curve of his box-office appeal but not enough to give him any clout in choosing projects. His employers still wouldn't take his wish for non-musical roles seriously, reasoning that Sinatra was barely passing muster in his 'natural' genre. The Voice and The Feet would shortly ride again in a movie that would make Kelly's MGM career and break Sinatra's.

ON THE TOWN 1949

*They're not going to get me into
another sailor's suit.*
Frank Sinatra, post *Anchors Aweigh*

*He wanted to see the beautiful sights of our
beautiful City of New York. And I
showed him plenty.*
Brunhilde Esterhazy

Three sailors find fun and romance on 24-hour leave in
the Big Apple. What *Anchors Aweigh* did for west coast
movie capital Los Angeles, *On the Town* does far better
for east coast New York. Inspired by the Leonard
Bernstein ballet *Fancy Free*, the original stage version
was a collaboration between Bernstein, the Comden-
Green team and respected Broadway director George
Abbott. When it came to obtaining the film rights for the
show, MGM had a head start. One of Mayer's personal
staff, story editor Lillie Messinger, was a close friend of
Bernstein and her enthusiasm was sufficient for Mayer to
make a deal for $250,000 before *On the Town* premiered
in December 1944, an investment the show's producers
badly needed to finance their musical spectacular. Once
he'd actually seen the show, Mayer rapidly regretted his
haste. He disliked *On the Town* intensely, regarding the
content as 'smutty' and, far worse, 'Communistic'. All
immediate plans to film *On The Town* were cancelled,
audiences obliged to settle for the nautical-themed
Anchors Aweigh.

Although neither Mayer nor Arthur Freed ever came
to appreciate the original show, Gene Kelly's enthusiasm
eventually persuaded them that *On the Town* did have
some film potential, especially the central premise. Kelly
also lobbied for the director's chair, arguing that the
project was ideal for his first official directing job. As co-
director Stanley Donen later explained to Fordin, the
theme could not have been better suited to cinematic
treatment: 'There was no stage, no theatre, simply the
street'. Impressed by the duo's work on *Ball Game*, Freed
agreed to Kelly's request, an extremely rare concession to

even the biggest stars at the time. Eager to reunite with
Sinatra and Munshin after their successful teaming in
Ball Game, Kelly found the former a little reluctant to
embark on a second Navy lark. Sinatra didn't like either
the costumes or the idea of repeating old concepts and
required extensive coaxing from his co-star/co-
director/co-choreographer. He also had doubts about his
leading lady, Betty Garrett, which is surprising given their
spot-on partnership in *Ball Game*. The most plausible -
and charitable - explanation is Garrett's second-lead
status. Already sensitive about his position at MGM,
Sinatra didn't need any further hints that the studio was
downgrading him. At least his contract still specified top
billing. There was little else about the project to persuade
viewers that Sinatra was the real star. Munshin was
paired with dancer Ann Miller, while Kelly got former
rockette Vera-Ellen, a new MGM signing.

Gaining his first directing assignment was not quite
enough for Kelly. He also wanted to shoot the entire
film on location in New York, giving *On the Town* a
very different look and feel to the largely studio-bound
quality of most MGM musicals. Persuading Mayer and
head of musical production Sam Katz proved a
struggle, neither understanding the effect Kelly wanted
to achieve. After protracted wrangling, Kelly agreed to
a compromise whereby he would film most of the
exteriors on location, still a first for a musical. Never
very comfortable with any kind of innovation, the
MGM executives would only sanction a modest $1.5
million budget for the production, $500,000 less than
Anchors four years earlier.

Freed's antipathy towards Bernstein's music made
radical changes to the score inevitable, despite protests
from Donen and Kelly. Only four Bernstein tunes were
deemed acceptable: the famous 'New York, New York'
opener, 'Miss Turnstiles Dance', 'Come Up to My Place'
and music employed by Gene Kelly for his 'A Day in
New York' ballet. By November 1948, *On the Town* was
well into preproduction, Comden and Green accepting a
$110,000 fee to rewrite the original show and produce
new lyrics. Kelly's central sailor character, Gabey, had to
be rendered less naive and helpless, attributes far more

On the Town – Chip and Brunhilde (Betty Garrett) atop the Empire State.

suited to Sinatra's screen persona. Roger Edens provided the new music and a useful piece of advice: keep the musical numbers intimate. Comden and Green substituted several new songs, notably 'Prehistoric Man', an enjoyably ridiculous showcase for Ann Miller's energetic tapping, and 'On the Town', which is even more fun and not a little sublime.

Rehearsals for *On the Town* began on 21 February 1949. For the first time, Kelly felt he could now teach Sinatra - and Munshin - some 'real' dancing, and his co-stars needed only four of the five weeks scheduled to learn their routines. More confident in his dancing ability, Sinatra had less faith in his appearance. At the age of 33, his hair was already thinning and the studio insisted on hair pieces for his film work. There was also concern over his lined face, which the Technicolor

process laid bare without mercy. Even the most careful make-up job could barely disguise the scars from his botched delivery back in 1915 and later mastoid operations. After all this cosmetic work, the taping-back of Sinatra's ears probably seemed a minor concession. The costume department provided a further headache for Sinatra in the form of his white Navy costume. The dark blue suit he wore in *Anchors* went some way to disguising his slender figure. White did him no such favours and it was decided that he needed a little rear padding for a more flattering shape. Extremely sensitive about this 'enhancement', Sinatra didn't tell any of his co-stars, leaving Betty Garrett to find out the hard way when she playfully patted him on the first day of filming.

The relatively straightforward studio work commenced on 28 March 1949, the cast and crew decamping to New York on 5 May. Filming the 'New York, New York' number on the crowded streets proved a major challenge. Kelly, Sinatra and Munshin had to synchronise with both their prerecorded voices and the tempo of the music for the choreography to work, a task further complicated by having to grab the shots out of sequence. Even when all these factors came together, there were still the problems of traffic, weather shifts and curious onlookers. Whatever his popularity nationwide, Sinatra still had his fans in New York. During filming in the Italian section of the city, he was close to being mobbed, with the police holding back thousands of fans until the scene was completed. The crowds still didn't shift and Sinatra had to be taken away in a patrol car.

While Sinatra's behaviour on *Ball Game* had exhibited only occasional flashes of boredom or laziness, his conduct during the *Town* shoot often resembled a return to the bad old days of *It Happened in Brooklyn*. No respecter of early morning starts, he arrived late for filming and recording sessions, further delaying work with more tiresome on-set horseplay. This was bad enough in the studio, downright unforgivable on location, especially with a novice director in need of maximum support and co-operation. Tolerating bad weather about as much as he did slow lighting cameramen, Sinatra quickly grew tired of arriving for morning calls, then sitting around waiting for the clouds to shift. Retreating to his hotel suite on Central Park South, he requested that he be summoned only when Kelly was ready to shoot. This was an absurd demand, given that the weather could change over a few minutes, with Sinatra miles away from the set. Executive wrath no longer cut much ice with the star and only the disapproval of his co-stars kept him from out-and-out rebellion. It is a measure of Sinatra's poor behaviour during filming that even Gene Kelly eventually lost patience with him. According to Garrett, Sinatra immediately backed down, giving up his lunch break to help Kelly out with the next camera set-up. Front-office suits could go hang but Sinatra couldn't bear losing the respect of fellow pros. The production wrapped back in Los Angeles on 2 July, a 47-day shoot at a cost of

$2,111,250, $600,000 over the original budget.

For all the various difficulties, *On the Town* was regarded as a largely harmonious production, with the exception of one poor-taste quip from Sinatra regarding Mayer's alleged love-life. Obviously short of recent gossip, he alluded to the latter's serious riding accident back in 1944: 'He didn't fall off a horse, he fell off Ginny Simms.' This was both cruel and inaccurate. Mayer had fractured his pelvis and developed pneumonia after the fall, and his relationship with singer Simms - which broke up the same year - was strictly platonic. Mayer could take the unprofessional behaviour, the bad press, the box-office flops. He could take Sinatra repeatedly defying his order to break off the affair with Lana Turner. He could even live with much of the star's open contempt for him. What Mayer couldn't take was any slur regarding himself and Simms. Still sensitive about the matter five years on, Louis B. Mayer finally blew his Sinatra fuse.

Plotwise, *On the Town* amounts to very little. Munshin's primitive allure nets him anthropology student Miller; Sinatra is cajoled into a romance with predatory taxi driver Garrett; Kelly pursues 'Miss Turnstiles' Vera-Ellen, a Coney Island kooch dancer from his hometown of Meadowville, Indiana. They are chased a bit by the police, Garrett's boss and an irate museum official. The spell of the film is all in the telling. In some ways, the best moment occurs right at the start, with none of the main cast present. At 5.57am, with dawn breaking over the New York skyline, a burly crane operator walks across the Navy dockyard towards his machine, hard hat on head, lunch pail in hand, singing 'I feel like I'm not out of bed yet'. Staging the action in single fluid crane shot, Kelly and Donen evoke a feeling of magical realism, their character believable as both a tough blue collar worker and a poetic romantic. What follows is fully deserving of its high reputation. Aside from the famous use of a regular on-screen time strip, Kelly's direction is as muscular as his dancing, making bold use of his hard-won locations - employing a 360-degree pan at one point - and stylised studio sets. Furthermore, the switches between the two don't jar the viewer. The film is marred only by some dated process work (obvious back projection), Vera-Ellen's bland persona and the curiously underwhelming ballet sequence towards the end of the film. For the latter, Kelly used professional ballet dancers as stand-ins for Sinatra, Munshin, Garrett and Miller, a switch which confused both MGM - who edited the scene down - and paying audiences. These lapses are more than atoned for by the stand-out musical numbers and some good jokes. Various 'exotic' night-clubs - The Sambacabana, The Dixieland, The Shanghai Review - all have the same signature tune; beer glasses contain a large amount of foam and about half an inch of liquid; there are humorous nods to *Anchors Aweigh* and *It Happened in Brooklyn*. There is even an Ava Gardner injoke, rather daring given Mayer's feelings regarding the ongoing Sinatra-Gardner relationship.

Though now a more assured dancer, Sinatra doesn't really get a lot to work with in the film, still lumbered with much of his standard MGM character. While his shipmates hope to score, he only wants to tour, his grandfather's guidebook in his hand. When Kelly is first smitten with Vera-Ellen, believing her to be a big local star, Sinatra just doesn't understand.

SINATRA: Hey, why do you have to run after girls all the time?
KELLY: I'll tell you when your voice changes, junior.

Not quite so girl-shy this time around, Sinatra still takes a little while to succumb to Garrett's advances. Their taxi-cab duet on the Bernstein-scored 'Come Up to My Place' isn't really suited to Sinatra's voice, the arrangement undercutting his smooth vocal technique, and the later love duet 'You're Awful...' works much better. Singing to Garrett on the roof of a studio-built Empire State building, Sinatra seems entirely at ease with her, delivering the Comden-Green lyrics with absolute conviction. When he throws the family heirloom guidebook off the edge of the roof to prove his love for Garrett, Sinatra's bashful youth seems finally to have grown up. What's more, *On the Town* offers the only chance to see Sinatra in drag, looking fetching in a red wig and harem girl outfit.

On 9 September 1949, MGM previewed their new musical at the Bay Theatre, Pacific Palisades. Even after viewing the final cut, the studio had found the film a puzzle, uncomfortably different from their standard output. Oblivious to such anxieties, the audience loved it and a second preview at Loew's 72nd Street Theatre, New York on 22 November confirmed the verdict. Encouraged, MGM put together a suitably eye-catching, if unsubtle promotional campaign. Posters bore the invitation: 'Come on, everybody, let's all go ON THE TOWN!', laying down the basic premise with commendable economy: 'Tour the town with three terrific tars and their tootsies!' Sinatra was placed on the extreme left of the artwork, his legs folded as he leapt in the air. Intentional or not, this had the effect of reducing his minimal figure even further, leaving Sinatra dwarfed by Munshin and Kelly.

On the Town officially premiered at the Radio City Music Hall, New York on 9 December 1949, with a general release on 30 December. By its fourth week at Radio City, the film was breaking all box-office records, attracting crowds of 10,000, and *On the Town* went on to gross nearly $4.5 million. Reviewers were equally enthusiastic, with Frank Quinn declaring: 'It has the tempo of the subway, the merriment of Coney Island and the glamour of Broadway.' Of the stars, Kelly inevitably drew the bulk of the praise. While the *Hollywood Reporter* praised Sinatra's efforts: 'Frank Sinatra's voice and harassed manner makes his role a delight', most critics passed him by. For the next three years, Kelly would be MGM's golden boy, triumphing in the Freed productions *An American in Paris* (1951) and *Singin' in the Rain* (1952).

For Sinatra, appearing in another box-office hit after a painful four-year gap proved an empty victory. Already humiliated when MGM changed the agreed billing, giving Kelly the top spot and demoting him to number two, he soon realised that his fall from favour didn't stop with the opening titles. By early 1950, Sinatra's inescapable day of reckoning drew near. Back in December 1949, with *On the Town* playing to capacity audiences, Mayer had threatened to terminate Sinatra's contract over his affair with MGM starlet Ava Gardner and the resulting media

On the Town – 'You Can Count On Me.' Alice Pearce, Ann Miller, Betty Garrett, Sinatra, Jules Munshin and Gene Kelly.

gossip. According to Nancy Sinatra, Mayer kept Sinatra on the studio payroll largely out of affection for the man. The singer's ever-multiplying back catalogue of personal and professional disasters would have damned any other contract player long before her father finally got the chop. On 27 April 1950, Frank Sinatra was formerly dismissed from Metro Goldwyn Mayer, the final straw being his on-set remarks regarding Mayer and Simms. The decision to fire him had been made months earlier, probably not long after his quip reached Mayer's ears, and the success of *On the Town* did nothing to change the general view that Sinatra would never be a big enough name to make up for his bad image and errant behaviour. His contract still had a year to run and the ex-star received an $85,000 pay-off by way of compensation. In a token effort to save face on both sides, the official MGM announcement stated that the split was by mutual agreement, Sinatra being keen to pursue work in other fields: 'As a freelance artist, he is now free to accept unlimited, important personal appearance, radio, and television offers that have been made to him.' Five years later he'd be back in triumph but at the time this looked about as likely as a movie star becoming President. The same month, Sinatra started coughing up blood, his vocal chords haemorrhaged. It was a very bad year.

4

Dead Ends

1950-1952

DOUBLE DYNAMITE 1951

As former *Dr Kildare* star Lew Ayres once remarked, there are certain kinds of film an actor only makes when they really need the work and *Double Dynamite* is a prime example. Moviegoers' first glimpse of Frank Sinatra following his departure from MGM was in this mediocre comedy from the RKO stable. Badly miscast as a timid bank clerk who wins a fortune on the racetrack but can't spend the money without being branded a thief, Sinatra found himself in a loser of a vehicle that made even *Higher and Higher* look like cutting edge wit. The one notable aspect of *Dynamite* is its troubled post-production history, with few of the film's small 1951 audience realising that it had been finished nearly three years earlier, shelved on the orders of new RKO boss Howard Hughes. *Double Dynamite* began life under the more prosaic, if accurate title *It's Only Money*, also one of Sinatra's songs in the film. Its belated release has led to some confusion over its exact place in the Sinatra filmography. According to Kitty Kelley, after Sinatra was dropped from MGM, Ava Gardner contacted old friend and hands-off admirer

Hughes to request film work for her lover at RKO, controlled by the eccentric millionaire since late 1948. Given Hughes' utter loathing of Sinatra, largely over his relationship with Gardner, this is unlikely. More to the point, principal photography on *Dynamite* was completed during November and December 1948, prior to Hughes taking hands-on control of RKO, before Sinatra started work on *On the Town*, and well over a year before his exit from MGM. Putting the disastrous reception of *Miracle of the Bells* behind him, the star had called on his loan-out clause once more, presumably to fill out the lengthy gap between *Ball Game* and *On the Town*. His choice of an RKO project can probably be attributed to a dearth of offers from the larger studios rather than loyalty to his old shooting ground. Had Sinatra been able to look just a little way into the future, he would surely have passed on *Double Dynamite*. A film intended as a throwaway between more weighty fare became a shabby reminder that his Hollywood star had not only dimmed but more or less burned out.

The key production jobs on *Dynamite* were taken by the father and son team of Irving Cummings Senior and Junior. Producer Cummings Junior was a former

Double Dynamite – Sinatra and Groucho Marx appear surprised to find each other in this dreary low budget comedy.

script writer for Twentieth Century Fox with credits such as *Lone Star Ranger* (1943) to his name. Director Cummings Senior had also served with Fox, directing vehicles for Shirley Temple, then Betty Grable, the studio's top star during World War II. *Dynamite* would be Cummings' only post-war film, the veteran director retiring after its commercial failure. Having agreed to take the nominal lead role for a $150,000 fee, Sinatra was provided with two interesting co-stars, a flimsy script and the character name Johnny Dalton, presumably a reference to the bank-robbing outlaw clan. Looking for some sultry sexual allure, RKO borrowed Howard Hughes discovery Jane Russell, noted more for her 38" chest than her acting ability. Still under personal contract to Hughes seven years on from *The Outlaw* (1941), she wasn't too thrilled about the RKO deal, later describing *Dynamite* as 'a big nothing'. Cast as Sinatra's fiancee and fellow bank employee, Russell's portrayal of Mildred Goodhug - 'Mibs' to her friends - certainly suggests an eagerness to be elsewhere. Less sultry but a little funnier is the official comedy relief, Groucho Marx. The glory days of the Marx Brothers were long gone, and Groucho had branched out into second-division solo film work, co-starring with Carmen Miranda in the so-so farce *Copacabana* (1947). His market value in obvious decline, Marx received a modest $60,000 for *Dynamite*, significantly less than either Sinatra or Russell. Marx's character, wisecracking waiter Emile J. Keck, hints at some attempt to recreate the old Marx Brothers zest but the script largely restricts him to acting as Sinatra's slightly shady friend and confidante, suppressing Marx the personality in favour of Marx the actor. The actor isn't so interesting.

The convoluted screenplay derived from the efforts of four writers, any initial invention or enthusiasm utterly obliterated in the end result. The characters were devised by one Manni Manheim, who handed them over to Leo Rosten for development into a storyline. This was transformed into a filmable screenplay by Melville Shavelson, with a few rewrites courtesy of Harry Crane. Two decades on, respected producer-director-writer Shavelson would recruit Sinatra for the more heavyweight drama *Cast a Giant Shadow* (1966, see Appendix 1), which wasn't much good either. Among the supporting cast was Don McGuire, a former journalist and press agent who'd been acting for a few years in movies such as *Pride of the Marines* (1945) and *Humoresque* (1946). A friend of Sinatra, McGuire later reunited with the star as the screenwriter and associate producer for *Meet Danny Wilson* and the co-writer-director of *Johnny Concho* (1956), Sinatra's first independent production. Despite his various changes of metier, McGuire never did display much in the way of discernible talent.

The on-set atmosphere was generally polite but cold, hardly conducive to the production of a supposedly high-spirited comedy. Russell felt she didn't get to know either Sinatra or Marx and the resultant lack of screen chemistry is very noticeable. His career heading for the doldrums, Sinatra couldn't invest his performance with much enthusiasm, let alone laughs, and his stormy affair with Ava Gardner further dampened his mood. Largely disillusioned with the movie business, Marx still behaved like a professional, always arriving on set early. As ever, Sinatra took a more casual attitude towards punctuality. The subsequent delays and hanging around displeased Marx, who retaliated in his own inimitable fashion by arriving for work later than Sinatra. Not one to be outdone, Sinatra started appearing even later, prompting a vicious circle of tardiness. Marx eventually called a truce, and made a deal with Sinatra for them both to arrive on time. To his credit, Sinatra stuck to the bargain.

The only moderately bright spot of the production for Russell was her duet with Sinatra on 'Kisses and Tears', a romantic number to balance the humorous Sinatra-Marx rendition of 'It's Only Money', both below par Cahn-Styne compositions that reunited the singer with his old collaborators for the first time since *The Miracle of the Bells*. Anxious to show off her vocal skills, Russell discovered that her pleasant, if underpowered singing voice was completely swamped by her co-star's more potent vocal flair. Balancing the two proved tricky, with Sinatra standing several feet away from the microphone while she got as close as was possible without distorting her voice.

With filming completed, RKO executives decided that the rough cut didn't add up to an acceptable product and an additional scene was shot in January 1949, presumably employing Harry Crane's material. According to one source, in 1950 Sinatra and Russell were summoned to record an additional song as a promotional gimmick for the film, hinting at some thought of releasing *Dynamite* at least a year before its eventual appearance. It was certainly previewed under its original title, to some enthusiastic audience response. Little concerned with other people's opinions, new boss Howard Hughes declined to do anything with the film. He disliked both the movie and its star, the latter consideration not open to negotiation. With Sinatra and Russell mightily glad to be free of the film and Hughes strongly inclined to leave it shelved, *Double Dynamite* found itself an unlikely champion in the form of Groucho Marx, who didn't like the idea of a star performance being buried, however mediocre. On 23 January 1951, Marx wrote to Hughes asking why *It's Only Money* hadn't been released. While he'd not seen the finished film, Marx saw little point in his 'minor masterpiece' being left to gather dust in the RKO vaults. Just how much effect this appeal had on Hughes is open to debate. If he didn't like a film, there was no-one at RKO who could force him to release it. Whatever the case, 11 months after Hughes received Marx's letter, the film finally appeared in public as *Double Dynamite*. Marx was certain that Hughes devised the new title himself, just one further manifestation of his fixation on Jane Russell's breasts. The title wasn't the only thing to be changed. Billed first on the original *It's Only Money* version of the film, Sinatra found himself once again demoted, this time to third place underneath Russell and Marx. Hughes still hated the star - a hatred intensified by Sinatra's recent marriage to Gardner - and wasn't shy about letting him know it. Sinatra was also excluded from the promotion for *Dynamite*. Instructed to play on the mammary angle, the publicity department came up with a poster depicting Russell in a low cut dress, with Marx leering over her shoulder, eyes bulging. Slogans such as 'Double Delicious' 'Double Delightful' 'Double Delirious' underlined Hughes' selling point(s).

Released in December 1951, *Double Dynamite* attracted largely negative reviews and minimal audience interest. Sinatra and Russell's failure to click as a romantic couple didn't go unnoticed, the former accused by one critic of walking through the film 'looking like an uninvited guest'. *Cue* magazine was a little kinder: 'Sinatra and Marx do yeoman comedy labours, and Miss Russell seems nicely typecast.' Despite its box-office flop in America, RKO elected to give the film a British release in January 1952, which suggests they were a little short of product at the time. *Picturegoer* gave it the thumbs up: 'If you're shopping for fun, this one's your buy', but there weren't many

takers. For Sinatra, *Double Dynamite* served as an appropriately underwhelming final act to his relationship with the company. Hughes' control over RKO ruled out any further work with the latter and Sinatra now felt reasonably confident he'd have no further need of them. Earlier in the year, he'd signed a contract with Universal-International and the first film under the deal was already finished and scheduled for release. Whatever the reception awaiting *Meet Danny Wilson*, it had to be a step upwards.

MEET DANNY WILSON 1951

All this trouble for a freak with a frog in his throat.
Crowd-control policeman

Personally, I'm a Crosby fan.
Nick Driscoll, gangster

While it possesses a lingering sordid interest, *Meet Danny Wilson* is by and large a tawdry, dishonest piece of work, a cheaply made melodrama that exploits its star and short-changes its audience. The plot comes across as a garishly fictionalised biopic of Frank Sinatra, a flimsy reworking of media myths that bizarrely panders to all the worst rumours surrounding the Sinatra legend. Danny Wilson, a quick tempered but amazingly talented New York bar singer, gets his lucky break through a shady nightclub owner, hits the big time, goes to Hollywood, grows big-headed, alienates his loved ones and nearly loses everything. The end. It's strange to think that the film was scripted by a friend of the star, even stranger that writer Don McGuire got to work with Sinatra again. While Sinatra would later speak favourably of the movie, rating *Danny Wilson* as '...the first role I could sink my teeth into', it's difficult to believe he could derive any pleasure or satisfaction from starring in a rip-off of his own story, the highlights of his moribund career indifferently recreated on a tinpot studio soundstage. Even taken as a straight rags-to-riches-to-near-tragedy morality tale, the film is fatally flawed by indifferent handling and a very uncertain tone, undercutting what little drama it has with nervous throwaway jokes and badly incorporated musical breaks. Still, *Danny Wilson* is an essential part of the Sinatra canon, if only to highlight the real quality of his best work. If *Miracle of the Bells* is an honourable failure, *Danny Wilson* is a dishonourable curio. The most detailed account of the film's production comes courtesy of co-star Shelley Winters, who claims that a standard medium-budget drama became a waking nightmare for Sinatra's co-workers thanks to the latter's crazed behaviour on the set.

From the start, the production offered very little to get excited about. Like RKO, Universal-International was now a minor league outfit, kept afloat largely as a 'B' factory. Sinatra's deal gave U-I a non-exclusive, three-year option on the star, hardly the greatest show of confidence. According to Arnold Shaw, Sinatra took the lead in *Danny Wilson* with some reluctance, his friendship with McGuire not blinding him to either the screenplay's glaring deficiencies or the dodgy parallels with his own life and times. Estimates for Sinatra's pay packet on the film vary enormously, from a respectable $150,000 to the bargain basement figure of $25,000. Richard Gehman states that Sinatra agreed to take a reduced fee in return for a percentage of the eventual profits. Given his need for ready cash at the time, this arrangement seems unlikely, though it's possible U-I took dubious advantage of Sinatra's declining fortunes to obtain his services for next to nothing. Not long after, Columbia boss Harry Cohn would get him for $1,000 a week. The star's return to film-making after a two-year gap prompted a little press interest. Sometime Sinatra-ally Louella Parsons predicted that *Danny Wilson* would relaunch the singer's career: 'Those crepe-hangers who said Sinatra was through in pix may now cheerfully choke on their words.' She was right, but not just yet.

Filmed during the period when Universal-International survived largely on a diet of Abbott and Costello and Francis the Talking Mule, *Meet Danny Wilson* is a modest black and white production with

credits to match. Sinatra was entrusted to producer Leonard Goldstein, whose filmography was unremarkable, and staff director Joseph Pevney, a former vaudeville song-and-dance man and nightclub entertainer. Despite his showbiz experience, Pevney proved uninspired on *Danny Wilson*, directing in a ploddingly orthodox style and relying on cameraman Maury Gertsman for a few moody night shots. Pevney's handling of the cast is similarly flat and sometimes downright careless, suggesting a lack of adequate rehearsal time. Sinatra's temperament may have exacerbated the problem but even the scenes without him often feel inert and lifeless.

Sinatra's co-stars were of a slightly higher calibre. For the role of fellow singer and reluctant girlfriend Joy Carroll, U-I selected contract star Shelley Winters, who'd just enjoyed her first decent part in the Paramount production *A Place in the Sun* (1951), cast as Montgomery Clift's doomed lover. Fellow Actors' Studio graduate Alex Nicol took the part of Mike Ryan, Danny's childhood friend, protector, accompanist, manager and conscience. The love triangle that develops between these three is utterly without surprises. The film did at least get a quality villain in the form of Winters' *Place in the Sun* co-star Raymond Burr, whose saturnine looks and sepulchral voice invest gangster-entrepreneur Nick Driscoll with a depth of menace lacking in his underdeveloped character. If Driscoll isn't quite in the same league as Burr's best known villain, *Rear Window*'s white-haired wife killer Lars Thorwald, his coldly matter-of-fact brutality does offer an effective contrast to Danny's hot-blooded aggression. Essentially a four-hander, *Danny Wilson* has no other roles of note. U-I deployed budding contract stars Tony Curtis and Jeff Chandler for brief cameo appearances in a nightclub sequence, their careful make-up, hair styling and lighting emphasising both the studio's grooming and Sinatra's intentionally haggard appearance. Chandler also gets a mention in the script during Danny's Hollywood sojourn with 'Majestic Pictures'. It's good to know that shameless studio self-promotion wasn't confined to MGM.

Along with the dubious script, *Danny Wilson* also offered Sinatra the highest number of solo songs per film to date, recorded under the supervision of Joseph Gershenson, head of U-I's music department. Belting out such standards as 'She's Funny That Way', 'That Old Black Magic', 'When You're Smiling' and 'All of Me', Sinatra performs beyond the call of duty, the potency of the music diminished by the shabby backdrop. McGuire's script confines most of the songs to Danny's stage and nightclub performances, with a few ill-advised attempts at outright musical-fantasy. Sinatra's impromptu rendition of 'I've Got a Crush on You' for Winters during an airport scene absurdly undercuts the otherwise relatively 'realist' style of the film. Backed by a quartet of close harmony porters - all black, naturally - and an unseen orchestra, Sinatra looks just a little desperate. The incidental music is similarly misjudged, overemphatic and overused.

Danny Wilson began production in June 1951, immediately running into a major problem: its leading man. Sinatra's career slump, poor press and questionable attitude to film work had already marked him as a star best avoided. The death blow was his imminent divorce from Nancy Barbato, played out against a backdrop of endless press coverage, with Sinatra attacked as a heartless adulterer. According to Winters, Sinatra made no effort to separate his personal and professional lives, regularly consulting with both priests and psychiatrists at the U-I studios during the *Danny Wilson* shoot. With the marriage break-up utterly dominating his thoughts, Sinatra had nothing left to offer the film. Had his career been in better health, the star would surely have dropped out of the movie or requested that the production be postponed, a more viable option given the tailor-made nature of the project. With over $100,000 in back taxes owing to the IRS, Sinatra could no longer afford such luxuries as breakdowns.

Sinatra and Winters couldn't even make it to the end of rehearsals before the rows began. Winters had just returned from a gruelling promotional tour for the forgettable U-I release *South Sea Sinner* (1950), notable only as Liberace's film debut. Rushed into the *Danny Wilson* production by the studio, she found her costumes ready-made on her wardrobe dummy and only a few days remaining for her to learn her big song, 'A Good Man is Hard to Find', first heard as a nightclub solo, then reprised as a duet with Sinatra during a party sequence. Unhappy over the lack of preparation time, she attempted to discover the reason for the haste. The only answer available was that Sinatra badly needed his fee for the film and couldn't wait any longer for shooting to start. This has a fair ring of truth yet Sinatra made no concessions to his parlous fiscal state when it came to getting the job done. Already wary of her co-star, Winters felt things were off to a poor start when Sinatra arrived 15 minutes late for the first day of rehearsal. Lacking any real experience in musicals, Winters couldn't keep up with her co-star's instant grasp of song lyrics, her nervousness further souring the atmosphere. Neither had any qualms about expressing themselves and the studio buildings soon echoed to the noise of their mutual dislike. That said, Sinatra did oppose studio plans to dub Winters' singing, arguing that she sounded more than acceptable once she was confident with a song (Sinatra was being charitable; Winters' voice is strained during their duet). He also taught her how to lip-synch to a prerecorded track during a take.

Having finally progressed to the filming stage, Winters took particular offence at one Sinatra remark during a night-time shoot at Burbank Airport and punched her co-star in the face. Sinatra responded all too predictably by storming off the set into his waiting limousine, leaving U-I executive Leo Spitz begging Winters to attempt a truce with the man. By Winters' account, Spitz didn't try to gloss over Sinatra's near-terminal film career problems: '...he is not famous as an actor but a singer...' A singer, it might be added, long out of fashion. Suitably appeased, Winters agreed to resume shooting the following day, only to find that Sinatra's mood had not improved. One late afternoon studio shoot involved Sinatra, Winters and Nicol riding in a mock-up car for a back-projected driving scene. After an apparently good take, director Pevney was informed by the projection machine operator that the device had malfunctioned, giving them a blank screen instead of the desired street footage. Feeling that his own performance was good enough, Sinatra declined to hear out the technical explanations and refused to do another take. The scene had to scrapped and the essential dialogue reworked into a subsequent scene [judging from the release print, the lost scene should come between Sinatra and Nicol's first encounter with Winters as she attempts to hail a taxi and their subsequent conversation in a bar]. Another two scenes would be cut from the script to speed up the production, giving the end result a slightly rushed, truncated feel, especially in the closing stages. If all this wasn't catastrophe enough, Sinatra had started to lose weight, roughly one pound a week, making Winters look increasingly bulky by comparison in the rushes.

For Winters, the last of many straws came during shooting on the final sequence, set in a hospital ward, where a penitent Wilson is reconciled with his old girlfriend and former best friend. She arrived for the 12.30 call, and prayed for a trouble-free afternoon. The scene progressed well until Sinatra's last line, when he allegedly deviated from the innocuous scripted dialogue: 'I'll have a cup of coffee and leave you two lovebirds alone', substituting 'I'll go have a cup of Jack Daniels, or I'm going to pull that blonde broad's hair out by its black roots'. Winters struck Sinatra with a well-aimed bed pan and walked off the set herself, staying away for two days. This time it took Nancy Snr's pleas to bring Winters back, the soon-to-be ex-Mrs Sinatra explaining that unless her husband completed the film he'd lose his fee and his family could lose their house. Winters returned once more, Sinatra stuck to the original dialogue and the film wrapped to a large gasp of collective relief.

Winters' tale makes for an interesting anecdote, with both drama and pathos, yet it's rather at odds with the existing film. There is a brief hospital scene, just after Mike is shot by Driscoll, but it bears no resemblance to the action she describes. Danny is seen pacing up and down a reception room, waiting for news of Mike, when Joy appears to berate Danny over his treatment of her wounded lover, informing the singer that it was she, not his ever-loyal best friend, who initiated their relationship.

Determined to put things straight, Danny leaves the hospital, to go after Driscoll telling Joy that it's time he grew up . The scene ends, the movie cuts to the ballpark showdown between Danny and Driscoll, and the hospital is not seen again. The film ends with Danny on stage at the London Palladium, singing 'How Much Do I Love You' to a sell-out house, while the newly married Joy and Mike watch from the wings. If the scene outlined by Winters was actually filmed, there would be little point in scrapping it after all the traumas and substituting a more elaborate sequence involving a new set, a prerecorded song and a dozen extras. The song in particular points to the existing finale being the one intended right from the start. Recalling the events nearly three decades on, Winters appears to have succumbed either to the mists of time or creative embroidery.

As Sinatra's one dramatic starring role prior to the *deus ex machina* of *From Here to Eternity*, *Danny Wilson* is of considerable interest. Looking decidedly tougher than the star's earlier movie incarnations, Danny is first seen hustling in a pool hall, Mike at his side to watch out for trouble. Quickly established as a cocky, hot-tempered ladies man - single ladies, of course - Danny is clearly going nowhere fast. Singing to unappreciative customers for $25 a night in Mother Murphy's bar, he knocks over a fat heckler to avenge an insult and is instantly fired. Sinatra's battered face has an appropriately lean and hungry look and his overall demeanour transcends the formulaic dialogue to give a sense of a gifted man dragged down by circumstances and his own weakness. Lacking much in the way of guidance from director Pevney, Sinatra's performance is uneven, with a tendency to overact. When Winters overdoes a drunk scene, her dubious and inconsistent New York accent coming and going, Sinatra attempts to follow suit, his lack of acting training showing through. Sinatra does better later in the film, more comfortable with the less savoury Danny. His reaction on discovering the budding affair between Joy and Mike offers an effective blend of mock-hurt and sneering malice, with not a shred of sympathy for the 'wronged' Danny. Turning up late for a performance at a charity dinner for

Meet Danny Wilson – Shelley Winters and Alex Nicol make bets on Sinatra's next walk-out.

the Damon Runyan benefit fund - a real event often supported by Sinatra - the obviously drunken singer staggers around throwing abuse at Mike, the band and the audience. This is an impressive piece of 'nasty' acting and for once McGuire's script does not throw in any alleged comedy to lighten the mood.

The borrowings from Sinatra's own career are predictable. Already a hit with the nightclub crowd, Danny becomes a teenage sensation, his fans screaming, swooning and giving him a big cake [?] His name makes the front page of all the big showbiz journals: *Newsweek, Colliers, Variety, Billboard.* Reliving the recent past in this way must have given Sinatra a strange

and uncomfortable sense of bogus *déjà vu*, not that the extras used in the big concert scene shriek with any great conviction. At 35, he looked just a little too old for the teenybopper crowd. The Hollywood scenes flatter neither Danny nor Sinatra, the former depicted as irresponsible and difficult, holding up shooting while he tries to contact Joy. The singer's image is further undermined in a scene where Danny and Mike become involved in a punch-up with two lorry drivers following a minor road accident. Danny is fighting mad but utterly useless with his fists, saved from a beating only by Mike's intervention. This is one troublemaker who can't fight his own battles. The most contentious element in the film is the gangster subplot, a piece of uninspired fiction that Sinatra's detractors were only too happy to interpret as fact. Absent for most of the film's middle section, Driscoll predictably reappears to demand his pound of flesh - 50 percent of Danny's total earnings - and Mike takes the bullet intended for his defiant friend. It's time for Danny to stand up for himself, walk like a man and generally do what he has to do. This boils down to shooting Driscoll in the back, a premeditated act of violence for which Danny incurs no legal retribution at all. The final shot of the film, a medium close-up of the back-on-top Danny in concert, rings equally false. While it can be argued with some force that *Meet Danny Wilson* provides the role closest to the real Sinatra, its cut-price blend of fact, half-truth, rumour, myth and outright invention renders the film void as any kind of insight into the man.

The exact release date for *Meet Danny Wilson* is the subject of some dispute, with February, March and April 1952 variously cited. According to Nancy Jnr, the film premiered on 8 February 1952 at the Orpheum Theater, San Francisco, Sinatra in attendance along with Ava Gardner and his parents Martin and Dolly. Comedian Milton Berle and actor Robert Preston lent extra showbiz support, the event duly recorded by newsreel cameras. Realising that his movie 'comeback' needed all the help it could get, Sinatra arranged a series of live singing engagements to accompany its run at the New York Paramount. The theatre didn't usually exhibit other studios' films and needed a fair amount of convincing from the star before the 2-in-1 show opened on 26 March to unspectacular box-office. While not overtly hostile, the reviews for *Danny Wilson* tended towards the lukewarm. There appears to have been some uncertainty over whether to pity or condemn the down-at-heels Sinatra for starring in a reworked version of his already

mythologised rise to fame. *The Los Angeles Times* argued that '...Sinatra is obviously unfair to himself', asserting that the story was 'so much like Frankie's that the parallel is inescapable'. *Time* magazine was less tolerant over the blatant 'cribs' from Sinatra's life: '...fans may expect Ava Gardner to pop up in the last reel'. The one positive note was sounded by Kay Proctor of the *Los Angeles Examiner*: '...for the first time on the screen he seems completely at ease, and sure of himself and what he is doing'. The debate proved entirely academic as *Danny Wilson* quickly earned itself flop status.

Accepting that both star and film had been subjected to some less than fair treatment by the media, U-I decided nevertheless that they no longer required Sinatra's services. Despite press speculation to the contrary, the option for a second movie wasn't taken up, Sinatra arguing and pleading to no avail. Needless to say, Universal-International later paid for their casual disposal of the star. Back on top only a few years later, Sinatra would never headline another film for the studio, agreeing only to a split-second cameo in the Kirk Douglas-Universal production *The List of Adrian Messenger* (1963, see Appendix 1).

For the time being, the star's career remained in a wretched state, his return to movies having come and gone with barely a whimper. In June of the same year, Sinatra was dropped by both his agency MCA and his recording label Columbia. On the personal side, the taxman was still knocking at his door and his marriage to Ava Gardner looked like heading for bust-up city. Had Sinatra been more religiously inclined, he might have thought about praying for a miracle. In the event, his unlikely saviour would be a foul-mouthed movie dictator who modelled himself on Benito Mussolini. The Lord does move in mysterious ways.

Fightback
1953-1954

FROM HERE TO ETERNITY 1953

*I just hate to see a good man
get it in the gut.*
Private Angelo Maggio

Now I'll show the bastards.
Frank Sinatra

It's a book, a film, a television series, a disco hit. It also gave Frank Sinatra the role that yanked him out of his Hollywood grave, placed him back among the major players and conferred his official career revival. With this in mind, it perhaps matters little that *From Here to Eternity* is a pretty mediocre film, better remembered for the much-parodied snogging-in-the-surf scene than its half-baked attempt to depict one man's struggle to retain his identity and integrity in the grip of a corrupt, dehumanising military regime. A professional but coldly dispassionate piece of work, *Eternity* offers little more than a monotonously negative image of army life, its last-minute burst of patriotism jarring as badly as the grainy stock footage of the actual Pearl Harbor raid. At least the Giorgio Moroder song is shorter.

By late 1952, the contrast between Ava Gardner's soaring career and Sinatra's run of abject failure could not have been much greater. Gardner had just been offered a new ten-year contract by MGM, paying $1.2 million for 12 films. Sinatra had no studio, no contract and no forthcoming projects. Anxious to keep both her husband and her marriage on the rails, Gardner fought with MGM to have Sinatra given prominent roles in at least some of her agreed vehicles. Wanting no further part of this burnt-out musical lightweight, the management decided to humour Gardner a little, agreeing to a dubious clause in her contract that guaranteed Sinatra a co-starring role in either *St Louis Woman* or another, as yet untitled film. The chances of these projects making it to the production stage were slim at best; with Sinatra attached they dwindled to zero.

Many industry insiders felt Columbia boss Harry Cohn had made a huge mistake buying the screen rights to *From Here to Eternity*. Published in 1951 to high critical praise, James Jones' unflinching portrait of army life at Schofield Barracks, Hawaii, just prior to the 1941 Pearl Harbor attack was controversial to say the least. Drawing on his own experiences as an enlisted man at Schofield, Jones pulled few punches when it came to depicting the brutality and corruption inherent in the military regime, with plentiful swearing, fornication, bloodshed and injustice. These elements covered just about every taboo in the MPAA's Production Code, rendering a successful film version nigh on impossible.

Having paid a tidy $82,000 for Jones' bestseller, Cohn stuck to his guns, intending to make the film using his studio's in-house talent on a low-risk budget of $2 million. He settled on staff producer Buddy Adler to oversee the production, a choice which proved fortuitous. A former lieutenant with the Signal Corps, the producer had a number of useful Pentagon connections, eventually securing official approval for the production with a minimum of fuss. The choice of director for *Eternity* fell largely to Adler, who wanted Austrian émigré Fred Zinnemann. Well respected for his sensitive character studies, Zinnemann had already directed two dramas of military life, *The Search* (1948), with newcomer Montgomery Clift, and *The Men* (1950), Marlon Brando's debut movie. Despite the shamelessly commercial nature of the *Eternity* project, director and screenplay appeared well matched, Zinnemann's interest in alienated loners following their own moral code in an amoral world finding a made-to-measure subject in Private Robert E. Lee Prewitt. As it turned out, Zinnemann could not inject any real depth of feeling into the film, he and his cast merely transforming thinly written ciphers into well-acted thinly written ciphers. The one striking directorial touch is a long overhead shot of a running, screaming soldier being gunned down by a Japanese Zero fighter, his body hurtling to the ground like a rag doll. Here, if nowhere else, the grim realities of combat are brought home with a vengeance.

After a number of false starts on the script, Cohn selected writer Daniel Taradash for the unenviable task of transforming Jones' 816-page novel into a coherent screenplay, the end result running a trim 161 pages. Taradash's final script for *Eternity* is a competent clean-up job at best, the whorehouse of the original becoming the absurdly euphemistic New Congress Club, and did not meet with the approval of James Jones.

Casting on the film took an eternity of its own, with Sinatra's tortuous saga just part of the story. Cohn wanted either Glenn Ford or Robert Mitchum for fair-minded Sergeant Milton Warden, with Joan Crawford as his unhappy married lover Karen Holmes, starlet Donna Reed as equally miserable club 'hostess' Alma Burke and new signing Aldo Ray as the doomed rebel Prewitt (unsubtly named after another of history's noble losers). Maggio had yet to be cast, though both Zinnemann and Adler were lobbying for stage actor Eli Wallach. Of this original line-up, only Reed made to the end of production. Ford, Mitchum and Ray soon fell by the wayside in favour of Burt Lancaster and Montgomery Clift. Joan Crawford got as far as the contract stage before demanding her own choice of wardrobe and cameraman. Cohn didn't care to be dictated to and dropped her as well, settling on the surprise choice of demure British actress Deborah Kerr. Though they shared no scenes together, Kerr and Sinatra would become good friends during filming, leading to inevitable press gossip about a romance. Both were unlikely casting for their parts and both worried that they wouldn't live up to people's expectations. As for Eli Wallach, the part was his for the taking, despite relentless lobbying from no-hoper Sinatra.

According to his own account, adventure-fan Sinatra had read *From Here to Eternity* soon after publication and immediately been drawn to the Maggio character. As he explained to daughter Nancy: 'For the first time in my life, I was reading something I really had to do.' This sounds rather similar to his reaction after leafing through *The Miracle of the Bells*, though his interest in playing Father Paul derived more from misguided career considerations than genuine empathy. There seems little doubt that Sinatra honestly believed himself to be the one natural choice for the role, as he explained in the oft-reproduced quote: 'I knew Maggio. I went to school with him in Hoboken... I might have been Maggio.' Ava Gardner agreed that the part would be perfect for him, tactfully neglecting to point out that Sinatra's flimsy track record as an actor was not going to make things easy. According to Gardner's memoirs, by the summer of 1952 Sinatra was obsessed with the character, certain that

Maggio represented his one remaining chance to get back to the top. Still in a fairly moribund state, Sinatra's career had recently experienced a tentative step out of the lower depths of showbiz oblivion. Humiliatingly dumped by MCA, he was now represented by the big league William Morris Agency in the person of Bert Allenberg. Even with this power behind him, Sinatra stood about as much chance of getting the part as a snowball emerging from hell lightly glazed.

The long campaign for the Maggio role commenced in early November 1952. Having publicly declared that he wanted the part on any terms, Sinatra arranged a meeting with Cohn. As related to Nancy Jnr, Sinatra's own account of securing the Maggio role is just a little too straightforward, not to say sanitised. He went to his good friend Harry's office, suggested himself for the part, and was offered a screen test the same day. The reality is slightly different, though exactly how different depends on which version of events is believed. There seems little doubt that Cohn initially regarded Sinatra's request with thinly veiled derision. According to Earl Wilson, an acquaintance of both men, the Columbia boss' reply was direct and to the point: 'You must be out of your fuckin' mind.' Aware that his controversial property required very careful handling, Cohn felt that the secondary-but-pivotal Maggio role called for an established dramatic actor. Casting a singer-dancer who couldn't even make it in musicals anymore would be a senseless move, detrimental to the overall film. The public might have long forgotten *Miracle of the Bells* but Cohn recalled the critical trashing very well. The recent failure of *Danny Wilson* only confirmed the painful truth that Sinatra simply didn't cut it as a straight actor. Hoping to appeal to Cohn's sense of opportunist thrift, Sinatra offered to play the role for the derogatory sum of $1000 a week (at one point, Sinatra supposedly offered to pay Cohn for the part). Cohn was intrigued by this unprecedented abasement but still didn't feel particularly moved by Sinatra's line of pleading, making vague noises about a possible screen test once the stronger candidates had been auditioned.

His overtures largely rejected out of hand, Sinatra

had little to do with his time except join Ava Gardner in Kagera, Kenya, for her location work on the MGM production *Mogambo* (1953), a lavish remake of *Red Dust* (1932), with original star Clark Gable. Still not entirely resigned to defeat, a bored Sinatra left instructions with his WMA agents to cable him when casting on *Eternity* began. According to biographer Arnold Shaw, Cohn had already promised Sinatra a screen-test prior to the Africa trip, but no-one at the singer's agency held out any great hopes for their troubled client. Sinatra himself worried that the casting of Clift in the Prewitt role could kill off his chances, apparently convinced that he looked too much like him. Clift, on the other hand, thought Sinatra ideal casting for Maggio.

Ava Gardner's role in pleading Sinatra's case with Cohn is as disputed as the rest of the epic *Eternity* casting saga. One story has it that, all too aware of her husband's easily hurt pride, she wanted to aid his near-hopeless cause without his knowledge. Another version points to a largely pride-free Sinatra imploring Gardner to exercise a little star power on his behalf. Whatever the case, Gardner first suggested Sinatra for the Maggio role at a dinner party thrown by Harry and Joan Cohn, whom she knew slightly from her obligatory rounds on the Hollywood social scene. Initially taken aback by the directness of Gardner's request, Mrs Cohn came to like the idea. She was also touched by Gardner's loyalty to her down-and-nearly-out husband and remained a useful ally throughout the prolonged process of tests and screenings and conferences. Placing a lot of faith in his wife's judgement, Cohn eventually summoned her to a Columbia screening room and ran the Sinatra and Wallach tests three times over. Deliberating between an inexperienced but believably vulnerable Italian-American and a Jewish-American equipped with considerably more dramatic and actual muscle, Joan Cohn advised her husband to go with ethnic authenticity.

Sinatra didn't restrict his campaigning to Cohn.

From Here to Eternity – Private Angelo Maggio in Sinatra's great film comeback.

Zinnemann recalled himself and Adler being bombarded with telegrams from Sinatra, all signed 'Maggio'. This cut little ice with the director, who shared Cohn's opinion that casting a has-been musical star in the film would hurt the end result. First choice Eli Wallach was a proven talent; he could be promoted as a new screen star in his debut role, and his lack of Hollywood clout meant he was available for a bargain price. Adler and Cohn agreed that Wallach seemed the best option and the deal looked fairly set.

After weeks of agonised waiting, Sinatra finally got his screen test. There is a case for arguing that it represented just part of a larger test conducted by Cohn to see how desperate the singer really was for the part. Cohn waited until Sinatra was on location with Gardner in Africa before summoning him back to Los Angeles, insisting that he pay his own travel expenses. Flat broke, Sinatra either borrowed the air fare from his wife (Gardner's version) or charged the ticket to her MGM expense account and embarked on the eight-day round trip, a total distance of 27,000 miles for a 15-minute audition. Back at Columbia, Sinatra met up with the unenthusiastic duo of Adler and Zinnemann, who regarded his 14 November screen test as a foregone conclusion. For the test, Sinatra had to enact a couple of Maggio's key scenes, notably a bar scene where the drunken soldier reveals that he's gone AWOL and plays dice with a couple of olives. Asked by director Zinnemann to ad-lib a little, Sinatra apparently improvised the latter touch himself. Whatever he made of Sinatra's initiative, Zinnemann was underwhelmed by the latter's acting, rating the overall test as no more than okay. Adler felt rather more positive about the performance, later claiming that he started thinking Academy Award right then. Scared to death during the filming, Sinatra began the long trip back to Nairobi the next day, feeling he'd given the test his best possible shot. Even Zinnemann was warming to him. Once Eli Wallach had filmed his test, however, the general consensus swung back the stage actor's way. Sinatra's commitment and spontaneity had gone a long way to making up for his lack of technique but Wallach's performance was easily the stronger of the two. Back in Nairobi, news of Wallach's red-hot screen test dampened Sinatra's spirits. For all his efforts, Cohn still didn't want him. His marriage was crumbling, his bank account was empty, the IRS wanted back-taxes dating from the mid-1940s and his career was apparently over.

Dedication and hard work aside, Sinatra's break back into movies came about largely through pure fluke, a factor he preferred not to dwell on in later years. Prior to the *Eternity* deal, Wallach had committed to starring in a new Tennessee Williams play, *El Camino Real*, to be directed on Broadway by Elia Kazan. Problems over attracting sufficient backing had stalled the production at the planning stage, leaving Wallach free to take the Maggio role and break into films. Kazan finally found the money for *Camino Real*, obliging Wallach to choose either stage or screen. Wallach claims that deciding between Tennessee Williams and James Jones was more or less a no-contest and he opted for the play with little hesitation (it flopped). Others assert that the real factor was money: Cohn offered only $16,000 for the Maggio role - $2,000 a week over eight weeks - while Wallach's agents would not settle for less than $20,000. Unwilling to cough up the extra $4,000, Cohn played on Wallach's career ambitions, arguing that the *Eternity* role was sure to get Academy Award attention. Wallach's camp wouldn't budge and he walked away from the deal, his enthusiasm for *Eternity* further eroded by Cohn's insistence on a standard seven-year contract. With their number one choice out of the picture and the start date looming, Cohn, Adler, Zinnemann and Taradash were faced with either taking Sinatra or resuming the whole audition process from scratch. After rerunning the latter's test several times, they still had reservations. Joan Cohn's vote and Sinatra's frail, vulnerable appearance finally won out, Taradash convincing the others that Sinatra would have no trouble winning over the audience as he suffered the slings and arrows of barrack life. Inevitably, there were rumours that Sinatra got the role only through Mafia intervention, Cohn being 'advised' that it would be in everyone's best interests if the singer was cast. These stories appear to have originated a good 15 years later with the publication of Mario Puzo's pulp epic *The Godfather*, which contained a character very loosely based on the young Sinatra (see Appendix 2). The scene where an inflexible movie producer finds the head of his favourite stallion at the bottom of his bed is undeniably effective. It is also a figment of Puzo's imagination. In January 1953, Adler dispatched a telegram to Sinatra offering him the part, the glad tidings heading back to Nairobi or possibly Montreal, Sinatra claiming to have been there for a nightclub spot when he heard the good news. He signed the contract on 9 January 1953, picking up the agreed paycheque of $1,000 a week. Never slow to exploit their merchandise, Columbia played on the unusual casting of both Sinatra and Kerr in the preproduction press releases for *Eternity*, hinting that audiences were going to get something a little out of the ordinary. The studio issued a publicity shot if Sinatra in uniform, his tunic undone, a broom in one hand, a copy of *Variety* in the other.

Scheduled at a tight eight weeks (41 shooting days), studio work on *Eternity* commenced on 2 March 1953, with the all-important location filming in Honolulu beginning in April. Sinatra's euphoria over winning the part was tempered by his enforced separation from Gardner at a time when their stormy marriage looked like reaching hurricane force. Based at the Roosevelt Hotel, Los Angeles during the studio shoot, Sinatra spent many drunken evenings lamenting his lost love while fellow residents Clift and James Jones made sympathetic noises. The hotel management were not impressed with the more aggressive star antics - shouting obscenities and throwing beer cans - threatening to eject them several times. Sinatra's growing depression over the relationship didn't let up during the location shoot, the star drinking himself into oblivion on the plane from Los Angeles to Hawaii. Co-star Burt Lancaster appeared not to resent Sinatra's dissolute behaviour, pointing out the latter's ongoing personal and professional difficulties during the *Eternity* shoot fed his angst-ridden performance in a way not possible either before or after.

Fortunately for them both, there was more to Sinatra and Clift's relationship than a shared passion for heavy drinking. Sinatra felt the same respect, if not

awe, for Clift that he'd had for Gene Kelly. Both were driven by an uncompromising sense of perfectionism, insisting on the highest standards from themselves and their co-stars. With Lancaster way off his wavelength, Clift latched onto Sinatra as his best buddy during the shoot, endlessly working through their dialogue together, helping Sinatra fine-tune his performance, and generally serving as his on-the-job acting tutor. Zinnemann had chosen to restrict his cast rehearsals to a script run-through the week before filming commenced - an unusual approach - and the normally rehearsal-shy Sinatra was grateful for Clift's help. With this kind of special attention, the near-novice actor could not help but grow in confidence during the shoot. Attuned to the workings of the Hollywood machine, Clift predicted a likely Academy Award win for Sinatra after watching him being shot in an intimate close-up. Zinnemann was similarly impressed by his second-choice Maggio. Rarely requiring retakes, Sinatra's spontaneous style enlivened his often so-so dialogue, which he occasionally reworked and added to in consultation with the director. Both Sinatra and Zinnemann cited Clift as the film's real dramatic driving force. As Sinatra put it: 'The way he pitched, I couldn't help shining as a catcher'.

By the end of the location filming, both Clift and Sinatra were arriving on set intoxicated, though the latter was never so far gone he couldn't work at all. On one of the last night shoots before the return to Los Angeles, Zinnemann intended to film the scene where Prewitt finds the AWOL Maggio drunkenly lolling about on a park bench. Left alone while his friend goes in search of a cab, Maggio spots two approaching military policeman and jumps up at them, looking for a fight. Quickly overpowered, he is taken off for court martial. As written by Taradash, Maggio's alcohol-fuelled hostility towards these authority figures is unmistakable. Dependent on military goodwill, Cohn apparently developed cold feet about showing an enlisted man behave in this manner and ordered Zinnemann to keep Sinatra seated and passive during his arrest. Here events become a little unclear, though

From Here to Eternity – Prewitt (Montgomery Clift) keeps Maggio out of Fatso's (Ernest Borgnine) range.

there was certainly friction between Sinatra, Zinnemann and Cohn over the scene. Unhappy with Cohn's dictate, the director intended to shoot the original version of the action, leaving Cohn with no option but to accept the footage, and rehearsed his cast accordingly, backed by Sinatra and Clift. No fool, Cohn did not intend to leave Zinnemann unsupervised and planted a spy among the crew present for the filming outside Fort De Russy. Word of the director's 'treachery' got back to Cohn as he dined with military brass at the Royal Hawaiian Hotel and the enraged studio boss sped his way to the location and demanded that his wishes be followed. Labouring under the eye of his employer, Zinnemann felt obliged to shoot the toned-down version. Sinatra hated this compromise, unfairly blaming Zinnemann rather than Cohn for the whole incident. One of the cinema's few true gentlemen, Fred Zinnemann's integrity is beyond question, yet he appears to have succumbed to the Shelley Winters syndrome in his account of events. The arguments prior to shooting the scene were doubtless protracted and fierce but in the finished film we clearly see Maggio get up from the park bench to attack the MPs, yelling

defiance and abuse as he is beaten to the ground. Perhaps Zinnemann recalled only the compromises he had to make on *Eternity*, forgetting the small battles he actually won.

Aside from some nervous, occasionally perfunctory delivery of his lines, Sinatra does well as Maggio, projecting qualities of warmth, defiance, pride and all-important vulnerability. First seen stripped to his vest as he crouches on the ground picking up stones, Sinatra's slight build is emphasised throughout the film. His Hawaiian shirt hangs off him like a small tent, his dancing partner at the Congress Club towers over him, and his puny challenges to bull-sized stockade Sergeant 'Fatso' Judson (Ernest Borgnine) are both absurd and touching. Written largely as Prewitt's confidante, the role doesn't give Sinatra much screen time, though Maggio's death provides the crucial impetus for Prewitt to temporarily turn against the army regime - as represented by Judson - that has been his whole life (a key failing of the film is its inability to explain why a man of Prewitt's stubborn individuality would choose to be a career soldier). Powerless to help out his pal against the intimidation sanctioned by their captain, Maggio can only suffer with him.

Aside from his scenes with Clift, Sinatra works best opposite Borgnine's brutishly stupid Judson, their wildly contrasting sizes emphasising Maggio's cruel fate as a born loser. He won't take racist insults from Judson - 'Only my friends call me wop' - but can't follow up his defiance with effective action. Here Sinatra definitely has the edge over original choice Wallach, conveying very well an inwardly scared man trying to act tough in the face of a bullying thug. Though not as large as Borgnine, the solidly-built Wallach would have looked genuinely tough, and close to his equal in a fight. As it is, Sinatra's dialogue during the olive-rolling scene - 'Snake eyes. That's the story of my life' - unnecessarily spells out what is already obvious. It is a measure of the audience sympathy for Maggio that he can strike Judson on the back of the head with a bar stool and still be regarded as a hero. Their final on-screen encounter as Maggio arrives at the stockade after his court martial is well staged by Zinnemann. The last shot of the scene has Sinatra placed at the centre of the frame, dwarfed by the looming figure of Borgnine on the right, the latter reaching for his billyclub. Taradash's original script included scenes of Maggio's prison ordeal at Judson's hands. The Pentagon asked that they be taken out to tone down the element of army brutality and Zinnemann happily complied, feeling that the audiences would fill in the blanks to greater effect.

The biggest screw-up in the film from Sinatra's point of view is his botched death scene. As Prewitt and Warden drunkenly converse in the middle of a road, Maggio suddenly staggers into shot from frame left, bloodied and battered. Collapsing into Prewitt's arms, he gives a deathbed speech, detailing the tortures inflicted by Judson for both his friend and the audience. Sinatra handles the overheated melodrama as best he can, but it cheapens what has gone before. In fairness, the scene was filmed under difficult conditions, which probably contributed to its unsatisfactory feel. Working during the early hours of the morning, Sinatra, Lancaster and Clift grew increasingly cold in their thin army uniforms, the resultant shivering becoming noticeable on camera. Someone had the bright idea of giving them coffee laced with brandy, which proved disastrous in Clift's case. He passed out cold (again), halting the shoot for another hour. Brought round with some difficulty, Clift managed to stumble through the scene, where he and Lancaster were supposed to be drunk, anyway, but couldn't deliver the final line. As Maggio's battered body is placed in the back of an army jeep, Prewitt is supposed to say: 'See his head don't bump'. Hours past the original schedule, Clift blew numerous takes, with Zinnemann finally obliged to concede defeat and cut the line from the film. Inevitably, there is an alternative version of events. Zinnemann stated that he did eventually get an acceptable take of the scene, only for the philistine Cohn to cut both the poignant last line and the body being taken away from the release print, determined to deliver an exhibitor-friendly two-hour film. Whoever

was to blame, the existing scene ends with Lancaster bending over Maggio's motionless body and solemnly intoning 'He's dead', the line slightly clipped at the end by an abrupt cut that suggests garden shears treatment in the editing room. Far more affecting is the subsequent shot of Maggio's bare camp bed, the mattress folded up and out of use.

The publicity campaign for *Eternity* did as efficient a selling job as the film itself. As with *Miracle of the Bells*, most of the posters emphasized the movie's origins as a hit novel, the title depicted as lettering on a hardback book, along with the legend: 'From the Boldest Best-Seller of All!' Audiences were invited to sample 'Courage! Gallantry! Emotion! Violence!', though not necessarily in that order. Fourth-billed behind Lancaster, Clift and Kerr, Sinatra did well out of the promotional material. Maggio was depicted on posters crouched over, clutching a bar stool, oppressed but defiant. He was prominent enough for everyone to be aware of his presence in the film, with bigger names above him to take the bulk of the flak should *Eternity* fail. Conversely, Donna Reed's fifth billing acted as a buffer against Sinatra being perceived as a mere afterthought in the advertising. His only reservation about the prerelease publicity was the decision to pick up on Cohn's original pitch to Eli Wallach and plug the Maggio part as certain Oscar material. Sinatra knew full well that such grandiose claims could easily backfire.

Premiered on 17 August 1953, *From Here to Eternity* proved an immediate smash success, grossing over $19 million during its initial release and reaching $80 million by the end of 1954. The critics were similarly ecstatic, Bosley Crowther proclaiming that 'It captures the essential spirit of the James Jones source...a shining example of truly professional moviemaking.' Sinatra got more than his share of praise in the press coverage. *New York Post* critic Richard Watts felt that Sinatra had finally arrived as an actor: '...playing the luckless Maggio with a kind of doomed gaiety that is both real and immensely touching'. The *Los Angeles Examiner* described his performance as '...simply superb, comical, pitiful, childishly brave, pathetically defiant'. Overseas audiences proved similarly enthusiastic; the critical response abroad was a little more measured. Reviewing the film on its British release in November 1953, Dilys Powell praised all the leading performances, '...Sinatra in particular acting with great ease and fluency', but found the overall effect rather numbing.

Sinatra's personal hit with the film sparked him to cash in on his new success and he recorded an *Eternity*-linked single supervised by his new arranger, ex-Tommy Dorsey trombonist Nelson Riddle. Whether or not he ever watched all of the film himself is uncertain. Clift biographer Patricia Bosworth states that Clift and Sinatra sneaked into a matinee showing at the Capitol Theater on the film's opening day. According to Michael Caine, Sinatra saw *Eternity* for the first time at a Soho cinema in London, walking back to his hotel through rain-swept streets in a state of exultation. Alternatively, he didn't even bother to look at the film until 1960, when he returned to Hawaii for location shooting on *The Devil at 4 O'Clock*, another Columbia production. A special open-air screening was arranged by unit publicist Bob Yeager, who later discovered that Sinatra had snuck off after his own death scene to spend quality time with his latest girlfriend.

Handed his biggest ever hit, Cohn didn't waste time getting Columbia's Academy Award campaign for *Eternity* under way. With *Look* magazine predicting a surefire nomination, it soon became clear that Sinatra had a date with the Awards ceremony, held on 25 March 1954 at the Pantages Theatre. *From Here to Eternity* picked up 13 nominations, with both Clift and Lancaster vying for Best Actor, an unfortunate split in voter loyalty which lost one of them the award in favour of *Stalag 17* star William Holden. Carefully billed just below the top-line stars, Sinatra could be nominated in the Best Supporting Actor category. Even here, the competition was tough, with Sinatra up against Eddie Albert for *Roman Holiday*, Robert Strauss for *Stalag 17* and both Jack Palance and Brandon De Wilde for *Shane*. Sinatra did worry that his past skirmishes with both the film industry and the media would count against him, yet most of the popular press declared the reborn star the clear favourite. However many actors he'd antagonised during his decade in films, the prevailing feeling among Sinatra's fellow thespians - or at least the ones voting - was that he deserved the award, ill-mannered sonofabitch or not. Attending with daughter Nancy and son Frank, he ran to the stage when his name was announced as the winner. Handed the statuette by actress Mercedes McCambridge, Sinatra's acceptance speech ran along predictable lines: '...I'm deeply thrilled and very moved and I really don't know what to say...' This was enough for the assembled masses and he received a huge round of applause, the longest ovation of the evening. Giving due acknowledgement to Cohn, Adler and Zinnemann, Sinatra later regretted his failure to mention Clift in his list of thank-yous. Some feel he should also have paid tribute to Ava Gardner, who valiantly fought his corner with Cohn when Sinatra's cause looked utterly hopeless. The Oscar win received widespread coverage in the following day's press, *Variety* hailing Sinatra's *Eternity* win as 'the greatest comeback in theater history'. Five decades on, it's difficult to think of a comparable Hollywood resurrection, with even John Travolta's *Pulp Fiction* renaissance qualifying only as an honourable also-ran. The only downside for Sinatra was the response to his performance from close friend and mentor Humphrey Bogart. Asked for an honest opinion by the newly anointed star actor, Bogart merely shook his head. The veteran star did have a point; Sinatra's Maggio is a competent, if slightly uneven piece of acting but the performance works largely on a surface level. Like the overall film, it fails to linger in the mind. Realistic about his own career failings - 'I made more lousy pictures than any actor in history' - Bogart worried that Sinatra's Hollywood resurgence could be quickly undone by his still doubtful commitment to the acting profession. For the time being, Sinatra had little to worry about. If he'd smelled of terminal failure a few months previously, the star now reeked of success. After a little pause for thought, Sinatra would spend the next two years working on an impressive total of six films. Even more amazing, four of them would actually be good.

SUDDENLY 1954

*Sinatra sears the screen...as a snarling
mad-dog killer!*
Publicity

*I got no feeling against the President. I'm just
earning a living.*
John Baron, hitman

Deluged with offers of lucrative, high-profile film roles after *From Here to Eternity*, Sinatra's biggest problem was deciding which parts to take. The $8,000 deal with Columbia gave the studio no further call on his services, leaving him a free agent in hot demand. Twentieth Century-Fox was waving a non-exclusive multi-film contract, kicking off with a starring role opposite Marilyn Monroe in the musical romance *Pink Tights* (see Appendix 2). Warner Brothers felt he'd be much better off appearing with Doris Day in *Young at Heart*. MGM had suddenly become very interested in Ava Gardner's pet project *St Louis Woman*. As for Columbia, there were tentative plans to offer Sinatra the studio's long-standing film adaptation of *Pal Joey*, but problems over casting and Cohn's resentment of Sinatra's misbehaviour during the *Eternity* shoot put the idea back on the shelf for several years (see Chapter 8). The star's first choice of project proved a miscalculation, though for reasons entirely beyond his control. Opting to take up Fox's offer of *Pink Tights*, Sinatra found himself with a generous paycheque but no film, Monroe running off to Japan with lover Joe DiMaggio. Anxious to retain their first call on Sinatra's services, the Fox executives kept him on their payroll without proffering any suitable alternative roles. (In the event, Sinatra wouldn't get to star in a Fox production until 1959.) Largely back to square one in his quest for a strong starring role, he placed his musical comeback plans on temporary hold and agreed to take the lead in a modestly budgeted thriller. Covering similar ground to *The Manchurian Candidate* with its story of an attempted political assassination, *Suddenly* has tended

to dwell in the latter's shadow, which is a little unjust. While it lacks the flamboyance and wit of the later film, not to mention its off-kilter style and acting strength, *Suddenly* is an effective piece of work, admirably uncompromising in its depiction of a small-town American family held hostage by a trio of hired killers. It also marked the beginning of Sinatra's career as a fully-fledged leading man, an accomplished and confident performer ready to tackle both light and dramatic parts, singing and non-singing.

Made by the independent outfit Libra Productions for distribution through United Artists, *Suddenly* was quite daring in its contemporary account of a plot to kill the president. Screenwriter Richard Sale based his script on Dwight Eisenhower's regular train trips to and from Palm Springs, constructing an ingenious what-if scenario revolving around a mysterious conspiracy to gun down the nation's leader during a stop-off in an innocuous, anonymous California town. While the script is careful never to mention Eisenhower by name, audiences could be in little doubt that he was the intended target. Elected in 1953, only a year before *Suddenly* went into production, Eisenhower's war-hero status gave the script an extra layer of irony, his chief would-be assassin being a decorated World War II veteran unable to make a living from anything but killing. If Sinatra felt that the subject matter might tread on a few nerves, it clearly didn't bother him for long (Eisenhower was a Republican). Nor was he perturbed by the fact that the starring role of professional hitman John Baron had been rejected by Montgomery Clift. After several years of being no-one's choice for anything much, substituting for Clift represented a considerable leap up the Hollywood ladder. Besides, Baron was a strong part, lacking any of Maggio's sympathetic attributes but a more intriguing example of battered humanity turned sour. *Suddenly* would also be the first of Sinatra's nine collaborations with UA, his company of choice until the early 1960s. Riding high after recent hits with *The African Queen* and *High Noon*, UA was less conservative than its competitors when it came to controversial subjects, as Sinatra later discovered with *The Man With the Golden Arm*.

While it offered few big names, the production team on *Suddenly* did serve as a keen reminder that the studio system largely despised by Sinatra was beginning to break down, irreparably hit by declining audiences, the anti-trust laws and some truly mediocre output. Producer Robert Bassler, writer Sale and cameraman Charles G. Clarke had all served terms with Twentieth Century-Fox before departing to work as freelance talents. The director, Shropshire-born Englishman Lewis Allen, was best known for the genteel ghost story *The Uninvited* (1943), the high point of his six-year stint with Paramount before the studio dispensed with his services.

Sinatra's co-stars for *Suddenly* included only one biggish name, former Paramount star Sterling Hayden. Tall and inscrutable in a vaguely disquieting way, Hayden's imposing screen presence had been largely wasted in his film work to date, only John Huston's *The Asphalt Jungle* (1950) standing out.

The endless hold-ups and wrangles over Fox's aborted *Pink Tights* project meant that *Suddenly* did not begin production until April 1954, a full year after filming on *Eternity* wrapped. Still on a high over his recent Academy Award win, Sinatra wasn't bothered by this lengthy gap between films and the famous temperament didn't surface once. This was a man in no doubt over the longevity of his new star status. Producer Bassler anticipated trouble when Sinatra approached him with a few suggestions for rewrites, but his fears were unjustified. Determined to make his all-important *Eternity* follow-up as successful a film as possible, Sinatra was concerned only with improving the overall script, not retailoring his role for show-off theatrics, and a lot of his ideas were used in the final version. Confident in his co-workers, the relaxed star even found time for a few jokes at his own expense, advising director Allen to get him a new revolver as his bulky Colt .45 automatic was making him list. Of the cast, he got on best with fellow assassin Christopher Dark, later giving the actor a similar role western-style in *Johnny Concho*. Interviewed during the shoot, Sinatra claimed to be taking his switch to 'serious' acting very much in his stride: 'There's no reason why a singer can't go

Suddenly – Hired killer John Baron taunts pacifist hostage Ellen Benson (Nancy Gates).

dramatic. A singer is essentially an actor.' This quote has been cited as proof of the star's lack of insight into the demands of the acting profession, a typically glib dismissal of the hard work and dedication required for a truly first-rate performance. Maybe so, but these words came from a man who'd spent nearly 20 years perfecting his singing technique and over a decade learning the ropes of movie acting. Judging by his performances over the next few years, Sinatra knew what he was talking about and Hollywood appeared to agree with him. Once he'd finished on Suddenly, there were co-starring roles in *Young at Heart* and *Not as a Stranger* waiting.

Owing more than a passing debt to *High Noon*, *Suddenly* sets its action over just a few hours on a quiet Saturday afternoon, with regular ominous cutaways to various clocks as the President's 5pm arrival draws ever nearer. The town of Suddenly is named after its hectic, often violent past, when gambling and gunslinging were the order of the day. Fifty years on, the only 'excitement' is the occasional stranger wanting directions to the next town. Peaceful in itself, Suddenly cannot remain untouched by the violence of the outside world, the intrusion of Baron's gang prefigured by the casualties of the more distant conflict in Korea. Army widow Ellen Benson (Nancy Gates) is firmly anti-violence, regarding her late husband's death on the battlefield as a wasted life. Her father in-law, Pop Benson (James Gleason), is a World War I veteran and retired secret service man, former bodyguard to President Calvin Coolidge. An unshakeable patriot, he looks on the loss of his son as a noble sacrifice in the line of duty. This view is endorsed by town sheriff - and Ellen's would-be boyfriend - Tod Shaw (Hayden), a proud World War II veteran who firmly believes in confronting the forces of evil, meeting violence with violence: '...guns aren't necessarily bad. Depends on who uses them.' Taking a firmly pro-gun stance, the script spells out the necessity of armed resistance, arguing that psycho-killers such as Baron cannot be dealt with any other way. Selecting the Benson residence for its vantage point overlooking the train station, Baron and his fellow assassins turn the house into a miniature battlefield where no-one can remain neutral. This is a contentious position to adopt, hinging on a situation few suburban American families would ever have to face, and it's a measure of the film's slightly dubious skill that it does not come across as blatant propaganda for the National Rifle Association. The gun is not a fetishised love object, merely a necessary tool of defence, perfectly safe in the hands of all right-thinking people.

First seen 15 minutes into the action, Baron poses as an FBI agent to win over the Bensons' trust, playing on their unquestioning faith in the forces of law and order. Civil, if a little abrupt, his cold smile and contemptuous treatment of Ellen's 'squirt' son Pidge soon arouse suspicions. His flimsy cover blown, Baron threatens to cut Pidge's throat at the first sign of resistance, a threat repeated at regular intervals (Sinatra clearly didn't worry about losing audience goodwill). Callous and sadistic, Baron takes great pleasure in pulling Tod's bullet-shattered arm back into place, his smiling face

contrasted with Tod's stoical wincing. The larger, stronger man has been cut down to size - Hayden towers over Sinatra - and is now in Baron's power. Sinatra is remarkably convincing throughout the film, whether threatening violence or mocking amateur presidential assassin John Wilkes Booth: 'I'm no actor.' Even when the script succumbs to clichés, such as Baron offering appalled pacifist Ellen his (empty) gun to see if she has the 'guts' to shoot him, he keeps the character plausible. Ellen can't even bring herself to hold the despised .45, letting it fall to the floor. The smirking Baron picks it up, showing Ellen the ejected clip with the petty triumph of a malicious child. An unfeeling, self-centred nonentity who thought he'd finally made it when the army taught him how to kill, Baron claims to be the product of a broken childhood - the usual unmarried mother and alcoholic father - and the dehumanising military machine. Tod questions his claim to have won a Silver Star for gunning down 27 Germans single-handed, a reckless move given Baron's obviously unbalanced mind, effectively reassuring audiences that killers such as Baron are born, not made. It's notable that the script gives Baron a World War II background rather than make him a product of the Korea conflict. Presumably the producers felt that depicting a veteran of the recent war in a negative fashion could cause serious offence. By the time of *The Manchurian Candidate* there would be few such qualms. Another interesting touch is Baron's utter lack of interest in his employers. Concerned only with earning his $500,000 fee, he couldn't care less about the people behind the conspiracy. A man of no convictions whatsoever, political or otherwise, Baron has only his perverse sense of professional pride to distinguish him. That and his habit of keeping his hat on at all times, which spared Sinatra the usual hairpiece make-over. Inevitably, the assassination plot is foiled, Baron gunned down by Ellen with her father-in-law's old service revolver. This predictable touch of irony is enlivened by the killer's effectively unheroic exit, whimpering as he dies.

Generally impressive, *Suddenly* has a few flaws. The script is overwritten, with patches of repetitive dialogue and a slight feeling of padding out even at a mere 76 minutes. With much of the action confined to a few rooms of the Benson's house, the verbose exchanges occasionally give the impression of a filmed stage production, a rather elementary failing for an original screenplay. Child actor Kim Charney is only adequate as Pidge - few will be too shocked when Sinatra hits him - and the normally excellent Paul Wexler seems almost amateurish as Hayden's dim-witted deputy. Another distraction is David Raksin's overcooked score, a surprising lapse given Raksin's acclaimed work on films such as *Laura* (1944). On the other hand, the key performances are all fine and Lewis Allen's brisk direction is never less than efficient, maintaining the suspense during the lapses in Sale's overly schematic script and staging some effectively brutal bursts of violence. The scene where electrocuted assassin Christopher Dark is locked to his rifle by muscle spasm, mindlessly firing off a volley of bullets, lingers long in the mind.

Released on 24 September 1954, *Suddenly* picked up a lot of critical praise, with Sinatra's killer acclaimed as both a skilful piece of acting and a potent change of image. There'd been some predictable post-*Eternity* murmurings that his performance as Maggio was nothing more than beginner's luck, voted to an Academy Award win on the strength of sentiment rather than merit. *Newsweek* had no time for such cynicism, rating Sinatra's work in *Suddenly* as 'superb'. *New York World-Telegram* critic Alton Cook agreed, though not without having an unsubtle dig at the star's earlier film work: 'Sinatra carries a one-man show on his once lifeless acting shoulders for almost the entire length of the picture.' *Newsweek* offered an unconditional endorsement of both film and star: 'As simple and startling as a good scream... Sinatra becomes one of the most repellent killers in American screen history.' Eager to promote his movie, Sinatra made at least one personal apperance in his hitman costume, signing autographs from the safety of a theatre ticket booth. Despite these efforts, audiences proved unenthusiastic, possibly because of the controversial subject matter,

more likely owing to the unilluminating title, and the film barely broke even. It's probably no coincidence that Sinatra never again played a character so completely lacking in redeeming features. This commercial disappointment had little effect on the steady upward curve of Sinatra's career. With *Young at Heart* awaiting release and *Not as a Stranger* mid-way through production, he didn't yet need to worry about the film roles running dry.

Largely forgotten after its original release, *Suddenly* later acquired a little notoriety thanks to Sinatra's one-time friend John Fitzgerald Kennedy. Around 1970, Sinatra discovered that alleged solo Kennedy assassin Lee Harvey Oswald had watched the film just a few days before the Dallas slaying on 22 November 1963. Still shocked by the episode and now something of a political conservative, Sinatra felt that such inflammatory material should not be in the public domain and withdrew *Suddenly* from circulation. This ban was not confined to the United States, the film vanishing from British television between 1971 and 1994. Unavailable for nearly 25 years, *Suddenly* eventually resurfaced to take its rightful place as one of Sinatra's finest hours on the screen.

YOUNG AT HEART 1954

Don't try to see all the films I directed, that would turn you off movies completely.
Gordon Douglas

Don't you ever get tired of being a nice guy, Alex? It would bore me stiff.
Barney Sloan

Doris Day and giant ants. In 1954 director Gordon Douglas worked with both, embarking on *Young at Heart* once the rampaging mutant hymenoptera of *Them!* (1954) were safely in the can. *Them!* was the bigger box-office hit of the two, and this nuclear-anxiety sci-fi classic remains his best known and most appreciated film. Remembered largely as an uninspired, if competent technician-for-hire, Douglas is one of the unsung heroes of Frank Sinatra's later film career, watching the star's back on *None But the Brave*, then directing *Tony Rome* and its sequel *Lady in Cement*, with the more weighty *The Detective* sandwiched in between (see Chapter 14). At the very least, these all deserve respect as class acts, highly professional entertainment on a level seldom achieved in Hollywood or elsewhere. Douglas also helmed *Robin and the 7 Hoods*, but no-one's perfect. A one-time actor, casting director and gagman for legendary comedy producer Hal Roach, Gordon Douglas was largely based at Warner between 1950 and 1965. Popular with cast and crew alike, the director always wore a baseball cap on set, turning the brim around to the back of his head when he wanted the cameras to roll. Assigned to the *Young at Heart* production in the summer of 1954, Douglas had little idea of the traumas ahead. Given Sinatra's poor behaviour during the shoot, it's amazing the two men ever talked again.

In a rational universe, *Young at Heart* shouldn't work at all. A softened reworking of Warner's 1938 hit *Four Daughters*, the film is schmaltzy, sentimental and shamelessly manipulative. Losing one daughter somewhere along the way, the story centres on the romantic entanglements of the three grown-up Tuttle sisters, who live with their widowed father and his all-seeing/all-knowing sister somewhere in suburban Connecticut. Youngest sister Laurie (Day) thinks she is in love with smooth composer Alex Burke (Gig Young), only to realise that she really cares for his troubled friend Barney Sloan (Sinatra), a gifted but unsuccessful pianist and songwriter. There isn't a great deal more to the film yet somehow it clicks, tapping the viewer's emotions in much the same way as the more acclaimed big-screen soap operas directed by Douglas Sirk for Universal-International (*Magnificent Obsession, All That Heaven Allows* et al). A cannily assembled package given unexpected resonance by its stars and their music, *Young at Heart* has the courage of its melodramatic convictions. A word or two of praise

should also go to director Douglas, whose assured handling keeps the ingredients from turning into purest gluten. Opening with a lengthy crane shot down the Tuttles' street and into their living room - where Pa Tuttle plays the flute while Aunt Jessie watches televised boxing - he rarely makes a false move.

The inspiration for pairing Sinatra with top Warner star Doris Day in a musical romance appears to have stemmed from his renewed recording success as much as his rising film career. The song 'Young at Heart' began life as an instrumental piece by Johnny Richards, with lyrics later added by Carolyn Leigh. Persuaded by composer Jimmy Van Heusen that the piece had potential, Sinatra recorded 'Young at Heart' on 9 December 1953. By March of the following year, the song had climbed to the number five spot in the US, giving Sinatra his first top ten hit in years and an impressive run of 22 weeks in the charts. Played over the film's opening and closing credits, the song doesn't actually have much bearing on the events in between, but it was certainly an astute way of pre-selling its motion picture namesake.

A Warner contract star since 1948, Doris Day had notched up 16 films over six years, most of them successful. The studio played on her ultra-wholesome, family-safe persona, promoting the much mocked 'eternal virgin' image in vehicles such as *On Moonlight Bay* (1951). *Young at Heart* was the last in Day's original run of films for Warner, her subsequent return to the studio for *The Pajama Game* (1957) a definite one-off. Increasingly disenchanted with Warner's handling of her career, Day and husband-manager Marty Melcher had decided to take more control over their films. *Young at Heart* would be made by Melcher's newly formed company Arwin Productions for release through Warner. While casting Sinatra was Warner's decision, Day had no problems with the studio's choice of leading man. Six years previously, Day had done a 20-week stint during the 1947-48 run of Sinatra's radio show *Your Hit Parade*. Uneasy performing live in front of a large theatre audience, she hadn't enjoyed the experience much, but claimed both to respect and like Sinatra.

Young at Heart – Laurie (Doris Day) thinks she loves another, but comes to realise it's Barney (Sinatra) who has a place in her heart.

Day's enthusiasm for her co-star would be sorely tested over the next few weeks. At least she got top billing.

The Day-Sinatra combo looked like a box-office winner - *Suddenly* hadn't yet flopped - and Warner protected their investment with a impressive selection of co-stars, led by the esteemed Ethel Barrymore. In failing health during the *Young at Heart* production, Barrymore was largely confined to a wheelchair between takes, requiring help to stand up when the cameras were ready to roll. The supporting cast also included former Warner contract actor Gig Young, who'd worked with Gordon Douglas on *Come Fill the Cup*, and Sinatra's old *Step Lively* comrade Dorothy Malone. While Day, Malone and sister number three Elisabeth Fraser all look slightly too old for their roles, Malone is the only member of the trio to appear miscast, her sultry glamour at odds with the wholesome, caring nature of the Tuttle clan. Day might occasionally resemble a perky, chirpy, peroxide chipmunk but she does it with conviction. The part of grouchy-yet-loveable family patriarch Gregory Tuttle went to Robert Keith, who would reunite with Sinatra on *Guys and Dolls* as a gruff-yet-likeable policeman.

Hoping to repeat the full impact of the original

film, Warner appointed *Four Daughters* producer Henry Blanke to oversee the remake. Adapted by Julius J. Epstein and Lenore Coffee from the Fannie Hurst novel *Sister Act*, much of the *Four Daughters* screenplay was retained for *Young at Heart*, which gave a misleading impression of the writers' contribution to the new film. Despite their prominent billing in the credits, neither Epstein nor Coffee did any work on the remake. The original script was revised by playwright Liam O'Brien, whose main brief was to give the Tuttle family a musical background. And lose that surplus daughter.

Supervised by Ray Heindorf, head of Warner's music department, the score for *Young at Heart* included a satisfying mix of standards by Cole Porter, George and Ira Gershwin, Harold Arlen, Jimmy Van Heusen and Johnny Mercer, with piano solos courtesy of Sinatra's old friend Andre Previn. There was a little consternation when Sinatra demanded the same number of songs as Day, though this turned out to be the least of his impositions. Extra tunes were squeezed into the script with minimal awkwardness, O'Brien giving Sloan the job of a bar piano player. If Sinatra's assured renditions of 'Someone to Watch Over Me' and 'Just One of Those Things' didn't quite obscure their questionable relevance to the main narrative, few in the audience were complaining.

The musical side of the production appears to have been partly responsible for Sinatra's utter loathing of Marty Melcher. At one of the preproduction conferences in the latter's Warner office, Sinatra refused even to acknowledge his co-star's husband, holding a newspaper in front of his face rather than look at Melcher. Following a mysterious conversation between the two men regarding the songs for *Young at Heart*, Sinatra informed Jack Warner that he would not shoot one frame of film if the 'creep' Melcher was anywhere on the studio lot (a nine-mile complex). The banished Melcher always professed to have no idea why Sinatra hated him. Given the later revelations regarding his extremely shady business practices - effectively stealing and squandering Doris Day's entire career earnings - it's possible Melcher hoped to interest Sinatra in a sneaky deal over the song rights. Music publisher Sam Weiss, a friend of Sinatra, believed that Melcher had attempted some kind of 'hustle'. For his part, Sinatra never explained his dislike of Melcher, presumably feeling that Day's shock discovery of bankruptcy and huge debts after her husband's death in 1968 told the whole story.

Triumphant over Melcher, Sinatra still felt dissatisfied with the production, expressing unhappiness about his character's climactic death in a suicidal car crash. In *Four Daughters*, this spectacular exit had topped a star-making performance from newcomer John Garfield. His own star largely secure, Sinatra didn't require this kind of splash. Besides, after *From Here to Eternity* and *Suddenly* he wanted to make it to the end credits alive. Day disagreed, arguing during the protracted preproduction meetings that the entire film built up to the tragic ending. Allowing Sloan to live would destroy the mood of the piece and leave audiences feeling cheated by the obvious cop-out. She also felt that killing off Sinatra would give his performance more depth, a point later made by Sinatra himself regarding Shirley MacLaine's character in *Some Came Running*. Unswayed by these arguments, Sinatra insisted that the ending be rewritten, flexing his still growing star muscle to get his way. As an Arwin production, the film was theoretically under the control of Day and Melcher but the Warner executives were not about to risk losing their leading man. With Sinatra refusing to sign his contract until the necessary changes were made, the studio hurriedly put O'Brien to work on the rewrite. Oddly, no-one seemed to consider Sloan's delayed entrance a problem. With the emphasis in *Four Daughters* firmly on the title characters, there was no pressing reason to put debutant John Garfield in the action early on. O'Brien's brief for *Young at Heart* obviously didn't include addressing this problematic aspect for the remake's rather better known male star, Sinatra not appearing until well over half an hour into the story.

Day and Sinatra also clashed over working hours, Day happy to keep to the standard filming routine, starting early in the morning. Not inclined to abandon his old habits, Sinatra failed to follow her good example, prompting lengthy - and expensive - delays in the shooting with frequent late arrivals. Already upset by the ultimatum over Melcher, which effectively barred her husband from his own production, Day failed to see the funny side of this screw-'em-they-need-me attitude. Sinatra didn't appear to care if he cost the production an hour's shoot or a whole morning's. There was worse to come, a prime example of Sinatra's tendency to throw a fit rather than articulate his problems. Just a few days into filming, the star announced that he was walking off the set and would quit *Young at Heart* altogether if cameraman Charles Lang wasn't replaced. A multiple Academy Award winner, Lang had a reputation as one of the industry's finest directors of photography, making Sinatra's demand all the more outrageous. As with the star's other dictates, Warner felt unable to say no and Lang made way for Ted McCord, who'd worked with Blanke on *Treasure of the Sierra Madre* (1948) and Day on *Young Man With a Horn* (1950). The most charitable explanation for Sinatra's treatment of Lang - and the one offered by co-star Day - is his old problem with hanging around between set-ups. Lang's careful, ultra-precise lighting took time, leaving the star restless and bored to distraction. Rather than explain his difficulty with this to Blanke or Douglas or Jack Warner or even Lang himself, Sinatra opted to have the latter thrown off the film without even telling him the reason. As Sammy Davis Junior later pointed out - to his cost - Sinatra's occasional tendency to tread on 'lesser' minions was unacceptable behaviour, far more offensive than the alleged Mafia dealings so beloved by the press. Needless to say, there was no friction between the star and the sufficiently speedy new cameraman. Aware that Sinatra was still suffering over the break-up of his marriage to Ava Gardner, Day felt nevertheless that his selfish behaviour undermined him as a supposedly professional actor. Much as she admired his spontaneous one-take style, agreeing that repeated takes could render a performance mechanical, there was only so much time Day could spend knitting in her dressing room while the company hung around waiting for Sinatra to appear.

If the *Young at Heart* production saw rather too much of Sinatra at his worst, he did redeem himself a little by throwing a surprise 75th birthday party for co-star Ethel Barrymore on the Tuttle living room set. Day was so moved by the gesture she burst into tears. A member of the company threw her a box of Kleenex tissues, which unfortunately struck her on the head. Outraged by this ungentlemanly act, Sinatra turned on the guilty party. Touched by his display of gallantry, Day thereafter always associated Sinatra with this particular brand of tissue.

Delayed it might be, but Sinatra's entrance in *Young at Heart* is undeniably impressive. Sloan is first seen in the doorway of the Tuttle house, his back to the camera, his hat tilted at an insouciant angle. Turning around to reveal a loosely knotted tie and a distinct lack of manners, he is clearly a man of contradictions, delicately picking out a tune on a harp while a cigarette dangles from his mouth, the ash threatening to drop on the instrument. This is a million miles from the old MGM persona, the colour photography detailing the battered Sinatra face in a way that now enhances rather than undermines his character. Throwing up a barrier of all-purpose surliness to protect his vulnerability and loneliness, Sloan doesn't fool wise Aunt Jessie (Barrymore) for a second. It is surely some measure of Sinatra's dramatic ability at this time that he could share centre stage with Ethel Barrymore and emerge with honours entirely even. He also works well with Day, whose shiny, beaming face and gleaming teeth make an effective contrast to his crumpled, careworn features. Outwardly confident and optimistic, Laurie Tuttle has a sharp mind to rival Aunt Jessie's, correctly guessing that sister Fran (Malone) doesn't love her fiance. Admiring Sloan's obvious musical talent, she has little time for his defeatism. Orphaned at birth, Sloan believes himself to be a born loser, a helpless pawn of cruel fate. Even changing his Italian name to something a little more WASP-friendly hasn't made any difference (an interesting reference to Sinatra's decision to keep his original name). Laurie dislikes this self-indulgent despair, typified by Sloan's refusal to finish a song she

feels sure will be a hit. This gulf between them is poignantly expressed in the scene where Laurie leaves Barney alone in a bar as she heads off to her intended wedding to Alex Burke. The final shot places the departing Laurie on the left of the frame, her bright blue dress standing out against the gloom of the interior, while the sombrely clad Sloan sits slumped over a piano on the right, at one with his surroundings. Even their subsequent elopement and marriage fails to transform him, Sloan regarding himself as a failure and fearing that Laurie still loves the far more successful Burke. Driving home in a snowstorm, he switches off the windscreen wipers and puts his foot down on the gas pedal (the image of the windscreen being steadily filled with snowflakes is highly effective). A fast driver off screen, Sinatra's expression of resolute despair is utterly convincing. Had Sloan died in the resulting crash as intended, audiences would have gone home weeping but the film wouldn't ring true. If his prediction of a sad end was borne out - albeit with a little help - Sloan's encounter with the Tuttle family and genuine love for Laurie would have counted for nothing, instead of being the life-changing experience he so badly needed. If *Young at Heart* has any point to make, it is that no-one's destiny is fixed, especially when there are others who care about them. Following the obligatory hospital scene, where the critically injured Sloan learns that Laurie is pregnant, the film cuts to the living room of the Tuttle house, with the family gathered around Laurie's baby son. The piano starts playing and we see Sloan singing the final version of his song. It may not be hard-hitting realism, but this rewritten finale does make for an affecting conclusion (Sinatra was sufficiently impressed with Liam O'Brien's work to hire him as scriptwriter for *The Devil at 4 O'Clock*.) Mirroring the opening shot, the camera pulls away from the house and back down the street, leaving the enlarged Tuttle clan at peace. Incidentally, the song, 'You, My Love' was released as a tie-in single with some success, just missing top ten placings in both the American and British charts.

Released on 15 January 1955, *Young at Heart* met

Young at Heart – Sinatra and Doris Day in the recording studio.

with a mixed reception. Warner's promotion for the film featured Day and Sinatra's smiling faces along with the legend: 'TOGETHER... and TERRIFIC' but many didn't agree. The *Saturday Review* cited the film as conclusive proof 'that Hollywood has not lost its knack for making indifferent new pictures out of good old pictures.' The British magazine *Films and Filming* felt the stars were simply mismatched: 'The cadaverous and undernourished Sinatra pairs oddly with Doris Day, whose rosy-cheeked tomboy vitality affords the only lively relief in two hours of pedestrian sentiment and platitude.' A solid box office hit, the film still made for a poor start between Sinatra and Warner Brothers,

leaving neither in a hurry to continue the relationship. While the smash success of *Four Daughters* had prompted two sequels featuring the original cast, *Four Wives* (1939) and *Four Mothers* (1940), a follow-up to *Young at Heart* looked highly unlikely. Sinatra wouldn't work with the studio again until 1960, and even then the deal resulted from a dubious clause in Natalie Wood's loan-out contract for *Kings Go Forth* (see Chapter 8). If anyone had told him that by 1963 he'd have a major production partnership with Warner and be regarded by many as a likely successor to studio head Jack Warner, Sinatra would surely have laughed a little bit.

Major Contender
1954-1956

NOT AS A STRANGER 1955

Gentlemen, this is a corpse.
Dr Aaron

While Sinatra never attempted to match Doris Day's impressive tally of 16 film roles in six years, during 1954 and 1955 he appeared in more movies than any other Hollywood star. If there was a slight feeling of making up for lost time in this non-stop film schedule, Sinatra's determination not to repeat the gap between *Eternity* and *Suddenly* needed little explanation and his choices of project were generally sound. Accepting a third-billed supporting role in the medical soap opera *Not as a Stranger* probably seemed a good idea at the time. He'd signed on for the film during the *Suddenly* shoot and the part of a dedicated, if fun-loving doctor and loyal friend was in marked contrast to the ice-cold killer of the latter film. Aside from one bout of hellraising, Sinatra's first collaboration with producer-director Stanley Kramer was relatively placid compared to the well-documented fireworks on *The Pride and the Passion* a few years later and *Stranger* has never attained the same prominence in

the Sinatra filmography. This is probably just as well, given the film's overall quality. Aside from Sinatra's confident, good-natured performance, *Not as a Stranger* is a dud.

Active in films since the early 1940s, Stanley Kramer had recently quit Columbia Studios – with minimal regret on either side – and made a new production-distribution deal with United Artists. *Not as a Stranger* would be his first such independent production and also his first film as a director. Married writing team Edward and Edna Anhalt were recruited to adapt the original Morton Thompson novel into a working script, having previously collaborated with Kramer on Fred Zinnemann's *A Member of the Wedding*. They had little success with either the story or the characters, and the resulting film is often laughably bad.

Much of the blame must fall on Kramer's shoulders, the producer-director making poor decisions in just about every department. Even allowing for Kramer's novice status, the direction is awkward and uncertain, demonstrating little feeling for either actors or the camera. The pace is sluggish, the performances exhibit little focus or conviction, and Kramer's lack of visual

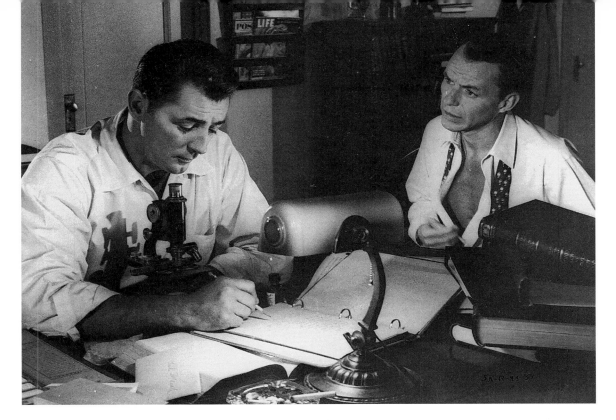

Not as a Stranger – Dedicated medical student Lucas Marsh (Robert Mitchum) fails to notice his friend's undernourished condition.

flair only highlights the overall sense of indifference. Even the expertise of veteran cameraman Franz Planer - a Kramer regular - couldn't prevent *Stranger* from looking static and dull.

Shot at the former Chaplin studios largely between September and November 1954 - some sources quote an October start - *Not as a Stranger* boasted a budget of around $2 million, easily Kramer's biggest to date. Determined to keep the medical details as accurate as possible, director and cast regularly attended real operations at the local university hospitals. The realism extended to the sound stages, with star Robert Mitchum surrounded by genuine surgeons as his character proved his skill with a scalpel. Between takes, Sinatra, Mitchum and supporting actor Broderick Crawford liked to perform mock operations on dummies. Arriving for work one day in less than glowing health, Sinatra was treated to a soothing alcohol rub by Mitchum as he lay stretched out on one of the mock-up operating tables. So soothing, in fact, that Sinatra fell asleep.

While Sinatra's behaviour on set was largely a model of decorum compared to his *Young at Heart* antics, he made up for it after hours. Following a particularly intense bout of socialising, Sinatra, Mitchum and Crawford went a drunken vandalism spree, tearing down the walls of Sinatra's dressing room, smashing the windows and ripping out the telephones. Faced with the hard evidence of the more or less demolished room, the hung-over trio informed the unamused Kramer that they'd only embarked on their DIY restructuring in order to converse more easily. Despite this episode, which left Kramer vowing never to work with Sinatra again, the producer-director looked back on the production as a generally happy experience.

First seen sandwiched between the looming figures of Mitchum and Lee Marvin during one of Crawford's pathology lectures, Sinatra gets relatively little to do in *Not as a Stranger*. His character is sketched in as a carefree ladies' man, but serves largely as a sounding board and conscience for Mitchum's Lucas Marsh. When the impoverished Marsh announces that he intends to enter into a loveless, money-making marriage with infatuated spinster nurse Kristina (a miscast Olivia De Havilland), Boone sees through the scheme straight away and berates his friend's cold-bloodedness: 'You're taking advantage of a poor squarehead who's afraid of being an old maid.' In one of his few animated moments, Marsh turns on Boone and shoves him against a bookcase, Mitchum's exposed torso emphasising his muscle and Sinatra's lack thereof ('Sometimes I wish I had 75 more pounds. I'd belt you one'). Unfortunately, there also appears to be an element of snobbery in Boone's disapproval of the marriage, as he tells Marsh that his intended simply isn't doctor's wife material, lacking the social connections to advance his career in the private sector. (In fairness, Boone later recants this opinion.) The character's likeable nature is also undermined by a scene where he does an unamusing imitation of Dr Aaron (Crawford), which comes across as vaguely anti-Semitic. Script aside, Sinatra delivers an honourable performance, though he blinks a little too much in the scene where Boone informs Marsh of his alcoholic father's death. He gets to wear the trademark fedora hat featured on numerous album covers and the forceps scars behind his left ear are particularly prominent, contributing - intentionally or not - to the hard-achieved atmosphere of surgical realism. Sinatra even sanctioned a sly reference to estranged wife Ava Gardner, with Marsh and Kristina seen leaving a cinema showing the Gardner-Bogart Hollywood satire *The Barefoot Contessa* (1954). Sadly, he largely vanishes from the film during the second half, where the newly qualified Marsh sets up as a country doctor in the unsubtly named small town of Greenville. Reappearing only to confirm Kristina's pregnancy and scold Marsh for his neglect of her, Sinatra doesn't even get to meet up with his old *It Happened in Brooklyn* co-star Gloria Grahame.

In December 1954, with post-production on the film not yet completed, Sinatra placed a full page advert in *Billboard* magazine, detailing his recent run of movie success. Plugging the new and forthcoming releases *Suddenly* and *Young at Heart*, the as-yet unfinished

Stranger and the still unscheduled *Guys and Dolls*, he gave the impression of a man very content with his career. In truth, he had severe reservations about *Guys and Dolls*, having seen the plum role of Sky Masterson go to Marlon Brando and learned that much of the original Frank Loesser score was to be discarded. He would also have to settle for third billing once again, an improvement on his *Eternity* placing but a noticeable slide from his number one spot in *Suddenly*. By now rather sick of his 'comeback' status, Sinatra knew full well that until he secured a starring role in an 'A' budget production, his hard-won career renaissance could be open to doubt.

An utterly bogus piece of work, *Stranger* picked up deservedly poor reviews following its release on 2 July 1955. No-one liked Mitchum's central performance, *Variety* arguing that the star simply lacked the ability to play the character: 'He's considerably over his acting depth.' There were kinder words for Sinatra, whose sheer professionalism kept his few scenes at least watchable. Mitchum agreed with the general verdict, conceding that only Sinatra's performance had saved the film from total mediocrity. The box-office response displayed more enthusiasm than either the critics or the cast and *Not as a Stranger* turned out to be Mitchum's biggest hit to date. Good reviews or not, Sinatra must have realised he was merely marking time with the film, notching up another commercial hit while he waited for the bigger, better roles to come his way. *Guys and Dolls* offered such a part yet it was beyond his reach, a hard lesson in the crucial difference between stardom and superstardom.

GUYS AND DOLLS 1955

These fucking New York actors! How much cheesecake do you think I can eat?
Frank Sinatra to Marlon Brando, somewhere between take eight and take thirty four

The late Montgomery Clift was of the opinion that *Guys and Dolls* sucked, which is a little harsh. A lavish, if carelessly packaged blend of half-baked and largely incompatible elements, the film is clearly the work of talented people under the supervision of a man lacking the slightest idea how to stage a film musical. Viewing *Guys and Dolls* 15 years on, writer-director Joseph Mankiewicz admitted that the end result was too slow and far too talkative. He could have added miscast, mismanaged, misogynistic and generally misconceived. On the other hand, it does offer the image of co-star Vivian Blaine on stage at the Hot Box club, singing 'Pet Me Poppa' while clad in a skimpy feline costume designed to give maximum emphasis to her breasts. They let children watch this.

Based largely on the Damon Runyan story *The Idyll of Miss Sarah Brown*, the original *Guys and Dolls* stage musical opened at the 46th Street Theater, Broadway on 24 November 1950. With music and lyrics by Frank Loesser and a book by Jo Swerling and Abe Burrows, the show was a smash hit, running over three years. When the film rights became available at the beginning of 1954, the major studios went into a bidding war frenzy, veteran independent producer Samuel Goldwyn leading the pack. Loesser had provided the songs for Goldwyn's most recent film, *Hans Christian Andersen* (1952), the success of which convinced the producer that family musical spectaculars were surefire winners. With a record $800,000 already spent on the film rights to the show, Goldwyn lavished $5.5 million on his movie version. Looking for a suitable director to helm the production, he decided upon Joseph Mankiewicz, one of the industry's most respected talents. Mankiewicz had no experience of musicals but Goldwyn hoped he could bring some dramatic depth to the story, which the newly appointed writer-director felt to be a little thin. Assembling a script that worked without any songs attached - not the best move for a major musical - Mankiewicz still managed to impress his employer, drawing the famous Goldwyn comment: '...the picture has warmth and charmth.' (sic)

Casting the lead role of gambler Sky Masterson should have been a cinch. Goldwyn felt Gene Kelly was the only real candidate and Kelly wholeheartedly agreed. Sadly, MGM's New York boss Nicholas Schenck disliked both Goldwyn and Mankiewicz and refused to loan out his contract star. Big names such as Cary Grant, Kirk Douglas, Robert Mitchum, Burt Lancaster, Bing Crosby, Clark Gable and even Dean Martin were proposed as possible replacements but none satisfied the producer. With his first choice of star a no-hoper, Goldwyn promptly abandoned all consideration of the skills required for the part and hired Marlon Brando on the strength of the celebrated 'method' actor's box-office standing. For the role of Sky's Salvation Army romantic interest Miss Sarah Brown, Goldwyn didn't even bother to look for a singer, offering the part to Grace Kelly. Kelly was committed elsewhere, second choice Deborah Kerr couldn't fit the shooting dates into her schedule, and the producer settled for Kerr's fellow British expatriate Jean Simmons, Brando's love interest in the turgid Napoleon biopic *Desiree* (1954).

With Brando cast, Sinatra's hopes of playing the lead evaporated. For all his renewed film success, he hadn't even made the original shortlist. Faced with either losing the film altogether or pursuing the negligible supporting role of Nathan Detroit, he opted for the latter. Star and director were both Bert Allenberg clients and Sinatra shamelessly exploited the connection to secure a meeting with the reluctant Mankiewicz. Impressed by the singer's personal bid for Detroit, Mankiewicz still didn't think Sinatra was right for the part, which barely used his singing talent, but Goldwyn saw the box-office potential. Looking for an all-star line-up, Goldwyn wanted Betty Grable to play Detroit's love interest, nightclub entertainer Miss Adelaide. His director disagreed, insisting on the show's Broadway and London star, Vivian Blaine. Less than objective about the production, Sinatra felt that both Brando and Simmons were miscast, arguing that a successful film adaptation needed trained singers for the leads. He also disliked the revisions inflicted on the score, though several of these alterations were made to accommodate his own casting. Detroit had only one song - 'Sue Me' - in the original show, and the additional material penned for Sinatra meant that other numbers were squeezed out. Similarly, Detroit's

Brooklyn background disappeared and the already verbose script was expanded to build the part up into an ersatz starring role.

Scheduled to begin production in January 1955, *Guys and Dolls* didn't start shooting until mid-March, Mankiewicz temporarily put out of action by an appendectomy. While Sinatra later played down the antagonism between himself and Brando, there seems little doubt that he disliked his co-star intensely. According to Nancy Jnr, Brando envied Sinatra's singing talent and appeared genuinely pleased to be co-starring with him. By contrast, Sinatra could barely manage a smile in Brando's direction. When *Vogue* photographer Richard Avedon arrived to snap pictures of the stars for Goldwyn's promotional campaign, Sinatra refused to appear for the shoot before Brando, obliging a publicity man to devise a signal that summoned both men simultaneously. Aside from the small matter of Brando swiping the Sky Masterson role, Sinatra hadn't forgotten or forgiven losing the lead in *On the Waterfront* to the bigger star (see Appendix 2) and regularly referred to Brando as 'the most overrated actor in the world' or just plain 'mumbles'. The lingering ill-feeling over *Waterfront* was exacerbated by Brando's Academy Award nomination for his performance in the film. With the ceremony to be held on March 30, while *Guys and Dolls* was in production, the tension on set grew steadily stronger. When Brando emerged victorious from the Pantages Theatre, Oscar in hand, his already antagonistic relationship with Sinatra withered and died.

Sinatra's personal clashes with Brando were well matched by their professional differences, the latter's slow, methodical, multi-take technique totally at odds with his co-star's approach to acting. Brando was further slowed down by his understandable difficulties with Mankiewicz's often clumsy Runyonesque dialogue, hence the cheesecake incident that drove Sinatra off the set in fury on the first day of shooting. Needing to fill the vast Cinemascope frame with something, the director wanted to have both stars in shot as often as possible, requiring Sinatra to eat while Brando talked.

With Brando unable to deliver his lines to the expected standard, Sinatra finally suffered a cheesecake overdose, threw the plate to one side and buried his fork in the tablecloth. Brando wasn't wild about Sinatra's acting, either, complaining to Mankiewicz that his co-star had transformed Detroit into a second romantic lead, rather than the comedy relief originally intended. Wishing to skirt over the fact that he'd largely rewritten Sinatra's role as a leading man, the director informed Brando that while he shared his reservations, he wasn't about to tell Sinatra how to act or sing (obviously not the director's job).

Sinatra wasn't alone in his frustrations over Brando's laborious and drawn-out acting style. Vivian Blaine respected Brando but preferred Sinatra's rapid one-take working method, feeling that Brando's endless appetite for retakes - 135 on one occasion - wore down the rest of the cast. It also slowed down filming to a worrying degree, leaving Mankiewicz desperate to get back on schedule for the film's intended Christmas release. He attempted to remedy the situation by working Brando's co-stars both faster and longer, ordering Blaine to remain on set after a full day for a series of close-ups. Exhausted from the day's work, Blaine felt unable to protest. Sinatra had no such reservations and took her off the set, with no argument from his director.

Aside from his undying hatred of Brando, Sinatra's behaviour during filming on *Guys and Dolls* was by and large reasonable, though there were rumours he disliked his part so much he never bothered to learn the lines properly. Mankiewicz later conceded that Sinatra sometimes criticised his dialogue, but insisted there had been no demands for further rewrites. Nor did he blame his rare line-fluffs on other performers, as several Brando allies later claimed. Concerned largely with getting the job over and done with, Sinatra turned up on time for his scenes, compensating for his general lack of enthusiasm with lavish meal breaks. Unimpressed by the catering laid on by Goldwyn, he sent out for Italian food every day of the shoot, sharing it with his entourage. Sinatra also found time for a one-off performance in Las Vegas, standing in for the indisposed Danny Thomas. Racing off to the airport after his day's work on set, he flew back in the early hours to resume filming the next morning. This relative lack of fireworks probably stemmed from a recent career move that reduced the tribulations with Brando to a mere distraction. Prior to shooting on *Guys and Dolls*, Sinatra had made a deal with United Artists to produce six films over five years, one of them also to be directed by the star. The first of these, an offbeat western entitled *Johnny Concho*, would go into production towards the end of the year, co-written and directed by its producer-star's old friend Don McGuire.

Preoccupied by more stimulating career matters, Sinatra's performance as Nathan Detroit, proud operator of the 'oldest established permanent floating crap game in New York', is largely a walk-through. Dressed in a natty blue-grey pinstripe suit and bow tie, with matching greyed temples (why?) and oversized hat, he shares Brando's difficulty with the script, sometimes appearing to deliver his dialogue in inverted commas. His scenes with Vivian Blaine lack spark, Sinatra overwhelmed by Blaine's overbearing New York accent, and the few encounters with Brando fall lifeless to the floor. This uneasy, overplayed approach is complemented by Sinatra's lacklustre singing. His rendition of 'Adelaide', one of the new songs written for Sinatra, is unremarkable and even the supposedly showing-stopping title number, sung with original cast members Stubby Kaye and Johnny Silver, fails to deliver. There are jokes about his weight and Ava Gardner but they're flogging a whole team of dead horses. In fairness, Sinatra's failure seems minor compared to the overall film. Mankiewicz's clumsy direction is plodding and poorly paced, with numerous awkward pauses between songs and dialogue. Shooting in Cinemascope for the first time on Goldwyn's order, the director's inexperience with the format is evident and only serves to highlight his lack of musical flair. Michael Kidd's energetic and highly stylised stage choreography is plainly unsuited to the big screen, the elaborate 'Crapshooters' Ballet' reduced to a risible 'Dance of the Halfwits'. Crouching down behind co-star B.S. Pully as

the prancing gamblers hurl themselves about, Sinatra looks understandably nervous. Similarly, Oliver Smith's interestingly abstract background sets simply hang about to no great purpose as real cars drive along studio-bound streets. Surprisingly, *Guys and Dolls'* one success is a brief scene between Brando and Simmons as they duet on 'A Woman in Love'. While the stars' singing voices are noticeably flat and blatantly untrained, Mankiewicz's intimate staging and their low-key approach to the lyrics work rather well.

The hostilities between the various *Guys and Dolls* factions didn't cease with the end of production. Much to Sinatra's irritation, his write-up in the souvenir programmes handed out at the 4 November Capitol Theater premiere played on the tired comeback angle: 'After soaring to what was almost national adulation a dozen years ago, a combination of poor roles, a bad press, and other things [?] sent his career zooming downward... Today his 'second career' is in high gear.' With this in mind, it is perhaps not surprising that Sinatra effectively vetoed the release of a proper spin-off soundtrack album for the film. While the Brando-Simmons duet 'A Woman in Love' was released on the Decca label, Sinatra's exclusive contract with Capitol meant that all tracks from the film featuring his voice were out of bounds.

Released on 14 November 1955, *Guys and Dolls* found few critical admirers but scored bigtime with audiences, the public response fuelled by Goldwyn's mammoth promotional drive for 'America's Own Musical'. Expressing disappointment rather than outright loathing, the reviews were a fair reflection of the movie. *The New Yorker* ran a piece entitled 'Sam, You Made the Film Too Long.' *Time* magazine protested the lack of spirit: 'Faithful in detail, the picture is false to the original in its feeling.' The film went on to become 1956's second biggest domestic hit, narrowly beaten to the top spot by *Giant*. Eventually grossing over $13 million in the United States, *Guys and Dolls* proved similarly popular abroad, making more than $1 million in Britain and $500,000 in Japan. Sinatra had found himself another hit, making an impressive three in a row, yet the abiding feeling was one of missed opportunity. Easily the most expensive of his four films shot in 1955, *Guys and Dolls* turned out to be the least significant. *The Tender Trap* would finally confirm his star status beyond all doubt, while *The Man With the Golden Arm* underlined his skill as a dramatic actor. Even the largely forgotten *Johnny Concho* marked the beginning of Sinatra's career as an all-powerful film producer.

THE TENDER TRAP 1955

You're even attractive in an off-beat, beat-up kind of way.
Julie Gillis

Four Fabulous Funsters in Cinemascope and Gay Color.
Publicity

Adapted by Julius J. Epstein from the Broadway hit by Max Shulman and Robert Paul Smith, *The Tender Trap* is a stern moral tract disguised as a swinging bachelor comedy. Back with MGM after five years, Sinatra plays New York theatrical agent Charlie Y. Reader, a fickle yet loveable single man with a taste in short-sleeved orange shirts (shared by the star) and a seemingly endless chain of attractive, intelligent women to fill his spare time. Given his selection of hot chat-up lines, notably 'You are the softest girl', it's hardly surprising. Reader's hedonistic existence is brought to an end by two events: the arrival of his married childhood friend, who feels tempted to stray from the righteous path of family life, and his relationship with aspiring housewife Julie Gillis (Debbie Reynolds), a talented young actress ready to throw her career away when the right man comes along. The conclusion is pretty obvious several miles off, yet *Tender Trap* is a good example of Class A Hollywood merchandise, its ultra-conservative views and questionable sexual politics rendered largely inoffensive by the bright performances and a generally smooth production. Despite the vaguely gynaecological connotations of the title, there is nothing very carnal

about the movie, which leaves the viewer a little uncertain as to what Reader and his numerous lady friends actually get up to. No open-mouth kissing, that's for sure.

For Sinatra, returning to his old shooting ground for the first time since 1950 was not particularly traumatic. Old boss and nemesis Louis B. Mayer was long gone, his 25-year reign over the studio brought to an ignominious end by a power struggle with rising production executive Dore Schary. Allowed the token dignity of cutting his own throat, Mayer's resignation took effect on 31 August 1951, barely a year after Sinatra's unceremonious departure. The following year, MGM lost most of the clout and protection of its parent company, Loew's forced to drop its exclusive relationship with the studio under the new anti-trust laws. Left ever more vulnerable in an increasingly competitive marketplace, MGM needed all the star power it could get, giving the biggest box-office names a level of control unthinkable just a few years earlier.

The personnel deployed on *Tender Trap* were all seasoned and respected professionals, reflecting MGM's desire to furnish their 'homecoming' star Sinatra with as solid a showcase as possible. Producer Lawrence Weingarten's recent hits included *Adam's Rib* (1949) and *Pat and Mike* (1952). Director Charles Walters had extensive musical experience, his films including *Easter Parade* and the Esther Williams vehicle *Dangerous When Wet* (1953). Here, Walters' rather cautious direction tends to emphasise *Tender Trap's* theatrical origins, with very few close-ups and little attempt to exploit the ultra-wide Cinemascope format. While this was partly due to the limitations of the relatively new anamorphic system - which didn't permit precise framing and suffered from noticeable distortion during panning shots - the lack of visual dynamism is a drawback. Walters is more successful with the film's pacing, the action only flagging during the protracted sequence where Sinatra and old flame Celeste Holm decide to get engaged and throw a party, a largely pointless episode which only delays the inevitable.

Teaming 39-year-old Sinatra with 23-year-old

The Tender Trap – Charlie and Julie (Debbie Reynolds). Sadly, the shoe-bashing episode didn't make it into the film.

Debbie Reynolds was a smart commercial move, though the age difference - heightened by Sinatra's world-weary visage - prompted enough concern for it to be mentioned in the film by one of the supporting characters. Former Warner starlet Reynolds had been with MGM since 1950, scoring her biggest success opposite Gene Kelly and Donald O'Connor in *Singin' in the Rain*. With a roll-up fringe, prim manner and lines such as: 'A woman isn't really a woman at all until she's been married and had children', her character in *Tender Trap* is definitely from another age (somewhere around the sixteenth century). It is surely a tribute to Reynolds' talent that Julie Gillis engenders at least a little sympathy when she discovers Charlie's wicked ways,

rather than derisive laughter.

The role of Sinatra's long-time married best friend went to David Wayne, who'd appeared in *Adam's Rib*, and more recently been the object of Marilyn Monroe's attentions in *How to Marry a Millionaire* (1953). Describing two of Sinatra's conquests as 'tomatoes', his character doesn't get off to the best start. Wayne's tentative extra-marital love interest was played by Celeste Holm, a Broadway star signed by Twentieth Century-Fox following her success in the 1943 musical smash *Oklahoma!* Happier back on the stage, Holm asked to be released from her Fox contract in 1950, which damaged her Hollywood standing. According to Walters, Dore Schary hadn't forgotten this act of 'mutiny' - even if it was against a rival studio - and didn't want her in the film. Sinatra insisted on Holm as his co-star and got his way, appreciating with some relish that it was the star not the studio head who now wielded the real power. Sinatra, Walters and Holm reunited less than a year later for *High Society*, though once again Holm had to be content with a secondary role.

Shooting began in early May 1955, running over two months. Reynolds thought Sinatra 'fabulous' to work with, amenable to retakes where necessary and never displaying the slightest hint of his notorious temper. The one sign of a little impatience occurs during a bar scene featuring all four main characters, where Sinatra fumbles a line slightly during a dialogue exchange filmed in long shot. Presumably neither Walters nor Weingarten felt the fluff was noticeable enough to press for another take. Sinatra's goodwill towards cast and crew was probably helped along by his fulfilling social life. He spent most weekends with Humphrey Bogart and Lauren Bacall on their boat, occasionally arriving for his Monday morning calls looking a little the worse for wear.

With production completed in August 1955, Sinatra could congratulate himself on a first-rate comedy performance, light years away from his listless turn in *Guys and Dolls*. Lacking only the chest hair and gold medallion, his smooth-talking playboy character stays just the right side of arrogant, selfish piggery. Charlie's shock at the idea of his friend leaving his wife shows early on that, deep, deep down, he's an alright kind of guy. Alone with Julie at her parents' apartment, Charlie's amorous advances meet a brick wall of virtue and he has to settle for watching an old Esther Williams movie on television, her erotic swimming routine only firing his thwarted libido even more. Sinatra conveys the character's sexual frustration very believably, Walters' homage to their mutual former colleague enhancing the scene nicely. He also gets to ask a dead fish out on a date, almost certainly a Hollywood first.

Making only token changes to the Broadway original, *Tender Trap's* one major addition was the theme song, an obvious move given Sinatra's

participation. Old hand Sammy Cahn was set to work on a suitable ballad. Inspired by the title, he quickly penned the lyrics for '(Love is) The Tender Trap', handing them over to composer Jimmy Van Heusen for the accompanying score, a reversal of standard songwriting practice. Working with Cahn for the first time, Van Heusen came up with a tune neither liked very much, scrapped it, and started again. The end result met with the approval of both Walters and Sinatra, who recorded it in September 1955. Sinatra's contract granted him full publishing rights to the song, held through his company Barton Music. As expected, '(Love is) The Tender Trap' made the top ten charts in both America and Britain, while its movie namesake cleaned up at the box-office. The film opens with a vast long shot of what looks like desert highway, the distant figure of Sinatra strolling towards the camera singing the title song. Wearing a hat with an implausibly wide band, he looks the archetype of the fifties swinger, laid back, confident and ready for action. Reprised three times over during the course of the narrative, the song is transformed into an ensemble piece for the film's finale, as Sinatra, Reynolds, Wayne and Holm stand in line and bow to the camera. A slight case of overkill, perhaps. The musical bookends were added to *Tender Trap* after principal photography was completed, MGM concerned that the movie proper was too obviously static filmed theatre. The incidental music for *Tender Trap* was entrusted to Jeff Alexander, one of Sinatra's regular conductors for his radio shows during the late 1940s. Fifteen years later, Alexander worked on the score for the MGM comedy western *Dirty Dingus Magee*, one of Sinatra's few out-and-out failures.

Released within a few days of *Guys and Dolls* on 17 November 1955, *Tender Trap* received far more favourable reviews, the *Hollywood Reporter* rating the film 'Colourful as a bright new lipstick and as merry as a sixth martini.' While it didn't enjoy the same blockbuster success as Goldwyn's folly, *Tender Trap* was an infinitely superior vehicle for Sinatra, his top billing well and truly earned. Eight years on, he revisited similar territory in *Come Blow Your Horn*, with rather less successful results, his ageing New York playboy in pressing need of a punch in the face.

THE MAN WITH THE GOLDEN ARM 1955

The monkey never dies. When you kick him off, he just hides in a corner waiting his turn.
Louie, drug dealer to the masses

During the early 1950s, fading star John Garfield was looking for a project to revive his ailing fortunes. He found what he wanted in Nelson Algren's prize-winning 1949 novel *The Man With the Golden Arm*, the downbeat story of war veteran trying to kick his morphine addiction. Buying up the film rights, Garfield commissioned screenwriter Lewis Meltzer to produce a faithful adaptation of the book, then dropped dead at the age of 39. Left with an unfinished and now redundant first draft on his hands, Meltzer assumed the project was shelved for good.

Algren's book had also impressed Austrian producer-director Otto Preminger. Having successfully defied the censorious Motion Picture Association of America (MPAA) with *The Moon is Blue* (1953), a largely indifferent drama featuring such shocking words as 'virgin', 'mistress' and 'pregnant', Preminger was on the lookout for some equally controversial material. Defying industry predictions of commercial disaster, *Moon* had grossed $6 million on a $500,000 budget, and the ever-growing popularity of television made backers unusually sympathetic to adult subjects forbidden on the small screen. Preminger bought the rights to *Golden Arm* from John Garfield's estate and hired Algren to adapt his book for $1000 a week. The author's lack of script-writing experience soon became apparent, obliging Preminger to replace him with Walter Newman, one of Billy Wilder's co-writers on *Ace in the Hole*. Lewis Meltzer got co-billing with Newman on the credits, which suggests a threat of legal action rather than fruitful collaboration.

Even in its reworked, softened version, *The Man With the Golden Arm* stood no chance of winning MPAA approval. The 25-year-old Production Code explicitly forbade any depiction of illicit drug use, whatever the context, rendering any film treatment of the subject unreleasable. Or so the MPAA believed. While the verdict was a foregone conclusion, Preminger made a token attempt to bring the Board around, arguing that his film would be very explicitly anti-drugs. The MPAA refused to reconsider, supplementing their main objection to the script with protests over the climactic suicide of the hero's fake-cripple wife and the final scene where he walks away a free man with his girlfriend of doubtful virtue. This stand against the Production Code, a body backed by the more intimidating religious muscle of the Catholic Legion of Decency, was not quite as bold as it sounds. After the 1948 anti-trust laws came into effect, many cinemas began showing 'hot' foreign films denied an MPAA Seal with considerable success. An astute businessman as well as a gifted film-maker, Preminger had simply been the first to perceive a lucrative gap in the market.

For the key role of Frankie Machine, the ex-junkie card dealer desperate to build a new life as a clean big band drummer, Preminger wanted either Frank Sinatra or Marlon Brando. He despatched the 70-odd pages of existing script to their respective agents and waited to see who would get in touch first. Third time around, Sinatra beat Brando to the post. He seized on the role of Frankie Machine, claiming that it was the first part since Maggio he felt he had to play. Sinatra's agent called Preminger two days later to inform the director that his client liked the character so much he didn't even need to see the rest of the script before signing on. Brando's MCA agents also responded at speed, only to be informed that the role had been filled. Sinatra had secured the part before Brando even read it, picking up $100,000 plus ten per cent of the profits.

After toying with the idea of casting wholesome *Moon is Blue* co-star Barbara Bel Geddes as Machine's manipulative wheelchair-bound wife Zosh, Preminger settled for Eleanor Parker, chosen on the strength of her Oscar-nominated performance as a genuinely disabled woman in *Interrupted Melody* (1955), a sentimental MGM biopic of Australian opera singer and polio victim Marjorie Lawrence. A highly respected actress, Parker certainly lent the production a touch of class, no small consideration given the 'sleazy' low-life nature of the story. The role of evil drug pusher Louie went to Darren McGavin, an actor excelling in understated villainy.

The last major part to be cast was nightclub hostess Molly, whose fierce devotion to Machine and his dream of a better life finally lifts him out of the gutter. Eschewing more established star names, Preminger set his sights on Columbia's new sex-goddess-in-waiting Kim Novak, 'discovered' by studio head Harry Cohn the previous year. Despite her lack of experience with dramatic roles, Preminger had decided that Novak was his first and only choice for the part. Reluctant to loan out his still insufficiently groomed sex symbol, Cohn demanded the extortionate fee of $100,000 for five weeks of his star's services. After some intense arguing, Preminger and United Artists agreed to the terms within 24 hours, the director little appreciating the task he had taken on. Drilled into an animated mannequin by her Columbia masters, Novak had no idea how to give an actual performance.

Blissfully unaware of his co-star's difficulties, Sinatra worked hard on his pre-filming preparations for the title role (a reference to Machine's card-dealing skills). His research included a visit to a hospital ward, where he was permitted a brief glimpse of a heroin addict going through withdrawal: '...the most frightening thing I've ever seen'. While Machine's drug of choice is never named in the film, all the clues point to him being hooked on heroin, the script dispensing with the war injury/morphine angle of the book. In point of fact, *Golden Arm* never explains precisely how Machine got addicted in the first place, other than Louie's seductive overtures, his own weakness and the everyday pain and frustration of being a nice guy in a generally awful world.

Golden Arm went into production during late September and October 1955. Preminger originally intended to shoot most of the film on location in Chicago, the setting for Algren's book. Budgetary

considerations prevailed and the director settled for a studio-bound setting, filming all the exteriors on the old RKO backlot. Breaking most of his usual movie habits, Sinatra arrived for work each day at 8am on the dot, rarely departing until the previous day's rushes had been screened nearly twelve hours later. His normally hectic social life dwindled to almost nothing, Sinatra's energies entirely consumed by the *Golden Arm* production. While many industry insiders predicted a stormy working relationship between director and star, the production proved to be one of the smoothest of both men's often fraught careers. After some initial reluctance, Sinatra actually got to enjoy rehearsing, pressing Preminger for more than even the director thought necessary. (This new-found enthusiasm for in-depth preparation didn't extend beyond the *Golden Arm* production.) According to Preminger's friend and biographer Willi Frischauer, the only source of contention was the film's camera operator, a somewhat unlikely offender. After looking at the first day's rushes, Sinatra told his director that the man clearly wasn't up to the job. Preminger responded by reminding Sinatra that all the personnel on the film were hand-picked by him. The matter didn't arise again and the camera operator stayed. Preminger related a different incident, where Sinatra lost his temper after discovering that a good take of a long and difficult scene had been ruined by an electrician's mistake. As with *Meet Danny Wilson*, the star refused to do a retake because of a technical fault and stormed off to his dressing room. Preminger pursued his errant leading man and, obviously being more persuasive - or fiercer - than Joseph Pevney, soon had Sinatra back on set, where he apologised to the technician concerned and redid the scene.

Both pleased and flattered by his star's enthusiasm for rehearsals and general hard work, Preminger knew full well that the quality of the role was not the only factor involved. Sinatra felt particularly inclined to rehearse his scenes with Kim Novak, widely rumoured to be the star's new girlfriend. Novak always denied this, asserting that she and Sinatra were just good friends. Whatever the case, this was a fortunate situation, as Novak's inexperience,

The Man With the Golden Arm – Kim Novak concentrates on Otto Preminger's instructions. Sinatra looks suitably mellow.

lack of confidence and general terror of 'real' acting sorely tested everyone's patience and understanding. Realising that Novak felt too intimidated to speak her lines much above a whisper, Sinatra responded by dropping his own voice, encouraging his co-star to follow his lead as he steadily increased the volume of his performance. Her confidence gradually built up during the pre-filming rehearsals, with Preminger often clearing the stage of all cast and crew save himself and Sinatra, Novak suffered a major relapse when shooting commenced. Even her shortest scenes could require up to 35 takes, a total to rival Marlon Brando's record. Preminger later claimed that Sinatra never once lost his cool or complained about the endless retakes. For all her extensive on-set coaching, Novak has been accused of being wooden in the film, which is unfair. Softly spoken and generally understated,

Novak is effective in her part, believably portraying a woman badly bruised by life. Her determination to help Machine beat his addiction is similarly plausible, Molly's innate tenderness tempered by her anger at him for screwing up his life. Novak's painted-on eyebrows are a little incongruous, yet this is hardly a big deal.

If Kim Novak finally displayed some genuine talent in *Golden Arm*, the rather more gifted Eleanor Parker proved a disappointment, despite her recognised flair for wheelchair acting. The only member of the cast to attempt a genuine Chicago accent, her mannered performance is a distraction, often resembling a misplaced Southern belle. It doesn't help that Zosh is an overly melodramatic character to begin with, ultimately defying all suspension of disbelief. Having blackmailed a guilt-ridden Machine into marriage after she was injured by him in a drunken car smash, Zosh wants her husband to stick with his old life, dealing for an illegal gambling joint. His dream of being a professional drummer will take him away from her. The big plot twist is that Zosh isn't crippled at all, her supposedly damaged spine perfectly healthy. Knowing that Machine stays with her only from a sense of duty, she's kept up the act for three years, Machine never once noticing that his wife's legs aren't wasted from lack of use. Furthermore, Parker's overwrought acting style doesn't really mesh with Sinatra's less affected playing, though she found working with him a largely pleasurable experience, as she explained in a 1969 interview: 'He can be a bad boy, but he does it charmingly. He is always a gentleman.' Sinatra was similarly taken with Parker, later hiring her for a supporting role in *A Hole in the Head*. Script-writer Walter Newman felt that Preminger had miscast the part, Parker looking far too elegant for a woman he'd envisaged as a 'low-life slob'. Newman wanted Shelley Winters for Zosh, an interesting choice but hardly a viable option after her screaming rows with Sinatra during the *Danny Wilson* shoot.

Parker's problematic character aside, *Golden Arm's* only real flaws lie in the script, which is a little drawn out and repetitive in places, with even Machine's visits to Louie losing their shock value third time around. Favouring long, fluid takes and a prowling camera, Preminger's handling of *Golden Arm* exhibits an impressive confidence and authority. While some felt the lack of location shooting hurt the film, the main street set is well used, with credit owing to MGM-trained cameraman Sam Leavitt, who'd paid his dues as a camera operator on films such as *Anchors Aweigh* before teaming up with the director for *Carmen Jones* (1954). Another plus is the moody trumpet-and-drums led jazz score composed by Elmer Bernstein, who would write the music for both *Kings Go Forth* and *Some Came Running*. Of the supporting cast, the most striking is McGavin, whose demonic exploiter of human frailty is one of the cinema's more memorable specimens of foul inhumanity. First seen taunting a one-armed drunk, Louie is equipped with a pencil moustache, a black hat and a perpetual sneer, his

veneer of cool elegance punctured by the necessity of hiding drugs in his shoes.

For all its merits, *The Man With the Golden Arm* would be little more than an intriguing period piece were it not for Frank Sinatra. Seldom has his vulnerable, victimised underdog persona been so well utilised. Seen at one point in a (shoplifted) dark suit and bowtie, he resembles a soured, crushed version of his character from *Higher and Higher*, Machine even wondering if his new musical career will give him bobbysoxer appeal. Thrown into jail for possession of the stolen clothes, he freaks out when a junkie in an adjoining cell goes manic, climbing up the bars and screaming. Huddling in a corner, his arm clamped over his mouth, Machine's understated terror at this stark reminder of his recent past is uncomfortably plausible. The first trip back to Louie's apartment for a fix still has a surprisingly strong impact. His arm bared and tourniqued for the hit, Machine watches as Louie prepares the heroin solution with professional ease. As the pusher approaches with his syringe, the camera fast tracks in to a close up of Sinatra's eyes, his fraught expression changing to bliss as the drug takes effect. The infamous cold turkey scene is similarly impressive, lacking the clinical detail of later efforts such as *Panic in Needle Park* (1971) or *Trainspotting* (1996), yet still harrowing. According to frequent set visitor Sammy Davis Jnr, Preminger had scheduled five full working days for the staging and filming of the lengthy, extremely demanding withdrawal scene. Sinatra arrived early on day one and requested that Preminger drop the rehearsals. He knew exactly how to play the scene and wanted the cameras rolling straight away. A little sceptical, the director agreed to his request and got the entire scene in one take, its impact barely spoiled by split-second boom microphone shadow on the set floor. Locked in Molly's bedroom at his own request, the strung-out Machine feels the worst effects of withdrawal kick in. Starting with an overhead long shot of Sinatra, Preminger's camera fast tracks in on his star and stays with him as he shivers, paces the room, drinks from a saucepan, writhes on the floor and hammers on the door to be let out. If Sinatra had never made another film, this one sequence proved beyond all question that he was a truly gifted actor. Interestingly, the film doesn't allow Machine to be too sympathetic. Well acquainted with the torments of substance abuse, he looks on Molly's alcoholic boyfriend with utter contempt, unaware of his hypocrisy. More to the point, while Louie, Zosh and the poker-hustler Schweifka all have a vested interest in keeping Machine a junkie, his victim status is by and large his own doing.

Hugely impressed by Sinatra's committed performance, Preminger scrapped his original release dates for *Golden Arm* and rushed it through post-production to hit the cinemas before the impending deadline for 1955 Academy Award consideration. The lack of an MPAA Seal was a minor hitch at worst, especially given the Legion of Decency's surprise decision to approve the film (Preminger believed the Legion was still embarrassed over its failure to ban *The Moon is Blue*). Openly defying the declining power of the Board, United Artists resigned its MPAA membership and submitted the film directly to local State censors, virtually all of whom passed it. Over one thousand theatre owners agreed to show *Golden Arm*, giving it a nationwide release impossible in the days before the anti-trust rulings. (Admitting defeat, the MPAA later revised its regulations on the subject of drug abuse.) The director's gambit paid off handsomely, with *Golden Arm* turning into one of United Artists' biggest hits - $4 million and the number nine spot at the US box-office - and Sinatra named as a contender for the Best Actor Academy Award. Staying on good terms with Preminger after their mutually beneficial collaboration, Sinatra never got to work with him again, despite a couple of mooted projects (see Appendix 2). Given the director's later tendency towards humourless, overblown melodramas derived from pulpy, if impeccably liberal source material, it's likely any reunion would have proved a letdown.

Released on 15 January 1956, *Golden Arm* hardly needed additional publicity to draw audiences yet the critics came out in force for Sinatra's acting. *Saturday Review* critic Arthur Knight liked what he saw: '...a truly virtuoso performance. The thin, unhandsome one-time crooner has an incredible instinct for the look, the gesture, the shading of the voice that suggests tenderness, uncertainty, weakness, fatigue, despair.' The overall film was not so well received, the *Los Angeles Times* running a less than complimentary headline: 'Sinatra's Acting Redeems Sordid Film On Drug Habit.' Riding high on his personal triumph in *Golden Arm*, Sinatra's movie career was looking exceptionally good. *Johnny Concho* had just finished shooting, *High Society* was about to start production and *The Pride and the Passion*, *The Joker is Wild* and *Pal Joey* were already lined up to follow. Interviewed at the time, Sinatra declared himself more than satisfied with the mix of roles: '...a pretty even split between straight parts and musicals'. Both *Pride* and *Joey* had been considered for Marlon Brando, which didn't hurt.

The only disappointment over *Golden Arm* was Sinatra's failed Academy Award bid. While his promotional material for the campaign made few concessions to modesty, describing the star as 'the hottest thing in show business', he didn't regard the result as a foregone conclusion by any means. It's even been suggested that Sinatra had written himself off as a winner by the time of the ceremony, feeling that the film's controversial subject would deter the Academy voters. In the event, Sinatra's old *Eternity* nemesis Ernest Borgnine took the Best Actor Award for his against-type performance as a gentle bachelor in *Marty* (1955). Resigned to his loss, Sinatra still regarded his performance in *Golden Arm* as his best ever. If ever he deserved an Academy Award, it was for this film.

Leader of the Pack

1956-1957

JOHNNY CONCHO 1956

Barely remembered today, the dreary 'adult' western *Johnny Concho* is largely of interest as the first Sinatra film made through one of his own companies, Kent Productions. It's also conclusive proof that some childhood fantasies are best left unfulfilled. As he later demonstrated with *Sergeants 3, 4 for Texas* and *Dirty Dingus Magee*, city-boy Sinatra never looked at home on the range, the cowboy clothes giving the effect of a lavish fancy dress costume rather than a hard-bitten westerner caught in a life-or-death struggle, comic or otherwise. He didn't even like riding a horse. Cast as a cowardly small-town bully whose easy life comes to an end when his protective gunfighter brother is murdered by outlaws, Sinatra's performance misfires as completely as the overall film. He did at least take the role seriously, recruiting veteran cowboy star Gary Cooper for a few lessons in authentic gunplay. Still not satisfied with his prowess, Sinatra employed a spring-loaded holster for the action scenes, a useful 'cheat' device that launched the prop gun into his hand, supposedly creating the impression of a lightning draw. Given that Concho is

meant to be inexperienced with firearms, one wonders why he took all this trouble. One also wonders why he hired Don McGuire to co-write and direct the film. Having shafted Sinatra with the *Danny Wilson* screenplay, McGuire compounded his earlier misuse and abuse of the star, playing on Sinatra's love of westerns to flog him a lame coyote.

Given *Johnny Concho's* minor position in the Sinatra canon, it's perhaps not surprising that the film's origins are now a little obscure. According to *Leonard Maltin's Movie and Video Guide*, the script began life as a *Studio One* television play, which could explain the predominance of dialogue over action, the latter being a rare commodity in 1950s small screen drama. The majority of sources credit a short story by one David P. Harmon, *The Man Who Owned the Town*, as the inspiration. Given that Harmon is listed as co-writer on the film's credits, he presumably participated in the project at some point. The controlling hand was undoubtedly that of McGuire, whose film career had trundled along in unspectacular fashion since his last collaboration with Sinatra. Another old Sinatra friend to get a break on *Johnny Concho* was conductor-arranger Nelson Riddle, who'd come to the star's attention with his arrangement for the early 1950s Nat King Cole hit 'Mona Lisa'. Having picked up a little Hollywood experience with orchestration work on films such as *Guys and Dolls*, Riddle now had the chance to compose a full score for his regular employer. As he later demonstrated with his work on *A Hole in the Head*, *Ocean's 11*, *Come Blow Your Horn*, *4 for Texas*, *Robin and the 7 Hoods* and *Marriage on the Rocks*, Riddle had a knack for brash, lively big band-style compositions that evaporated from the mind the minute the accompanying film was over.

The nepotism didn't stop with the producer-star's fellow professionals. Shortly after *Johnny Concho* was announced, the *Los Angeles Examiner* ran a story claiming that Sinatra intended to cast heiress Gloria Vanderbilt, his then-girlfriend, as the film's leading lady. Socialite Vanderbilt had no acting experience whatsoever and the news was treated as a throwaway publicity stunt. In fact, she really was hired to play Concho's saloon singer girlfriend, though whether or not she ever made it as far as the set is disputed. Earl Wilson states that Vanderbilt dropped out when *Johnny Concho* was still in preproduction, annoyed that her role was not the big star part she wanted. Other sources claim that while Vanderbilt did start work on the film, her ineptness in front of the cameras became painfully evident after only a few hours. With the crew and co-stars unable to conceal their growing disquiet, Sinatra put on his producer's hat and sent Vanderbilt home. Hunting around for a last minute replacement, Sinatra decided on Phyllis Kirk, Vincent Price's intended victim in the 3-D horror show *House of Wax* (1953). The cast and crew hoped in vain that Kirk's arrival would add a little sparkle to the proceedings. Thoroughly flattened under the leaden hand of director-co-writer McGuire, *Johnny Concho* was already a goner.

Disrupted by the Vanderbilt episode, the production dates for *Johnny Concho* are as uncertain as her participation. Arnold Shaw states that the film began shooting in December 1955 under the odd title *The Loud Law*. Sinatra's commitment to co-star in *High Society* back at MGM necessitated a speedy shoot, aggravated by

the time-wasting false start with Vanderbilt. Despite the pressures heaped on the novice producer, he remained fairly cool and level-headed throughout the shoot, the various tensions never prompting a show of temper. It probably helped that he'd finally arranged to make a film on his own terms. As Sinatra later explained to columnist Joe Hyams, the shift away from the industry's standard working hours was of particular importance to him:

I work better later in the day...But nobody wanted to break the precedent about filming in the afternoon and early evening. I did, with the first independent production, because I was boss...it cost a few dollars

Johnny Concho – Hanging tough in an offbeat western.

extra for the crew's overtime, but the picture came out a week ahead of schedule. It balanced out, and everybody was a lot happier.

This affable mood lasted until the end of the shoot, when Sinatra held a lavish wrap party for his cast and crew. With a jazz combo playing on the main set, the star presented each of his fellow actors with a framed photographic portrait of themselves.

Running a compact 84 minutes, *Johnny Concho* still manages to be tedious and overstretched, McGuire's plodding, lacklustre direction merely highlighting the flaws in his half-baked script. The novelty of watching Sinatra stroll around the unsubtly named Cripple Creek in cowboy garb soon wears thin, as does his against-type coward persona. The supporting cast is respectable, including William Conrad and Christopher Dark as the invading bandits and Keenan Wynn as the local pistol-toting parson, but the material leaves them largely stranded. The film's finale is particularly mishandled. Having fled Cripple Creek with his girlfriend, Johnny decides he can no longer live with running away from his troubles and heads back to town for a showdown. Badly injured in the ensuing gunfight, he looks doomed until the militant parson leads the previously passive townspeople against the bad guys. While there are laudable messages here about conscience, duty and the necessity of communal resistance to oppression, McGuire's utter lack of film-making flair renders all good intentions void. Shooting in poky black and white, he doesn't even provide any decent scenery.

Distributed without much enthusiasm by United Artists, *Johnny Concho* premiered in August 1956. Sinatra realised he had a doubtful property on his hands and set about flogging it as hard as he could. On 19 August, he did an exhaustive round of the television circuit, making appearances on *The Ed Sullivan Show*, *The Steve Allen Show* and ABC's *Famous Film Festival* to plug his western. During the film's first week at the New York Paramount, the star appeared in person as a support act, singing an impressive 26 numbers on the opening night. A high-powered performance, but not

enough to save *Johnny Concho* from box-office apathy. Forced to drop out of three shows by an attack of laryngitis, Sinatra could do little more as his film slowly headed for oblivion. While its poorish reception made for a less than impressive start to his new career as an independent film-maker, Sinatra had little cause to worry over *Johnny Concho*. Released in the same month, *High Society* would be one of the year's biggest hits.

HIGH SOCIETY 1956

Hi. Bing! Hi. Grace! Hi. Frank!
Oddly punctuated poster caption

A Newport society wedding, a Jazz festival and two reporters from *Spy* magazine (15 cents a copy). MGM's musical reworking of *The Philadelphia Story* (1940) could have been a pleasant, if inevitably inferior imitation but emerged instead as a shoddy piece of goods, lacking even the studio's customary professionalism. At one point, uptight rich-bitch divorcee Grace Kelly and her even tighter fiancée John Lund have a tedious argument in her bedroom. Generating about as much on-screen chemistry as a broken test tube, their efforts are insufficient to distract the viewer from the top of the screen, where a microphone shadow is clearly visible. Soiled goods shoddily packaged without a hint of imagination. Casting ill-used guest star Louis Armstrong as Kelly's love interest would have fused the otherwise disparate romantic and musical elements and made for a much more interesting story. Sadly, middle-America just wasn't ready.

Barely finished with the *Johnny Concho* production, Sinatra arrived at MGM to find preparations for *High Society* in full swing. Preproduction work on the film had started back in December 1955, around the same time that Grace Kelly announced her engagement to Prince Rainier of Monaco. Looking for a suitably classy vehicle to serve as Kelly's farewell appearance, MGM settled on Katherine Hepburn's 'comeback' triumph, adapted by

High Society – Sinatra and Crosby discuss Grace Kelly's choice of husband.

Donald Ogden Stewart from Philip Barry's Broadway original. Aside from Kelly's lack of acting ability, non-existent comic flair and even more doubtful musical skill, she was just about perfect for the part. Cary Grant's debonair ex-husband part went to the less elegant Bing Crosby, who could at least carry a tune. Inheriting a cut-down version of the James Stewart role, third-billed Sinatra astutely weighed up a no-win situation, banked the $250,000 pay check and did his job with irreproachable professionalism. Casting Sinatra as the kind of sleaze journalist he so loathed in real life suggests someone had a sense of humour. Unfortunately they didn't get to write the script.

Having recalled their *Tender Trap* star for active service, MGM also recruited director Charles Walters, cameraman Paul C. Vogel and co-star Celeste Holm from the earlier film, Holm playing Sinatra's loyal

photographer and would-be girlfriend. *High Society*'s producer, Sol C. Siegel, had recently defected from Twentieth Century-Fox, where he'd overseen such hits as *Three Coins in the Fountain* (1954), which featured a Jule Styne-Sammy Cahn title song sung by Sinatra (see Appendix 3). Siegel brought along *Three Coins* writer John Patrick, a respected playwright, to adapt the original *Philadelphia Story* script into an ersatz musical, with mediocre results. Producer and screenwriter both worked on the far superior *Some Came Running* two years later and it's fair to suggest that the low quality of *High Society* lies more with MGM's blatant commercial pandering than any great failing on their part.

With much of the film resting on the inadequate acting shoulders of Kelly and Crosby, the studio counted on the musical numbers to give the proceedings a touch of style. A year or so earlier, top agent Irving Lazar had made a lucrative deal with MGM that gave the studio the film rights to Cole Porter's recent - if not very successful - musical *Can Can*, and the esteemed composer's services on both *High Society* and *Les Girls* (1957). Porter came up with 'Who Wants To Be A Millionaire?', 'You're Sensational' and 'True Love' among others, only to see his efforts largely thrown away. Inserted into a script that works perfectly well without them, the songs are largely irrelevant and also disruptive. Pop composer Crosby's intriguing 'Choo Choo Mama' is never heard, more's the pity.

Filming on *High Society* ran from 17 January to early March 1956. Constantly restless on the set, Sinatra was given the nickname 'Dexedrine', while the resolutely laid-back Crosby earned the moniker 'Nembutal'. Despite this apparent difference in attitude, Crosby shared his co-star's preference for fast work, completing most of their scenes together in a single take. Kelly's impending marriage had put the film on an unusually tight schedule for an MGM 'A' production, a mere five weeks, which suited both men just fine. Playing a comparatively small role, Sinatra found time to perform in Las Vegas during the shoot, the break from filming further enhancing his good mood. His only flash of temperament stemmed from a disagreement with musical director Johnny Green over one of his songs. Green felt the first recording fell short of the singer's normal high standard and requested a retake, which Sinatra refused to do.

Looked at four decades on, *High Society* has a strangely remote, uninvolving feel to it, as if the events depicted were being viewed under a microscope. After struggling a little with Cinemascope on *Tender Trap*, Walters and Vogel appear to have experienced even more difficulty with the VistaVision process employed for this film. Developed by Paramount as a cheaper, less complicated rival to the anamorphic system, this new technical marvel simply masked off the top and bottom of the standard Academy frame, concentrating the action in the middle section to produce a pseudo-widescreen effect. Even allowing for this studio-imposed limitation, Walters' lacklustre direction is absurdly static, with far too many dull long shots, making the film's stage origins more obvious than they were in *The Philadelphia Story*. Walters had more success as the film's choreographer, taking Sinatra through a little light tap-work. The performances show some signs of life, without ever suggesting any great faith in the material. Looking too old for Kelly's love interest, Crosby is pleasant enough in a detached, overly casual manner. Appearing 20 minutes in, complete with his now trademark wide hatband, Sinatra duets with Holm on 'Millionaire' and carries the intoxicated Kelly around while clad in a bathrobe. His duet with Crosby on 'Well, Did You Evah' is enjoyable, if hardly the hoped for *tour de force* joining of vocal titans, with the supposedly inebriated Sinatra having a not very subtle poke at his old rival: 'Don't dig that kind of crooning, chum.' Probably the best song in *High Society*, it was also the only one not written for the film, originally performed in Porter's 1939 Broadway show *DuBarry Was a Lady* by Walters and Betty Grable. Crosby also gets to punch Sinatra in the face, but it's nothing personal. While both Crosby and Sinatra are occasionally allowed flashes of their undeniable star quality, Grace Kelly never quite makes the grade. Her performance gives little hint of her enthusiasm for the original play, Tracy Lord emerging as an unprepossessing snob.

Confident they had a failsafe hit on their hands, MGM released *High Society* on 9 August 1956, a few months after the Kelly-Rainier marriage. The film was deservedly shredded by most reviewers, with Hollis Alpert pointing out one of the biggest flaws: 'The principals perform, most of the time, with a kind of glum cheeriness.' Sinatra did better in the reviews than most but no-one suggested he'd got himself anything more than another career-friendly audience pleaser. Reaching number four at the US box-office, *High Society* was MGM's biggest hit of the year, later climbing to the number one slot in Britain. The Crosby-Kelly 'duet' on 'True Love' sold over a million copies. 'Choo Choo Mama' would have been better.

THE PRIDE AND THE PASSION 1957

I am Miguel of the Gun...Those of you who are still Spanish can follow me.
Miguel, guerrillero

He is a gasser. I dig him.
Sophia Loren on Sinatra

Of the numerous historical epics produced during the 1950s, few are as reviled as *The Pride and the Passion*, a tale of nineteenth-century Spanish freedom fighters loosely based on C.S. Forester's novel *The Gun*. Variously described by its own director as a 'bomb' and a 'bust', the film appeared to have pleased absolutely no-one, drawing scorn for succumbing to all the weaknesses of its genre. Sinatra's own contribution, with strange accent and even stranger hairpiece, is seldom counted among his career highs, his infamous mid-production walkout drawing more attention than the actual movie. While the film is certainly underwhelming as human drama, this dismissive attitude is largely unfair. If the dialogue scenes are sometimes static and the love triangle subplot fairly perfunctory, there are compensations elsewhere. As spectacle, *The Pride and the Passion* is impressive, with a potent central image of militant peasants towing a huge cannon across the rugged Spanish countryside to liberate a French-held city. Compromised during production by script problems, uneasy casting and Sinatra's dislike of the far-flung locations, the finished product is no-one's finest hour, yet it carries a sense of conviction and integrity that merits more than a contemptuous dismissal. Working with a $3.8 million budget, a 400-strong production crew, 9400 extras, 1,500 livestock, six giant replica cannons, 25 exotic Spanish locations and General Francisco Franco's personal seal of approval, Stanley Kramer made a better film than he realised.

With *Not As a Stranger* scoring a very respectable hit, Kramer had little difficulty interesting United Artists in his change-of-pace Napoleonic-era epic. Most of the key production personal from the earlier film were retained, notably scriptwriters Edward and Edna Anhalt, cameraman Franz Planer, composer Georges Antheil, production designer Rudolph Sternad and editor Frederick Knudtson. The switch from low key black and white to Technicolor and VistaVision caused no apparent problems, Kramer and Planer making exemplary use of the short-lived format. Kramer's biggest headache was attracting two male stars with sufficient combined drawing power to make up for his less commercial choice of leading lady, Italian newcomer Sophia Loren. A fervent admirer of Cary Grant, Kramer felt the *Pride* script would be an ideal vehicle for the star, playing straitlaced British Naval Officer Anthony Trumball. Assured by both Kramer and C.S. Forester that he was perfect casting for the role, Grant finally agreed despite reservations over the script.

The second-billed role of illiterate-but-noble guerrilla leader Miguel was originally intended for Marlon Brando, who'd given a forceful, if mannered performance as a Mexican freedom fighter in Elia Kazan's biopic *Viva Zapata!* (1952). Unable to interest his *Wild One* star in the part, a reluctant Kramer bowed to pressure from United Artists and cast Sinatra, whose star appeal was felt to be a virtual guarantee of an extra $1 million at the box-office. The contract agreed paid $250,000, plus $25-a-day expenses, a baggage allowance and the proviso that neither Grant nor Loren would be given better accommodation than Sinatra. For his part, the star undertook some in-depth research into his role. Determined to match the authenticity of the Spanish locations with a suitably convincing accent, he asked his friend Victor Gomez, a gifted guitarist, to record the character's dialogue onto tape, which Sinatra listened to repeatedly until he could duplicate the intonation. While Gomez hailed from Argentina rather than Spain, the language was still his native tongue. As Kitty Kelley rather snidely points out, copying an accent from the wrong country was probably not the best start, yet it's a respectable stab at least, incongruous largely because Sinatra's standard speaking voice is so familiar. Critics just weren't prepared for a new accent, good, bad or indifferent.

Committed to 16 weeks of location filming, Sinatra headed out to Spain on 17 April 1956. Before departing he cabled Kramer at the Madrid Hilton to request that no reporters or photographers be notified of his arrival time. The slightest hint of a flashbulb or notebook and he would take the next plane home. Once in Spain, he appeared to lighten up a little, joking with Loren, introducing her to his favourite Ella Fitzgerald records and ordering pastrami from his regular New York delicatessen, but the alien landscape would quickly bring out the worst in him.

Depressed over his impending divorce from Ava Gardner, Sinatra initially dealt with the trauma by throwing himself into his work, then switched to treating the whole *Pride* production with utter contempt. Largely dispensing with a double, the star ran through explosions and fires, waded across rivers, climbed up steep hills and fell over in mud. Concerned at first that Sinatra was arriving for work without the slightest idea what to do, Kramer soon realised that the star needed just a few minutes to get his performance up to speed. This driven professionalism couldn't last, especially under the hot sun of Franco's Spain, and Sinatra was soon pressing Kramer to speed up the filming. With a large number of elaborate crowd scenes to stage, the director could do little to shorten his schedule and the tension between the two men grew steadily worse. The deteriorating working atmosphere and increasingly hectic pace of filming affected the entire company, with even consummate professional Grant feeling the stress.

Off-camera, Sinatra's attitude towards his living arrangements was inflexible from the start. Rejecting the make-shift location accommodation used by the rest of the company, he demanded his own suite at the Castellana Hilton, Madrid. Most of the locations were over three hours' travel from the capital, involving prolonged and uncomfortable trips along dirt roads, yet Sinatra insisted on returning to Madrid each night after filming, often setting off for the next day's work at four o'clock in the morning. According to unit publicist Richard Condon, Sinatra halted production during a night shoot in a small village to warn Kramer that he expected to be back in his hotel room by 11.30. Should the producer-director fail to meet this deadline he would be urinated upon. More amused than appalled by this outrageous ultimatum, Condon became friendly with Sinatra during the shoot, later providing the source novel for one of the star's best ever films, *The Manchurian Candidate*. Others weren't so inclined to see the funny side of the incident.

Having rescheduled the remaining scenes to finish with Sinatra as quickly as possible, Kramer eventually ran out of time. On 1 July, Sinatra informed him that he would quit there and then unless Kramer guaranteed he'd be finished by 25 July. The director needed another week at the very least and pleaded with his star to stay on until the beginning of August. Sinatra refused to work after 28 July and quit on that day with several weeks' worth of scenes still unfilmed, advising Kramer to contact his lawyer. The location shoot struggled on a little longer, Grant and Loren gamely playing several scenes to a coat on a hanger instead of the absent Sinatra, but the film could not be finished, even patchwork style, without additional footage of the mutinous star.

Back in Los Angeles, intensive negotiations between Kramer, UA and Sinatra's agent bought the director one week of the star's services on a soundstage, with potted palm trees standing in for the Spanish landscape. Reunited with Grant and Loren on a none too convincing set, Sinatra failed to capture the already negligible chemistry of the location shoot. The incident also reaffirmed his reputation as a difficult talent whose bad moods and lack of commitment did a lot more harm than merely upsetting his co-workers. Not only had Sinatra's behaviour affected the schedule and budget, he'd also compromised the final film. While Kramer and UA would have been fully justified in suing the star for breaking his contract, no-one wanted a drawn-out and costly court case, especially given *Pride's* already inflated budget. Largely unaware of this friction, the paying public continued to endorse Sinatra. By the end of 1956 he was a regular in the annual list of Top Ten Box-Office Stars, making his way steadily up the chart until 1961.

As a piece of film-making, *The Pride and the Passion* is by and large first-rate, its recreation of rural Spain circa 1810 carrying a real sense of authenticity. Having refined his directing skills a little after the clumsiness of *Not As a Stranger*, Kramer exhibits an assured visual style, making good use of the vast landscape as his characters travel through mountain ranges, forests and arid plains to reach the southern city of Avila. The dominant image of the film is, of course, the gun itself, first seen from an imposing low angle as its barrel appears on the edge of a cliff. Supposedly 42 feet long and weighing seven tons - the replicas used were rather smaller - the weapon is suspended in mid-air, floated on a raft, slid down a ramp, towed across country, pulled uphill, rolled downhill and hidden in the cathedral of San Lorenzo del Escorial, all the while surrounded by swarming peasants. Several critics remarked that the cannon has more personality than the people with it, yet this is in many ways the point of the film: for Miguel, Trumball and their guerilla band to triumph, everything must be subordinated to their instrument of liberation. They unquestioningly endure discomfort, exhaustion, starvation, injury and death in the name of freedom. Images of a fireball attack on a French camp, a knifefight at a windmill, a mountain pass strewn with Spanish corpses, Trumball and Miguel riding the gun downhill and a religious procession hiding the weapon beneath an altar convey the drama with a resonance

The Pride and the Passion – Captain Trumball (Cary Grant) is stunned into silence by Miguel's (yes, it's Sinatra) haircut.

that renders the prosaic script largely irrelevant.

Of the three stars, Sinatra emerges as the most comfortable, despite his scant regard for professional dedication during production. First seen nonchalantly cutting a piece of leather, his shoemaker's son-turned-warrior makes an effective spokesman for the fighting masses. Ruthless against even unarmed French prisoners, Miguel expresses his unrequited love for Juana by making her a new pair of shoes, a nicely understated touch. His most amusing moment appears to have been unscripted. Leaning against a gate, Miguel is butted by the bull penned inside, the startled look on Sinatra's face suggesting a touch of bovine improvisation. His co-stars earn more points for effort than achievement, largely owing to circumstances beyond their control. Kramer later announced that he'd simply miscast Grant, though the latter's uneasiness with his part works quite well for the uptight Trumball, a reserved Englishman stranded among a more earthy, volatile people. Working in a language she did not as yet speak with any fluency, Loren gives a fair enough reading of her token glamour role, aided by extensive coaching from Kramer and his wife Ann. It says a lot about the character that her biggest scene involves no dialogue at all, Juana arousing Trumball's passion as she performs a sensuous dance. Unfortunately, Loren is done no favours by the lighting and make-up, her dyed hair, sharp nose and wide mouth giving her the appearance of a shark in a red wig. With some kind of irony, the only member of the production team to have any enthusiasm for the finished film was Sinatra, whose earlier desertion resulted in the blatantly fake studio inserts that punctuate the location footage and undermine the otherwise flawless visual elements. The soundstage shots are very obvious, with distracting shifts in lighting and sound quality. In one sequence the extras grouped behind Sinatra change in the space of seconds from authentic Spaniards to shifty-looking Americans and back again, the jolt badly disrupting the mood of the scene. At least the all-important climax was finished as intended. Miguel is killed during the

attack on Avila and Trumball carries his body across the square to rest at the feet of the statue of Saint Teresa, bringing Miguel's long journey to its end. Given Sinatra's snotty behaviour on the shoot, he was lucky Grant didn't drop him.

Anxious to recoup their hefty investment in the film, United Artists pulled out all the stops for *Pride*'s promotional campaign. The press release spelt out the theme in easy to follow detail, emphasising that this was a story 'of human strength of body, mind and spirit; of human faith, poured into the symbol of the gun'. The poster legend dispensed with such wishy washy understatement:

MIGHTIEST EVER MADE!... CARY GRANT as the pride! FRANK SINATRA as the passion! SOPHIA LOREN as the flame!... in STANLEY KRAMER'S MONUMENTAL FILMING OF "THE PRIDE AND THE PASSION"

The accompanying illustration depicted the three stars standing suitably proud against a gaudy red sky, hordes of Spanish peasants pulling the gun along at their feet. The artwork is fairly risqué, Loren clad in a revealing sleeveless blue top, Grant's sabre pointed at her left breast, with Sinatra clutching a furled bullwhip in his hand.

Considering its less than sparkling reputation, many contemporary reviews for *The Pride and the Passion* were surprisingly favourable, with *Newsweek* rating the film: 'One of the year's best... A rousing paean to the spirit of nationalism.' Even Sinatra attracted a measure of praise. *Saturday Review* critic Hollis Alpert felt the star should 'be commended for his restrained and appealing guerrillero leader.' *Time* magazine thought Sinatra reasonably credible 'despite spit-curl bangs and a put-on accent'. With prints, advertising and distribution pushing the final cost up to $5 million, Kramer and United Artists were praying for a hit and got one, *Pride* eventually turning in a more than adequate profit. Not bad going for a bomb. Or a bust.

8

Tragi-Comedy

1957-1958

*Frankie enjoyed playing my life more
than I enjoyed living it.*
Joe E. Lewis

One of Sinatra's more personal projects, *The Joker is Wild* is a well-made, if conventionally romanticised biopic of comedian Joe E. Lewis, a 1920s nightclub singer forced into a major career change after a rival club owner hired gangsters to cut his vocal chords. An old friend of Lewis, Sinatra had often co-starred on theatre bills with the veteran comic and picked up the sought-after film rights to Art Cohn's biography while the book was still in galley form, Lewis rejecting all other bids from rival producers. Both men were represented by the William Morris Agency, making the deal nice and simple. Lewis also served as a consultant during production, which must have produced a strange sense of pseudo-*déjà vu*. If the dark, mob-influenced underside of the entertainment business held any particular resonance for Sinatra, it doesn't really show on screen.

After a little deliberation, Sinatra took his project to

Paramount, reuniting star and studio for the first time since *Las Vegas Nights* (1941, see Appendix 1). The deal paid Sinatra $125,000 through his new company Bristol Productions, which owned 25 percent of *Joker* and a corresponding share of the box-office gross. Sinatra's major creative partner on the film was Hungarian producer-director Charles Vidor, a former Columbia employee whose recent freelance credits included *Hans Christian Andersen*, another musical biopic. Sinatra and Vidor made for a harmonious team, handpicking their collaborators-in-faction to generally good effect. The task of transforming Art Cohn's book into a screenplay was allotted to Oscar Saul, who'd successfully adapted *A Streetcar Named Desire* for the big screen. Paramount cameraman Daniel L. Fapp had previously worked with Bob Hope, Danny Kaye and the Dean Martin-Jerry Lewis combo, which certainly gave him some behind-the-scenes insight into star comedian temperament. Sinatra used Fapp again on *Kings Go Forth*, a film notably lacking in laughs. For the score, Vidor recruited composer Walter Scharf, who'd contributed to *Hans Christian Andersen*, while Sinatra called upon the services of Sammy Cahn and Jimmy Van Heusen, who came up with the memorable theme song 'All the Way',

orchestrated by Nelson Riddle.

Sinatra's co-stars included Mitzi Gaynor and Jeanne Crain as the two women in Lewis' life, and veteran screen heavy Ted de Corsica. The one cast member to have matched Sinatra's level of celebrity was former child star Jackie Coogan, still in career freefall after co-starring in Charles Chaplin's *The Kid* (1921).

Another useful addition to the supporting cast was burlesque comic Hank Henry, who had to be expensively bought out of a Las Vegas engagement. Hired also as a consultant on the burlesque style, Henry was given a free hand to rewrite and stage his scenes.

Beginning in late October 1956, the generally easygoing shoot was marred only by Sinatra's antipathy towards certain members of the press, the star drawing up a list of reporters barred from the set while his scenes were being shot. Media loathing aside, Sinatra was very much the benevolent boss towards his cast and crew, throwing another of his surprise birthday parties when Jackie Coogan turned 42 during the shoot (also his 40th year in the film business). Shot in moody, low-key black and white, the finished film offers an enthusiastic turn from its star, careful period detail, better-than-adequate supporting performances, a believably tacky showbusiness backdrop and a suitably melancholy atmosphere. This is almost enough to offset *Joker*'s membership of a largely useless Hollywood subgenre: the sanitised, simplified screen biography of a still living/recently deceased celebrity. Given that the story hinges on a man having his throat cut, it's all just a bit too tasteful.

Released on 12 December 1957, *The Joker is Wild* received the expected high-profile launch, the star attending the film's Los Angeles premiere accompanied by new girlfriend Lauren Bacall. One of the few regular visitors to the Bogart household during his friend and mentor's battle with cancer, Sinatra had become close to Bacall after Bogart's death in January 1957, their friendship eventually turning into a romance.

For the more swingin' Las Vegas first night, Sinatra and Lewis decided to ride a horse to the theatre. Reluctant to enter the building, the uncooperative animal defecated in the lobby. Critics were less hostile, the reviews for *Joker* ranging from respectable to highly appreciative. The only friction between Sinatra and Lewis over the film occurred during the post-premiere party held at El Rancho Vegas. Having performed his own stage act, a drunken Lewis called on Sinatra for a song or two, forgetting that his friend had specifically asked him not to do this. Refusing Lewis' repeated entreaties, Sinatra eventually walked out of his own party. The incident did no lasting damage to their relationship, with both men apologising for their poor behaviour, but it was another gift for the Sinatra-hostile press. Lewis later made an unbilled guest appearance in *Lady in Cement*, playing a somewhat nervous massage parlour client.

A solid commercial success, *The Joker is Wild* proved a worthy addition to the Sinatra filmography without really lingering in the public's collective

The Joker is Wild – Relatively placid joker Sinatra confers with director Charles Vidor.

The Joker is Wild – Joe E. Lewis before the fall.

memory. While it can be argued that the 1920s period songs were not ideally suited for Sinatra's voice, the music caught on more than the accompanying movie. A hit in both America and Britain, 'All the Way' later picked up an Academy Award for Best Original Song. Eager to cash in on the film's major selling point, Paramount later reissued *Joker* as *All the Way*, an interesting example of a movie being not so much upstaged by its own theme tune as hijacked.

PAL JOEY 1957

How did I know she was jailbait? She looked like she was thirty-five.
Joey Evans, indiscriminate womaniser

You have all the subtlety of a battering ram.
Vera Simpson. Indiscriminate woman

Pal Joey should have been one of the undisputed highlights of Frank Sinatra's film career, the star perfectly cast as the amoral yet beguiling nightclub hustler and ladies man. A big fan of the Broadway show, Sinatra had wanted to play the role for years, claiming that Joey Evans was as important a part for him as Angelo Maggio. Instead he was lumbered with an utterly bland, family-safe reduction of the original, with many of the show's songs sanitised, thrown away as background music or dropped altogether. Divested of his more unsavoury traits, this Joey is a lovable rogue, pulling a few harmless scams here and there as he attempts to build his own deluxe 'Chez Joey' nightspot in swinging San Francisco. Yes, Sinatra gets to sing 'The Lady is a Tramp', but the film is a spineless cop-out, the reformed Joey literally walking into the sunset with true love Linda (Kim Novak) as the Golden Gate Bridge gleams on the horizon.

Based on a series of *New Yorker* short stories by John O'Hara, George Abbott's original 1940 production of *Pal Joey* had an immaculate musical pedigree, its Rodgers and Hart score enhanced by

Robert Alton's choreography, O'Hara's own book adaptation and the charismatic playing of newcomer Gene Kelly. By no means run of the mill fare, the lyrics emphasised sexual appetite rather than romance and the ending was atypically downbeat, with the double-dealing, two-timing Joey losing both the women in his life and his own nightclub. Hurt by some unfavourably puritanical reviews, *Pal Joey* scored only a modest commercial success. A decade on, it was revived on Broadway in a softened version, drawing rave reviews and sell-out audiences at the expense of its original edginess and bite.

Despite the concerns over the show's 'immoral' content, there was some Hollywood interest back in 1940, the film rights eventually going to Columbia. Delighted by the success of *Cover Girl*, Harry Cohn wanted to reunite stars Rita Hayworth and Gene Kelly for a follow-up vehicle and Kelly's original Broadway success appeared made to measure. Unfortunately, Louis Mayer didn't feel inclined to give his rival another hit and demanded an exorbitant loan-out fee for rising star Kelly. With the project hot again in the early 1950s after the show's second coming on Broadway, Cohn looked around for a new star, his interest in Kelly waning along with the latter's box-office appeal. Around 1952, word spread that Columbia hoped to make the film with the intriguing, if unlikely combination of Marlon Brando and Mae West under the direction of Billy Wilder. Hot off *The Wild One*, Brando expressed serious interest but negotiations led nowhere, partly because West wouldn't play a character who lost her man. By October 1953, Harry Cohn had changed tack and proposed to co-star *Eternity*-hot Sinatra with veteran *femme fatale* Marlene Dietrich. Somewhat fickle with his affections, Cohn then decided he was still annoyed with Sinatra over the latter's Honolulu antics, informing Dietrich she would now be playing opposite newcomer Jack Lemmon. Dismissing the latter as an ill-chosen nonentity, Dietrich begged to differ and withdrew from the project, much to Cohn's rage.

By early 1957, Sinatra seemed the only serious candidate for the lead and Cohn finally gave in to him.

Pal Joey – Vera takes centre stage. A decade on from Gilda,
Rita Hayworth still had what it took.

Working through Essex Productions this time around,
Sinatra made a similar deal to the one on *Joker*, taking
a $125,000 fee and 25 percent of the gross profits.
Anxious to finally get the film made, Cohn ate an
unusually large quantity of humble pie, agreeing to the
star's terms with only a token amount of haggling. *Joey*
reunited Sinatra with *Anchors Aweigh* director George
Sidney, who also served as the film's executive producer.
Now an independent film-maker affiliated to Columbia,
Sidney had recently worked with Kim Novak on two
mediocre biopics, *The Eddie Duchin* Story (1956) and
Jeanne Engels (1957), experiences he enjoyed very little.
The screenplay was entrusted to Sidney's fellow MGM
exile and *Bathing Beauty* collaborator Dorothy Kingsley.
Cohn's man on the spot was producer Fred Kohlmar,
who'd overseen the Columbia hit *Picnic* (1956) the
previous year, providing Kim Novak with a much
needed half-decent co-starring role. Kohlmar later
worked with Sinatra on *The Devil at 4 O'Clock*, an

unsuccessful but interesting effort.

Nearly 15 years on from the first preproduction
discussions, Harry Cohn still intended to use Rita
Hayworth in the film, his former 'Love Goddess' a long
way from the glory days of *Gilda* (1946). Absent from
films for three years, she only returned now to fulfil her
contractual obligations to Cohn. His decision to cast
her in the long-delayed film version of *Joey* was
interpreted by many as a calculated act of revenge and
humiliation. At 38, Hayworth no longer qualified as
sufficiently youthful to partner the 41-year-old Sinatra
and her intended role was given to Kim Novak,
Columbia's new sex goddess-on-the-block. Playing the
older woman in *Joey's* life, Hayworth would be
perceived as the loser both on and off-screen. This
unveiled insult hardly made for a conducive working
atmosphere yet the expected fireworks between
Hayworth and young pretender Novak never happened.
Pal Joey was Hayworth's last film under her Columbia

Pal Joey – Milk-drinking, dog-loving Joey puts the squeeze on Linda.

contract and she just wanted to get the production finished, with no tantrums or walk-outs. According to director Sidney, her only gripe was portraying a character supposedly older than middle-aged lust-object Sinatra. The one source of mild cheer for Hayworth was the agreed billing order, with her name appearing first, followed by Sinatra, then Novak. Sinatra could have insisted on the top spot for himself, but felt perfectly happy placed between his co-stars. It's been claimed that Hayworth's existing contract with Columbia stipulated first billing, yet she was currently a little short of front-office goodwill.

Beginning in March 1957, filming on *Pal Joey* ran over eight weeks in total, with most major scenes completed by the end of May. Unwelcome press visitors once again provided the only serious disruption to an otherwise even-tempered production. As with *The Joker is Wild*, Columbia executives were under orders from Sinatra not to allow certain journalists onto the set. When *Time* reporter Ezra Goodman arrived to interview Kim Novak, Sinatra expressed outrage that a banned name had been admitted, threatening to walk out mid-take unless Goodman departed immediately. Hardened by his experiences on *Anchors Aweigh*, Sidney had no problems with Sinatra's preferred working method, as he

later explained to Nancy Jnr: 'His first take is better than most people's tenth.'

Location shooting in San Francisco often took place during extremely cold weather, with the stoically uncomplaining Hayworth turning purple at one point. Aware that she wasn't really up to the part, Novak rapidly grew disenchanted with the film and Sidney didn't relish their reunion. Exhausted after the prolonged *Jeanne Engels* shoot, Novak wasn't ready to take on another starring role so soon, fainting in her dressing room during her first week on *Joey*. Looking for a major hit, Columbia supplied cinemas with a specially shot *Pal Joey* trailer, Sinatra explaining his character's 'jargon' and philosophy to prospective audiences.

If the 1950s revival had toned down some of the show's more controversial elements, Columbia's ultra-safe adaptation went for total emasculation, even adding four unconnected songs to build up the severely diminished score. The showstopping 'Bewitched, Bothered and Bewildered' might have been retained but the lyrics were so heavily bowdlerised the song lost most of its impact. Similarly, while Hayworth and Novak are both fairly eye-catching in the slinky black outfits provided for the film's famous 'What Do I Care For A Dame?' fantasy sequence, their singing had to be dubbed. Looking decidedly uneasy in her unwanted role, Novak was obliged to reloop much of her dialogue in the old Columbia style, undermining an already strained performance. Cast as an ex-showgirl turned wealthy society widow, Hayworth's faded glamour at least lends her character some authenticity. George Sidney's workmanlike direction lacks both pace and inspiration, most of the action staged in unexciting medium shots. The film only comes to life during the vigorous 'Lady is a Tramp' number, Joey seducing Vera with his vocal magic as he sits at a bright red upright piano. The use of actual San Francisco locations is counter-productive, slowing down the narrative with regular travelogue inserts. There are several awkward cuts between studio and location shots and the usual use of long shot doubles and back projection.

As for Dorothy Kingsley's increasingly glutinous

script, it's probably best to let the lady speak for herself: 'I never think of myself as a 'real writer'. I only wrote because I needed the money'. Some of the original show's sexual banter and one-liners survive, but never quite enough. Sinatra's performance as the scheming, love-'em-and-leave'-em Joey matches Sidney's direction, professional yet flavourless. Good-natured and mildly amusing at times, he seems a little cold overall, delivering Joey's quick-fire patter without much flair. The Hayworth-Sinatra-Novak combo generates almost no chemistry, Sinatra working much better with his cute pet dog and *Joker is Wild* actor Hank Henry, cast here as a milk-drinking, head-banging nighclub manager. *Pal Joey*'s biggest surprise is Rita Hayworth's revealing shower during the 'Bewitched, Bothered and Bewildered' number, her breasts clearly visible behind a glass screen.

Accompanied by a soundtrack album release on 14 October, *Pal Joey* opened in the late autumn of 1957, with Sinatra and Bacall on hand once again for the Los Angeles premiere. Opinions vary greatly on the film's box-office fate, with *Joey* often rated as both a big hit and a huge commercial disappointment. Predictably, the truth drifts between the two extremes. Despite its relatively modest budget of just under $3 million, the film took nearly two years to recover its costs, not showing an actual profit until it was sold to television.

KINGS GO FORTH 1958

If you're going to kick a guy in the teeth be sure to use both feet.
Lieutenant Sam Loggins

Any film featuring a symbolic chunk of brown bread hanging on a wall has got to give the viewer a little pause for thought. Sadly, a little is all *Kings Go Forth* really deserves. Set during the American Army's San Tropez campaign towards the end of World War II, this uneasy blend of action, romance, character study and moral tract is a classic example of good intentions gone astray. Centring on an inter-racial love triangle with no

happy ending, *Kings* should have been even more explosive and controversial than Stanley Kramer's *The Defiant Ones* (1958), made just before it. Fourteen years on from *The House I Live In*, Sinatra reteamed with producer Frank Ross to make a feature-length pro-tolerance fable. For *Kings* they recruited director Delmer Daves, who'd helmed Ross' successful biblical melodrama *Demetrius and the Gladiators* (1954). The mix of religiosity and arena brutality brought the crowds running and Ross presumably hoped that *Kings* would manage a similar trick, its taut combat sequences offsetting the worthy anti-racism message. Made in partnership with United Artists, the film was budgeted at around $1.5 million, relatively little for an 'A' production, reflecting some executive concern over its 'daring' inter-racial romance subplot. In the event, fatal miscasting largely nullified this supposedly central element and even the conventional excitements of the battlefield failed to deliver.

Along with Ross, *Kings Go Forth* also reunited Sinatra with Tony Curtis, briefly glimpsed in *Meet Danny Wilson* a few years back. Now one of Universal-International's biggest stars, Curtis had successfully made the transition from lightweight costume romps to more substantial fare such as *Sweet Smell of Success* (1957). *Kings* offered him the role of cocky, confident rich kid Britt Harris, a combat-shy Sergeant who begins to bond with Sinatra's war-hardened Lieutenant Loggins before a woman comes between them. For the role of Monique Blair, an American girl raised in France by her white mother and black father, Sinatra and United Artists went for the cop-out choice of Natalie Wood, who despite her dark hair and eyes looked nothing like a woman of mixed-race. Discovered at the tender age of five by *Miracle of the Bells* director Irving Pichel, Wood subsequently signed with Warner as a teenage hopeful, displaying an attractive face and doubtful acting ability. Warner's high expectations for her performance in *Marjorie Morningstar* (1958) were largely shared by their rivals, making the 19-year-old actress a hot property. Keen to work with Sinatra and Curtis, Wood feared Jack Warner would decline to loan her to United

Artists for *Kings Go Forth*. In the event, Sinatra and UA negotiated a deal even Warner couldn't refuse, paying $75,000 for Wood's ten weeks on the film. Sinatra also agreed to make one of his future projects in association with the studio, netting Warner a profitable share in *Ocean's 11* a few years later.

Sinatra's insistence on including Wood in the star line-up inevitably prompted rumours that his interest in her was more than professional. In fact, she currently had eyes only for fiancée Robert Wagner, a contract player over at Twentieth Century-Fox. Their forthcoming marriage complicated an already difficult situation regarding the scheduled location work on *Kings*. Tony Curtis' ongoing commitment to *The Defiant Ones* meant he was unavailable for the Nice shoot in late December 1957. Wood and Wagner's wedding plans involved them staying in Phoenix, Arizona for the two weeks she was supposed to be in France, though Sinatra could have insisted on Wood meeting her contractual obligations. Instead, he granted his leading lady an unusual wedding gift, reworking her scenes so that a double could be used for all the required French location shots. While Sinatra's generosity towards Wood undoubtedly made for a happy working relationship, his decision hurt the finished film. With Curtis at work and Wood at the altar, only Sinatra could make it to Nice and Villefranche, Antibes, the resulting footage having to be blended with later shots of Curtis and Wood filmed in Monterey, California. As Arnold Shaw points out, this logistical trade-off severely limited the film's use of its French locations, largely wasting Nice's eyecatching coastline.

Despite the loss of his co-stars and the inevitable media attention in France, Sinatra found his experience of continental film-making practices enlightening in at least one respect. French crews liked to work from noon till eight in the evening, the kind of hours Sinatra had lobbied for since the beginning of his movie career. As with most of his independent productions, Sinatra played the perfect host to *Kings'* cast and crew back in Hollywood, throwing regular Friday night parties with catering courtesy of the Villa Capri. One of the more notable visitors to the set was Lauren Bacall, who apparently laughed out loud watching Sinatra and Curtis film the scene where Loggins urges Harris to marry Monique.

Attractively photographed in sharp black and white by Daniel L. Fapp, *Kings* is probably most effective in its opening sequence. As the titles roll, a platoon of American soldiers march down a country road, flanked by cheering French villagers. An elderly lady stands clutching a bottle of wine and an empty glass, offering a drink to the largely uninterested troops. Loggins comes into view, halts, pauses and courteously accepts the woman's hospitality. Having exchanged appropriate pro-American and pro-French sentiments - 'Vive le Radio City Music Hall' - Loggins gives the woman a kiss and moves on. A contrived yet affecting moment, this brief exchange achieves a depth of feeling largely missing from the rest of the film.

While it's probably a little unfair to heap criticism on the ill-fated Natalie Wood, her inadequate performance is *Kings'* most glaring flaw. Burdened with a dodgy French accent, Monique is supposedly a woman of insight and compassion beyond her years, rapidly perceiving the tenderness beneath the besotted Loggins' brash manner. Working with some admittedly so-so dialogue, Wood just can't bring the character to life. Worse still, once Harris catches her eye, Monique's supposedly sharp appreciation of human nature goes straight out the window. One glimpse of Harris blowing his horn with Red Norvo and Pete Candoli at Le Chat Noir jazz club and she's gone, leaving the heartbroken Loggins dumped on the sidelines. Helped little by Merle Miller's script, Wood fails to generate any real sympathy for Monique, her attempted suicide after Harris' cruelly racist brush-off prompting only the desire to slap her around the face for being so stupid. The character is further undermined by the odd casting of Leora Dana as her mother (Mr Blair is conveniently deceased). Only 15 years older than Wood, Dana needed heavy-duty ageing make-up to effect a credible age gap, the end result looking very fake. An accomplished performer, Dana had previously appeared in Delmer Daves' western *3:10 to Yuma* (1957) and the director was perhaps over-eager to use her again. Recognising a top professional when he saw one, Sinatra cast Dana more successfully as his nagging bitch of a sister-in-law in *Some Came Running*.

Well aware of her limitations as an actress, Wood was grateful for the support of her co-stars and director, all of whom realised they were stuck with a no-win situation. A good friend of Wood off screen, Curtis felt her miscasting destroyed any chance of the film's already timid race angle being credible. More sensitive to the issue than many of his fellow countrymen, Curtis found the scene where Harris dumps Monique very difficult to play. With his shiny, chubby face and slicked hair, he looks too 1950s to entirely convince in his own role, yet Curtis renders Harris just about as plausible as the script will allow. Speaking fluent French, this womanising, college-educated, trumpet-playing heir to a textile fortune is a cold-hearted opportunist, using and discarding people with no regard for their feelings. With his boyish good looks, easy charm and winning smile, Harris has gone through life knowing what to say to get what he wants, never having to think about the cost. Eventually killed during a mission behind enemy lines, Harris is first given a misjudged speech of self-abasement, confessing to Loggins that he feels like an empty shell (Loggins wisely falls asleep). This last-ditch attempt to redeem the character a little falls flat, diminishing Curtis' creditable portrayal of a man both contemptible and pathetic.

As a piece of film-making, *Kings Go Forth* is professional but lifeless, exuding technical know-how rather than any discernible feel for the characters or subject matter. Daves allows the film to unreel at too leisurely a pace, failing to generate the kind of tension he'd sustained so well in *3:10 to Yuma*. The French locations work more as travelogue than atmosphere or setting, which can't have been entirely due to the absence of Curtis and Wood. Interestingly, Wood's failure to make it over the Atlantic is the more noticeable, her outdoor scenes with Sinatra involving an awkward blending of location footage, studio sets and indifferent back projection, with Wood obviously

doubled in several long shots. There is also far too much voiceover from Sinatra's character, pedantically spelling out plot points and feelings that should be evident within the film proper.

The saving grace of *Kings Go Forth* is Sinatra himself, his wrong-side-of-the-tracks character both likeable and sympathetic. A blue collar worker made good, Loggins is almost as girl-shy as Clarence Doolittle in *Anchors Aweigh*, his nervous courtship of Monique far removed from Harris' well-honed routine. Resentful of the latter's self-impressed arrogance, Loggins has Harris demoted for reckless behaviour, later conceding that his motives were not entirely honourable: '...he was born rich and handsome and I was born poor and not handsome.' A decent man at heart, Loggins is forced to confront suppressed feelings of bigotry when Monique reveals her mixed parentage. Recalling how as a boy he regarded his black neighbours as the faceless, hostile 'them', he needs an entire week to conquer his racist instincts. It's a tribute to Sinatra's acting skill that he prevents this rapid turnaround from being merely risible. Some of the credit for this impressive performance should go to veteran star Boris Karloff, who served as Sinatra's unofficial acting coach during the studio shoot. Karloff's principal criticism of his pupil's approach was Sinatra's tendency to neglect his vocal performance, over-relying on his striking, expressive face. Valuing the opinion of one of the cinema's premiere talents, Sinatra followed Karloff's advice. He needed all the dramatic ability he could muster for the final section of the film, where reality and logic take a prolonged absence of leave. Having punched out Harris for his cruel treatment of Monique, Loggins determines that his former friend must die (emotional betrayal = capital crime?) The German army saves him the trouble of a more personal execution and Harris expires in Loggins' arms, neither reconciled nor rejected. Losing his right arm during the climactic bombardment of a hidden enemy base (a symbolic amputation?), Loggins returns to Monique, now a dedicated schoolteacher. At the fade-out, their relationship is presumably one of reunited friends, yet it's difficult to tell exactly what the film-makers intended. Having treated

Kings Go Forth – Kings stay put under enemy bombardment.

their subject matter with several pairs of kid gloves throughout the film, Ross, Daves and company clearly hadn't the slightest idea how to resolve it. Sinatra's missing arm is quite convincing.

Kings Go Forth received its American premiere on 4 July 1958, drawing poor reviews and negligible audiences. Sinatra fared a little better than his film, *News* critic Wanda Hale declaring that the star 'may not be the best actor in the world, but there is none more interesting to watch'. The *Hollywood Reporter* dished out superlatives for both leading men: 'Sinatra is

superb. Curtis is equally fine as the feckless show-off who arouses pity by his very shallowness.'

One of the star guests at the Los Angeles opening night was Dean Martin, now branching out into a solo acting career following his acrimonious split with Jerry Lewis. Martin had heard that Sinatra's forthcoming screen version of the James Jones novel *Some Came Running* featured an alcoholic gambler as one of the main characters. Cornering Sinatra, Martin informed the star that his search for the right actor was at an end.

Dramatic Irony
1958-1960

9

SOME CAME RUNNING 1958

Bumming around can only help make you a bum.
David Hirsh

Dave, you have a very exciting talent.
Gwen French

The first in a new three-picture deal with MGM, *Some Came Running* is probably the high point of Sinatra's late fifties output, a superior piece of schlock melodrama that flaunts the courage of its dubious convictions to largely successful effect. Combining Sinatra with Dean Martin and Shirley MacLaine for the first time, the film also reunited its star - albeit indirectly - with *From Here to Eternity* author James Jones, whose follow-up novel provided the source material. Intended by Jones as a pseudo-sequel to *Eternity*, the story features another of his rough-hewn poet-warrior characters, Dave Hirsh, returning home from army service in 1948 to stir up a hotbed of hypocrisy, frustration and repressed emotion. Jones described the book's theme as the coldness of human relationships, the way people seek affection from others without wanting to give any in return, and this idea is largely retained in the film version. Set in the fictional small town of Parkman, Indiana, *Running* offers a relentlessly sour take on humanity, its characters emerging from their selfish, self-protecting shells only after one of their number is violently killed. Even hero/anti-hero Dave Hirsh is often contemptible, squandering his writing talent in pursuit of unfulfilling low-life seductions, and treating those who care for him like dirt.Extremely well crafted in bright, pin-sharp Technicolor and Cinemascope, *Running* does contain the odd flaw, the cast being generally superior to the soap de luxe script. Unable to overcome the harsh truth that writing is a fundamentally uncinematic activity, the film is more seriously flawed by its blatant misogyny, arranging its female characters along the old virgin/whore divide. Dominating the proceedings from frame one, Sinatra's full-blooded performance conceals most of *Running*'s faults, his second visit to Jones country outshining his first in all respects.

Published in January 1958, Jones' 1,266-page novel was snapped up by MGM at the galleys stage. Recalling the author's abortive stint on the *Eternity* screenplay, the studio did not attempt to involve Jones in the production, entrusting the adaptation to John Patrick and Arthur Sheekman. Aiming to make *Running* one of their top releases for 1959, the studio looked to premiere craftsman Vincente Minnelli, an Arthur Freed recruit who'd been with MGM for 18 years. The director had just given the studio another hit with *The Reluctant Debutante* and in May 1958 new MGM head Sol C. Siegel asked Minnelli to take the *Running* project. With Sinatra already cast, they were on to a surefire winner.

Sinatra's supposedly on-the-spot decision to cast Dean Martin in *Running* as professional gambler Bama provided one of the film's biggest strengths, surprising many who still regarded Martin as nothing more than Jerry Lewis' former singing straight man. His first solo vehicle, the indifferent MGM comedy *Ten Thousand Bedrooms* (1957), flopped badly, confirming the popular view that Martin without Lewis was a box-office no hoper. MCA came to the rescue, deciding that all their troubled client needed was an *Eternity*-style comeback in the forthcoming war drama *The Young Lions* (1958). *Running* is often cited as Martin's breakthrough as a serious actor, which is something of an overstatement. His performance in *Young Lions* had already arrested the downward curve of his film career, and Martin was cast in *Rio Bravo* (1959) before he made *Running*. That said, Sinatra had to exert a little star muscle to have his choice accepted. For all the prerelease buzz on *Young Lions*, MGM had not forgotten the fiasco of *Ten Thousand Bedrooms* and didn't want Martin back, singing or non-singing. Sinatra refused to consider anyone else for the role, impressed by the novice actor's show of confidence. Martin certainly earned his $150,000 fee.

Cast before Martin, Shirley MacLaine had a rather bumpier ride getting her part. A struggling newcomer, she was under personal contract to producer Hal Wallis who appeared unsure what to do with his new recruit. MacLaine had recently lost the lead part in *Marjorie Morningstar* to Natalie Wood and *Running* represented a major career break for her. Competition for the role of dim but loveable 'hostess' Ginny Moorehead was

intense, with former roommates Marilyn Monroe and Shelley Winters regarded as the frontrunners. Unconvinced by the various star names suggested, Sinatra and Minnelli spotted MacLaine dancing and singing 'Blue Moon' on the *Dinah Shore* television show, the answer to their dreams. The MGM front office weren't impressed with the choice, rating neither MacLaine's talent nor her box-office draw. More to the point, she didn't have the requisite sex appeal. Unperturbed by this resistance, Minnelli shot a screen test with MacLaine, the actress dressed in figure-hugging black satin. She got the job, MGM paying her the derisory sum of $10,600 under the terms of the Wallis loan-out contract. MacLaine's immediate chemistry with both Sinatra and Martin was helped by her earlier meetings with the stars. She'd co-starred with Dean Martin and Jerry Lewis in *Artists and Models* (1955) and become acquainted with Sinatra while he was shooting his brief cameo role in *Around the World in 80 Days* (1956), MacLaine's third film.

The secondary role of uptight schoolteacher Gwen French was as fiercely contended as Ginny Moorehead, with former Sinatra co-stars Deborah Kerr, Jean Simmons and Eleanor Parker all under consideration for the part. No-one regarded second string Universal-International starlet Martha Hyer as a likely candidate. Determined to get her shot at the role, she secured a meeting with Sinatra's agent Bert Allenberg, who agreed to take her on as a client. Introduced to Siegel and Minnelli, Hyer met with their approval. Once Sinatra had given his okay, the part was hers. Having taken a chance with their casting for Bama, Ginny and Gwen, Siegel and Minnelli opted for safer ground when it came to the role of Frank Hirsh, hiring Arthur Kennedy to play Dave's wealthy, straitlaced businessman brother. Academy Award-nominated for his recent performance in Fox's film version of *Peyton Place* (1957), Kennedy certainly knew how to handle lush melodrama.

Production on the film ran over August and September 1958, with extensive location shooting in the small town of Madison, Indiana, on the Ohio River. The arrival of a 130-strong Hollywood production team

Some Came Running – Dave and Bama (Dean Martin) –
a superior piece of schlock melodrama.

in early August caused understandable excitement. Sadly, the feeling wasn't entirely mutual. The prospect of nearly three weeks in Madison rapidly lost all appeal for Sinatra and he began pushing Minnelli to drop some of the scheduled location work for an early finish, abruptly cancelling one night shoot to make his point. Unwilling to compromise his film for the sake of star pampering, the director refused, prompting an uncomfortable stand-off. Word of their increasingly frequent disagreements filtered back to Hollywood, obliging Siegel to pay a visit and act the peacemaker. After a little strategic rescheduling, Sinatra declared himself satisfied and filming resumed, the production later relocating to Kentucky for a few more days of exteriors.

Blessed with a healthy respect for his star, Minnelli later acknowledged the benefits of Sinatra's rapid-fire working methods, agreeing that both time and money could be saved if the rest of the company matched his speed. As it happened, most of the *Running* cast required the standard amount of rehearsal time, Minnelli taking them through a scene until he was satisfied, then bringing on Sinatra for one last rehearsal just before the cameras rolled. Never once did the star let his director down: 'He gave me everything I wanted.' Sinatra also gave Minnelli a scare the day they were scheduled to film the scene where Dave finally breaks down Gwen's resistance to his amorous advances, announcing that the director had only two hours to get the elaborate, single-take sequence as he was catching the train to Las Vegas for Judy Garland's opening night. Having rehearsed the scene with Hyer and Sinatra's stand-in, Minnelli called his star onto the set, showed him his moves and marks, and got the take he wanted first time. Heading off to the railway station, Sinatra told Minnelli and Hyer that their success was a tribute to true professionalism, the seduction scene turning out

Some Came Running – Dave and Ginny (Shirley MacLaine).

to be Minnelli's favourite of the whole film. Back in Los Angeles, Sinatra persuaded Minnelli to adopt his noon-till-eight working day, breaking for lunch at 4pm on a rehearsal stage transformed into a temporary commissary. The director was happy to oblige and Sol Siegel offered no objections, tactfully acknowledging a level of star power that would have infuriated the late Louis B. Mayer.

According to MacLaine, neither Sinatra nor Martin ever really took to Minnelli personally, regarding the director as a little too 'precious'. It probably didn't help matters when he instructed them to play their roles like two respectable Beverly Hills matrons who both know that the other used to be a hooker, a singularly useless piece of advice. Then there was the director's sometimes obsessive attention to detail. Unable to track down an operating carnival for the climactic sequence, the

production team hired the various components needed, their gradual assembly chronicled on screen throughout the course of the film. With the entire funfair built and ready for shooting, Minnelli suddenly realised that the giant Ferris wheel was obscured behind buildings to the right of the picture in his long master shot up the main street. As the focal point of the scene, the wheel had to be visible from all camera angles. Cast and crew would have to wait while it was moved a vital six feet to the left. Having spent hours on call surrounded by screaming fans, Sinatra reacted to the news that the director was shifting the wheel rather than the camera by ordering his driver to take him back to Los Angeles. Once again, Sol Siegel rode to the rescue.

The presence of a big Hollywood production in Madison inevitably drew massive outside interest from both the public and the media, rendering Sinatra and many of his co-workers virtual prisoners during their stay. This enforced confinement led the star to seek release in a heavy-duty night life, often appearing for work the next day looking decidedly wrecked after just one hour's sleep. The national press picked up on several alleged incidents: Sinatra had described Madison as a dump to rival Los Angeles' skid row; he'd ripped a telephone off a wall when he thought the local operator was listening in; an elderly hotel clerk was roughed up by the star's entourage after failing to deliver their exact hamburger order. *Time* magazine took the stories seriously enough to print a formal censure against Sinatra, which doubtless caused him many sleepless nights. Based in the grounds cottage of the hotel occupied by the rest of the cast, Sinatra and Martin entertained a large and raucous circle of acquaintances. Minnelli noticed one shifty-looking man he took to be a small-time Chicago gangster, one of the star's long-rumoured Mafia friends. In fact, he was a state censor from Illinois, so the director was half right. MacLaine paints a less savoury picture of Sinatra's social life during the shoot, claiming that one of the star's regular guests was infamous Chicago mob leader Sam Giancana, who pulled a .38 revolver on her when she waved a water pistol at him. She also objected to

Sinatra and Martin's love of juvenile pranks, which included lobbing firecrackers into people's beds and spilling spaghetti bolognaise over brand new tuxedos.

Utilising the improved, composition-friendly Cinemascope system, Minnelli's direction of *Running* is almost beyond reproach, employing extremely long, fluid takes without ever rendering his scenes static. Hirsh's seduction of Gwen is staged in tantalising silhouette, her submission to his kisses signalled by Dave literally letting down Gwen's hair (subtlety is neither required nor displayed). The film's tragic final act begins with an ominous shot of Ginny's shunned would-be boyfriend, framed as a black shadow against deep red backlighting. Minnelli visualised the night-life scenes as resembling the interior of a juke box, with the emphasis on bright, garish colours. He extended this vulgarity motif to MacLaine's character, Ginny wearing horrendously overdone make-up and clothes to match. So confident is Minnelli's handling of the material, the few technical faults are both surprising and disruptive. Aside from some negligible, if obvious overdubbing early on in the film, the sequence where Frank takes Dave home for dinner with the family is peculiarly beset with slip-ups. When Frank and Dave arrive at the house, it quickly becomes apparent that Kennedy parked the car too close to a hedge bordering the driveway, the actor unable to get out of the driver side without brushing the foliage. Once inside the house, Dave is introduced to Gwen's father Bob French (Larry Gates). They shake hands in one shot, their hands then dropping to their sides, followed by a reverse set-up which shows their hands clasped again, a continuity error which should have been spotted at the rough-cut stage. A quibble, maybe, but this elementary fault spoils the effect of an important and otherwise well-handled scene.

Minnelli's highly effective use of both Technicolor and Cinemascope owed a lot to the talent of cameraman William H. Daniels, whose 11-film partnership with Sinatra started here. Active in the industry since 1917, Daniels had prospered at MGM thanks to the patronage of Greta Garbo, who used him on 19 of her 24 Hollywood films. Aside from honing his technical skill,

Daniels picked up plenty of experience dealing with 'difficult' talent, shielding the reclusive Swede from crew and bystanders between takes with strategically placed black screens. His more recent credits included *Cat on a Hot Tin Roof* (1958), another lavish MGM melodrama. Just how much Daniels prospered under Sinatra's wing is open to question. While his work on *Never So Few*, *Can Can* and *Von Ryan's Express* is impressive, the flat, over-lit style of *A Hole in the Head*, *Come Blow Your Horn*, *Marriage on the Rocks* and *Assault on a Queen* suggests that Sinatra's customary impatience with intricate lighting set-ups often led to Daniels' talent being wasted. Despite being made a co-producer on *Robin and the 7 Hoods*, *Marriage and Assault*, he broke with Sinatra after the mid-1960s for reasons never fully explained.

Running's visual dynamism is easily matched by its three starring performances. Cutting a distinctive figure in his ever present stetson, Dean Martin's Bama is a heavy-drinking, heavy-smoking card hustler more than content with his dissolute way of life. Affable as opposed to likeable, his cruel dismissal of Ginny as a 'pig' is at least more honest than Dave's treatment of her, Hirsh using and abusing Ginny as it suits him. Sharing Sinatra's preference for minimal rehearsal time, Martin's attitude to film-making displayed few signs of his co-star's impatience or short attention span. A consummate professional, he always knew his lines and turned up on time, delivering the goods even in unmitigated trash such as *4 for Texas* and *Marriage on the Rocks*. Here he had the edge over Sinatra, whose lacklustre showing in these efforts is deeply unimpressive. While his role in *Running* doesn't call for much in the way of dramatic fireworks, Martin imbues Bama with a sense of conviction that goes deeper than the more emotive playing of trained thespians such as Kennedy, Leora Dana and Larry Gates. It probably helped that Martin had once been a professional card dealer at The High Hat gambling joint in his home town of Steubenville. Whatever the secret, he had a grasp of film acting to rival Sinatra's in his handful of half-decent movies. With a total of ten joint appearances - cameos included - Martin qualifies as Sinatra's most enduring co-star, though none of their subsequent on-screen pairings matched *Running* in terms of quality.

For all her standing as one of the grande dames of modern American cinema, Shirley MacLaine's performance as Ginny has survived less well, her interpretation of the pathetic, dim-witted loser veering too often into strident over-acting. First seen slumped on a seat of the Greyhound bus that brings Dave to Parkman, Ginny's personality matches her cuddly rabbit purse, cute at first in a kitsch kind of way but ultimately cheap and garish. Not to mention empty. An aspiring model, Ginny takes a job in the town's brassiere factory to stay close to Dave, enduring his contempt with minimal complaint and gratefully taking him on the rebound when Gwen loses her nerve. There is presumably some irony intended in the fact that Ginny's sacrificial murder bestows on her a dignity and heroism she could never have attained in life. Her funeral is attended by all the other main characters, with even Bama sufficiently moved to take off his hat. This is an affecting denouement, almost making up for the fact that the living, breathing Ginny is often simply tiresome, notably in the scene where she attempts to join in a nightclub performance of the specially written Cahn-Van Heusen number 'To Love And Be Loved'. Not so much tone deaf as tone deceased.

Despite some reservations over Sinatra's aversion to rehearsals, MacLaine found working with him an enjoyable and rewarding experience, the stars establishing an easy rapport. She even forgave him for removing one of her big scenes from *Running*, Sinatra responding to concerns over schedule overruns by ripping out 20 pages of unfilmed script, with no thought as to the dialogue contained within. The revised schedule did not allow for the discarded material to be reinstated and a remorseful Sinatra atoned for his bad behaviour by insisting on a major rewrite of the climax in MacLaine's favour. In the original script, Dave Hirsh is shot dead by one of Ginny's old pick-ups, an obsessive psychotic. Sinatra persuaded Minnelli and some rather nervous MGM executives that Ginny should die instead, cut down as she shields the injured Hirsh from the

gunfire. Aside from generating more audience sympathy for the character, it greatly increased MacLaine's chances of critical recognition and Academy Award attention. As *Eternity* demonstrated, everybody loves a heroic victim. MacLaine's performance was a particularly big hit with Sinatra, who regularly screened a print of the film for his house guests.

His hair enhanced and dyed a severe shade of black, Sinatra's burned-out writer is largely a triumph of well-guided star power over substance. Explicitly depicted as a tortured soul torn between creative sensitivity and empty hedonism, Dave Hirsh is a little too schematic to convince entirely as a character. This is the kind of man who keeps his money in the crotch of his army trousers and his copies of Faulkner, Steinbeck and Wolfe in his army rucksack. Estranged from his successful older brother for 16 years, Dave is unable to forgive Frank for dumping him in a children's home while he pursued his career in the retail jewellery business. Married with an adolescent daughter, Frank represents the kind of self-made man held up as a role model for all good Americans, the polished façade of his life and career masking an empty, spite-filled and lonely reality. In a predictable, if efficiently handled subplot, affection-starved Frank seeks short-lived solace with his secretary (*Suddenly*'s Nancy Gates), and it's up to the supposedly amoral Dave to steer his brother's resentful daughter away from a retaliative walk down the path of teenage delinquency. Dave's more overt lust for creative writing teacher Gwen is similarly doomed, the latter admiring his literary talent but shying away from his aggressive carnal instincts. Largely discarded after the chaste seduction scene, Gwen is inadequately developed by the script, making Dave's longing for her and what she represents - self-respect, creativity, commitment - seem a little bogus. His relationship with Ginny gets a lot more screentime, despite Sinatra's impromptu revision of the screenplay. Having casually picked Ginny up after a drunken fight with her eventual killer, Dave wants little more to do with her, tolerating Ginny's presence out of indifference rather than growing friendship. Treating her earnest declarations of love with polite disdain, he puts

Ginny to work as his housekeeper, eventually losing his temper over her 'inferior' childlike mind: 'You haven't got enough sense to come in out of the rain unless somebody leads you by the hand.' Dave's out-of-nowhere decision to marry Ginny completely fails to convince, his explanation ringing false - 'I'm just tired of being lonely, that's all'. Dave's tears as he holds Ginny's bullet-torn body are probably as much for his own failures as her death. The gun shots bring Gwen, Frank and their respective families running, the subsequent en masse attendance of Ginny's funeral vaguely hinting at some kind of group reconciliation hardly borne out by earlier events in the film. Sinatra certainly suffered for his art during the shooting of Ginny's death scene, which required MacLaine to fall on him as her character was riddled with bullets. Still feeling a little guilty over trashing one of his co-star's major scenes, Sinatra did five takes of the difficult shot without complaining, the repeated impact of MacLaine's bulk leaving him somewhat bruised.

Predictably, the advertising for *Some Came Running* played on the *Eternity* connection: 'From the bold, new novel by the author of *From Here to Eternity*...Dave was back and the whole town knew that trouble - and women - were close behind!' Following its west coast premiere at the Hollywood Paramount on 18 December 1958, *Running* opened on 4 January 1959 at New York's Radio City Music Hall, drawing impressive crowds and widely varying critical responses. *Mirror* reviewer Justin Gilbert dismissed the film as '...acceptable screen entertainment - but not much more'. *Time* magazine continued its attack on the production, lamenting 'the spectacle of director Vincente Minnelli's talents dissolving in the general mess of the story, like sunlight in a slag heap'. *Running* did better in the trade press, with *Variety* rating it as '...certainly one of the most exciting pictures of the season'. Making several Ten Best lists for 1958, the film went on to become one of MGM's biggest hits of the year. Sinatra's Oscar prediction for MacLaine was promptly borne out, with his co-star picking up a Best Actress nomination, accompanied by Martha Hyer's less expected

nomination for Best Supporting Actress. Neither of them won, but then they didn't really deserve to.

A HOLE IN THE HEAD 1959

A Very Fresh, Very Funny...Very Frank Capra Look at Life!...The Most Wonderful Entertainment In The Whole Wide Wonderful World!
Theatrical trailer, a clear breach of the Trade Descriptions Act

There are those who argue that director Frank Capra should have quit after *It's a Wonderful Life* (1947), thereby ending his mostly glorious career on a high note, with more than enough triumphs for any self-respecting auteur. *Wonderful Life* and *State of the Union* (1948) aside, his return to feature films following World War II service proved a failure, Capra finally calling it a day after the Paramount comedy *Here Comes the Groom* (1951). The director's wartime experiences also included a brief near-encounter with Frank Sinatra at Los Angeles Station, Capra little realising that 13 years later he'd be relying on Sinatra to kick-start his dead-and-buried film career.

Derived from an unremarkable stageplay by Arnold Shulman, *Hole in the Head* offers an uneasy balance of sentiment and laughs, indifferently staged by a sadly burned-out talent. The story concerns feckless, bankrupt Miami hotelier Tony Manetta (Sinatra), who attempts to realise his wild entrepreneurial fantasies by cadging money from older brother Mario Manetta (Edward G. Robinson), former business partner Jerry Marks (Keenan Wynn) and wealthy widow Eloise Rogers (Eleanor Parker). In the tear-jerking subplot, Mario decides that Tony's young son Allie (Eddie Hodges) is being led astray by his loser father, offering to finance his brother's latest scheme if the boy is given up to him and his wife for adoption. Having toyed with renaming the film version either *All My Tomorrows* - one of Sinatra's songs - or *The Garden of Eden*, the makers opted to retain the original title. Based in a specifically Jewish milieu, Shulman's play premiered on Broadway in early 1957, qualifying as a success rather than a hit. Bert Allenberg saw *Head*, decided it could make a useful vehicle for Sinatra and suggested he check it out. Unable to catch an actual performance, Sinatra read through the text in July 1957 while on a San Pedro-to-Coronado holiday cruise with Lauren Bacall. Back in Los Angeles, he endorsed Allenberg's initial verdict, instructing the latter to buy up the film rights for $200,000. By Capra's account, *Head*'s Broadway producer-director Garson Kanin urged Sinatra and co. to use Shulman for the screen adaptation, the New York playwright rapidly regretting his decision to take the Hollywood dollar. To begin with, Schulman was advised that the family in the story should become Italian-American to accommodate the star, his antipathy to the project increasing when Sinatra announced that they needed a softened, happy ending, with the reformed Tony finding love, success and fraternal harmony. While Shulman was contractually guaranteed sole writing credit on the film, his script didn't meet with much enthusiasm and Capra recruited old collaborator Myles Connolly (*State of the Union*, *Riding High*) to undertake a few strategic revisions, including a new racetrack scene where Manetta attempts to interest Marks in his latest deal.

Now firmly ensconced in television, Capra had spent the last six years making Bell Telephone-sponsored science films for children. Realising that Capra was not exactly up to speed regarding the new Hollywood, Allenberg made it clear to him that the stars now called many of the shots, the studios and top directors obliged to yield much of their coveted power. No longer a bankable commodity, Capra needed to be part of a Sinatra deal to get his career running again. With fellow Allenberg client Edward G. Robinson included in the package, *Hole* was guaranteed to attract finance. A fan of Capra's work, Sinatra agreed to make the film a co-production between their two companies, a UA-backed alliance christened SinCap. Star and director would have a 50/50 vote on all matters pertaining to the production, with WMA head Abe Lastfogel on hand as official

mediator. Ownership of the film was not so evenly split, Sinatra holding two-thirds to Capra's third. Given their respective levels of power in the industry, even this percentage was something of a sentimental concession on the star's part. Meeting up at Sinatra's WMA office in August 1957, director and star made their deal the same day, Sinatra pocketing $200,000 to Capra's $100,000. Allenberg then informed Capra that Sinatra's schedule meant he could not actually begin work on *Head* until November 1958, well over a year away. Capra later protested that no-one had mentioned this delay before, taking a little of the edge off his 'comeback' euphoria. A native Sicilian, Capra felt seriously short of respect.

Burdened by a mediocre script and an extremely rusty director, *Head* at least had a strong supporting cast, headed by former Warner screen gangster supreme Edward G. Robinson. *Head* would be Robinson's first film since *The Ten Commandments*, a gap of nearly three years. The role of Mario's wife Sophie went to Thelma Ritter, who'd memorably upstaged James Stewart and Grace Kelly as the former's plain-speaking nurse in *Rear Window*. Sinatra found a smaller part for his friend Joi Lansing, who'd known the star since playing a bit role in *Take Me Out to the Ball Game*. Cast as Wynn's girlfriend, she got little to do in *Head* other than admonish the former for dropping cigar ash on her. For the role of Sinatra's son, Capra picked 11-year-old Eddie Hodges, who'd recently appeared in Meredith Wilson's Broadway hit *The Music Man*. Aside from Parker and *Johnny Concho* co-star Wynn, Sinatra also recruited old hands Carolyn Jones (*The Tender Trap*), as Tony's on/off girlfriend Shirl, and B.S. Pully (*Guys and Dolls*), cast as a local hoodlum.

Shot over 40 days between 10 November 1958 and 9 January 1959, *Head* did not enjoy the smoothest of productions, especially during the location filming at Miami Beach. Even by Sinatra's standards, his relations with the assembled press were appalling, the media seizing on every anti-Sinatra rumour they could find. Intrigued by the endless reports of the star's supposedly monstrous behaviour, Sinatra-friendly journalist Joe Hyams paid a visit, discovering no evidence whatsoever

A Hole in the Head – Sinatra and Eddie Hodges quail under the hard stare of Edward G. Robinson.

to support the rumours. When the company left Miami a week ahead of schedule, many conjectured that Sinatra had become sick of the endless press sniping, though both star and director insisted that they'd simply speeded up the work pace and completed all the required scenes earlier than expected.

According to his weighty and rather depressing autobiography, Capra rated Sinatra as a 'great' actor, despite sharing the fashionable opinion that he'd become a little too casual with his talent. The director quickly learned that the trick with Sinatra was to keep him busy, leaving the star no time to become impatient or bored. During the second night of filming at Miami's West Flagler Kennel Club dog track, Sinatra grew annoyed at Capra's insistence on two rehearsals before shooting, acting on autopilot once the cameras were rolling. Anxious to resolve the problem as fast as possible, the director called a ten-minute break, then took Wynn and Lansing aside, instructing them to ad-lib on the scripted dialogue, giving Sinatra fresh material to play with.

Capra even switched the extras in the track crowd around, Sinatra returning to find a new set-up requiring his full concentration.

Back at the Goldwyn Studios, the director found that Sinatra's rehearsal phobia presented more serious difficulties. Aware that Robinson required extensive rehearsals prior to shooting, Capra intended to run him through the scenes with Sinatra's stand-in delivering the absent star's lines. On learning that Sinatra refused to rehearse with him, Robinson threw a star tantrum of his own, walking off the set to sulk in his dressing room and threatening to quit the film. A combination of remorse, career advice and sound financial acumen brought the wayward actor running back two hours later, Robinson tearfully embracing Capra in front of the cast and crew. Unaware of this mini-drama, Sinatra arrived on set to be similarly greeted. Putting their initial clash aside, Sinatra and Robinson did become good friends, the latter making an unbilled cameo appearance in *Robin and the 7 Hoods* five years later. Sharing 12 December as a birthday, they held a joint party during the *Head* shoot. Fours months after the completion of filming, Sinatra recorded the Cahn-Van Heusen theme song, 'High Hopes' on 8 May 1959. Better remembered than the film itself, the song proved a big hit in Britain, later picking up some home-grown acclaim in the form of an Academy Award.

Despite the sterling efforts of Sinatra, Robinson, Ritter et al, *Hole in the Head* is a resolutely unmemorable experience. Superior to such desperate later Sinatra efforts as *Marriage on the Rocks*, its sporadic flashes of wit or style make the flavourless end result all the more frustrating. For all his boasts to the contrary, Capra's use of colour and 'scope betrayed his inexperience with both, resulting in a maladroit, thinly textured piece of film-making. The director appears to have been content to get the script onto film as fast as possible, relying on the cast to give the proceedings some pretence of life. Sinatra's performance offers what film historian David Shipman described as a 'quizzical, casual charm', taking the edge off his character's somewhat mercenary behaviour. Along with 'High Hopes', he delivers an agreeably smooth

rendition of 'All My Tomorrows'. Denied his co-star's Terpsichorean gifts, Robinson wins out in the comedy stakes, his assuredly droll handling of the dialogue rendering the somewhat bogus Jewish-Italian metamorphosis largely irrelevant.

Aided by William Daniels' expertise, Capra completed *Hole in the Head* a full eight days ahead of schedule, its final production cost of $1.89 million well under the allotted budget. The film was then rushed through post-production, enabling SinCap to beat a tax deadline. Capra's first cut ran over the agreed two-hour limit, a problem the director remedied by chopping out a short scene where Manetta takes Eloise to dinner at a swish restaurant, reducing Eleanor Parker's already small role to a glorified cameo. After a successful preview for UA bosses Arthur Krim and Robert Benjamin at Loew's Bronx theatre in New York, the film opened on 17 June 1959 to some positive reviews. The *Hollywood Reporter* certainly liked what it saw: '...a comedy that registers its success not in chuckles but in roars'. Bosley Crowther rated *Head* a near-instant classic, '...a thoroughly fresh, aggressive and sardonic comedy', later naming the film as one of the year's Ten Best. His appreciation of Sinatra's performance fell little short of ecstatic: '...a soft-hearted, hardboiled, white-souled black sheep whom we will cherish as one of the great guys that Mr Capra has escorted to the American screen.' Like Shulman's original play, *Head* proved only a modest box-office success, grossing $4 million in America, which placed it joint 11th with the dubbed Italian epic *Hercules* (1959) in *Variety*'s annual list. Capra hoped to work with Sinatra again, with projects such as *Pocketful of Miracles* (1961) and unlikely biopics of Jimmy Durante and Saint Paul discussed at various stages (see Appendix 2). As so often happened, Sinatra's initial enthusiasm soon waned in all cases.

NEVER SO FEW 1959

*I kiss you and the bells ring
wildly in my temples.*
Carla Vesari

Frank Sinatra with a stick-on goatee. Steve McQueen standing in for Sammy Davis Jnr. A pompous Churchillian title. Peter Lawford. The signs aren't good for *Never So Few* and this World War II drama is seldom cited as anyone's finest hour. Directed by John Sturges between his far better known westerns *Last Train from Gun Hill* and *The Magnificent Seven*, the film is undeniably flawed, suffering from redundant romantic interludes, risible dialogue - see above - and a disappointingly flat ending. That said, *Never So Few* is a lot better than its mediocre reputation would suggest. The goatee soon comes off, McQueen delivers a star-calibre performance, the title doesn't linger and even Lawford is basically inoffensive. Moreover, the combat sequences are first rate, displaying all the flair later on show in *The Magnificent Seven*. The second film in the star's new MGM deal, *Never* had been brought to Sinatra's attention by Sturges, regarded as a top-of-the-range action director after *Bad Day at Black Rock* and *Gunfight at the OK Corral* (1957, see Appendix 2). Based on a bestseller by Tom T. Chamales, the plot concerns a small contingent of Overseas Special Services troops leading 600 Kachin guerillas against 40,000 Japanese soldiers in North Burma. The $3.5 million budget was entrusted to producer Edmund Grainger, whose credits included the hit war movie *Sands of Iwo Jima* (1949). Sinatra's performance as the cynical, battle-hardened liberal Captain Tom C. Reynolds is impressive, if not quite a career best, and *Never* deserves at least a footnote in movie history for the behind-the-scenes shenanigans that cost Sammy Davis Jnr one of his few decent film roles and launched Steve McQueen on the road to superstardom.

The Tale of Peter Lawford. Following his triumph in *It Happened in Brooklyn*, Lawford appeared to lose his magic touch, and was dropped by MGM in 1952. By the mid-1950s, the fading ex-juvenile lead could only find steady employment on the small screen, starring as Nick Charles opposite Phyllis Kirk's Nora in *The Thin Man* television series (1957-58). Lawford's social contacts were in somewhat better shape, thanks to a canny choice of marital partner. In 1954, he married Patricia Kennedy, sister to Joseph Junior, Kathleen, Robert, Edward and John Fitzgerald. Sinatra didn't immediately figure on the Lawfords' guest list, the star having ostracised his former friend in 1951 after Lawford was seen out on the town with Sinatra's temporarily estranged *amour* Ava Gardner. The immediate factor behind their reconciliation in 1959 had little to do with either friendship or Lawford's impressive connections to the Democratic Party. Sinatra had become hooked on the story outline for the caper

Never So Few – Captain Tom Reynolds and friend in an underrated World War II drama.

movie *Ocean*'s 11 and Lawford owned the rights. This alone was sufficient to restore the latter to the star's inner circle. Shortly before production on *Never* was due to begin, Sinatra gave Lawford the small role of an Army doctor, his first film work for over six years. Unimpressed by Lawford's unexpected return to the studio, MGM vice president Benny Thau offered him a contract paying a mere $4,500 for three weeks' work. Playing on the actor's renewed friendship with Sinatra, Lawford's agents demanded $75,000. The parties eventually agreed on a figure between $40,000 and $50,000, Thau not wishing to be left explaining Lawford's absence to Sinatra.

The Saga of Sammy Davis Jnr. Of all Sinatra's celebrity friends, Davis probably owed the most to him in terms of career assistance. Eager to break into big budget movies, Davis's prayers were answered by his old friend and patron, though neither Chamales' novel nor Millard Kaufman's original script featured a black character. When Sinatra informed his MGM partners that he wanted Davis written into the film as Corporal Ringa, they pointed out that there hadn't been any negro soldiers in the Burmese campaign. Never a stickler for pedantic historical accuracy, the star was unfazed: 'Now there are.' Davis was hired for $75,000, with Bill Ringa's dialogue suitably revised. He then proceeded to shoot himself in one foot while placing the other firmly in his mouth. During an engagement at Chicago's Chez Paree nightclub in February 1959, Davis granted an interview to local radio reporter Jack Eigen. Talking in the relaxed atmosphere of the club lounge, he discussed his good friend Sinatra with reckless, never-to-be-repeated candour: 'I love Frank... But there are many things he does that there are no excuses for. Talent is not an excuse for bad manners... It does not give you the right to step on people and treat them rotten.' Having committed virtual social and career *hara-kiri*, Davis stuck the sword in even deeper by claiming he'd now overtaken Sinatra as America's number one popular singer. Word of Davis' indiscreet remarks inevitably got back to Sinatra, who summoned his friend for an explanation. Unconvinced by Davis'

dismissal of his comments as nothing more than inconsequential ad-libs, Sinatra contacted Eigen to request a copy of the original tape, which reputedly sent him into a rage. Shortly afterwards, Sinatra advised MGM that Davis was no longer in the film, obliging Kaufman to undertake a further rewrite. No one even questioned the abrupt switch-around. Sturges was busy scouting locations in Ceylon - now Sri Lanka - when a telegram arrived advising him that Ringa would now be played by 'a medium-size Caucasian'. Never entirely happy with the choice of Davis, the director didn't feel he'd suffered any great loss. After two months hard grovelling, Davis finally earned Sinatra's forgiveness, clearing the way for his co-starring role in *Ocean*'s 11. Davis made no mention of *Never So Few* in his two volumes of autobiography, an understandable omission given the circumstances, but offered a completely different version of the incident in his movie reminiscences book *Hollywood in a Suitcase*. According to this entertaining, if factually suspect volume, Davis' departure from the film was entirely down to an argument over how his role should be played. This isn't very convincing.

The Story of Steve McQueen. In the late 1950s, Steve(n) McQueen was pretty much a Hollywood nobody, few studio executives having caught his starring role in the science fiction shocker *The Blob* (1958). Unable to make much headway in films, McQueen had found a useful television break as the bounty-hunting lead of *Wanted: Dead or Alive* (1958-61), an ideal vehicle for his rugged good looks and charismatic cool. There are numerous conflicting accounts of exactly who first spotted and selected McQueen as a likely replacement for Davis, though the initial move appears to have been made by agent Hilly Elkins, who represented both actors. According to Nancy Sinatra Jnr, her father had been impressed with McQueen's work on *Wanted* and suggested that Sturges arrange a meeting with the young actor. The director knew the show and was either a) already an admirer of McQueen, having urged Sinatra to watch him in *Wanted* or b) decidedly underwhelmed, not warming to the actor until they met in person. Whatever the case, Sturges quickly decided they'd found their man. For all the career benefits of co-starring in a big budget film, McQueen did not immediately jump at the offer of $25,000 and fourth billing, wary of Sinatra's reputation as a difficult, unpredictable talent. Like most of the latter's co-stars, he soon realised his concern was unwarranted: '...we sort of found ourselves on the same wavelength - we dug one another. We're like minds; we're both children emotionally.' Liking McQueen as both an actor and a man, Sinatra asked Sturges to favour his co-star during filming, giving him more than one unscripted close-up. Introduced with an appropriately imposing low camera angle as he sits nonchalantly in his jeep, Ringa tangles with Military Policemen as readily as he battles the Japanese, displaying considerable prowess with a hand-held mortar during a surprise attack by the latter. At the end of the production, Sinatra accurately predicted a highly favourable response for McQueen: 'It's a good movie, kid - and it's all yours.' Sturges was similarly impressed, placing McQueen under contract for *The Magnificent Seven*.

The Mild Bunch. McQueen aside, Sturges and Sinatra assembled a largely high quality supporting cast on *Never*. For the role of sultry woman-of-mystery Carla Vesari, they agreed to take Italian star Gina Lollobrigida, who'd recently achieved a short-lived Hollywood breakthrough in *Trapeze* (1956). Her performance in *Never* is lacklustre, Lollobrigida's apparent problems with English dialogue heightening her utter lack of chemistry opposite Sinatra. It comes as no great surprise that the stars didn't get along, Lollobrigida unable to cope with Sinatra's speedy, one-take working method. Saddled with 'profound' lines such as: 'You found in yourself a rare ability. For violence. You are a gifted killer', she makes far more impression just lying in a bubble bath, the water line obstinately staying the right side of decency. It's a sure sign that something is wrong when her scenes with Sinatra are dominated by the scars on his neck. MGM 'discovery' Richard Johnson played Captain Danny De Mortimer, Reynolds' doomed British comrade-in-arms. He has more success than Lollobrigida

with lines such as: 'You can't murder a man without killing part of yourself', though the most memorable aspect of his performance is De Mortimer's mildly masochistic relationship with Reynolds. In order to demonstrate the staying power of his monocle, Danny likes his good friend Tom to punch him in the face. Further down the *Never So Few* cast was Dean Jones, as Sergeant Norby, the actor completing his last film under a rather unproductive MGM contract. Norby regularly tangles with uptight Native American Sergeant John Danforth, played by Charles Bronson. Nicknamed 'Hiawatha' by the playfully insensitive Norby, Danforth's protestations of racist victimisation ring a little hollow given his own contempt for the 'gook' Kachins. The script doesn't allow the Norby-Danforth relationship to go anywhere much, yet both actors make a strong impression, with Bronson earning his place among *The Magnificent Seven* a little while later. As with *Seven*, he gets to expire heroically on the battlefield, sharing his last moments with Norby.

War Games. With location work in Burma, Ceylon and Thailand, *Never So Few* required a lengthy production schedule, beginning in July 1959. Sinatra and Lawford decided to initiate shy boy McQueen into their on-set fun by placing a lit firecracker in a loop of his ammunition belt while he was absorbed reading the script. Blown out of his chair, McQueen responded to their violent 'humour' in kind, opening fire on his co-stars with a handy tommy gun, emptying the entire clip of blanks in their direction. This kind of retaliation was unheard of, and the set went dead while the assembled cast and crew awaited Sinatra's reaction. After ten agonisingly slow seconds, the star laughed and there were regular firecracker wars between the two men from then on. Sturges professed not to mind the gunpowder antics, arguing that actors tended to behave like children anyway. A grip suffered an eye injury when a cracker exploded next to him, yet even this serious accident failed to halt the fun for more than a few days. Sinatra only lost his cool when McQueen continued the running battle off the set and lobbed a cracker into his dressing room, blowing out a wardrobe man's hearing aid. Even

Never So Few – Philip Ahn and Steve McQueen. Ahn's Kachin guerrilla leader marked a step up from his wise-yet-humble Chinese waiter in *The Miracle of the Bells*.

the scheduled fire fights staged for the cameras caused potentially serious injuries. During the filming of one studio battle sequence, a gun was fired a little too close to Sinatra's head, the muzzle blast scorching the cornea of his left eye. Temporarily blinded, the star was led off by Lawford to the studio infirmary, where the doctor informed Sinatra that he'd nearly lost the eye for good. A taste of harsh poetic justice, some might say, though only Nancy Sinatra's *Frank Sinatra. An American Legend* makes any reference to what would have been a highly newsworthy accident. Given the frequent explosions on the *Never* set, it's surprising Sinatra could hear anything else at all, let alone feel that the television crew shooting *One Step Beyond* on an adjoining backlot were making too much noise.

The Frank Sinatra Masterclass. Interviewed during the *Never* production by *Newsweek* journalist Betty Voight, Sinatra offered some insight into his approach to acting. While his protest of lack of time for drama classes sounds a little glib, the star's comments reveal the amount

of thought and hard work put into his best film work:

I wish I had some formal dramatic training, but I never have enough time. I have my own technique that I've evolved from discussing acting with Spencer Tracy and Bogie... Before starting to shoot a picture, I read the script half a hundred times. I pick it up and read maybe two or three pages one night and two days later I pick it up again and read halfway through it. By the time I start working I have a good idea of the dialogue and the story and the character I'm playing. Once we've begun shooting, I rarely open the script. I feel that you don't have to go by the script verbatim. If two good actors in a scene listen carefully to what the other is saying, they'll answer each other intelligently. Actors who go only by the lines never seem to be listening to the other actor, so the scene comes out on the screen as if you can see the wheels going around in their heads.

One of the cinema's least heralded advocates of on-camera improvisation, Sinatra's technique certainly works well here, even if he does cut across another actor's line during a hospital sequence.

Never So Few's strongest assets are undoubtedly John Sturges and Frank Sinatra. Blessed with a fine eye for composition and tracking shots, Sturges' use of the ultra-wide Cinemascope frame is exemplary, with no dead screen space at all. The two jungle battle set-pieces are very well staged, with a careful build-up of suspense before the first and a sudden shock explosion opening the second. Making good use of his locations, Sturges conjures up some memorable images as Reynolds' platoon wade across a wide river or advance cautiously through a forest. Uncomfortable with prolonged non-macho dialogue scenes, Sturges does allow the pace to falter away from the combat zone, though the failure of the civilian scenes is largely due to their clumsy scripting. Given Millard Kaufman's success with *Gun Crazy* (1949) and *Bad Day at Black Rock*, his screenplay for *Never* is disappointingly trite in places. The best sequence with Tom and Carla doesn't involve dialogue or even the actual stars, Sturges framing their location doubles against gigantic stone Buddhas, dwarfing the petty human drama into insignificance.

A fair-minded, monkey-loving man of action, Sinatra's Captain Reynolds is a commendably understated piece of acting, the low key approach helping to counter the script's less plausible elements. Confronting the brutal realities of jungle warfare head on, Reynolds' respectful treatment of his Kachin troops supposedly balances the slightly uncomfortable master-servant aspect of their relationship. Early on in the film, he shoots a mortally injured Kachin fighter without hesitation, unwilling to watch the man suffer from his agonising stomach wound. His fellow OSS soldiers react with 'civilised' horror, yet the natives see Reynolds as a wise and courageous leader. When bigoted Sergeant Danforth protests at having to take orders from senior Kachin Nautaung (Philip Ahn), the Captain gives him a verbal slapping. Hospitalised after the second skirmish, Reynolds is outraged by the staff's ignorance of the local diet, the injured Kachins unable to digest standard western invalid food. Sadly, the final section of the film lets Sinatra down, petering out at speed after a promising scene where Reynolds' company illegally crosses over the Chinese border to track down the warlord-backed bandits who murdered and robbed an American convoy. When De Mortimer is gunned down by one of the bandit chiefs, Reynolds loses his cool and orders the summary execution of the entire gang. Shooting unarmed Chinese civilians stirs up a minor international incident, yet he gets off the hook with little apparent difficulty. Explaining his actions to General Sloan (Brian Donlevy) while his feet soak in a tub of whisky, Reynolds convinces his superior to tell the Chinese officials where to go: 'I know I'm right about this, and if you don't know it I pity you.' Staged and performed like exceptionally static filmed theatre, the scene carries no dramatic charge whatsoever. Reynolds' subsequent reunion with Carla is similarly underwhelming. A disappointing end to a good movie.

Prior to its release, *Never So Few* ran into some difficulty with the MPAA. Unperturbed by the film's fairly graphic scenes of violence, the board objected to the number of 'damns' and 'hells' on the soundtrack,

though they'd presumably approved this use of profanity at the script stage. Accepting that the oaths were vital to the film's impact and integrity at certain points, notably Reynolds telling both his superiors and the Chinese government to 'Go to Hell', the MPAA agreed to a compromise. The essential swearing could stay, providing the more gratuitous cursing was removed from the soundtrack. The end result of this last-minute clean-up job is a number of exchanges with key words clumsily muffled mid-sentence. After Danny suffers an attack of cerebral malaria, Reynolds informs his convalescent friend: 'You scared the *mmmph* out of me.' This blatant censorship probably rattled audiences far more than the original dialogue would have.

The promotional campaign for *Never So Few* was peculiarly cack-handed, MGM obviously not knowing whether to sell the film as a lush romance or a Boy's Own action-fest. The press pack synopsis tried for the former angle, with questionable results: '...a lusty but tender love story of a man and woman set against the background of Burma during the hectic fighting days of World War Two'. This looked like a model of low-key advertising compared to the trailer:

Sooner or Later This Had to Happen
SINATRA meets LOLLOBRIGIDA
And the Screen Catches Fire!

Aside from its blatant dishonesty, this hard sell smacks of imaginative poverty. Having got the soppy love interest out of the way, the overextended promo packs in a few action highlights and a brief character sketch of Reynolds: 'A bomb who lighted his own fuse.' A intriguing image, but little to do with the actual film. Following a series of previews that saw McQueen singled out as the film's biggest hit, *Never So Few* received a New York premiere in January 1960, with Sinatra, Lawford and McQueen in attendance. The critics weren't too impressed, Arthur Knight complaining: 'What might have been an explosive and searching drama turns out to be just another war adventure film.' Bosley Crowther took an even harsher line: '...a romantic fabrication by which intelligence is simply repelled... Most sober people will just sit there appalled'. McQueen continued to draw praise, with *New York Herald Tribune* reviewer Paul Beckley announcing: 'He possesses that combination of smooth-rough charm that suggests star possibilities.' Overall, *Never So Few* was unfairly written off as a damp squib, the literally explosive atmosphere during production regarded as far more exciting than anything on the screen. Audience response proved similarly disappointing, the film's domestic receipts leaving MGM with a $1.15 million net loss to be recouped by overseas ticket sales. Just how much this affected Sinatra's relationship with MGM is unclear, but neither star nor studio appear to have been in any great hurry to make the third film due under the terms of their contract. Over a decade would pass before Sinatra returned to star in *Dirty Dingus Magee*.

CAN CAN 1960

This movie is about a bunch of pretty girls and the fellows who like pretty girls.
Sinatra's plot rundown for Nikita Khrushchev

The face of humanity is prettier than its backside.
Khrushchev's critique of the Can Can

The otherwise inexplicable existence of this drab song-and-dance show derives from two equally mundane factors. Twentieth Century-Fox put the film into production hoping to cash in on MGM's surprise success with the Gallic musical romance *Gigi* (1958). Sinatra agreed to star in it as token settlement with the studio for walking off *Carousel* five years earlier (see Appendix 2). Reunited with producer Jack Cummings for the first time since *It Happened in Brooklyn*, he treated *Can Can* with all the care and attention his enforced participation merited. Not that there was much for Sinatra to work with, anyway. Set against the

supposedly 'naughty' backdrop of 1890s Paris, the original Broadway show opened in 1953 to no great interest from the critics, public or Hollywood studios. Despite the involvement of Cole Porter and *Guys and Dolls* co-writer Abe Burrows, the ingredients just didn't blend into a successful whole, the story of a Parisian lawyer attempting to legalise his girlfriend's 'sinful' dancing lacking American appeal. Reluctantly acquiring the film rights to the show as part of a larger deal with Porter (see Chapter 7), MGM decided it had invested in a dud, selling the property to Fox in May 1958. Obtained as a possible vehicle for Marilyn Monroe and veteran Frenchman Maurice Chevalier, the *Can Can* project was postponed by the studio when Monroe signed up for *Some Like It Hot*. Had *Gigi* not briefly revived the ailing musical genre, it's likely *Can Can* would have mouldered on the shelf, lacking any real aesthetic or commercial value of its own.

Unfazed by his doubtful casting as a Frenchman, Sinatra accepted the film with little argument, agreeing on a $200,000 fee plus 25 percent of the gross profits (net profit shares tending to pay out precious little). He also insisted on Shirley MacLaine as his leading lady, which necessitated Fox buying MacLaine out of her contract to co-star in George Sidney's Columbia comedy *Who Was That Lady?* (1960). MacLaine's market value had risen considerably after her appearance in *Some Came Running* and Fox paid Hal Wallis $250,000 for his star's services. MacLaine would have done better to skip *Can Can*, her raucous, overbearing performance impressing absolutely no-one. Similarly miscast, Sinatra is at least inoffensive in his role, played in the manner of someone keen to get their job done with minimum fuss and be elsewhere. Briefly toying with the idea of attempting a French accent for the part, Sinatra decided to err on the side of caution, co-star MacLaine reminding him of the reception afforded his Spanish accent in *The Pride and the Passion*. Given *Can Can*'s origins as a piece of opportunistic exploitation, its star shouldn't be blamed too much for his lacklustre showing.

Fox's attempted duplication of the *Gigi* 'magic' extended to hiring its two genuine French co-stars,

Can Can - Foot fetish frenzy.

Chevalier and Louis Jourdan. While this would appear a fairly obvious ploy, it seems that Jourdan wasn't the original choice for Sinatra's smooth-talking rival in love, neither *Gigi* nor his role in the Fox hit *Three Coins in the Fountain* counting for much with the studio. Hired by MGM only after Dirk Bogarde declined the part of Gigi's lover, Jourdan inherited his role in *Can Can* from first choice Cary Grant, the latter still wary of Sinatra after the *Pride and the Passion* fiasco. Chevalier and Jourdan were joined on the film by fellow compatriot Marcel Dalio, whose Hollywood credits included *Gentlemen Prefer Blondes* at Fox.

Unhappy with many aspects of *Can Can*, the Fox front office dictated a few strategic revisions. The admittedly below-par Cole Porter score underwent extensive alteration, with the alleged 'smut' of the original show largely eliminated and several songs discarded altogether. It's likely Sinatra insisted on the substitution of four different Porter numbers for his character, the Fox executives readily agreeing that the existing song line-up lacked popular appeal. His rendition of 'It's All Right With Me' has been acclaimed by some as one of the star's best ever on-screen musical performances, though in truth even this doesn't quite justify sitting through the film. Elsewhere, Chevalier's performance of 'Just One of Those Things' makes an interesting comparison with the Sinatra version used in *Young at Heart*. The direction of *Can Can* was entrusted to studio veteran Walter Lang, who'd worked on the popular, if pedestrian musical hits *There's No Business Like Show Business* (1954) and *The King and I* (1956). *Pal Joey* writer Dorothy Kingsley adapted Burrows' book in collaboration with Ben Hecht's old scribbling partner Charles Lederer, who would shortly co-script the more watchable *Ocean's 11*.

Shooting on *Can Can* commenced in September 1959. Interviewed by Michael Freedland 25 years later, producer Cummings recalled the film as a traumatic experience, with Sinatra more than living up to his less palatable reputation. Unresolved problems with the script necessitated daily rewrites by Lederer, making it impossible for Sinatra to memorise all his scenes prior to the start of production. He also clashed with Cummings over rehearsal time, Lang's direction and the standard working hours. Neither producer nor director knew how to deal with their star, obliging MacLaine to act as an unwilling go-between. According to Cummings, she was reduced to tears by Sinatra's rudeness and bad attitude more than once, though MacLaine makes no reference to this in her various accounts of the film. Conversely, Arnold Shaw describes the production as largely trouble-free, with only Sinatra's unscheduled time-outs to attend World Series baseball games causing any concern. MacLaine recalled that her co-star displayed a remarkable lack of vanity in many respects, not caring if people looked into his dressing room while his bald spot was being painted over to match the remaining hair. Sinatra didn't even complain if the rushes showed the retouched area shining under faulty lighting. Denied a steady supply of firecrackers, the star still managed a few practical jokes during the shoot. One scene required an enraged MacLaine to burst into Sinatra's office, finding him cowering in a closet. Opening the door, she was instead greeted by Sinatra's back and the admonishment 'Sorry, lady, this is the men's room.' It's funnier than anything in the script.

One of the least interesting entries in its star's filmography, *Can Can* is probably best remembered for its connection to the biggest media event of the day. While working on the film, Sinatra agreed to act as

Master of Ceremonies for a gala lunch held in honour of visiting Soviet Premier Khrushchev on 19 September 1959. Around 400 stars were in attendance, with only such die-hard right-wingers as Ronald Reagan and Adolphe Menjou boycotting the occasion. Once the eating was done, the party moved on to *Can Can*'s large nightclub set, where Chevalier and Jourdan duetted on the mildly risqué 'Live and Let Live' ('...strip and let strip'), followed by Sinatra's rendition of 'C'est Magnifique'. Then MacLaine and her fellow dancers staged the main event, a performance of the Can Can. Pictured smiling during the show, Khrushchev later denounced the performance as 'lascivious, disgusting and immoral', a typically depraved example of western capitalist decadence. MacLaine felt he was just disappointed that the dancers had worn non-traditional, if MPAA-friendly underwear. Advance ticket sales for *Can Can* were reputed to be higher than *Ben Hur*'s, leading *Newsweek* to comment that '...being condemned by Khrushchev may be an even bigger commercial asset than being banned in Boston'. Only in the short term.

Fox decided on a spring 1960 premiere for *Can Can*, with Capitol releasing the accompanying 'Full Dimensional Stereo' soundtrack album on 4 April. The film earned the poor reviews it deserved, only Juliet Prowse's amusingly kitsch 'Adam and Eve' ballet drawing much critical appreciation. Like *Gigi* before it, *Can Can* met with an especially frosty reception in France, where the distributor inexplicably cut Chevalier's supposedly showstopping rendition of 'I Love Paris'. Audiences everywhere soon decided that neither Sinatra nor MacLaine made an acceptable substitute for *Gigi* star Leslie Caron and *Can Can* proved a serious commercial disappointment. With *Ocean's 11* already completed and presold all over the world, Sinatra barely cared.

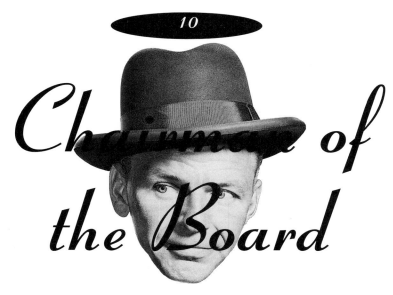

10

Chairman of the Board

1960-1962

OCEAN'S 11 1960

*You wouldn't call it a gang.
Just Danny Ocean and his 11 pals...
the night they blew all the lights
in Las Vegas...*
Publicity

*Why waste all those cute little tricks that the army
taught us, just because it's sorta peaceful now?*
Danny Ocean

*Let's not make the movie,
let's pull the job!*
Jack Warner

All things considered, it's fortunate that 'Ocean's
Eleven' rhymes with 'O O Seven'. Otherwise, Sinatra's
famous but facile caper movie wouldn't have made it
into Desmond Decker's reggae hit 'Shanty Town', the
film's one significant contribution to global popular
culture. Usually categorised as a light-hearted comedy

adventure, *Ocean's 11* is in fact a rather downbeat piece
of work, depicting a group of weary middle-aged losers
desperate to recapture the energy and excitement of
their wartime exploits. Sadly, neither the script nor the
stars' 'swinging' images allow the film to develop this
intriguing theme, the gang's ultimate failure brought
about by sheer misfortune rather than their own sad
delusions of criminal genius. Strolling around his drab
hotel room in an orange pullover and black trousers,
Sinatra's Danny Ocean resembles an older, seedier
version of his easygoing bachelor boy in *The Tender
Trap*, obliged to fend off countless nubile women with
a stick. (The theme from the earlier film is heard during
a scene in a strip club, the pursuit of love and marriage
now shunted aside in favour of more carnal appetites.)
While it may have been true to life, the ladykiller image
fails to convince in *Ocean*, the sight of Sinatra and a
bare-chested Peter Lawford being pawed by matching
blondes prompting only mild distaste. The star appears
to have been aware of the film's limitations, describing
Ocean and its follow-ups in defensive rather than

Ocean's 11 – Ring-a-ding-ding.

enthusiastic terms: 'Of course, they're not great movies... We gotta make pictures that people enjoy. Entertainment.' The production saw the rise of the largely meaningless 'Summit' tag applied to Sinatra and his co-stars, principally Dean Martin, Sammy Davis Jnr, Peter Lawford and Joey Bishop. This label supposedly derived from the 1959 Eisenhower-De Gaulle-Khrushchev Summit Conference, the United Nations event that had given *Can Can* a little free publicity. For whatever reason, this new 'gang' of showbiz buddies drew international press attention, *Ocean's 11* selling to distributors worldwide before the first week of shooting was completed. Not so much canny marketing as a cynical con trick.

The story outline for *Ocean's 11* supposedly originated with a mysterious gas station attendant, who'd once served as part of a 25-man team that smuggled stolen enemy radio equipment out of Germany during World War II. Peter Lawford first heard about the idea in 1955, from an assistant director named Gilbert Kay who hoped to turn it into his directorial debut.

Realising that Kay stood no chance of attracting studio interest in a novice-director deal, an intrigued Lawford bided his time while the budding auteur did the rounds. By early 1959, Kay had given up on the project, agreeing to sell Lawford the rights for $10,000. A little short of ready cash, Lawford persuaded his wife Patricia to put up half the amount, confident that such a hot idea would bring the big stars running. Credited to George Clayton Johnson and Jack Golden Russell, the basic plot was developed into a script by Harry Brown and Charles Lederer, Kay receiving no mention on the finished product. Brown's credits included *Sands of Iwo Jima* and *A Place in the Sun*, not that anyone would have guessed from this screenplay.

Following a failed attempt to secure William Holden for the project, Lawford found himself suddenly back in favour with Sinatra, who approached his former friend at a party to express an interest in the story. He felt *Ocean* would make an ideal vehicle for himself, Dean Martin and the other in-favour members of his social circle. With Lawford cast in *Never So Few* as a gesture of good faith, the has-been MGM reject was one of the in-crowd again. Sinatra still owed Warner Brothers a film as part of Natalie Wood's loan-out deal for *Kings Go Forth*, and offered his new caper movie to the studio. Jack Warner liked the idea a lot, agreeing to pay out $50,000 for the script, $10,000 of which reimbursed the Lawfords' original investment. Granted a free hand by Warner over casting and salaries, Sinatra expressed his gratitude to Lawford with a $50,000 acting fee plus 16.6 percent of the gross profits to split with Patricia Kennedy. Sinatra awarded himself $700,000 and a correspondingly generous cut of the box-office take. Lawford later claimed to have requested the right to select *Ocean*'s director as part of the deal with Warner. Given Sinatra's power as both the film's star and executive producer, this seems unlikely. In any event, the job went to veteran Lewis Milestone, one of Hollywood's greatest whatever-happened-to talents. Having risen to prominence during the early sound era with *All Quiet on the Western Front* (1930) and *The Front Page*, the Russian-born director-producer gradually lapsed into routine professionalism, scoring a few modest hits such as *Of Mice and Men* (1940) along the way. His recent Korean War movie *Pork Chop Hill* (1959) had earned some acclaim for acknowledging the contribution of black American soldiers, personified by actor Woody Strode, which probably appealed to Sinatra's sense of liberal fair play. The choice of Milestone proved fortuitous in several respects. Sharing his employer's antipathy towards early starts, the director was more than happy to work a noon-till-seven day for *Ocean*. According to *Front Page* co-star Adolphe Menjou, Milestone didn't function properly until midday, shooting his independently produced newsroom classic between the unorthodox hours of 1pm to 7pm, then 10pm to 1am, with a meal, a Turkish bath and a short nap in between. He enjoyed equally harmonious relationships with *Ocean*'s writers, having worked with Lederer on *Front Page* and Brown on *A Walk in the Sun* (1946) and *Arch of Triumph* (1948).

All the major roles were taken by friends of the star, with Dean Martin coming on board for around $300,000. His performance in *Ocean* as a two-bit club singer is both affable and vaguely contemptuous of the whole business. Martin's motivation wasn't entirely derived from the script, the actor largely indifferent to the whole Clan image. Significantly, his is the only character to suggest that the gang are indulging in a pipe dream, their commando skills blunted by 15 years of dreary civilian life. Having dumped Sammy Davis Jnr from *Never So Few*, a still aggrieved Sinatra was toying with the idea of replacing him in *Ocean* as well. Luckily for his co-star, they were reconciled on 14 May 1959 at a Moulin Rouge charity event for retarded children. Still a relative novice in motion pictures, Davis was grateful for the part, the $100,000 fee and Sinatra's patient on-set tuition. His later attempt to rationalise the blatant nepotism involved in the *Ocean* production is singularly unconvincing, comparing the Summit get-together with such star teamings as Katherine Hepburn and Spencer Tracy or James Cagney and George Raft. Martin's rising film profile gave him some box-office clout, but neither Davis' nightclub success nor Lawford's television exposure meant anything

to cinemagoers. Unhappy about this 'Sinatra Show' element of the production, Davis' *Never So Few* replacement Steve McQueen declined Sinatra's personal invitation to co-star. Initially keen to work with his benefactor again, McQueen sought advice from columnist Hedda Hopper - one of Hollywood's top star manipulators - who offered him a stark choice: 'Do you want to be a movie star or a Frank Sinatra flunky?' McQueen opted for the former career direction.

Others weren't so bothered by the 'flunky' label. The gang line-up included comedian Joey Bishop, who'd known Sinatra since appearing with him at Bill Miller's Riviera nightclub, New Jersey in 1952. Cast as former boxer 'Mushy' O'Connors, Bishop's previous film work amounted to bit roles in *The Deep Six*, *Onionhead* and *The Naked and the Dead* (all 1958). Resembling a smaller, milder version of Sinatra, he plays the part with all the indifference it deserves. A little token glamour was provided by Martin's *Rio Bravo* co-star Angie Dickinson, cast in the thankless role of *Ocean*'s estranged yet still loving wife. Briefly linked with Dickinson off screen, Sinatra enjoyed a longer acquaintance with character actor Richard Conte, an Elia Kazan discovery who'd done time with Twentieth Century-Fox. Best remembered as the villainous Mr Brown in Joseph H. Lewis' brutal cult favourite *The Big Combo* (1955), Conte had also co-starred in two of Milestone's more potent war dramas, *The Purple Heart* (1944) and *A Walk in the Sun*. Sinatra used Conte again in the aquatic caper movie *Assault on a Queen*, his noble attempt to prop up this waterlogged vehicle earning him the part of long-suffering Lieutenant Santini in the *Tony Rome* movies. Puerto Rican actor Henry Silva - cast in *Viva Zapata!* by Kazan - got the only other significant gang member role, playing smooth-talking recruitment officer Roger Corneal. A character actor much admired by Sinatra, Silva accepted the star's unshakeable belief in the potency of the first take: 'when you work with him, he sets the tone'. Well able to match Sinatra's shooting pace, Silva went on to roles in *Sergeants 3* and *The Manchurian Candidate*, the latter featuring a highly impressive karate battle between the two men. Stranded in the thankless role of Lawford's dodgy prospective step-father, former *Gay Caballero* Cesar Romero displayed the same unbending professionalism-in-the-face-of-crap he later brought to *Marriage on the Rocks*, investing Duke Santos with a hard-edged, easy charm. The part of perpetually flustered criminal mastermind Spyros went to Moscow Art Theatre graduate Akim Tamiroff, memorably strangled by Orson Welles in *Touch of Evil* (1958). Sinatra also found a small role for actress Patrice Wymore, recently left a struggling single parent by the premature death of husband Errol Flynn, hellraiser *extraordinaire*. Sinatra gave each member of the cast a leather-bound script holder, though flimsy cardboard would have been more appropriate.

Obtaining official permission to shoot *Ocean* on the required Las Vegas locations presented few problems, though the local police chief expressed reservations about the script, fearing possible imitation. Filmed over a two-month period, the *Ocean* production commenced with the extensive Vegas shoot, completed between 26 January and 16 February 1960. The Desert Inn, The Sands, The Sahara, The Riviera and The Flamingos had all consented to the production using their casinos, thereby earning themselves both film immortality and a once-in-a-lifetime publicity break. The hotels also agreed to keep their Christmas decorations up for the filming, in keeping with the festive backdrop essential to the plot. With all five establishments retaining their round-the-clock opening hours during the shoot, Sinatra often needed eight hotel security guards to clear his way through the crowds.

Still the benevolent boss, Sinatra arranged to have specially catered lunches delivered every day of the shoot for the cast and crew on call. The star also insisted on everyone joining him in his dressing room to eat – a friendly if somewhat cramped arrangement. Sinatra and Lawford resumed their firecracker battle from *Never So Few*, which at least provided a contrast to the otherwise extremely relaxed working atmosphere. Aware that the non-Summit gang members had precious little to do, Sinatra attempted to redress

the balance, giving two of his own lines to Buddy Lester in one scene rather than have the actor rendered mute. Present on set even for the scenes without his character, Sinatra liked to stand next to Milestone when not in front of the camera, ensuring that his director didn't want for creative input. This direction-by-proxy sounds like a blatant usurpation of Milestone's authority, yet the latter appeared not to mind at all, later remarking that Sinatra was really quite easy to work with once a director understood his needs. As Angie Dickinson explained to biographer Nick Tosches: 'He knew exactly who was signing his check.' The finished film certainly bears little sign of creative clashes, not that creativity of any kind is much in evidence. The location shoot threw up a few technical headaches, some of them insurmountable. A short scene in a hotel bathroom had to be scrapped after highly audible airplane noise ruined four takes in a row. One unexpected slowdown in the production resulted from Davis' insistence on occupying his hands with a lit cigarette during a conference scene. Having advised against this particular prop, Sinatra permitted his co-star the humbling experience of attempting to match multiple cigarettes between shots, each one carefully burned down to resemble its predecessor.

Along with their day job on *Ocean's 11*, Sinatra, Martin, Lawford, Davis and Bishop all agreed to play evening dates at The Sands Hotel's Copa Room during the location shoot. Interestingly, the idea came from hotel boss Jack Entratter rather than Sinatra, the latter presumably feeling that The Sands had already done pretty well out of the deal. Whatever his reservations, the attraction of parading the new Summit group before a live audience proved irresistible. Both Sinatra and Martin owned shares in The Sands, which doubtless helped sway their minds in Entratter's favour. If Warner had any doubts about this arrangement, there was little they could do to stop it, the after-hours shows not open to negotiation. Sinatra originally intended to ration out the Copa performances evenly, with his fellow Clansmen not working at night if they had a heavy shooting day lined up, but the arrangement didn't last beyond the first

Ocean's 11 - The Clan hog centre stage while Akim Tamiroff holds forth.
Richard Conte and Henry Silva steal the scene with a left-right pincer action.

evening. Supposedly on stage for a solo act, Bishop was rapidly joined by his co-stars, first as onlookers, then participants. The Summit members often did two shows a night, their 5am finish leaving them precious little time for sleep before getting back to work on the film the next day. This sounds like an arrangement guaranteed to provoke complete physical and mental breakdown after a few days, yet it appeared to suit Sinatra perfectly well. Awaking mid-morning, the star took care of his various business interests while relaxing in the Sands' steam room, filming not beginning until noon. After the day's shoot, he returned to the steam room around 7pm, grabbing a bite to eat before the first show. Sinatra even found time for a cameo appearance in George Sidney's epic all-star comedy flop *Pepe* (1960, see Appendix 1), recruiting most of *Ocean*'s principal cast for split-second guest roles. The other Summit members weren't quite so robust, Davis in particular flagging badly towards the end of the shoot. Diagnosed with nervous exhaustion, he was later hospitalised for a week. A huge draw for both

press and paying customers, the five-man Sands shows would never be repeated. According to Tosches, the Summit members finished their last Copa Room performance on 16 February and caught the night train to Los Angeles, ready for work at the Warner studio complex the next morning. The interior scenes were completed by 23 March, leaving only the two Cahn-Van Heusen songs written for the film. Working with Nelson Riddle, Martin recorded 'Ain't That a Kick in the Head' on 10 May, with Davis contributing the theme song a little later.

It's usually a bad sign when a caper movie can't even establish the number of men in the gang. The title *Ocean's 11* implies a grand total of 12, as does the original promotional material, yet there are clearly only ten men under Danny Ocean's command, making them one short of a dirty dozen. True, 'Ocean's Ten' doesn't have quite the same ring, but this basic error reflects the kind of sloppy thinking that pervades the entire film. Given half-competent handling, *Ocean's 11* could at least have delivered a few professional thrills, with even a little suspense thrown in. The storyline is sound, if unexceptional, with a group of ex-army buddies developing an elaborate scheme to rob five Las Vegas casino safes simultaneously under the cover of New Year's Eve celebrations. Unfortunately, this premise is wasted by a script that relies on cheap melodramatics and absurdly contrived plot devices, displaying all the thought and craft of a mediocre television episode. Milestone's bland direction doesn't help, doing very little with the characters, locations or the wide Panavision format. Aside from some quite effective tracking shots of the luminous footprints used to map out the gang's routes through Vegas, he brings almost no visual flair to the proceedings, underlining the sense of professional indifference that characterises the film. The prolonged, extremely detailed build-up to the multiple robberies generates no excitement at all, with too many of the procedures laboriously repeated five times over. Sinatra is rumoured to have removed several scenes from the overlong script, in which case he should have ripped out a few more pages. Not that this would have remedied the monotonous, plodding pace. Nelson Riddle lapses into his usual tendency to overscore, and both Martin and Davis are obliged to reprise their songs twice, as if they were being paid repeat fees.

The former members of the 82nd Airborne Division are mostly a very sorry bunch. Spoiled rich kid Peter Lawford is a reluctant mother's boy, her smothering attention sapping him of the will to strike out and make his own life. He says. Sammy Davis Jnr's character is a Distinguished Service Medal winner turned failed baseball player turned garbage truck driver, his sporting career wrecked by blindness in one eye (wartime injury?), a curious reference to the 1954 car accident that cost Davis his left eye. Despite having his role built up during filming at Sinatra's request, Joey Bishop's slow-witted ex-boxer still gets precious little to do, not even throwing a punch. Richard Conte plays a cancer-ridden ex-convict, estranged from his wife and young son, whose sudden death provides the film with its ironic final twist, an MPAA-friendly 'Crime Does Not Pay' coda. The only member of the gang to generate any sympathy, Conte's role appears to have been reduced during post-production, as stills depict a street scene where Sinatra and Lawford help their ailing friend that doesn't feature in the existing film. Henry Silva aside, the remainder of the 11 are there just to make up the numbers. Even with the wide frame at his disposal, Milestone only manages to get them all on screen together in two scenes. If *Ocean* doesn't care about its characters, there is little reason for the audience to take an interest. The oft-mentioned cameo appearances from George Raft, Red Skelton and an unbilled Shirley MacLaine are a waste of space, the latter's turn as a drunken reveller seeming to go on forever. MacLaine subsequently referred to the film as '...some stupid Mob-caper-Vegas movie', revealing how much attention she'd paid to the script. Warner paid her with a new car, though a rusty second-hand bicycle would have been over-generous. Sinatra's own performance as an Army Sergeant turned professional gambler is a disappointing walk-through, his occasional attempts at humour falling painfully flat. Other than his leadership abilities and irresistible attraction to much younger women, Ocean is barely characterised at all. Separated from wife Bea, he attempts to explain himself to her with a singularly unrevealing mini-speech: 'I did not invent myself...I do not own the patent and I can't change it any more than you can...' Intense.

Nearly four decades on, the most interesting aspect of *Ocean's 11* is the highly unflattering portrayal of Las Vegas. Given the co-operation afforded the film by the casinos and the stars' own professional interests in the place, this cannot have been intentional, yet Vegas emerges as a vulgar, glittering trash pile, a leeching, amoral playground for the rich, idle and dim. With poor security no less. Perhaps there was just no way of glamorising or sanitising its true character. Sammy Davis Jnr once described Las Vegas as 'my spiritual home', which is very depressing.

Safely in the can, *Ocean's 11* looked certain to turn a serious profit months before it opened. On 15 June, Warner announced that the film had attracted over $1 million in advance bookings. Anticipating a major commercial success, the studio devised an appropriately bold advertising campaign: 'That Big One!...Nobody else would have dared it because nobody else would have the nerve!' Premiered at the Fremont Theatre, Las Vegas on 13 August 1960, *Ocean* was a smash hit with audiences, no-one overly bothered by the now out-of-season Christmas setting. It broke the record set by *From Here to Eternity* during its run at the Capitol Theater, New York, ending up as the year's ninth biggest domestic hit. Reviewers weren't so enthusiastic, several bothered by *Ocean*'s depiction of its criminal heroes. The *Los Angeles Examiner* felt obliged to issue a parental warning: 'something you should keep your children away from'. Bosley Crowther, often a Sinatra ally, expressed outrage at the film's approach to its subject, condemning 'the surprisingly nonchalant and flippant attitude toward crime, an attitude so amoral it roadblocks a lot of valid gags'. *Ocean* didn't deserve such impassioned outrage. Crowther wasn't much impressed by the style, either: 'an admiring wide-screen color travelogue of the various effluvia - animate and inanimate - of Las Vegas'. Untouched by *Can Can*'s poor showing earlier in the year, Sinatra finished 1960 at number six in the movie star top ten, beaten only by Rock Hudson, Cary Grant, James Stewart, Doris Day and Debbie Reynolds. His good friends the Lawfords went on to make $480,000 from their share in the profits, a pretty good return on the original $10,000 stake.

THE DEVIL AT 4 O'CLOCK 1961

It is hard for a man to be brave when he knows he is going to meet the devil at four o'clock.
Old proverb (apparently).

God? Who's he?
Harry the convict.

Filmed nearly a decade before *Airport* (1969) set the great disaster movie cycle in motion, *The Devil at 4*

O'Clock offers most of the staple ingredients plus a strong dose of Hollywood preachiness: three convicts, two priests, an ex-prostitute, assorted leprous yet photogenic children, a beautiful blind girl, a cynical ace pilot, an isolated island, numerous frightened townspeople and a volcanic mini-apocalypse. Burdened with an awkward script, by-the-numbers characters and variable special effects, the film is a clear triumph of competence over inspiration, directed with detached professionalism by Mervyn LeRoy. Somehow *Devil* works better than it should, spicing up the adventure storyline with such lofty themes as spiritual faith in a secular world, social prejudice, human frailty and moral relativism. Set on the fictional island of Talua, a French colony somewhere in the South Pacific, the film matches Sinatra's amoral career criminal against Spencer Tracy's disillusioned, booze-slugging priest, both men finding personal redemption through their brief encounter before sacrificing themselves to save others. Sentimental, ponderous and in several ways rather stupid, this is still a curiously affecting experience, transcending the hackneyed absurdities of the script with its sense of heroism through sheer pig-headedness. *The Devil at 4 O'Clock* is not prime Sinatra by any means but one has to admire a star prepared to portray a character who shouts abuse at a sick child, attempts to steal from a church poor box and takes sexual advantage of a blind woman.

Sinatra had become friendly with Tracy during their regular visits to the dying Humphrey Bogart back in 1957. A star since the early 1930s, Tracy had recently finished work on Stanley Kramer's evolutionary courtroom drama *Inherit the Wind* (1960), and *Devil* would be his only non-Kramer film of the 1960s. Intrigued by Liam O'Brien's script, Tracy passed up a chance to go on a world tour with his *Inherit* sparring partner Fredric March, the proposed dates clashing with the production schedule. *Devil* marked his fourth outing as a movie priest, following on from *San Francisco* (1936), *Boy's Town* (1938) and *Men of Boy's Town* (1941). Raised as a devout Catholic, Tracy had seriously considered taking holy orders for real at the

The Devil at 4 O'Clock – Sinatra waits between shots with Gregoire Aslan, Bernie Hamilton and Spencer Tracy.

age of 17, impressed by the power, authority and respect accorded his Jesuit teachers (gangsters could produce much the same effect). Tracy told his friend and biographer Garsin Kanin that he felt completely at home impersonating a holy man, more so than in any other role: '...Those were always my most comfortable parts.' Furthermore, he hadn't enjoyed a major box-office hit since *Bad Day at Black Rock* in 1955 and

Devil looked a highly commercial property on paper. Sinatra's agreement to give Tracy top billing on the film received wide press coverage, the former declaring he wouldn't have conceded the number one spot to any other star. Sinatra hadn't been second-billed since *Pal Joey* - a charitable gesture towards fading co-star Rita Hayworth - and *Devil* marked the last time. Even here, it was more a case of equal billing, Tracy's name given the preferential left-side placing on the credits, with Sinatra across to the right.

Devil also saw a belated reunion between Sinatra and his *House I Live In* collaborator Mervyn LeRoy (see Appendix 3). A cousin of *Miracle of the Bells* producer Jesse L. Lasky, LeRoy had made his name at Warner Brothers, directing such acclaimed Depression-era melodramas as *Little Caesar*, and *I Am a Fugitive from a Chain Gang* (1932). His most notable recent work was the strange moral fable *The Bad Seed* (1956), another Warner release. According to LeRoy, Columbia had owned the rights to Max Catto's novel *The Devil at 4 O'Clock* for several years, investing a substantial preproduction budget in the projected film version. Despite the Sinatra-Tracy star teaming, a number of directors had already turned *Devil* down, put off by the logistics of staging a series of natural disasters in the service of an indifferent script. Unenthusiastic about the story, LeRoy accepted the assignment at the personal request of Sinatra and Tracy, reworking O'Brien's screenplay in collaboration with producer Fred Kohlmar. With William Daniels unavailable, the director of photography job went to Joseph Biroc, whose credits included *It's a Wonderful Life, Bwana Devil* (1953) - the first film shot in 3D - and *Attack!* (1956). A fast-working craftsman, Biroc earned the Sinatra seal of approval on *The Devil at 4 O'Clock*, rejoining the star for *4 for Texas, Tony Rome, The Detective* and *Lady in Cement*. Columbia house composer George Duning had worked on the previous Sinatra efforts *From Here to Eternity* and *Pal Joey*, his score for *Devil* more impressive than either of these, complete with a heavenly choir.

If the supporting cast for *Devil* lacked the big-name cameos later common in the disaster genre, the actors largely made up for it in dogged conviction. For the part of a womanising pilot the producers chose French star Jean-Pierre Aumont, whose American credits included *The Cross of Lorraine* (1943) and *Jean Paul Jones* (1959). The role of Tracy's idealistic young successor went to Kerwin Mathews, taking time out from battling assorted animated monsters as Sinbad,

Gulliver and Jack the Giant Killer. Sinatra's fellow convicts were played by Gregoire Aslan and Bernie Hamilton, the latter nearly 15 years away from ordering Starsky and Hutch into his office at regular intervals. Barbara Luna got the role of innocent blind orphan Camille, who attracts Sinatra's lust, then his affection ('That's a chick, man'). She's not a particularly good actress, but then it's not a particularly good part.

Filming commenced in early October 1960, with extensive location work on the Hawaiian island of Maui, second largest of the group. Shooting mostly in the Lahaina district, the production crew constructed an entire village to be shaken and burned up by the forces of nature. Their own accommodation was a little less flimsy, most of the personnel based at Kula Lodge up on Haleakala mountain. Katherine Hepburn accompanied the 60-year-old Tracy to Maui, spending most of her time on-set watching him at work. Amicable for much of the shoot, Tracy became annoyed when Columbia allowed journalists onto the location to interview him without his prior consent, unit publicist Bob Yeager receiving the brunt of the star's wrath. Tracy also contracted severe diarrhoea, for which Yeager was entirely blameless. Co-star Aumont recalled the production as extremely fraught, claiming that LeRoy would shout at Biroc, who shouted at soundman Josh Westmoreland, who shouted at assistant directors Carter De Haven Jnr - Gloria's brother - and Floyd Joyer. They, in turn, shouted at the extras. One suspects Aumont exaggerates just a little, the level of noise being no higher up the decibel scale than most other busy location shoots. Aumont also claims that Kennedy-supporter Sinatra spent his mornings out on the Democrat campaign trail with Peter Lawford, touring all over the islands in his private plane. He certainly staged a Kennedy benefit performance during the production, presumably with the blessing of LeRoy and Columbia. Ineligible to vote in the forthcoming election, Aumont and fellow French co-star Marcel Dalio got little out of Sinatra other than an occasional brief 'Hello'. According to Aumont, Tracy was noticeably unwell, only able to work a few hours during the morning. By the time Sinatra returned from his political canvassing in the early afternoon, his co-star had already quit for the day. Given the number of scenes they share, not to mention the physical demands of Tracy's role, this account smacks of amusing apocryphal anecdote. According to LeRoy, Tracy was in relatively good health, as yet unaffected by the lung disease that eventually killed him. LeRoy turned 60 himself during the location shoot, celebrating with over 70 guests and a specially written musical tribute from Sinatra, lyrics courtesy of Sammy Cahn.

The Maui shoot wrapped on 1 November, with Sinatra departing immediately to make a guest appearance on Dean Martin's television show that evening (he arrived a little late). The studio work proceeded smoothly enough until 16 November, when Tracy's old MGM comrade Clark Gable died of a heart attack. Aumont felt the news had a beneficial calming effect on *Devil*'s Hollywood crew, no-one wishing to follow Gable into cardiac arrest. Taking three day's compassionate leave from the production, Tracy served as a pallbearer at his friend's funeral. This unexpected hold-up obliged the Columbia executives to both reschedule and relocate the subsequent filming, switching from the Fox Ranch in Malibu to their own studios on Sunset Boulevard. Sinatra's representatives immediately protested this move, pointing out that the star's contract guaranteed him a Class A lot for all studio filming. Regardless of its undoubted merits, the Sunset complex was definitely Class B. With a large mock-up airplane set already built, Columbia was effectively forced to up sticks once more and shift the production to their unquestionably Class A studios on Gower Street, constructing another expensive dummy aeroplane from scratch. LeRoy's biggest technical challenge was the 'Devil's' climactic eruption, culminating in the entire island blowing up. While some of the required footage was shot on Maui, most of the sequence had to be filmed on a sound stage, with a fake mountain built out near La Jolla, on a farm belonging to one Gil Hodges. Filming finally wrapped in January 1961, LeRoy pronouncing himself satisfied with the end result.

Given their enduring friendship both before and after the *Devil* shoot, it's surprising how much conjecture surrounds the Sinatra-Tracy relationship during filming. Several insiders on the *Devil* production attributed Sinatra's petty-minded attitude over studio sizes to mounting tension between himself and Tracy, and the assembled press were certainly hoping for a few star tantrums. It's true that Sinatra had no previous professional experience of the man he nicknamed 'Grey Fox', despite earlier talk of them co-starring in the film version of *Exodus* (1960, see Appendix 2). There was certainly some trouble over Sinatra's dislike of rehearsals, which once again proved incompatible with his co-star's more disciplined approach. The star was also accused of refusing to deliver his lines off camera while LeRoy shot close-ups of Tracy, the latter having to make do with a script girl and a broomstick substituting for Sinatra. Providing the required dialogue and reactions for another performer's close-up is regarded as a basic professional courtesy by most actors and Tracy is said to have resented his co-star's bad manners. For the defence, Sinatra responded to the rumours by claiming that he'd been present for all Tracy's scenes, even when he wasn't needed on the shoot, keen to learn from an old master. They did at least share an antipathy towards multiple takes, Tracy seconding Sinatra's view that freshness and spontaneity were invariably lost with repetition. Acknowledging the differences in their working methods, Tracy denied any serious arguments, promoting his co-star as a benevolent boss. Despite the billing, Tracy could be in no doubt that the production was controlled by Sinatra, as he explained to visiting reporters: 'Nobody at Metro ever had the financial power Frank Sinatra has today'. For all his status as one of the industry's revered elder statesmen, Tracy was no longer a major box-office name, with even *Inherit the Wind* proving a commercial disappointment. Tracy's biggest worry over his co-star was Sinatra's lack of sleep, the latter occasionally joining him for an early breakfast less than two hours after he'd gone to bed. Six years on, Tracy broke his reclusive habits to attend Sinatra and Mia Farrow's wedding reception in July 1966. A year

The Devil at 4 O'Clock – Spencer Tracy as Father Doonan.

later, Sinatra served as a pallbearer at Tracy's funeral on 12 June 1967. LeRoy claimed to have had minimal trouble with Sinatra, director and star only disagreeing over one close-up. Sinatra felt it was unnecessary, consenting to LeRoy's request with obvious reluctance, then asking to be released from the afternoon shoot two hours early. Sensing a possible mutiny, the director agreed, returning from the shoot at seven o'clock to discover an apologetic note under his hotel door. That evening, Sinatra cooked a spaghetti dinner for the entire cast and crew.

Adapted without much finesse from a lengthy novel, the script for *Devil* is serviceable at best, struggling to juggle characters and subplots while forging ahead with the main storyline. The dialogue includes such gems as 'Some priest. Cognac and sex magazines' and 'Like I said Mr Priest, I don't dig chapels.' Kerwin Mathews' character serves largely as a device for developing Tracy's Father Doonan, hearing the latter's sad story from the leprosy hospital's atheist doctor. Once Doonan's struggle to care for the diseased children in

the face of local prejudice and hostility is established, Mathews has little else to do, invalided out of the action with a convenient broken leg. The film works better on a visual and emotional level, though even here there is often a feeling of uninspired Hollywood production-line. The effective location work is undermined by very obvious studio shots, with far too much of the climactic escape down a treacherous mountain filmed on sound stages, the cast dodging outrageously fake lava streams. LeRoy does come up with a few nice touches, notably the smouldering 'Old Devil' volcano ever present in the background, and the earthquake effects - shaking camera and all - are still impressive. At the tender age of six, LeRoy had lived through the 1906 San Francisco earthquake, giving him rare first-hand experience of the phenomenon.

With his craggy, imposing features and whiter-than-white hair, Spencer Tracy is a dominating screen presence with or without decent dialogue. A survivor of New York's Hells Kitchen, the Irish-American Doonan was his first drunken priest, the former element uncomfortably close to home. Still a fierce humanitarian despite his loss of faith in God, Doonan protects the rights of Sinatra's not very likeable convict band, only to punch out Sinatra when he makes a move on Camille. His church boycotted by the resentful islanders, Doonan has survived only on his devotion to the leprous children, their steady recovery mirrored by his gradual physical and spiritual dissolution. Biographer Bill Davidson claims that Tracy had become increasingly drawn to his childhood faith as he grew older and more aware of his own mortality. He certainly plays his role for all it's worth and some more on top. Sinatra's Harry is not quite so impressive, largely because the character is too sketchily drawn to generate much interest or sympathy. All Harry's actions and abilities blatantly stem from the requirements of the script rather any sense of personality or motivation. He served in Korea and can thus show Doonan and his fellow convicts how to parachute down to the isolated hospital. He agrees to help rescue the children in the hope of having his prison sentence reduced, enabling his later sudden transformation from sinner to saint. Even Harry's rough New Jersey childhood serves only to contrast his and Doonan's wildly different lives after starting from similar backgrounds. The trip down the mountain to save the children who previously repelled him becomes Harry's journey into salvation, marked by his off-screen marriage to Camille (as unbelievable as it sounds). Preoccupied with the Kennedy campaign during the *Devil* shoot, Sinatra allegedly rushed through his location scenes in order to get back to the mainland and lead the east coast showbusiness support for the Democrat's struggling presidential candidate. The Kennedy connection had been partly responsible for Sinatra's public humiliation during the *Private Slovik* fiasco earlier in the year (see Appendix 2), and there's a case for arguing that *Devil* also suffered from the star's commitment to the JFK bandwagon. That said, Sinatra plays his scenes with more than professional competence throughout, bringing Harry to melodramatic life as the character approaches his martyrdom. With the children and hospital staff safely

stowed on a departing boat, Harry chooses to return up the mountain where Doonan is trapped on the wrong side of a ravine by a collapsed bridge. Having bid new bride Camille a fond farewell - 'Be good and be happy' - he waits with Doonan for the final eruption, apparently unfazed by their imminent demise: 'Just you and me, pops. New Jersey and New York.' There is presumably some irony intended in a priest's faith being restored by a godless convict, though Sinatra crosses himself just before the big bang. Trite and sentimental, perhaps, but it's a strangely haunting finale.

Released on 16 July 1961, *The Devil at 4 O'Clock* was an unqualified flop in the United States, interesting neither critics nor filmgoers. For the record, LeRoy later claimed that his film did much better at the international box-office than was generally thought and it's safe to assume that *Devil* eventually broke even. Tracy expressed surprise at the lack of audience interest, though he'd never actually seen the finished film, unwilling to look at his ageing features magnified on a cinema screen. Back with his fellow clansmen for *Sergeants 3*, Sinatra hoped to counter *Devil*'s poor showing with another *Ocean's 11*-style hit. Second time around, audiences were wise to him.

SERGEANTS 3 1961

It probably seemed a good idea at the time: a western remake of the Indian North-West frontier adventure *Gunga Din* (1939), with cavalry officers standing in for the original British soldiers, hostile Red Indians/Native Americans instead of murderous Indian Thugs and an ex-slave bugler replacing the heroic native water bearer. The male-bonding element of the story was tailor-made for the Clan image and the post-Civil War setting gave Sinatra the chance to flaunt his liberal credentials in light-hearted fashion, Sammy Davis Jnr's character treated as an equal by his army buddies. Hot from his success with *The Magnificent Seven*, John Sturges agreed to take up the director's chair, guaranteeing first-rate battle sequences if nothing else. Davis rated the end result as the best of the Clan efforts, with the strongest storyline and most action. Sturges certainly orchestrates the latter element with much of his usual flair, yet the elements largely fail to blend. As with *4 for Texas* two years later, the knockabout antics and in-jokes sit uneasily with the more realistic bloodshed, while the often frantic pacing soon becomes tiresome. The leading performances exhibit little sign of directorial control, the Summit gang playing 'themselves' rather than making any discernible attempt at characterisation. Sinatra and friends appear to have had a good time making it but there's little in *Sergeants* to let audiences in on the joke. Besides, no film with a leading character called Mike Merry was ever much good.

With United Artists lined up as the distributor, *Sergeants* marked the first and only co-production between Sinatra's Essex subsidiary and Dean Martin's Claude Productions, Incorporated, founded in 1960. This arrangement gave Martin both a bigger cut of the profits and more say in the production, enabling him to cast old friend Sonny King in a small role. A western fanatic all his life, Sammy Davis Jnr possessed an in-depth knowledge of the role played by black soldiers and cowboys in the history of the American West and had long wished to play such characters on screen. His costume for *Sergeants* included the hat worn by John Wayne in *Stagecoach* (1939), a personal gift from the Duke. Davis' original deal with Sinatra and Essex paid him a straight salary of $125,000. After Davis' marriage to Swedish starlet May Britt on 13 November 1960, Sinatra revised the contract, paying his co-star $75,000 up front plus seven percent of the box-office gross. Aware of Davis' rather casual treatment of money, Sinatra felt he needed a steady income to support his future family, reckoning that the *Sergeants* profits should net Davis around $250,000 over the next few years. If this sounds a little too paternalistic, not to say patronising, Davis appeared grateful for his mentor's consideration. The role of Sergeant number three went to Peter Lawford, making his fourth appearance in a Sinatra movie. His Kennedy connections ensured it would also be his last, though for reasons no-one

appeared to envisage at the time. Joey Bishop had to settle for the non-titular role of a Sergeant Major, his second and final appearance with Sinatra, the comedian abruptly dropped from the latter's circle after a disagreement. Of the second division *Ocean* gang members, only Henry Silva got a look-in here, cast as a very non-PC Indian renegade. The token glamour role went to Ruta Lee, who'd impressed Sinatra with her performance in Billy Wilder's *Witness for the Prosecution* (1958). Rating Martin as the most laid-back and amiable of the Clan, Lee felt he kept Sinatra's more volatile character in check, though not enough to prevent the latter from regularly telephoning acquaintances and firing blanks down the receiver. As a favour to Bing Crosby, Sinatra handed out bit parts to three of the crooner's sons, Phillip, Dennis and Lindsay, none of whom make any impression at all.

Essex Production's executive producer for *Sergeants* was poverty row auteur Howard W. Koch, a former assistant editor, assistant director and second-unit director who'd spent much of the 1950s churning out such 'B' efforts as *The Black Sleep* (1956), *Bop Girl* (1957), *Jungle Heat* (1957) and *Frankenstein 1970* (1958). Boris Karloff, star of the latter film, didn't rate Koch's directing talent at all and his change of metier for Frank Sinatra Enterprises proved a fortunate career move. The selection of collaborators for *Sergeants* promised results that the finished film could never hope to deliver. For the made-to-measure script, Sinatra and Sturges turned to respected novelist W.R. Burnett, whose film credits included *Scarface* (1932), *High Sierra* (1941) and *The Asphalt Jungle*. Burnett would shortly reunite with Sturges for *The Great Escape*, a more profitable use of both men's talents. Academy Award-winning cameraman Winton Hoch was a John Ford regular, working on *She Wore a Yellow Ribbon* (1949), *The Quiet Man* (1952) and *The Searchers*. The score came courtesy of ex-jazz trumpeter Billy May, one of Sinatra's regular arrangers. May's subsequent contribution to his employer's film career was limited to scoring *Tony Rome* and arranging *Lady in Cement*, both better suited to his 'swinging' style than *Sergeants*.

The biggest headache engendered by *Sergeants 3* derived from its problematic intended title. Burnett's script began life as *Badlands*, which no-one particularly liked, leaving Terrence Malick free to use it a decade later. Before shooting began, the title was officially changed to *Soldiers 3*, retaining the distinctive, if pointless, numbering system pioneered by *Ocean's 11*. MGM immediately objected to the new moniker, justifiably concerned over its similarity to *Soldiers Three* (1951), a more faithful - if equally unofficial - *Gunga Din* remake starring Stewart Granger, David Niven and Robert Newton. Hoping to retain the title while avoiding any legal action, Sinatra attempted a peace-making deal with his old studio. In exchange for MGM waiving their objection, he would make a guest appearance in their forthcoming all-star production *How the West Was Won* (1962) free of charge. Already well-stocked with star names for the film, the studio did not immediately respond, leaving *Sergeants* untitled for much of the shoot. Somewhere along the line, either MGM finally said no or Sinatra lost interest in the deal and the less resonant compromise title came into being.

Sergeants was filmed over May, June and July 1961, with a break between the location and studio shoots. Koch arrived in Kanab, Utah a few days before the bulk of the production team to film second unit footage with a skeleton crew, led by *Frankenstein 1970* colleague Carl Guthrie. Sinatra unexpectedly appeared the next day, flying in from Las Vegas onto the local schoolyard employed as an impromptu landing strip by the production (the school got $5,000 worth of equipment from Sinatra as a thank-you). The producer-star wanted to look at the rushes immediately, unfazed by the lack of suitable projection equipment. Sensing that Sinatra's insistence represented some form of initiation test, Koch sent an SOS message to Kirk Douglas, whose downbeat modern-day western *Lonely Are the Brave* (1962) was shooting in nearby New Mexico. Douglas agreed to lend the beleaguered producer a projection unit, which Koch collected by plane. Four hours after his original request, Sinatra sat down to view the footage. One hopes the results were worth it. Koch

certainly benefited from his show of quick-thinking. Post-*Sergeants*, he would oversee five more Sinatra productions.

Working on the isolated Kanab desert locations with no Vegas-style entertainments to divert them after-hours, the stars rapidly succumbed to intense boredom. Tiring of poker games and fun with imported prostitutes, they took to watching Laurel and Hardy films, not that any comic inspiration rubbed off onto the work in progress. Despite having his pals all based on the same floor of the local hotel, Sinatra felt they were still too distant from each other, ordering the management to install connecting doors between their rooms, an alteration charged to the film's budget. Martin's 44th birthday on 7 June provided the stars with an excuse for a Las Vegas party, attended by the likes of Elizabeth Taylor and Marilyn Monroe, the latter rumoured to be dating Sinatra. With so little happening off the set, the actual shooting seemed like undiluted pleasure by comparison, and little of the Sinatra temperament surfaced. Always happy to perform as many of his own stunts as possible, Sinatra agreed to be dragged underneath a runaway wagon while Martin was thrown about inside, the only injuries incurred during the sequence caused by the latter's boots crushing his fingers. Lawford couldn't match his co-stars in the action stakes, afflicted by an arm crippled during childhood when he'd put it through a glass pane. The severed muscles, tendons and arteries had never properly healed, obliging Lawford's stand-in Ken DuMain to handle even relatively simple 'stunts' such as climbing a ladder. If Lawford found this a little humiliating, there was worse to come. Every evening, Sturges assembled his cast for a screening of the daily rushes in the basement of the ever-obliging local school. Largely inactive since the *Ocean* production over a year earlier, Lawford had put on 30 pounds of flab, the surplus weight particularly noticeable on screen. According to James Spada, fun-loving joker Sinatra liked to greet his co-star's scenes with a cry of 'There's fat boy'. Stung by this jibe, Lawford responded by knocking back Dexedrine to effect a rapid weight loss.

Sergeants 3 – Plus Bugler 1.

Having shed his excess bulk less than halfway into the shoot, he took some satisfaction in shutting Sinatra up, though the wardrobe people probably didn't thank him for the extra work on costume alterations. Unbeknown to most of the cast and crew, Martin was suffering from a rather more serious condition during the shoot, his arthritic spine giving him long periods of intense discomfort.

Back in Hollywood, the stars continued their by now traditional pursuit of on-set practical jokes. Dressing rooms were the preferred target, with smoke bombs regularly thrown in to cause maximum inconvenience. Martin went one better, filling Sinatra's room with so many balloons that the star couldn't get inside. Back on the set, the cast and crew were obliged to take drastic measures when the balloons began to

burst, spoiling several takes in a row. One mass balloon popping later, work resumed with no further setbacks.

With *Sergeants* well into post-production, the Essex-Claude office received a communication from the owners of the original *Gunga Din* film. Perhaps inspired by MGM's earlier action, they pointed out that the RKO production was still under copyright, which *Sergeants* clearly breached. Unless the new film's producers paid up for the remake rights, they would launch a plagiarism suit. Given MGM's failure to obtain official permission for *Soldiers Three*, it's highly unlikely such a court action would have succeeded but with the legal wranglings threatening to postpone *Sergeants*' release, Sinatra was persuaded to pay out a token sum. Original author Rudyard Kipling was unavailable for comment. United Artists premiered the film on 7 January 1962, with Sinatra attending a benefit screening for handicapped children at the Capitol Theater, New York on 10 February. Despite this charitable gesture and radio support in the form of several high profile 'Frank Sinatra Days', *Sergeants* failed to match *Ocean*'s success by a long way. If the latter film had been indifferently reviewed, response to the second Clan outing was downright hostile, *Time* magazine sneering: 'Sinatra and his cub scout troupe are pioneering in a new art form: the $4 million home movie.' *Sunday Express* critic Thomas Wiseman expressed a sentiment that would haunt the Summit players until the end of their brief screen alliance: 'Sergeants 3 gives the impression of having been made for the private amusement of members of Sinatra's Hollywood clan...' With domestic receipts far less than expected, *Sergeants* was saved from box-office oblivion only by its surprise success in Europe.

The film also marked the end of the Clan buddies line-up established with *Ocean*. The original idea had been for a five-year, five-film deal where the group took it in turns to receive the lion's share of the profits. No-one objected to Sinatra getting first go, but Lawford expressed unhappiness over the star's alleged refusal to reduce either his fee or his percentage for the later outings. Now working for *Golden Arm* producer-director Otto Preminger, with supporting roles in *Exodus* and *Advise and Consent* (1962), Lawford evidently felt he no longer needed Sinatra's patronage for his movie career to prosper, a delusion shortly to be shattered. Martin would be back for four more Sinatra films, Davis just the one, but the Rat Pack phenomenon would soon breathe its last.

THE MANCHURIAN CANDIDATE 1962

Raymond Shaw is the kindest, bravest, warmest, most wonderful human being I've ever known in my life.
Bennett Marco, brainwashed

I think it's a damn good film...
Frank Sinatra

Controversial, ahead of its time, unseen for many years, *The Manchurian Candidate* is probably Frank Sinatra's finest 126 minutes as a film performer and the one project that could not have made it to the screen without his assistance. Based on an intriguing what-if novel by Richard Condon, the scrupulously faithful film adaptation has lost none of its potency or surprise over the decades, standing as a tribute to creative ambition in the face of industry timidity. First published in 1959, Condon's nightmarish political satire outlines an alarmingly plausible international conspiracy between far-right and far-left to seize control of the United States. Set in 1954, the year after the end of hostilities in Korea, the story centres on Congressional Medal of Honour winner Raymond Shaw. Hailed as a war hero, Shaw is in fact a brainwashed killing machine, the product of a Sino-Soviet-backed plot to put his half-witted ultra-conservative Senator stepfather into the White House. The villain of the piece is Shaw's own mother, controlling both her son and husband like wind-up toys. As much an absurdist black comedy as a paranoia thriller, *Candidate* is a joke with a very serious point, the nervous laughs gradually tailing off as the body count rises and innocent

lives are crushed. When an essentially decent, if alienated young man can be transformed into a dispassionate killer triggered by a pack of cards, all notions of individual morality, conscience or social order become irrelevant. Sixties analyst Ethan Mordden describes the film as simultaneously conservative and innovative, yet it appears more the product of a cynical liberalism, exposing monstrous corruption while at the same time pronouncing it near unbeatable. Cast as dedicated yet impotent army investigator Bennett Marco, a fellow brainwash victim, Sinatra gets the despairing last words: 'Hell... hell'.

Initially seized upon as prime material for filming, *Candidate* rapidly proved to be dangerous goods. A major star snapped up the film rights soon after the book's publication, only to panic over the too-hot subject matter and drop the option. As studio interest in the project cooled off, the rights fell into the hands of director John Frankenheimer, who intended to make the film in collaboration with co-producer and screenwriter George Axelrod. One of the most impressive talents to emerge from American television's 'golden age' of live drama, Frankenheimer's fine debut film *The Young Stranger* (1957) proved a traumatic experience for the movie novice and his big screen career stalled until he teamed with Burt Lancaster for *The Young Savages* (1961) and *Birdman of Alcatraz* (1962). Best known for his Broadway hits *The Seven Year Itch* (1953) and *Will Success Spoil Rock Hunter?* (1955), Axelrod's screen credits included Billy Wilder's 1955 film version of the former, plus *Bus Stop* (1956) and *Breakfast at Tiffany's* (1961). Frankenheimer regarded *Candidate* as his first truly personal project, feeling that the story made an all too valid point regarding the political manipulation and conditioning of American society. The director did his own in-depth research into genuine brainwashing techniques, including some allegedly used during the Korean War to prevent American POWs from attempting to escape. He rated Axelrod's screenplay as one of the best and most faithful book-to-film adaptations ever done. Determined to retain as much of the novel's flavour as possible, Axelrod even used some of Condon's narrative prose as dialogue in his adaptation. With the script completed, Axelrod and Frankenheimer went looking for commercial backing, only to find all the major studios extremely wary of the material. The anti-McCarthy jibes were felt to be too inflammatory, despite the Senator's public, career-killing humiliation back in 1954. Their overtures to independent producer Sinatra - a friend of Axelrod and admirer of Frankenheimer - met with considerably more success, the star eager for an adventurous vehicle free from the growing Clan stigma. A big fan of the book, he was very enthusiastic about starring in a movie version and gave them an immediate yes, intending to make the film through regular distributor United Artists. Both director and writer felt Sinatra was a good choice for the part of Bennett Marco. As Axelrod explained to Robin Douglas-Home at the time, he especially liked the idea of the often bizarre dialogue being delivered by the down-to-earth star, with his '...marvellous, beat-up Sinatra face'. The project then hit a major snag, UA president Arthur Krim informing the producer-star and his associates that he wanted nothing to do with *Candidate* and would try to dissuade any other studio they approached from backing it. About to take office as national finance chairman for the Democratic party, Krim felt that the political storyline - complete with corruption, communist infiltration and assassination - could be both embarrassing and harmful to Kennedy, especially given the ongoing American-Russian negotiations over limiting nuclear tests. Krim also happened to dislike Condon, a former employee during his years as a publicity man. Undeterred, Sinatra visited President Kennedy at his Hyannisport base in September 1961, hoping to obtain an official seal of approval for his project. According to popular legend, Kennedy responded to Sinatra's proposal for the *Candidate* film with: 'That's great, and who's playing the mother?' Whatever the truth of this, the President certainly had no objections to the movie, sharing Sinatra's enthusiasm for Condon's book and his belief in its film potential. At Sinatra's request, Kennedy made a phone call to Arthur Krim, expressing his support for the production. With Krim's objections laid to rest, United Artists finally gave *Candidate* the

The Manchurian Candidate – Bennett Marco tries a yak dung cigarette. Raymond Shaw (Laurence Harvey) isn't impressed.

green light, Sinatra announcing to the press that his role as Marco was the most exciting of his career. He especially liked the character's 'long, wild speeches' in Axelrod's script, though at least one of these would be removed after the first previews. Sinatra was so enamoured of the screenplay, he liked to carry it around with him at all times, reading out his favourite passages to anyone within earshot.

The supporting cast assembled for *Candidate* is one of the strongest ever to grace a Sinatra movie. The biggest surprise was Lithuanian-born British star Laurence Harvey, whose international success as ruthless social climber Joe Lampton in *Room at the Top* (1958) had been largely dissipated by such Hollywood dross as *Butterfield 8* (1960) and *Walk on the Wild Side* (1962). *Candidate* offered a $270,000 fee and Harvey's first decent role since *Room at the Top*. Like Sinatra, he was a fan of the novel and had met Condon during the latter's visit to the *Alamo* set in 1960. Already eager to play brainwashed anti-hero Raymond Shaw on screen, Harvey expressed serious interest in obtaining the film rights, only to be cautioned by the author that the bidding war was very fierce, the figures mentioned way beyond anything he could afford. The more token part of Marco's girlfriend Rosie went to former MGM contract player Janet Leigh, completing her unofficial trilogy of classic paranoia films (*Touch of Evil* and *Psycho* making up parts one and two). Now separated from Tony Curtis, Leigh had been absent from movies for a year, devoting her time to their two young children. An old friend of both Sinatra and executive producer Howard Koch, she didn't need much persuading to sign on for *Candidate*. Angela Lansbury won the role of the evil Mrs Iselin, despite being only three years older than screen son Harvey. Another ex-MGM player, memorably singing 'Goodbye Little Yellow Bird' in *The Picture of Dorian Gray* and 'How D'Ya Like to Spoon With Me?' in *Till the Clouds Roll By*, Lansbury had recently played two more conventional mother roles, nurturing Elvis Presley in *Blue Hawaii* (1961) and Warren Beatty in Frankenheimer's *All Fall Down* (1961). John McGiver, the scene-stealing Tiffany salesman in the Axelrod-scripted *Breakfast*, featured in a brief but highly memorable role as one of Mrs Iselin's ill-fated political opponents, Senator Thomas Jordon. Henry Silva, largely wasted in *Ocean* and *Sergeants*, contributed a first-rate performance as devious Soviet agent Chunjin, the Korean translator and guide who leads Shaw, Marco and their fellow platoon members into the 1952 pre-credits ambush.

Silva aside, Sinatra entrusted most of the support casting to Frankenheimer. James Gregory, Whit Bissell and James Edwards had all appeared in *The Young Stranger*, Albert Paulsen in *All Fall Down*. Cast as Red-baiting Senator John Iselin, Gregory possesses a rubbery, petulant face to rival Leon Errol's, perfectly capturing Iselin's idiot-child character as the Senator endlessly spouts the communist subversion rhetoric drilled into him by his string-pulling wife. Frankenheimer also selected much of the off-camera talent. Director of photography Lionel Lindon was an Academy Award winner for his work on *Around the World in 80 Days* (1956), his only previous, if brief, experience of Sinatra (see Appendix 1). A long-time Bob Hope regular, Lindon had photographed both *The Young Savages* and *All Fall Down* for Frankenheimer. Composer David Amram had also worked on *Young Savages*, his score for *Candidate* capturing the ominous, slightly discordant feel of the overall film.

Production began on 22 January 1962, Frankenheimer committed to a fairly tight schedule despite some major technical challenges. The famously off-kilter brainwashing sequence had to be shot three times over with three sets of actors, staged on differently dressed versions of a set built to allow the 360-degree camera pans essential to the disorientating atmosphere. Aware of how important the film could be to his flagging American career, Harvey threw himself into the role of Raymond Shaw with total dedication and scant regard for his own safety. For the scene where the accidentally triggered Shaw walks into Central Park Lake, he volunteered to take the plunge himself, unconcerned by the freezing cold water on a chill February morning. A potentially hazardous shot such as this would normally be undertaken by a stuntman fitted with a wetsuit underneath his costume. Harvey declined both the double and the insulation, hitting the water to Frankenheimer's satisfaction on the first take, after which he was rushed back to his suite at the Sherry Netherlands Hotel across the park to shed his soaking clothes and dry off. While the subsequent Shaw-Marco dialogue by the lake is fairly obviously faked in a studio, Frankenheimer can be forgiven on this occasion for not insisting on absolute authenticity. Sinatra respected Harvey's dedication to his role, recognising all too well the latter's need to prove critics of his recent work wrong. Sinatra hadn't picked up much acclaim for his own acting since *Some Came Running*, nearly four years earlier.

Most of the climactic assassination sequence was filmed at New York's Madison Square Garden over four days in early February, with hundreds of extras recruited for the political rally where Shaw is supposed to kill the presidential candidate. Shots not requiring the vast background crowd were staged at the smaller Olympic Auditorium, Los Angeles, and back in the studio. Immersed in a supposedly fictional political world, Sinatra's work schedule had to be slightly altered after President Kennedy asked him to perform at a dinner for Senator George Smathers in Miami on Saturday 10 March. The Thursday before the event, the star backed out, supposedly afflicted by laryngitis. Given Sinatra's ongoing commitment to Kennedy, this doesn't appear to have been a deliberate snub, yet it proved strangely prescient in view of subsequent events.

Back on set, Sinatra's most physically demanding scene involved a brilliantly staged and edited karate fight with Henry Silva, Chunjin's reappearance as Shaw's valet acting as the vital catalyst for Marco's recovering memory. Punching, kicking and throwing each other into most of Shaw's furniture, both men end up cut and bruised, Marco finally pinning Chunjin down and stamping on his ribs until the police arrive. Using a double only for the shot where Marco is hurled across the room, Sinatra suffered for his art while shooting the sequence. Karate-chopping a wooden table, he broke both the furniture and his little finger, though the injury went unnoticed until shooting on the sequence was completed, the star having shown no sign of discomfort. The brutal end result was effective enough to give British censor John Trevelyan serious worries over possible imitation, not that there are any records of sudden Karate-mania following *Candidate*'s release. Sinatra appears to have been a model of commitment and good humour during the shoot, impressing cast and crew alike with his hard work. Following Vincente Minnelli's example on *Some Came Running*, Frankenheimer would rehearse the rest of the cast prior to filming, then bring on Sinatra for one last pre-shoot run-through, seldom needing to ask for retakes. Janet Leigh later confessed to having felt a little apprehensive about co-starring with Sinatra, aware of his reputation for unorthodox working methods. She soon realised her worries were groundless; Sinatra treated his fellow actors with courtesy and consideration, rehearsed with them when necessary, contributed his ideas for scenes and never questioned Frankenheimer's authority. With Axelrod on set throughout the filming for consultation and dialogue changes, *Candidate* proved to be one of the smoothest productions of Sinatra's career, Frankenheimer

completing the film in 39 days.

As a piece of film-making, *Candidate* offers a near-faultless blend of technique and imagination, enhanced by the pin-sharp black and white photography and Frankenheimer's astute use of his old television techniques. The scene where Shaw returns home from Korea to a hero's welcome has a surreal documentary style, complete with pompous voice-over. A later press conference uses frenetic camera movements, fast cuts, overlapping shouted dialogue and strobing television screens, making Marco's exposure to the political media circus almost as disorientating as his experiences back in Manchuria (*Candidate* was the first film to employ actual television images rather than fake the small-screen pictures post-production). Featuring some of Richard Sylbert's most innovative production design, the brainwashing scenes - depicted as dream flashbacks - are probably the most distinctive. The captured American soldiers believe they're whiling away a dull afternoon at the Spring Lake Hotel, New Jersey, listening to Mrs Henry Whittaker deliver her lecture 'Fun with Hydrangeas'. As Frankenheimer's camera slowly circles around the room, the middle-aged ladies in the audience and on stage abruptly transform into a gallery of exceptionally ugly, high-ranking communists, a superb piece of editing. The double murder of Senator Jordon and his daughter Jocie (Leslie Parrish), Shaw's new wife, is another *tour de force*. Shaw's gunning down of his father-in-law is chillingly matter-of-fact, the bullet passing through a milk carton clutched in the Senator's left hand, the liquid pouring out like ersatz blood as Jordon drops to the floor. Frankenheimer employs a haunting low angle shot of the zombie-like Shaw exiting the murder scene, Jordon lying dead in the foreground, Jocie's casually bullet-ridden body slumped in the background.

Given the level of cold-blooded carnage in *Candidate*, there is a surprising amount of humour at times. The captured American platoon unwittingly smoke yak dung cigarettes during their mindbending treatment. When a black member of the platoon dreams of the brainwashing sessions, all the ladies at the lecture are black as well. The jokes are viciously undercut by Shaw's test-run murder of

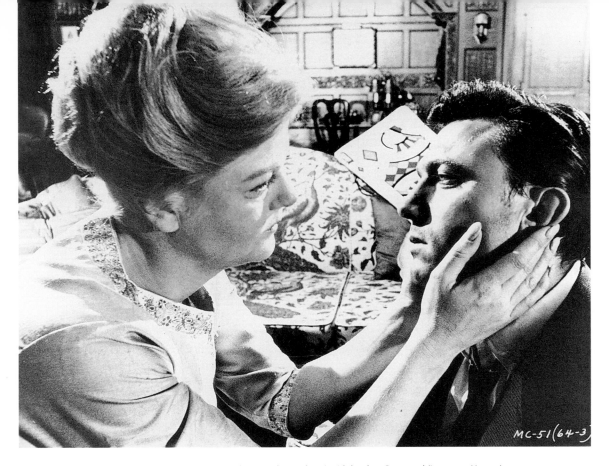

The Manchurian Candidate – Family romance. Mrs Iselin (Angela Lansbury) with her boy Raymond (Laurence Harvey).

two fellow soldiers, one strangled, one shot through the head, his blood spattering onto a blow-up photograph behind him. Elsewhere, a top Soviet scientist takes time out to visit Macy's department store, Marco looks at a book on the history of Mafia financing and Mrs Iselin throws a costume party dressed as a shepherdess, all the better to control the political sheep around her. At the same party, Jocie Jordon unwittingly frees Shaw from his mother's control by turning up dressed as the Queen of Diamonds, the trigger card in his conditioning.

There are a few weaknesses and contrivances in *Candidate*, mostly the result of Axelrod's script shortcuts. Shaw's abrupt marriage to Jocie may lend his subsequent murder of both her and Senator Jordon an added poignancy, but fails to entirely convince. Similarly, Marco's decision to allow Jocie 48 hours alone with Shaw while she tries to 'cure' her highly dangerous husband seems unlikely given his knowledge of the man. The scene where Marco attempts to deprogramme Shaw with 52

Queen of Diamonds cards is quite effective, yet all too obviously an excuse to clarify both earlier events and the basic plot. Interestingly, Marco comes to believe his reversal treatment failed - it does appear a little too easy - when in fact he succeeded one hundred percent, leaving Raymond free to alter his targets at the political rally. The Marco-Rosie scenes have been criticised as both trite and irrelevant, though their out-of-nowhere romance does serve to give the former a life-saving dose of comforting normality. Largely unconnected to the central narrative, Rosie is a puzzling character, a gratuitous love interest with a line in baffling *non sequiturs*. Leigh found her difficult to play, requiring extensive help and input from Sinatra and Frankenheimer to deliver a performance she felt happy with. Lovers of movie anachronisms should look out for the location shot of a New York cinema screening *Pirates of Tortuga* (1961), made over five years after the film's supposed mid-fifties setting.

Acting honours for *The Manchurian Candidate*

should be split evenly between Lansbury, Harvey and Sinatra. A twisted, soured perversion of wholesome motherhood, Mrs Iselin is despicable and strangely alluring at the same time, coolly selling out her country for political power yet displaying a depth of maternal love quite ferocious in its intensity. The famous scene where she incestuously kisses Shaw on the mouth still carries a charge, her son's trance-like state only adding to the taboo-breaking *frisson*. Furious at her Soviet masters' use of her own child as their supposedly foolproof killing machine, Mrs Iselin plots a terrible revenge for this betrayal, leaving audiences in no doubt that she could achieve it, her primly affable veneer masking a fist of hardest steel. Despite the controversy surrounding *Candidate*, Lansbury's performance later netted her a much deserved Golden Globe Award and Academy Award nomination. Seldom a particularly expressive or likeable performer, Harvey's deadpan Raymond Shaw stands as either an exceptionally fine piece of low-key acting or an extremely troubling reflection of the man himself. Despite the critical jibes that he was just a little too convincing as an emotionless zombie, there's a lot more to the performance, Harvey's unexplained British accent quickly becoming irrelevant. Shaw is given a much-needed injection of humanity during a drunk scene with Marco, the latter comparing his old Army colleague's maternal relationship to that of Orestes and Clytemnestra. Via the ever-handy flashback device, Shaw gets to tell the sad story of his one true love, Jocie Jordon, destroyed by his ever-dominating mother. Conditioned to have no memory of his murderous acts, leaving him both guiltless and fearless, Shaw's 'liberation' at Marco's hands restores his freedom at the cost of his sanity. With the plot to kill the presidential nominee thwarted, Shaw has only one course of action left. Having slain his wife, his father-in-law, his stepfather and, lastly, his mother, he turns the gun on himself, his medal hung around his neck. Shaw's death is both pathetic and heroic, his act of matricide finally earning him his previously unwarranted status as a national hero. Axelrod's script visualised the suicide as a point-of-view shot of the rifle, a gimmicky touch Frankenheimer wisely rejected in favour of focusing on

Harvey's tortured face. Sinatra conveys Marco's own angst very well, the loyal career soldier verging on mental breakdown as his sense of reality becomes dangerously unhinged. Placed on indefinite sick leave by his commanding officer, Marco sits slumped in a train seat on a ride to nowhere. Unable to clear his mind, he twitches, sweats and shakes, even dropping a cigarette into his drink, until offered a lifeline by intrigued fellow passenger Rosie. The ensuing conversation is one of the film's less successfully weird scenes, but provides Marco with enough background to prevent *Candidate* from becoming entirely Raymond's show. Marco's closing citation for Shaw is genuinely touching, Sinatra framed in haunting close-up as he delivers the film's coda:

> *Made to commit acts too unspeakable to be cited here, by an enemy who had captured his mind and his soul. He freed himself at last and in the end, heroically and unhesitatingly gave his life to save his country.*
> **Raymond Shaw**

In mid-June 1962, Sinatra and United Artists arranged a sneak preview of *Candidate* at a cinema in London, where the star was recording his 'Great Songs from Great Britain' album. Audience response to Frankenheimer's first cut of the film proved highly favourable, with only minor problems such as mild confusion during the opening scenes. Pleased by the reaction, Sinatra made few alterations to his director's version, though the deletions included one of Axelrod's favourite Marco speeches regarding the application of Theobald Boehm's fingering system to clarinet playing. Even with these trims, Sinatra rated *Candidate* as easily his best film since *Golden Arm*.

Premiered on 27 September 1962, with a general release on 12 October, *The Manchurian Candidate* did much to restore Sinatra's industry standing after all the flak directed at the Clan movies. *Variety* expressed a common sentiment: 'After several pix in which he appeared to be sleepwalking, Sinatra is again a wide-awake pro creating a straight, quietly humorous character of some sensitivity.' The popular press delivered a more mixed verdict, though reviewers dubious of the overall film were generally impressed by its star. Opening in Britain the following month, *Candidate* did equally well with the critics, rated by Dilys Powell as 'an insolent, heartless thriller'. Audiences didn't register anything like the same level of enthusiasm, Axelrod later commenting that the paying public appeared unable to swallow *Candidate*'s audacious treatment of its extremely sensitive subject matter. The idea that the extremes of the political spectrum were not only equally dangerous but also virtually indistinguishable didn't go down too well in many quarters. Similarly, Angela Lansbury's demonic, incestuous mother figure was seen as a savage, below-the-belt lampoon of the sacred All-American family matriarch. According to Mordden, many concerned parents forbade their children to see the film. Despite Kennedy's endorsement, none of the United Artists front office ever warmed to *Candidate* and it's likely this affected the distributor's handling of a property requiring careful marketing. Unable to resolve their differences over *The Manchurian Candidate*, Sinatra and UA came to a parting of the ways shortly afterwards, the star setting up house with Warner Brothers (see Chapter 11). Aside from his cameo in *Cast a Giant Shadow*, Sinatra would never grace another United Artists release. *Candidate* soon disappeared from circulation altogether, not resurfacing until 1986, though Sammy Davis Jnr did manage to obtain a copy for a private screening at Laurence Harvey's Los Angeles wake in 1974, a year after the latter's death from cancer. Various rumours spread as to the reasons why, with many commentators arguing that Sinatra was uneasy about the plot's similarity to the subsequent Kennedy murder. More down-to-earth observers guessed that disagreements over the film's ownership made any reissue or television sale impossibly complicated to negotiate, consigning it to cultural limbo. The latter theory proved to be closer to the eventual explanation, Sinatra claiming that he simply didn't realise he now held all rights to *The Manchurian Candidate*. Taking only a nominal interest

in the finer points of his business operations, he'd never looked at the small print on the United Artists agreement. Free from any possible contractual wrangles, *Candidate* was rereleased to American cinemas in March 1987, receiving highly favourable reviews.

While early 1960s cinemagoers quickly lost their chance to see *The Manchurian Candidate*, President Kennedy briefly enjoyed the luxury of his own print, courtesy of Sinatra and United Artists. In August 1962, the star contacted Kennedy's press secretary Pierre Salinger to offer a copy. Sadly, this appears to have been less a gesture of thanks for his part in getting the film made than a last ditch attempt on Sinatra's part to repair their flagging relationship. On the weekend of 24-26 March 1962, not long after *Candidate* finished production, Kennedy was scheduled to stay at Sinatra's Palm Springs home, specially refurbished for the occasion. At the last minute, Sinatra was informed by Peter Lawford that the President's security people were unhappy about the house being exposed on all sides. Bing Crosby's home, backing onto a hillside, was deemed a safer option, his openly Republican loyalties not seen as in any way incongruous. Rumours rapidly spread that the security explanation was merely a convenient cover story for the real reason behind the switch. Always wary of Sinatra's alleged Mafia connections, Attorney General Robert Kennedy had decided that his brother could not be seen as a house guest of the man rumoured to have entertained Sam Giancana in the same house. It mattered little that the Kennedy family's links to organised crime were far stronger - and far more definite - than Sinatra's, their public image still relatively spotless. Enraged by the apparent snub from his most esteemed acquaintance, Sinatra took his wrath out on Lawford. The Kennedy in-law/go-between/alleged procurer immediately lost his scheduled roles in *4 for Texas* and *Robin and the 7 Hoods*, cast out from Sinatra's circle forever.

11

Hollow Laughter
1963-1964

COME BLOW YOUR HORN 1963

Take a bite out of the real fruit of life.
Alan Baker, reluctant wax fruit salesman

*If I was in the bum business
I'd want ten like you.*
Harry Baker, father of the above

Just over half-way into *Come Blow Your Horn*, ageing bachelor boy Alan Baker (Sinatra) emerges from a New York restaurant with neglected true love Connie (Barbara Rush). A vagrant approaches him, hand outstretched, begging for spare change to buy food. Baker gives the man a piece of raw steak he's been using to nurse a recently obtained black eye. A fair enough joke on which to end the scene, but it's not over just yet. As Sinatra and Rush exit the shot, the vagrant turns around to reveal himself as Dean Martin. Having topped the steak gag with a Rat Pack cameo, the film-makers still won't let go of the ever-expanding punchline. Speaking straight to camera, Martin laments his unsuccessful hustle for booze-money: 'Why didn't I tell him the truth? Why did I have to lie? Why didn't I tell him what I really wanted?' This absurdly

overextended in-joke reflects the overall flaw in *Horn*: everything is too forced and drawn out, overplayed to the point of no return, as if no-one felt the material was strong enough to stand on its own merits. Sharing the casual misogyny of *The Tender Trap*, with none of the earlier film's redeeming style or hint of ambivalence, *Come Blow Your Horn* sees Sinatra's swingin' single running out of momentum. The film also closes with the caption 'The End?', consigning itself to eternal comedy damnation.

Adapted from Neil Simon's 1961 Broadway hit, *Horn* was a co-production between Sinatra's Essex company and Tandem Productions, founded in 1959 by Bud Yorkin and Norman Lear. Co-producer and director Yorkin had enjoyed major success in television comedy during the 1950s, *Horn* marking his debut as a film director. Another small screen veteran, co-producer Lear retailored Simon's play as a Sinatra vehicle, distributed through Paramount for the first time since *The Joker is Wild* in 1957. Offering a return to the more humanised pre-Rat Pack Sinatra lothario, the role also gave him a pseudo-paternalistic side, Baker educating impressionable younger brother Buddy in the ways of high-living and good-natured promiscuity. The star also got to perform a theme song, provided by the ever dependable Cahn-Van Heusen team ('I tell you chum/It's time to come blow your horn'). Yorkin was very satisfied with the end result, orchestrated by Nelson Riddle, using the song to underpin some otherwise gratuitous location footage of Alan taking Buddy on the town for a style make-over. Singing on the streets of New York for the first time since his sailor-suit days, Sinatra displays an easy exuberance sadly lacking from the rest of the film.

Most commentary on *Come Blow Your Horn* tends to highlight a supposedly controversial piece of casting. The negligible bit role of Mrs Eckman, one of Baker's clients and presumed conquests, went to Phyllis McGuire, better know as a third of the McGuire Sisters singing act. McGuire was allegedly cast at Sinatra's request as a favour to boyfriend Sam Giancana. According to Kitty Kelley, the Chicago Mafia honcho regularly visited the set to watch McGuire at work, his presence intriguing rather than dismaying the cast and crew. Once the rumour mill got moving, additional details flew thick and fast. Giancana and McGuire were already secretly married. Robert Kennedy had sent undercover special agents onto the set to confirm the Mafia connection, dubious that Sinatra would have cast McGuire for her talent alone. For the record, the hard-faced, heavily made-up McGuire appears in only two scenes and delivers her lines adequately, exiting well before the end of the film. Kelley claims that Sinatra also attempted a little nepotism on behalf of his favourite offspring. Married since September 1960 to singer-actor Tommy Sands, Nancy Sinatra wanted her father to give him a high-profile film role that would boost his decidedly minor league movie career. Sinatra supposedly agreed to cast Sands as Buddy Baker, despite Yorkin and Lear's strong reservations. More sensitive to the prevailing feeling than his wife and father-in-law, Sands declined the role on the grounds of miscasting. While the 25-year-old juvenile could probably have passed for the required 21, it seems highly unlikely that Sinatra would have risked damaging the film by placing an inexperienced performer in a leading role. Unless he'd learned nothing

Come Blow Your Horn – Fraternal bonding from Alan Baker rearranges younger brother Buddy's (Tony Bill's) face.

at all from *Johnny Concho*. Director Yorkin offers a rather different version of events:

> *...Frank Sinatra had very little input in the casting of* Come Blow Your Horn. *He was however very much concerned with who would play the young brother. For this reason, we had quite a manhunt until we discovered Tony Bill. We tested him and Frank loved the test.*

Sinatra certainly found a worthy screen partner in 22-year-old Bill. Like Yorkin, he was making his movie debut, which may account for his enthusiastic overplaying. Bearing more than a passing resemblance to Frank Sinatra Jnr, Bill impressed Sinatra Snr enough to merit an 'introducing' credit for *Horn* - a kiss of death for many screen hopefuls - and co-starring roles in *None But the Brave* and *Marriage on the Rocks*, neither of which did a lot to advance his career. The rather cringe-making part of Alan's ditched pick-up Peggy Dawn went to Jill St John, also just turned 22 at the start of production. Married at the time to one Lance Reventlow, St John inevitably became labelled as the latest Sinatra girlfriend, her subsequent co-starring role in *Tony Rome* re-igniting the speculation a few years later. Few such rumours grew around the casting of Barbara Rush, despite her rapid reappearance in *Robin and the 7 Hoods*. A mere 11 years younger than Sinatra, Rush got the chance to invest Connie with marginally more dignity than the other female characters but precious little substance. If nothing else, *Horn* offered Sinatra the chance of a reunion with old co-star and sometime friend Lee J. Cobb, cast as Alan's inflexible, disapproving father and employer Harry Baker. Sinatra did not appear to hold Cobb's career-saving HUAC testimony against him, fully supporting Yorkin's decision to use him in *Horn*: 'Frank enjoyed the experience of this film in particular because he was a great fan of Lee J. Cobb.'

Shooting began on 13 September 1962, the amicable working atmosphere ensuring a strife-free production, whether or not Sam Giancana and accompanying FBI agents were lurking just off-camera. All too aware of his novice status and the career damage that could result from failing with a supposedly foolproof hit property, Bud Yorkin had suffered some preproduction anxiety:

Due to the fact that this was the first picture I directed, I approached it with some trepidation. I am grateful, however, that Frank Sinatra did everything possible to make me feel comfortable.

So comfortable in fact, that *Horn* completed production one week ahead of schedule and $100,000 under budget.

Lightweight material to begin with, *Come Blow Your Horn* appears to have been doomed as movie material from the start, crushed by the double blow of its stage origins and the heavy-footed, television-style handling. From the crass use of production stills in the credits sequence to the touchy-feely, happy-families conclusion, *Horn* resembles an overexpanded situation comedy, most of the action taking place on a large and outrageously fake-looking apartment set. The feeling of staginess is not helped by the relentlessly broad acting and overwritten script, which makes half-hearted jokey references to Khrushchev and Kennedy, Alan obliged to impersonate the latter at one point. As with *A Hole in the Head*, the Jewish milieu of the original appears to

have been half-heartedly reworked as a nod to Sinatra, though both Cobb and screen wife Molly Picon seem unaware of this. Technically competent, the film never settles into a comfortable style, Yorkin apparently unsure what to do with the larger canvas of the cinema screen. The Panavision format was presumably stipulated by Paramount, as the director makes very little use of the wide frame, tending to arrange his actors in television-safe compositions. Yorkin's major stylistic innovation is framing his characters through the open door of a refrigerator, a shot he uses in two scenes. Riddle overscores as usual and there are shameless plugs for Paramount, Alan pretending to have an influential friend at the studio to impress Peggy.

Aside from his song and a passable Bogart imitation, Sinatra is on autopilot for most of *Horn*. Often clad in his standard playboy colours of orange and black, whether ski parka or pyjamas, the star failed to recapture the loveable philanderer of *Tender Trap*, doomed by time and inferior material. Twenty-five years older than Bill and only four years younger than Cobb, he missed the thirtysomething age range envisaged for the character by at least a decade. The broadened, world-weary face so effectively used in *The Manchurian Candidate* now looks merely tired. Sinatra's first scene sets the tone, Alan returning from a clandestine dirty weekend with airhead would-be actress Peggy:

PEGGY: You didn't press my floor.
ALAN: I'd rather press you.

Appearing to hold easy-lay Peggy in the utmost contempt, Alan treats sensible, long-suffering Connie with more respect but shows no inclination to take their relationship seriously. Educating Buddy in the ways of free 'n' easy bachelorhood, Alan creates a younger version of himself, only to decide he no longer likes what he sees. As Buddy takes on Alan's persona - right down to the orange/black colours and bogus Paramount contact - he becomes increasingly obnoxious. Their angry confrontation at Buddy's supposedly wild party

Come Blow Your Horn – Harry Baker (Lee J. Cobb) displays a little paternal affection.

is easily the most effective exchange between the characters, both Sinatra and Bill handling the mutual recriminations well, despite the so-so dialogue: 'You're seeing yourself for the first time, Alan. I'm just a carbon copy.' Transformed into a milder version of their work-ethic oriented father, Alan ends up both more likeable and responsible, finally realising that business success and marriage to Connie are what he really wants, after all. This endorsement of traditional, conservative values is somewhat undermined by the film's failure to seriously criticise Alan's old lifestyle. Far from accepting that women should be treated as more than interchangeable organic sex toys, Alan 'reforms' simply because he's too old to get away with it anymore. *Horn*'s final shot is of Buddy ensconced in his brother's abandoned bachelor pad, smooth-talking his landlady on the telephone, the baton successfully passed on.

The film's one saving grace is a 'guest' appearance from *Bonanza* star Dan Blocker, taking a little time out from playing Hoss Cartwright in the hit western series, filmed on the Paramount lot. Playing McGuire's irate husband, a two-fisted good ol' boy from Dallas, Blocker puts the rest of the *Horn* cast to shame. The bear-sized,

stetson-wearing Eckman is supposed to be loud, aggressive and overbearing yet appears almost understated compared to the other characters, Blocker turning in a well-judged performance finely attuned to the film medium. Eager to pick up a contract with Eckman's company, Alan tries to tempt Mrs Eckman with a new line in artificial fruit, the not-so-subtle stemless purple plums. Having punched Baker out - an act deserving much applause - Eckman proceeds to crush the man's plums in his hand, accompanying the humiliation with a memorable caution: '...I'm gonna jump on you until your eyes bug out like a stomped-on toad-frog.' If only. Impressed by both Blocker's talent and his 6' 4", 270-lb frame, the still relatively slender Sinatra used him again on *Lady in Cement*, their wildly contrasting sizes serving as one the latter film's key ingredients.

Evidently convinced that their movie would sell itself, Paramount made no discernible attempt to market *Come Blow Your Horn* with any imagination. The promotional material included an inane shot of Sinatra playing a snake-charmer's flute, surrounded by the evidently transfixed Rush, St John and McGuire. In

February 1963, the star attended a charity preview at the Plaza Theatre, Palm Springs, raising $15,000 for the City of Hope Hospital. An extra-lavish Las Vegas press screening followed in May, Paramount flying in scores of reviewers and columnists from both the west and east coasts, treating them to an accompanying press conference and buffet dinner. Officially premiered at the Radio City Music Hall on 6 June 1963, *Horn* drew mixed reviews and better box-office. *Variety* felt the star more than equalled his similar *Tender Trap* role: 'Sinatra's jaunty performance is his best in some time', having apparently forgotten its enthusiasm for *The Manchurian Candidate* the previous year. Dismissing the overall film as 'vapid boredom', Bosley Crowther reserved the brunt of his contempt for Sinatra, a one-time favourite now irretrievably fallen from grace: 'He appears so indifferent and coolly self-satisfied that he moves and talks in the manner of a well-greased mechanical man.' A useful commercial winner after three disappointments in a row, *Come Blow Your Horn* failed in most other departments, suggesting that *Manchurian Candidate* represented a one-off revival of the old Sinatra star power rather than a general upswing in the quality of his work. There was, however, a lot worse to come.

4 FOR TEXAS 1963

I'm anybody's man. Mostly my own.
Joe Jarrett

Grown men. Acting like little schoolboys.
Elya Carlson

4 for Texas is surely one of the most shameless wastes of time, talent and film-stock ever to emerge from Hollywood. As producer, director and co-writer of this dismal effort, respected film-maker Robert Aldrich warrants much of the blame, aided and abetted by Sinatra at his most indifferent. While the movie features most of Aldrich's standard macho themes, it's still a

badly written, flatly directed, lazily acted piece of drek. Cast as loveable hustlers Zack Thomas and Joe Jarrett, Sinatra and Dean Martin cruise through 1870s Galveston, Texas like two nineteenth-century playboys, treating the minimal plot with a kind of good-natured contempt. Something is seriously wrong with a comedy when the only laugh involves ageing Three Stooges frontman Moe Howard being struck on the head with an umbrella.

Made by the SAM Company (Sinatra And Martin?) for release through Warner, *Texas* employed only a few of the star's regulars, notably Howard Koch and Nelson Riddle, with most of the cast and crew selected by Aldrich. Riding high after the unexpected success of his psycho-horror drama *Whatever Happened to Baby Jane?* (1962), Aldrich hoped to make *Texas* an amusing, mildly satirical spoof western. The script was written in collaboration with Teddi Sherman, who'd previously worked with Aldrich on *Ten Seconds to Hell* (1959), a watchable tale of bomb disposal experts in post-war Germany. Cameraman Ernest Laszlo was another old Aldrich hand, photographing *Vera Cruz* (1954), *Kiss Me Deadly* (1955) and *The Last Sunset* (1961).

The showy supporting role of arch bad guy Matson went to Charles Bronson, who'd worked with Aldrich on *Apache* and *Vera Cruz* before serving with Sinatra in *Never So Few*. Aldrich regulars Victor Buono, Nick Dennis, Richard Jaeckel and Wesley Addy were also included in the supporting cast, variously overplaying and underplaying in the service of a lost cause.

Appreciating that intermittent hijinks and gunplay might not be enough for paying audiences, Sinatra and Aldrich attempted to spice up their meagre concoction with a double dose of well-endowed Scandinavian glamour, hiring Anita Ekberg and Ursula Andress as the film's love interests. Ekberg's casting in *Texas* was probably the result of her friendships with its leading men rather than any great box-office appeal. Martin knew her from the dying days of his partnership with Jerry Lewis, Ekberg appearing in *Artists and Models* and *Hollywood or Bust* (1956). Sinatra's acquaintance with Ekberg dated back to 1954, when she turned up for his

4 for Texas – Director Robert Aldrich attempts to extract performances from Sinatra and Anita Ekberg.

December opening at the Copa, New York, informing the assembled press that the star had personally paid for her round trip from Hollywood. Andress' international career was starting to take off thanks to her attention-grabbing role in *Dr. No* (1962), 1963 also seeing the release of her Elvis Presley venture *Fun in Acapulco*. International but not very good.

One prominent absentee from *Texas'* star line-up was the now-banished Peter Lawford, the finished film bearing no trace of his exclusion. Despite the initial casting of Lawford, presumably as a more refined version of Buono's crooked banker character, Nancy Sinatra claims that her father never intended *Texas* as part of the 'official' Rat Pack series. It certainly didn't offer a suitable role for Sammy Davis Jnr, who failed to meet the requirements of the only significant black character. Lacking the stature and muscle for Prince George, Jarrett's street-fighting, coach-driving gentleman's gentleman, Davis could hardly complain when the part went to West Indian actor Edric Connor,

best remembered as one of the champion harpoonists in John Huston's *Moby Dick* (1956).

4 for Texas was filmed over the summer of 1963, the studio work beginning on 24 May. According to Michael Freedland, Aldrich initially rated the production as the funniest, most enjoyable experience of his career. If so, he rapidly changed his mind as the intended 'fun picture' fell apart before his eyes. Never at home with broad comedy, Aldrich dismissed the final film as a total failure. The director's biggest problem during shooting was his uneasy, unproductive relationship with Sinatra, who declined to put any great effort into his leading role. Out for a good time playing cowboys with Martin, the star had no intention of treating *Texas* as anything more significant than another Clan-style lark. Frustrated at the latter's refusal to follow or even listen to his advice, Aldrich regularly argued with Sinatra, their fierce conflicts recalled by Howard Koch at the director's memorial service over 20 years later. Aldrich got on much better with Martin, rating the actor as a true professional. Martin certainly emerged from the debris with more credit than Sinatra, his affable, what-the-hell performance bearing no trace of his co-star's occasional sulkiness. The director also had problems with long-standing cameraman Laszlo, the latter's meticulous, time-consuming methods sorely testing Aldrich's patience. With the ever-restless Sinatra instantly on his back over any delays, the director finally decided he could no longer work with Laszlo, the final straw being the cameraman's insistence on more creative autonomy over his lighting set-ups. Midway through production, Joseph Biroc took over from Laszlo, diplomatically accepting second unit billing on the credits. Well attuned to Sinatra's requirements after *The Devil at 4 O'Clock*, the fast-working Biroc helped ease some of the tension between star and director, the latter close to reaching the end of his tether. Co-star Richard Jaeckel felt that Aldrich simply gave up on the film at some point, finishing the remaining scenes in perfunctory fashion to be free of the project as soon as possible.

According to rumour, Sinatra's idea of fun during

the *Texas* shoot amounted to more than firing off blanks from his six-shooter. Kitty Kelley claims that the star arranged for prostitutes to be on call throughout the production, playing the standard 'saloon girls' during working hours and providing the usual services off-camera. While no-one objected to the morality of this unorthodox casting, the production manager had a difficult time deciding what to pay the star's special bit players and how to list their contribution in the accounts. Given the total lack of saloon scenes in *Texas*, this story bears the aroma of ripest bullshit. Ekberg's entourage of giggling maids could have numbered a few of the world's oldest profession but none of the visiting reporters appear to have asked them. Keen to sustain the party atmosphere of the shoot, Sinatra announced that the filming of the climactic fight scene would be open to all spectators, attracting a large audience from the Hollywood community. Despite the scale of the mass punch-up, there were relatively few injuries. Squaring up to Sinatra for the initial *mano a mano* fisticuffs, Martin forgot to duck in one shot and was accidentally hit in the face by his co-star. With doubles standing in - very obviously - for the more risky moves, neither man suffered overmuch.

Even allowing for the poor quality script, something evidently went badly wrong with *Texas* along the way. The pre-credits chase sequence where Matson pursues Thomas and Jarrett through the desert is well enough staged, second unit director Oscar Rudolph throwing in a coach crash for good measure. From here on, it's flabby, flimsy and very, very long. The subsequent 'humorous' Thomas-Jarrett stand-off drags on forever, paying spurious homage to the much sharper Gary Cooper-Burt Lancaster encounter that opens Aldrich's *Vera Cruz*. What storyline there is revolves around an uninvolving series of crosses and double-crosses as the various characters pursue $100,000 of stolen money, used by Jarrett to finance a floating casino. As the pace slackens to a near standstill, the phoney back projection, blatant redubbing, lumbering background score and general sense of apathy have a numbing effect, the end result

resembling a below-par television movie, showing off a series of okay sets and costumes with nothing going on in the foreground. Victor Buono belches and sweats in a most unappealing fashion and Bronson's dead-straight performance as the nasty, black leather-clad villain belongs in an entirely different film, his insane giggle failing to counter the joke-free menace. Struggling with their dialogue, Ekberg and Andress are little more than barely animated mannequins, the former proving beyond all doubt that she has very large breasts. Having left his cast to get on with it, Aldrich only perks up during the infrequent bursts of inappropriately realistic violence, the succession of bloody gunshot wounds, fist-fighting and burned eyes culminating with Matson's fatal bullet in the head. The director also half-heartedly employs some pointless punctuation devices, bridging a few scenes with either Jarrett's narration or still pictures or both. There is an interesting touch of old lady victimisation, one struck in the rear with a peashooter, another ejected from her wheelchair, and a vaguely troubling, if historically accurate multitude of humble black servants, but these are fleeting moments in a mountain of dross.

Unable to duplicate Dean Martin's self-mocking lightness of touch, Sinatra appears to be living out a dirty old man's wet dream for much of *4 for Texas*, surrounded by Ekberg's nubile, ever-worshipful servant girls. Adorned with a gold cravat, Zack Thomas lies back in an easy chair, drinking champagne, smoking a large cigar, very much the bossman as the women cater to his every whim. As Andress later explains to Martin: 'A man as a partner I don't understand, but a master...a master, him I know how to handle.' Martin's reaction shows he knows not to take this claim too seriously. With Sinatra, it's not so clear-cut.

Released for the Christmas season in December 1963, *4 for Texas* received a comprehensive Yuletide kicking from the critics. Robin Bean's verdict in the British magazine *Films and Filming* echoed the popular sentiment regarding earlier Clan films: 'One suspects that the most amusing antics were those that went on off-screen... there is not very much on screen which will entertain the audience.' The paying public evidently agreed, *Texas* doing only mediocre business. At some point after the initial press showings, the film was edited down from its unpalatable premiere length of 124 minutes, existing prints running nearly ten minutes shorter. A brief post-punch up scene where the four principals visit Jarrett's old friend Miss Emmaline was cut, making their subsequent departure from Galveston somewhat abrupt. The other deletions are more difficult to determine, though at one point Martin and Andress refer to some crockery throwing and face slapping not found in the revised 115-minute version. One of the lowest points in Sinatra's post-*Eternity* career, *4 for Texas* provided ominous proof of a star out of touch with both audience demands and his own talent.

ROBIN AND THE 7 HOODS - OR WHO MAID MARIAN? 1964

Like we've taken the Robin Hood legend and changed the bows and arrows to machine guns...! Like with songs yet!..Like WILD!
Poster caption

Promising a wacky, zany, tuneful parody of the man from Sherwood Forest, *Robin and the 7 Hoods* is a resolutely underwhelming experience. Undeniably superior to *4 for Texas*, thanks largely to some decent Cahn-Van Heusen songs and Gordon Douglas' no-nonsense direction, the film lacks any real verve or enthusiasm, as if all the creative energy had been expended on the basic idea. While many would have expected the part of a benevolent gang leader to be Frank Sinatra's dream role, *Robin* suggests otherwise, the star walking through the film at his most detached. Set in 1920s gangland Chicago, the script offered the surviving Rat Pack regulars such remodelled characters as Robbo, Little John, Will, Guy Gisborne and Allen A. Dale, none of the stars coming close to topping Edward G. Robinson's brief appearance as Big Jim, whose violent death sets the story in motion. Notable largely

as both the last Clan outing and Sinatra's final musical, *Robin* also proved to be one of the star's most troubled productions, though this time for reasons beyond his control. Despite the title, there is little trace of inspiration from either *Snow White and the Seven Dwarfs* or *Seven Samurai*, which could have produced a far more interesting film. Still, this must be the only spin on the Robin Hood legend to depict Maid Marian as a cold-blooded, double-dealing slut.

Shortly before *Robin and the 7 Hoods* went into production, its star consolidated his already enviable position in the entertainment industry, securing an apparently foolproof pact with Jack Warner. In September 1963, following a month of fierce bargaining, Sinatra's management negotiated a deal with Warner selling the studio his Reprise record label for $3 million. In return, Sinatra would pay Warner $2 million for one third ownership of the newly formed Warner Brothers-Reprise label. This new-found harmony between man and corporate machine should have extended to Sinatra's film-making partnership with the studio, Warner's belief in his drawing power as yet unshaken by *4 for Texas*' poor showing. *Robin* was the last film made under an earlier deal and the studio rapidly proffered a new multi-project contract, starting with *None But the Brave*, a script promoted by United Nations ally Jack Warner as good propaganda for American-Japanese relations. In the event, there would be only two follow-ups, the flop ventures *Marriage on the Rocks* and *The Naked Runner*, and rumours that Sinatra would eventually succeed Warner as head of the studio quickly subsided.

Returning to full-blown musicals for the first time since the mediocre *Can Can*, Sinatra evidently felt in need of a little expert help. The star originally intended to co-produce *Robin* with old MGM shipmate Gene Kelly, the first in a projected multi-film deal between the former dancing partners. Once their gangster parody was in the can, Kelly would co-star in the second film and direct the third, Sinatra acting in all three. No longer in any great demand as either an actor or director, Kelly was duly grateful for Sinatra's patronage, happy to accept the latter's senior position in the deal. Sadly, their renewed screen partnership soon fell apart, Kelly unable to adapt to Sinatra's working methods. The two men clashed early on in preproduction, Kelly unhappy over both the 'excessive' number of songs planned for the film and Sinatra's insistence on producing as well as starring. Keener on the idea than the reality of sharing executive responsibility with Kelly, Sinatra appeared unwilling to give up any of his authority, leaving Kelly both powerless and largely irrelevant. Sinatra's old aversion to rehearsals also reared its head, the star repeatedly delaying his arrival from New York to begin work on the film at Warner. According to Kelly's version of events, Sinatra refused to give any reason for his non-appearance, simply informing Howard Koch that he'd show up the next day, then the day after and so on. Unable to take the hard line with Sinatra that he'd used during the *On the Town* shoot, Kelly felt the tension rising to an unbearable level. Feeling that his compromised 'shared' producer role reduced him to nothing more than another Sinatra lackey, with no effective say in the project, Kelly resigned from *Robin* before filming commenced. Howard Koch issued a standard 'artistic differences' statement to the press, Kelly's involvement in the film quickly forgotten.

With Gene Kelly making an undignified exit from the *Robin* production, Sinatra could take solace in a more successful reunion with director Gordon Douglas, now reaching the end of his long tenure with Warner. Having recently thrown a snake eyes with Robert Aldrich, one of Hollywood's more esteemed directing talents, Sinatra had no problem working with self-proclaimed technician-for-hire Douglas, the latter moving *Robin* along at a commendably brisk pace after *Texas*' snail-plod. Specialising in smooth, unshowy crane and tracking shots, Douglas makes effective use of the camera throughout *Robin*, filling the Panavision frame with well-judged compositions. He appears to have had a curious fondness for 'saucy' close shots of bent-over female rears, a motif repeated in both *Tony Rome* and *Lady in Cement*. Probably not most people's

idea of an authorial signature, but Sinatra was evidently impressed.

While Kelly felt that *Robin* had too many songs clogging up the storyline, Sammy Cahn protested the loss of what he considered his finest composition for Sinatra, 'I Like To Lead When I Dance'. Cahn and Van Heusen produced this number for the scene where Robbo is approached by Marian to avenge Big Jim's death. The song would subsequently be reprised as Marian worked her way through Little John, Guy Gisborne and Sheriff Potts. Turning up at the recording studio to hear Sinatra put the number on tape, Cahn was informed by Koch that the song wouldn't be used. Upset by this development, Cahn attempted to discover why his hard work had been rejected, the probable reason being that Sinatra was either hung-over on the day or simply unrehearsed. All pleas for a second try were rejected, the song existing in the finished film only as background music for the relevant scenes.

As with *4 for Texas*, the intended cast line-up for *Robin* underwent a few changes, both Peter Lawford and Joey Bishop unceremoniously dumped along the way. Lawford's role as ageing orphan Allen A. Dale went to Bing Crosby, Sinatra bearing his *High Society* co-star no apparent grudge over the previous year's Kennedy incident. Semi-retired from film acting, Crosby happily accepted the part, anticipating a Clan-style good time during the shoot. Pleased to have Crosby on board, Sinatra also hired his son Phillip, handing the *Sergeants 3* veteran a single-line bit part as one of Robbo's gang. Bing Crosby's participation in *Robin* created a minor disagreement between Sinatra and Warner, the studio wanting to give him third billing on the credits after Sinatra and Martin. The star disagreed, having already reserved this all-important above-the-title spot for Sammy Davis Jnr. Sensing they were heading for a confrontation, the Warner executives backed off, agreeing to Crosby's compromise 'special guest star' billing further down the credits.

Cast in the poorly written, near unplayable role of Marian, *Come Blow Your Horn* co-star Barbara Rush at least got to wear a series of expensive, if tasteless, 'flapper'-style costumes, her dignified performance going some way to masking the howling misogyny. The remaining supporting roles were doled out to a job-lot of interesting character actors, notably *4 for Texas* co-star Victor Buono and *Columbo*-in-waiting Peter Falk, veteran of such no-kidding gangster movies as *Pretty Boy Floyd* (1960) and *Murder Inc* (1960). Anxious to inject some old-style class into the proceedings, Sinatra asked *Hole in the Head* co-star Edward G. Robinson to make an unbilled cameo appearance as kind-hearted crime lord Big Jim, Robbo's old friend and mentor. Another nod to the old-time screen gangster was the casting of character actor Allen Jenkins, whose in-joke turn as the smoke-allergic mobster Vermin Witowsky is one of *Robin*'s few bright spots.

While the period setting limited the use of actual Chicago locations, Sinatra and Koch felt it was worth their while obtaining some authentic footage of the city, production starting there on October 31 1963. Up until a fateful day in late November, filming appears to have been largely harmonious, the preproduction grief forgotten. Crosby certainly enjoyed the on-set camaraderie, despite some reservations over his co-stars' very casual approach to their roles. Engaged at The Sands for much of the studio shoot, Davis was obliged to commute between Las Vegas and Los Angeles on a daily basis, his growing exhaustion not helped by an awkward situation with wife May Britt. Britt disliked Davis' relationship with employer/friend Sinatra, feeling that he crawled to the star, and refused all invitations to visit her husband on the set. The songs were recorded at the Warner studios during the evenings, when Sinatra felt his voice was at its best. Davis became so fascinated by Crosby's easy professionalism as they rehearsed 'Mr Booze', he missed his own cue five times over.

Sinatra's dealings with *4 for Texas* were now behind him, but an event in the real Lone Star state was about to have a shattering effect on both his personal and professional lives. While it's long been claimed that anyone over a certain age can remember where they were when President Kennedy's murder was announced, there appears to be some doubt over Frank Sinatra's exact whereabouts. According to most sources, on 22 November the *Robin* cast and crew were on location at a cemetery in Burbank, Los Angeles when news of the Kennedy assassination came in. Already dressed in respectful black for Big Jim's burial scene, Sinatra went into mild shock. Leaving the cemetery for a solitary walk, Sinatra called the White House for any further news before returning to finish the scene, unwilling to work at the depressingly apt location a second day. Once Gordon Douglas had all the graveyard shots he needed, Sinatra shut down the production for three days, retreating to his Palm Springs home.

The rival version of events places Sinatra on Stage 22 of the Warner lot when the tragedy was announced, filming the courtroom scene where the innocent Robbo is tried for the murder of Sheriff Potts' predecessor. Calling an immediate halt to all work on *Robin*, the star made an out-of-character visit to a nearby church for prayer. Back on set a few days later, Sinatra overheard some disparaging remarks from cast and crew regarding the natives of Dallas. Disturbed by this attitude, he requested a brief time-out to address his co-workers over a loudspeaker system, exhorting them not to give in to malice and hatred. Stunned into silence by this impassioned entreaty, the assembled crowd gave their boss a spontaneous round of applause, the incident making the Hollywood trade papers. Inevitably, the trauma of the Kennedy tragedy and the resulting delays had a noticeable effect on the production, Crosby later remarking that they never recaptured the pleasant atmosphere and easy chemistry of the pre-22 November filming. Making any kind of a comedy would have been difficult under the circumstances. A musical comedy involving murderous, gun-toting gangsters and corrupt policemen now seemed in the worst possible taste. It's probably no coincidence that *Robin* keeps all but one of its killings off screen.

Already burdened by his share of grief, Sinatra suffered a more personal nightmare on Sunday 8 December 1963, when Frank Sinatra Jnr was kidnapped by three men and held for a $240,000 ransom. The gang turned out to be fairly inept amateurs, with Sinatra Jnr

Robin and the 7 Hoods – How to steal a scene even when reduced to a poor quality wall hanging.

returned unharmed three days later, followed by most of the ransom money. The defence counsel at the later trial provided a tasteless epilogue to the incident, claiming that the whole affair was a publicity stunt for *Robin*. Rightly contemptuous of this approach, Sinatra declined to attend the final days of the trial and subsequent convictions, spending his time more constructively in Tokyo, negotiating the deal for *None But the Brave*. With production finally completed, Sinatra, Crosby, Martin and Davis recorded *Robin*'s accompanying stereo soundtrack album in Los Angeles between 8-10 April 1964.

Robin and the 7 Hoods opens in quite promising fashion, Big Jim gunned down by 'friends' at his birthday party in an explicit homage/rip-off of *Some Like It Hot*, where George Raft's Spats Columbo is shot by an assassin concealed in a giant cake. Always top value for money, Robinson continues to dominate the film, portraits of Big Jim hanging on various walls.

Sadly, there isn't much worth dominating. Like the earlier Clan films, *Robin* lumbers on towards the two-hour mark for no very good reason, a steady downward slide with precious few redeeming features. David Schwartz's script is workmanlike at best, its half-baked Runyonesque dialogue failing to conceal the lack of characterisation, mood and plot development. This careless approach is typified by Marian's unsubstantiated claim to be Big Jim's long lost daughter. What should have been a crucial story point is simply abandoned a few scenes later, playing no part at all in the long-delayed denouement. The film's visual elements are similarly unremarkable, William Daniels' additional credit as *Robin*'s associate producer making no apparent difference to his flat, television-style photography. Looking rather more 1960s than 1920s, the period detail is shaky, badly undermined by a succession of elaborate but tacky sets, decked out in strangely drab colours. With two large-scale nightclub demolition jobs in the film, plus a gambling joint that transforms into a religious mission, the designers appear to have gone for utility rather than atmosphere, which unfortunately renders their hard work null and void. Watching mock gangsters trash equally bogus furniture quickly loses its entertainment value. Even Robbo's office is adorned with ugly, shiny brown leather chairs, suggesting that Koch and Sinatra negotiated a special bulk-buy deal with the local thrift shop.

The acting in *Robin* is surprisingly uneven, exhibiting cold professionalism rather than enthusiasm. Peter Falk is disappointing as Gisborne, overacting and singing flat. Dean Martin offers his usual laid-back persona, the pool-hustling Little John 'accidentally' prodding a waitress in the behind with his cue handle ('It's the other end you play with, buster'). In one shot, where Robbo's Lincoln green-clad 'hostesses' are handing over their charity takings, Martin simply grins as one of the actresses forgets to retrieve the lid for her tin.

Sammy Davis Jnr impresses as Robbo's right-hand man Will, looking cool in a bowler hat and dark suit. More confident on camera than during his early Rat Pack days, Davis gets to perform the lengthy, energetic 'Bang Bang' song and dance routine, informing the audience that gunfire is 'Just like heavenly music to my ears'. A real-life gun fanatic, he'd wanted to play a black gangster for years and certainly makes the most of his underwritten part, gleefully firing off what seem to be 36 shooters. Appearing an hour into the action, Bing Crosby delivers the Cahn-Van Heusen numbers 'Mr Booze' and 'Don't Be a Do-Badder' in his usual good-natured favourite-uncle style but appears less comfortable with the straight dialogue. Praising Robbo's decision to donate his vice profits to the poor and needy, Dale announces: 'This act of serendipity will produce abundant results', Crosby's delivery as self-conscious as the writing.

Aside from his genuinely show-stopping rendition of 'My Kind of Town (Chicago Is)', Sinatra is at his least inspired for much of *Robin*, failing to conceal a distinct lack of interest as he goes through the motions. There is one brief spark of life as Robbo slaps Marian across the face with her own financial statement, the sole moment of genuine tension in an otherwise inert drama. Following the trial scene, the film simply falls apart as Robbo's empire does likewise, Marian plotting to turn public opinion against their former hero. Seducing both Little John and Allen A. Dale into her service, this *femme fatale* evidently possesses a shrewder, more cynical business sense than any of the gangsters. With Robbo, Little John and Will reduced to playing street Santas at the film's conclusion, there appears to be an unambiguous Crime Does Not Pay coda on the cards, yet Marian's clear triumph as she steps from her limousine with Allan in tow renders the film strangely amoral. Crime does pay, if you're smart enough.

Robin and the 7 Hoods was released on June 27 1964, Sinatra attending the New York premiere. While there were no serious accusations of the film glorifying organised crime or trivialising violence in the wake of the Kennedy assassination, few critics had much to say in its favour. Noting that 'the usual Sinatra arrogance is subdued', Bosley Crowther had no time for the 'artless and obvious film...about as humble and harmless as a romp with the Keystone cops'. The box-office take marked a slight improvement on *4 for Texas*, but still fell a long way below the returns generated by *Ocean's 11*, Sinatra's one hit for Warner since *Young at Heart* a decade earlier. *Robin*'s biggest success was its theme song, 'My Kind of Town'. An impressive spin-off hit record, it later received an Academy Award nomination for Best Original Song, losing on the night to *Mary Poppin*'s 'Chim Chim Cher-ee'.

12

Wartime Heroics

1964-1965

NONE BUT THE BRAVE 1965

Ordinary men blown together by a big wind called war.
Lieutenant Kuroki, Japanese commanding officer

None but the brave deserves the fair.
John Dryden, Alexander's Feast

Sometime in 1964, writer and former POW Kurt Vonnegut was discussing war stories with registered nurse Mary O'Hare, who dismissed the Hollywood versions as dangerous lies and stars like John Wayne and Frank Sinatra as 'war-loving, dirty old men'. While the jury remains out on Wayne, Mrs O'Hare's sweeping statement did Sinatra an injustice, the star producing and directing his aggressively anti-bloodshed drama *None But the Brave* the same year. Picking up the pacifist banner dropped by the aborted *Private Slovik* project, this World War II story is a flawed piece of work, schematic, sentimental and very variably acted. It's also courageous, unflinching and uncompromising, Sinatra's assured direction revealing a talent that should have been developed, whatever Gordon Douglas' uncredited contribution. The premise is simple and

effective: a small group of American soldiers crash-lands onto a nameless, uncharted Pacific island, only to discover an abandoned Japanese platoon already in residence. With neither side able to contact their outside forces, the enemies are faced with a choice: either they resume the conflict, needlessly throwing away lives, or they agree to an uneasy truce. It's to Sinatra's credit that the outcome emerges as sadly inevitable rather than tediously predictable.

A co-production between Tokyo Eiga Co. Limited, Toho Film and Sinatra's new movie label Artanis ('Sinatra' backwards), *None But the Brave* was a *bona fide* Japanese-American collaboration rather than a Hollywood film employing Japanese talent. In February 1964, producer Sinatra flew to Tokyo for final negotiations on the deal with opposite number Kikumaru Okuda and the all-important casting of native Japanese actors. The challenge of directing performers who spoke little-to-no English didn't deter the novice auteur one bit, Okuda providing Sinatra with a Japanese interpreter, dialogue coach and assistant director to ease the language barrier. With *None But the Brave* a go-project, Nancy Sinatra gave her father his own official chair, THE VOICE of *Anchors Aweigh* now

THE DIRECTOR. The film was proudly trumpeted as the first ever American-Japanese co-production, though some claim the honour really belongs to the forgotten sci-fi-horror *The Manster* (1959).

Working from Okuda's original story, writers John Twist and Katsuya Susaki produced a script stronger on liberal sentiment than dramatic force, the end result still an effective moral fable. With Howard Koch in place as the film's executive producer, William Daniels signed on in his new associate producer role, leaving the actual camerawork to *Pal Joey* veteran Harold Lipstein. For the melancholy score, Sinatra took a chance on relatively untried talent John Williams, a promising television composer .

Casting himself in the showy top-billed supporting role of Chief Pharmacist's Mate Francis Maloney, Sinatra gave the nominal lead to giant-sized actor Clint Walker, playing haunted pilot Captain Dennis Bourke. With Nancy Sinatra still lobbying for husband Tommy Sands, her father cast him in the third-billed part of Second Lieutenant Blair, an inflexible by-the-book marine. Sinatra also cast his second cousin Richard Sinatra, son of the modestly successful bandleader Ray Sinatra, whose refusal to make his surname more WASP-friendly spurred young Francis to keep the family moniker. The most significant addition to the *None But The Brave* supporting cast was burly character actor Brad Dexter, equally at home playing affable and malignant tough guy roles. With the kind of inverse logic probably only possible in Hollywood, Dexter is best known as the forgotten member of *The Magnificent Seven*. Playing the insubordinate Sergeant Bleeker as an unsubtle, cigar-chewing loudmouth, Dexter's performance in *None But the Brave* is largely run-of-the-mill, the actor's importance to Sinatra not apparent until filming was under way. Smaller roles were handed out to Tony Bill, Phil Crosby, fellow *Hood* Richard Bakalyan and *Suddenly/Johnny Concho* veteran Christopher Dark.

Basing the production on the small Hawaiian island of Kauai, Sinatra commenced the location shoot on 27 April 1964. The producer-director-co-star took up

None But the Brave – Maloney checks in at the Japanese camp.

residence in a $2,000-a-month beachfront property, redecorated by its owner in Sinatra's favourite shade of orange. His co-stars and production team were mostly installed at the Coco Palms Hotel, their carelessness with both cigarettes and firecrackers resulting in an unusually large laundry bill. For all the juvenile antics, Sinatra had remained a popular figure with Hawaiian hotel staff after *From Here to Eternity* and *The Devil at 4 O'Clock*. His habit of leaving behind desirable consumer goods such as television sets and expensive bottles of whisky probably helped.

Work on *None But the Brave* was temporarily overshadowed by an off-camera incident early in the production, initial local reports announcing that Sinatra was dead. On Sunday 10 May, Sinatra and Ruth Koch were swimming close to the beach in Wailua Bay when she was suddenly swept out to sea. Attempting to rescue her, Sinatra got caught in the undertow some distance from the shore. While Mrs Koch was quickly recovered, he struggled in the water for close on half on hour, succumbing to hypoxia before strong swimmer Brad Dexter could get to him. Given artificial respiration on the beach by Dexter, Sinatra slowly began to revive, his rescuer later receiving a citation from the Red Cross. Never comfortable being in anyone's debt, Sinatra rewarded Dexter with a bigger supporting part in *Von Ryan's Express* and the producer role for *Naked Runner*, the actor also enjoying a brief executive post on Sinatra's Warner staff. Their subsequent falling-out over the *Runner* project prompted some revision of the drowning story, Dexter's role in the star's rescue considerably reduced in many accounts. Dexter himself claimed that the incident had little bearing on his later work with Sinatra, the star retaining his services because he was a good film actor with serious ambitions to produce (see Chapter 13).

Even as producer, director, co-star and near-drowning victim, Sinatra still found time to become restless during the Kauai shoot, obliging Howard Koch to rework the schedule for an earlier finish, fearful his boss might up and quit without filming all the necessary footage. *None But the Brave* proved to be his last film as a Sinatra employee, Koch departing for an executive position at Paramount. Star and producer remained on good terms, Koch later attempting to recruit Sinatra for the Barbra Streisand musical *On a Clear Day You Can See Forever* (1970, see Appendix 2). Back at the Warner Brothers complex in Hollywood, Sinatra completed the relatively small amount of studio work required for *None But the Brave*, recording his 'It Might As Well Be Swing' album with Count Basie and Quincy Jones during the evenings.

None But the Brave flaunts its noble intentions from frame one, the opening credits rolling over a Japanese painting of the island, the film's title first appearing in Japanese characters. Even the supporting cast billing is carefully arranged, the American actors balanced with their Japanese counterparts. While *Never So Few* depicted the Emperor's forces as a ruthless, faceless killing machine, here they are people first, professional soldiers second, their daily routine sketched in over a good ten minutes before the Americans show up. The film is narrated - in English - by Lieutenant Kuroki (Tatsuya Mihashi), a civilised and cultured man torn between his humanitarian instincts and loyalty to the

Japanese flag. His soldiers are similarly humanised, laughing, singing and playing games when not on-duty, their amicable conversation carefully subtitled. After a few minor skirmishes between the opposing forces, one American soldier decides he can't shoot an unarmed Japanese counterpart as the latter returns from a fishing trip, opting instead to trade his cigarettes for some of the man's catch. When Maloney saves a Japanese soldier's life by amputating the man's gangrenous leg, a formal peace is agreed.

Inevitably, the uneasy truce is undercut by lingering feelings of patriotic duty on both sides. Kuroki's fiercely militaristic second-in-command, Sergeant Tamura (Takeshi Kato), disapproves of his superior's liberal regime, their antagonism paralleled by Blair's frequent arguments with the less regulation-bound Bourke. At one point, both Tamura and Blair disobey orders to avoid enemy confrontation, their subsequent dressing-downs intercut in no uncertain fashion. Kuroki and Bourke share more in common with each other than their men, a bond articulated by the Japanese officer: 'In the loneliness of command we are brothers.' Sinatra even gives the characters matching flashbacks, Kuroki recalling his marriage the day he left for the war, Maloney relating the death of Bourke's fiancée, killed in an air-raid after Bourke rejected her wish to bring their wedding forward ('I'll never let him forget that the bomb was his mistress'). One of the film's many ironies is that Kuroki doesn't survive to be reunited with his wife Keiko - this story is being told by a ghost - whereas Bourke is left alive but with no-one to go home to. Sick of endless fighting, both Kuroki and Bourke accept that their truce must come to an end once either side re-establishes contact with the outside world. Even as they co-operate to protect the island's only fresh water supply from an impending monsoon, the peace is threatened by the Americans' repaired radio.

While the film is successful in its determined attempt to break with the usual Hollywood stereotyping of Japanese soldiers, the American troops are mostly the standard mix: inexperienced young officer, good-natured country boy, tough-talking

None But the Brave – Director Sinatra between takes. Co-star Clint Walker shows off his profile.

bigmouth, cynical veteran, firm-yet-caring leader. This wouldn't matter too much were it not for the fatal miscasting of Tommy Sands, whose stunning inadequacy reduces a pivotal character to unintentional caricature. Contemptuous of the 'dirty Japs', Second Lieutenant Blair wants no part of Bourke's fraternisation with the enemy, his attitude only changing after Kuroki saves his life during the monsoon sequence. Having finally learned to accept the Japanese as fellow human beings, Blair expresses his admiration for Kuroki's courage and compassion: 'You can take this for whatever it's worth, and maybe that's not much, but you're a hell of a guy.' When a US Destroyer finally shows up, Blair attempts to warn the Japanese against a suicidal attack, only to be jumped on by Bourke, their initial attitudes now apparently reversed. If there was anything to made of this part, it vanished into the vacuum of Sands' risible acting, a prime example of nepotism gone horribly wrong. Barking out most of his

lines, Sands twitches and grimaces, his nondescript face in constant danger of disappearing into his oversized helmet. Sinatra's son-in-law apparently took his film career very seriously, enrolling at Lee Strasberg's famous Actors Studio in 1960. If so, he should have demanded a full refund. Cast in the minor role of radio operator Air Crewman Keller, Tony Bill would surely have done a lot better as Blair. Perhaps Sinatra felt he owed Sands a break after allegedly dropping him - albeit at his own request - from *Come Blow Your Horn*. Giving Bill the favoured role a second time would have seemed an unconditional put-down. At least Bill gets a memorable death scene in *None But the Brave*, shot through his right eye during the final firefight on the beach.

Making effective use of the Kauai locations, a usefully contrasting mix of sandy coastline and verdant forest, Sinatra the director displays a sure grasp of film grammar, his sense of composition and camera movement balancing out some loose, overbroad acting in the American camp. The action scenes are well staged and edited, especially a prolonged and costly fight for possession of a crudely made boat, which results in the vessel being blown up. Sinatra is slightly less effective in front of the camera, his drunken, disreputable Irish medic serving largely as Bourke's confidante, Maloney well aware that the latter's solid frame masks a host of insecurities and regrets. Aside from a cynical running commentary on the follies of his fellow man - '"Dirty Jap", lieutenant? They invented the bathtub' - Maloney's big moment is the amputation scene, a prolonged sequence that spares audiences the gore but not the grimly detailed procedure. Equipped with a scalpel sterilised in burning whisky, Maloney crosses himself with the knife before proceeding. Staging much of the scene in a long master shot of Maloney surrounded by anxious, mistrustful Japanese soldiers, Sinatra's blend of drink, religion and merciful blood-letting is quite potent, alcohol depicted as both a life-wrecker and a vital instrument in saving life. Just as Maloney is about to cut into the infected leg with a woodcraft saw, Sinatra cuts away to the night-time forest, the patient's echoing scream telling the whole story. Sadly, Maloney's valiant efforts are later put to waste, his patient gunned down along with the other surviving Japanese soldiers at the climax. Refusing Bourke's offer of peaceful surrender - the ultimate shame for a Japanese warrior - Kuroki initiates a mutual wipeout between the two sides, leaving only five American soldiers standing. Lingering on bloody, smoking bullet wounds during the hectic battle, Sinatra's camera roams over the dead of both armies, closing the film with an unambiguous caption: 'NOBODY EVER WINS'. Point taken.

The prerelease media coverage for *None But the Brave* predictably focused on Sinatra's new director role. Interviewed shortly after the film finished post-production in July 1964, the star talked enthusiastically about his behind-the-camera venture: 'Directing's my favourite medium. It keeps me busier and I like that. I also like the sense of responsibility.' He later admitted to a few difficulties during the shoot, largely a result of

his inexperience: 'The director has so many things to worry about - pace, wardrobe, the performances... Next time I won't try to perform when I direct.' Reaffirming this desire to helm another movie in an interview with *New York Times* reporter Peter Bart, Sinatra proved surprisingly candid regarding his less successful recent efforts: 'I guess the trouble has been that at the time, nothing better seemed to be available. It all boils down to material.' This search for better scripts had already led him to Twentieth Century-Fox and *Von Ryan's Express*, continuing the upturn in quality before his abrupt plunge into the awfulness that is *Marriage on the Rocks*. Out on the publicity trail with *None But the Brave*, Sinatra liked to reiterate the anti-war message: 'I have tried to show that when men do not have to fight, there is a community of interests.' Indeed.

Opening in late January 1965, *None But the Brave* drew mixed, often favourable reviews and respectable box-office. *Los Angeles Times* critic Kevin Thomas praised Sinatra for the 'provocative and engrossing' drama, though many reviewers felt the star's confident directorial debut was undermined by the clichéd script. Tommy Sands' risible performance did not escape attention, Thomas dismissing the latter's efforts as 'hopelessly hammy'. Following his appearance in the so-so Mexican western *The Violent Ones* (1967), Sands retired from the screen for good.

VON RYAN'S EXPRESS 1965

That's what the bloody Bosch have - style.
Major Eric Fincham

Reunited with Twentieth Century-Fox after a five-year gap, Sinatra's immediate and highly astute return to World War II territory following *None But the Brave* suggested he was finally getting his movie act back together, the ill-advised Clan sojourn into self-indulgent parody now ancient history. Offering an exciting locomotive variation on *The 'Great Escape, Von Ryan's Express* is tense and well-paced entertainment, capturing the excitement of a mass allied POW breakout without over-sanitising the terrible cost involved. Generally regarded as superior to *None But the Brave*, it's certainly a slicker, more assured piece of film-making, yet lacks the earlier film's resonance. The brutalities and mayhem depicted are conventional, if well-turned genre ingredients rather than a serious attempt at a personal statement, provoking the desired reactions without lingering in the mind. Sinatra's performance as doomed escape leader Joseph Ryan works on a similar level, his often antagonistic relationship with director Mark Robson resulting in a confident display of star power that carries the film but doesn't transcend its in-built limitations. Offering the star's fifth and final on-screen death, *Von Ryan* was also one of the last films shot in Cinemascope, Fox shortly abandoning their pioneering widescreen format in favour of new market leader Panavision.

Associated with Fox since the early 1950s, Sinatra's track record at the studio didn't exactly sparkle, consisting of the Marilyn Monroe-killed *Pink Tights*, his own *Carousel* walk-out and the flop musical *Can Can*. Things had changed a little at Fox since 1959, former vice-president turned independent producer Darryl F. Zanuck returning to the fold in 1962 after Spyros Skouras' disastrous mismanagement of the *Cleopatra* (1963) affair. Sinatra certainly benefited from Fox's reinvigoration, which is a little ironic given his supposedly 'special' relationship with rival outfit Warner. Following the career-throttling post-*Von Ryan* trio of *Marriage on the Rocks*, *Assault on a Queen* and *The Naked Runner*, Sinatra would return to the studio for his final flourish as a major film player, starring in *Tony Rome*, *The Detective* and *Lady in Cement*.

Based on a novel by David Westheimer, the *Von Ryan* project originated with producer-director Mark Robson. Recognising the book's similarity to John Sturges' recent smash hit *The Great Escape*, Robson acquired the film rights and made a deal with Fox. The director's contract gave him the executive production position on *Von Ryan*, leaving the hands-on producer role to Saul David. Looking for a faithful adaptation of the book, Robson and Zanuck turned to experienced

writers Wendell Mayes and Joseph Landon, the latter's credits including the recent Fox western *Rio Conchos* (1964). Impressed with the resulting script, Sinatra's enthusiasm for *Von Ryan* was tempered a little by the lengthy location shoot in Italy and Spain, thousands of miles from his preferred base of operations. Having sworn never to return to the latter country after the *Pride and the Passion* debacle he felt torn between turning down an almost certain hit and taking on conditions likely to bring out the worst in him. In need of advice, Sinatra turned to old friend Harry Kurnitz, respected novelist, playwright and scriptwriter. Kurnitz shared the widely held view that Sinatra had been wasting his talent on the Clan 'home movies'. *Von Ryan* offered a solid, well-constructed war-adventure vehicle, just the kind of film to build on the success of *None But the Brave*. Convinced, the star signed on the dotted line, contributing cameramen William Daniels and Harold Lipstein to the technical crew, the latter serving with *Von Ryan*'s second unit.

Lacking *The Great Escape*'s line-up of stars in the making, *Von Ryan* still boasted an impressive supporting cast, headed by British character actor Trevor Howard as Major Eric Fincham. Zanuck also obtained the services of Howard's fellow countryman John Leyton, who'd appeared in the Sturges film. The part of nice, anti-Nazi Italian officer Oriani went to Sergio Fantoni, previously cast by Mark Robson in *The Prize* (1963). Oriani's evil fascist counterpart Major Battaglia was played by Adolfo Celi, shortly to achieve international recognition as the one-eyed villain of *Thunderball* (1965). For the German camp, Zanuck cast his *Longest Day* colleague Wolfgang Preiss as Major Von Klementz, a typical example of ruthless efficiency. Aside from Brad Dexter, the Sinatra-picked supporting cast included Richard Bakalyan and famed Hollywood restaurateur 'Prince' Mike Romanoff, a friend of the star who later appeared in *Tony Rome*.

Venturing out onto far-flung locales for the first time since *Never So Few*, Sinatra lapsed into some of his bad old ways during the *Von Ryan* shoot in Italy and Spain over August and September 1964. Fox originally planned to base their star in Rome for the first leg of the production, Robson having found a prime location site in Cortina D'Ampezzo, high up in the Dolomite Alps. Booed off stage during a concert in the Eternal City back in the early 1950s, Sinatra refused to stay there, settling instead for the 18-room Villa Apia on the outskirts, protected from prying reporters by four bodyguards. Once installed, the star resumed his old cherry bomb antics as the chief after-hours diversion. The villa came with its own helipad, from which Sinatra was flown out to the location every day, arguing that the standard limousine transportation would inevitably draw the paparazzi during the one-hour drive. The rest of the cast and crew had to be content with a car ride, not that anyone felt inclined to cry foul.

Sinatra's working relationship with Mark Robson could best be described as fraught, one of the few times in the star's career where he appeared actively to dislike his director. Priding himself on being a painstaking craftsman, Robson would probably have clashed with Sinatra on the easiest of shoots, the latter ever-eager to work through his scenes at top speed. Out on difficult, isolated locations, a clash was inevitable, the star failing to show Robson the kind of respect he'd afforded to Otto Preminger or John Frankenheimer. Deaf to all explanations of production logistics, Sinatra demanded that his scenes be filmed consecutively, with minimum waiting time between set-ups. Robson's initial protests were swiftly countered by a show of star power, Sinatra walking off the set until he got his way. The subsequent hasty rescheduling proved a nightmare for Robson and producer Saul David, Sinatra's 'entourage' contributing to the grim working atmosphere with their arrogant, insulting behaviour. With filming costs running at $25,000 a day, Robson could not afford any serious delays, his anxiety over the schedule driven by both professional and personal concerns. While Sinatra's deal with Fox gave him a gross share of the box-office take, Robson had only been granted a percentage of the net profits, which were steadily shrinking with every wasted minute. According to Earl Wilson, *Von Ryan's*

subsequent commercial success left its director feeling seriously cheated by his star's unreasonable behaviour.

Sinatra's frequent disagreements with Robson did not prevent his fellow actors from having a reasonably good time on locations such as Rome, Malaga and Cortina. Trevor Howard certainly enjoyed making *Von Ryan*, rating the end result as one of his best Hollywood films. Having weathered Marlon Brando's tantrums during the tortuously drawn-out production of *Mutiny on the Bounty*, he found Sinatra largely affable by comparison. Usually surrounded by his entourage on set, the star could appear a little remote but was never deliberately rude or unpleasant. Sinatra's visitors during the Italy shoot included Ava Gardner, then working in nearby Sicily on John Huston's *The Bible* (1966). The star was disturbed by his ex-wife's heavy drinking, which probably didn't help his mood on the *Von Ryan* set.

With the Italian scenes finally completed, the production team relocated to Spain in early September, setting up home at the Pez Espada Hotel, Torremolinos. Unenthusiastic about returning to Generalissimo Franco's Republic, Sinatra had initially refused to leave Italy, eventually swayed by executive pleading and a free yachting holiday. While the star's opinion of Spain hadn't improved much since *The Pride and the Passion*, the shoot went more or less to schedule until the last day. Out on the town the previous evening, both Sinatra and Brad Dexter were detained by the local police after a young woman falsely accused them of assault. Faced with the possibility of a drawn-out legal battle, Saul David bailed his actors out of prison, settling the matter with a minimum of fuss.

Back on safer Hollywood ground, *Von Ryan* commenced studio work at the Fox lot in October 1964, running over 30 days. Trevor Howard took a little time out for a cameo role in Fox's other 1965 World War II drama, the Marlon Brando-Yul Brynner flop *Morituri*. The studio's Nuns 'n' Nazis family extravaganza *The Sound of Music* was also in production at the time, which must have placed a considerable stretch on the wardrobe department's supply of German uniforms.

Von Ryan's Express – Sinatra upstages Sergio Fantoni and Adolfo Celi with the old head wound trick.

Away from the mock battlefields, the hit television series *Peyton Place* was shooting on a nearby soundstage, one of its stars soon becoming a regular visitor to the *Von Ryan* set. Mia Farrow initially turned up to see her friend John Leyton, whom she'd met while filming *Guns at Batasi* (1964). Watching Sinatra shoot one of his train scenes with Raffaella Carra, Farrow became drawn to his 'beautiful' face. The rest is well known, if brief history, the Sinatra-Farrow affair becoming the media hit of the year. While Sinatra's preoccupation with Mia Farrow would later take its toll on the productions of *The Naked Runner*, *The Detective* and *Lady in Cement*, her appearance late into the *Von Ryan* shoot appears to have wreaked little damage.

Set in 1943, just after the allied invasion of Sicily, *Von Ryan's Express* is very much a film in two acts, switching from POW camp stoicism to captured train excitements as the escapees head up Northern Italy towards neutral Switzerland. Having crashlanded his plane during the precredits sequence, former civilian pilot Colonel Joseph L. Ryan arrives at the camp just as the previous allied commanding officer is being buried, a premonition of his own demise in the film's closing moments. Aware that liberation is close at hand, Ryan advises co-operation

with the Italian jailors, his passive attitude placing him in direct opposition with Fincham. Offering a stiff-upper-lip version of Sinatra's battered integrity, Howard's British Army Major is obsessed with continuing the war from within the prison camp walls, organising breakout attempts on a regular basis. While their relationship runs along the expected course of hostility-distrust-wary co-operation-mutual respect, the Ryan-Fincham combination provides a solid centre for the story, both actors investing the serviceable script with an extra depth. It takes an unusually - and commendably - long time for the characters to abandon their initial antagonism, Fincham wary of Ryan for most of the film.

Making good use of his vivid, hard-won location footage, Mark Robson's direction is generally first rate. Another camera crane specialist, he keeps the action flowing, his fluid style masking the story cracks and stock characterisation. Memorable images include the backlit figures of escaping POWs advancing across the roof of a train carriage and the climactic set pieces involving a Messerschmitt attack on the bridge-bound train and a shootout in a railway tunnel. The carnage is balanced by injections of black humour, marred only by Jerry Goldsmith's overdone 'comedy' music. The Italian soldiers obviously hate their German 'allies', making obscene gestures at the backs of Nazi officers. Battaglia's overfed stomach is held in place by a corset. Protesting over their ragged, unwashed clothes, Ryan leads the prisoners in a mass burning, the soldiers standing in line naked as their uniforms go up in smoke (new arrival Ryan doesn't shed his shiny dark green jumpsuit). The film's dialogue is noticeably less sanitised than *None But the Brave*'s, Fincham's heartfelt cry of 'Bastard' at Battaglia making Tommy Sands' ludicrous 'Son of a buck' look pretty tame.

Inevitably, some of the flaws show through. The escape plan hinges almost entirely on the British chaplain's ability to speak near perfect German, his accent arousing no suspicion at all. Aside from embellishing the title, the disparaging nickname 'Von Ryan' seems a little pointless after the first Ryan-Fincham clash, even Trevor Howard delivering the put-down without much conviction. A brief subplot involving attractive-but-treacherous Nazi mistress Mariella (Raffaella Carra) appears to have been taken from the 'dangerous glamour' file, rendering her subsequent shooting by Ryan as she attempts to escape largely unshocking.

Overweight during most of the filming by as much as 15 pounds, Sinatra still carries himself well on screen. First seen swigging from a whisky bottle, apparently unperturbed by his recent aircrash, Ryan appears a man out for the easiest time possible. He quickly pulls rank on Fincham to make a deal with Battaglia, putting a stop to the escape attempts in return for more humane treatment. Interestingly, Ryan is depicted as man of flawed judgement, his decision to spare Battaglia's life after the breakout later resulting in the deaths of many allied soldiers. Reluctantly accepting his destiny as a leader of men, Ryan leads the takeover of the prison train, donning full German uniform as disguise. In a rather contrived moment of heavy irony, he is mistaken for a real Nazi by an anti-fascist Italian youth, the latter watching in mute horror as Ryan shoots Mariella in the back. This necessary brutality is neatly mirrored by his own climactic death, machine-gunned from behind as he runs down the line towards the train. One of the best known movie endings, Ryan's death on the tracks was Sinatra's idea, included in the film only after protracted arguments. The original script retained the book's ending, Ryan escaping over the Swiss border with his fellow POWs. Sinatra disliked this straightforwardly upbeat finale, feeling that Ryan's cold-blooded killing of a young woman - fascist collaborator or not - should be balanced by his own death. As things stood, the act had no real effect on later events, Ryan quickly getting over his guilt and self-loathing. Sensing a hit, Fox bosses Darryl and Richard Zanuck were not happy with the idea, their minds already focused on Westheimer's sequel to *Von Ryan*. Zanuck Jnr also felt that the tragic ending could hurt the film's box-office. The argument continued throughout the shoot, the Zanucks eventually offering a compromise where both Ryan and

Fincham are wounded during the final escape, left bleeding on the tracks while the train speeds into the distance. The film would close with a shot of the injured men surrounded by jackboots, leaving the door wide open for a follow-up. Adamant that Von Ryan should die, Sinatra wouldn't buy minor bullet wounds. Audiences had been moved rather than turned off by the deaths of Maggio in *From Here to Eternity* and Ginny in *Some Came Running*, creating a level of sympathy not possible if the characters had lived. More to the point, *The Great Escape*'s downbeat conclusion hadn't stopped it from becoming a blockbuster. Impressed by this line of reasoning, the Zanucks agreed to Sinatra's choice of ending. Placing his camera on the departing train, Robson offers a poignant long shot of Ryan's prone body, cut down within seconds of getting away. Fincham's closing voiceover reiterates his earlier argument with Ryan, now a martyr to the cause: '...if only one gets out, it's a victory'.

Von Ryan's Express premiered at Loew's State Theatre, New York on June 23 1965, Sinatra turning up for the screening with daughters Nancy and Tina. The largely favourable reviews were more than endorsed by the audience response and the film quickly proved a major box-office success, Sinatra making close on $2 million from his percentage deal. The generally favourable response to the film prompted talk of a third Academy Award nomination for Sinatra, though in the event the star had to settle for preserving his hand and footprints in cement outside Grauman's Chinese Theatre. The only significant shadow hovering over the *Von Ryan* success story was an astonishingly hostile review from Bosley Crowther, who condemned the film as '...an outrageous and totally disgusting display of romantic exhibitionism in a pseudo-wartime environment'. Criticised himself for being increasingly out of touch with the changing face of sixties American cinema, Crowther's uptight moralising was occasionally balanced by spot-on dissection. A few months later, he dismissed *Marriage on the Rocks* as 'a tawdry and witless trifle'. There weren't many dissenters.

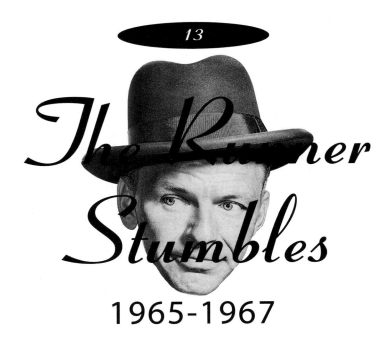

13

The Runner Stumbles

1965-1967

MARRIAGE ON THE ROCKS 1965

I work hard at being married. I'm a great father and a good husband.
Daniel Edwards, divorcee in the making

Film up the creek. Tedious, poorly made and utterly uninventive, *Marriage on the Rocks* is one of the few truly terrible entries in the Sinatra filmography, a project that can't have looked good even on paper. Tired of distant foreign locations after *Von Ryan's Express*, the star shouldn't be blamed for selecting a smaller scale, home-based vehicle, yet he appears to have picked the first script that came along, quality be damned. Aside from the ill-advised participation of *From Here to Eternity* co-star Deborah Kerr, the film's only notable feature is its punning title, changed from original non-starter *Community Property*. In his one and only screen appearance as a conventional family man - complete with the statutory wife and two kids - Sinatra plays workaholic advertising executive Dan

Edwards, a man too wrapped up in his business to notice the cracks in his 19-year-old marriage. Kerr is his bored 30-something wife Valerie, beginning to feel she made the wrong choice of husband. A therapeutic second honeymoon in Mexico leads to moment-of-anger divorce, immediate reconciliation, remarriage to the wrong person and general mayhem. A witless blending of marital and generation gap comedy, the film is further doomed by incompetent direction, tatty sets, an unbearable 'swinging' score and some truly desperate acting. While nothing quite equals the sight of 43-year-old Deborah Kerr getting down to the magical sound of guitar-strumming, hip swivelling popster Trini Lopez at the Cafe a Go Go, there's an awful lot of competition.

While the blame for *Marriage On the Rocks* should fall on several heads, it seems fair enough to begin with the man who came up with the idea. Veteran gag writer Seymour 'Cy' Howard appears to have concocted his script as a twisted act of revenge upon the entire comedy genre, offering approximately two passable

Marriage on the Rocks – Cesar Romero gives co-stars Sinatra and Deborah Kerr a good look at the script.

jokes and about enough plot to fill a 25-minute television episode. It's doubtful anyone could have salvaged a half-decent movie from this feeble effort, yet Sinatra did himself no favours entrusting *Marriage*'s direction to his former dance teacher Jack Donohue. With Gordon Douglas tied up on the Paramount release *Harlow* (1965), the star hastily chose a replacement with nothing like the same level of competence. A regular television collaborator, Donohue hadn't directed for the cinema since the flop Disney extravaganza *Babes in Toyland* (1961) and his unexpected return to the medium proved a big mistake. With cameraman William Daniels serving as the film's full-fledged producer, there was no-one running the show who hadn't been promoted from the ranks by Sinatra. This lack of outside talent and experience showed in the end result, suggesting that both Donohue and Daniels were struggling with roles beyond their ability.

Casting for *Marriage* presented few problems,

Sinatra simply doing the rounds of friends, relatives and esteemed fellow professionals. For the role of Edwards' bachelor colleague and best friend Ernie Brewer, the star naturally looked to Dean Martin, who said yes without taking a close look at the script. The part of Edwards' disenchanted wife could have been played by just about any actress in the late-30s/early 40s bracket, yet Sinatra had only one candidate in mind. Nearly 12 years had passed since *From Here to Eternity* and he wanted an on-screen reunion with his old friend Deborah Kerr, perhaps looking for a touch of class otherwise lacking from *Marriage*. Kerr had decided largely to retire from film work when she received the *Marriage* script in late 1964. Reluctant to go back on this decision, she declined to give Sinatra an answer straight away, her reservations over the project countered by a desire to work with him again. Sinatra's pre-existing commitments meant that the film could not begin production until early spring 1965, leaving Kerr plenty of time to decide. A telephone conversation with Sinatra made up Kerr's mind, the star promising her an enjoyable, fun-packed shoot. *Marriage* would be Kerr's first Hollywood-based production for six years and by a long way her worst.

Press speculation over Sinatra's new friendship with Mia Farrow prompted him to use the *Marriage* shoot as a none-too-convincing cover for their liaisons. Seen out on the town with Farrow during the film's preproduction period in November 1964, Sinatra claimed he was merely discussing business with the *Peyton Place* star, one of several actresses under consideration to play his daughter in the forthcoming film. While the press were not slow to pick up on the irony of the situation, it appears to have been lost on Sinatra. Casting his own daughter Nancy in the part didn't seem to give him any pause for thought, either. Five years older than her father's current *amour*, Nancy Sinatra was briefly in vogue as a film performer during the mid-1960s, debuting in *For Those Who Think Young* (1964), a Sinatra Enterprises-Paramount production overseen by Howard Koch (see Appendix 3). Never a screen natural, Nancy Sinatra's movie appeal derived largely from her chart success with hits such as 'These Boots Are Made For Walking', a Reprise release. She doesn't get to sing in *Marriage on the Rocks*, her role requiring little more than a dose of teen petulance. The part of Sinatra's fiery Scottish mother-in-law went to British actress Hermione Baddeley, who'd played a similar role in the recent marital comedy *Do Not Disturb* (1964). Sinatra filled out the remaining key roles with old hands Joi Lansing, Cesar Romero, John McGiver and Tony Bill.

Filming commenced on 8 March 1965. Dispensing with the firecrackers and balloons of earlier shoots, Sinatra and Martin devoted most of their energies to breaking each other up on set. Sinatra's favoured tactic was to stick black electrician's tape on his upper lip, an ersatz 'moustache' reused to equally hilarious effect during the production of *Assault on a Queen*. Deborah Kerr recalled the filming of *Marriage* as non-stop fun and laughter, Sinatra's promise of a good time more

than fulfilled. She even found the star's time-saving habit of tearing out scenes from the script amusing, obviously not feeling that anything noteworthy was being lost. For all this star-foolery, co-star Nancy Sinatra regarded the working atmosphere as generally brisk and professional. An inexperienced film performer, Nancy Jnr felt extremely nervous acting opposite her father, veteran of 36 leading roles. Sinatra went out of his way to put her at ease, carefully rehearsing their scenes together and offering advice when she came unstuck. Her mood wasn't improved by off-screen traumas during the shoot. As Frank Sinatra grew closer to Mia Farrow, Nancy Sinatra's more conventional relationship with Tommy Sands fell apart, the latter informing her that their marriage was over.

While some of the Clan films had appeared rather indifferently put together, *Marriage on the Rocks* often looks downright incompetent. Attempting to replicate his fairly basic television techniques on the Panavision screen, Jack Donohue's direction is barely professional at times, displaying a misplaced preference for long, static takes that only serve to highlight the wretched writing and struggling performances. Sam O'Steen's editing is surprisingly clumsy in some sequences, suggesting that Donohue left the post-production team a little short of usable footage.

Given the useless script and hands-off direction, it seems unfair to make too much of the supporting actors' failings. Nancy Sinatra felt her own performance would have been better had she overcome her nervousness, yet the part has nothing to offer. Cesar Romero does a lot better as Miguel Santos, presumably a near relative of *Ocean's 11*'s Duke Santos. The cheerfully corrupt attorney-hotel manager-doctor is certainly the high point of Dan and Val's trip to Warner's Mexican village backlot, hustling his services with a broad smile and outstretched hand. For the rest, Hermione Baddeley wears tartan, plays the bagpipes and sports a bad accent, while Tony Bill, cast as Nancy Sinatra's psychiatrist boyfriend, does little other than take notes on human behaviour, observing rather than participating in the action: 'I don't need the stimulation of alcohol.'

Having put together a triumphantly third rate vehicle, Sinatra pitches his performance at the same low level, acting with an eye on the studio clock. The star's only noticeable concession to the demands of his role is donning a pair of thick-rimmed glasses, obviously the mark of a dedicated professional (Tony Bill has a similar pair). Jaded by two decades of marriage, Dan Edwards has forgotten how to make a lady feel special, relying on Ernie to pick out anniversary gifts for Valerie. A creature of monotonous habit, he is no longer sensitive to her feelings, blithely assuming that she is content with the daily routine. While both Sinatra and Deborah Kerr could have shone in a more considered study of crumbling relationships, *Marriage* offers no real drama and only a pitiful trickle of tired comedy standards. Sinatra fails to show much enthusiasm even when Dan gets the chance to sample Ernie's single lifestyle, living it up in his friend's Malibu beachfront pad while Ernie attempts to control the Edwards household. This brief role-reversal sees the star back in his familiar bachelor orange, yet the spirit is gone and he looks bored.

Marriage on the Rocks does offer two memorable star turns, though most would prefer to forget the first. The word most commonly applied to Deborah Kerr's acting in *Marriage* is 'embarrassing'. Lumbered with some highly unflattering costumes, notably an absurd fur hat and a figure-revealing 'Vive La Derrière' negligée, Kerr's performance is awkward and mannered, her supposedly humorous dialogue falling hopelessly flat. Kerr's comments to biographer Eric Braun are revealing, the actress claiming that *Marriage* was just a fun time not to be taken seriously. Throwing herself into the film with enthusiasm rather than any noticeable comedy expertise, she delivers little more than amateur dramatics, pointlessly overemphasising certain words as if this would automatically make them funny. Left stranded by director Donohue, Kerr's performance in *Marriage* earned her the first truly bad reviews of her career.

By contrast, Dean Martin is commendably understated, his delivery and reactions displaying a sense of timing that leaves the other actors standing. If, as Nick Tosches claims, Martin was 'suckered' into the film by good buddy Sinatra, he rose to the awful challenge with admirable professionalism. A former rival for Valerie's affection, Ernie appears content with his easy come-easy go relationships, negotiating his multiple amorous liaisons like business deals. Popular with Valerie and the Edwards kids for his laid-back manner, Ernie learns the hard way that true, full-time marital and parental responsibility requires discipline and sacrifice. Martin doesn't appear to take this conservative endorsement of middle-American family values with any measure of seriousness, mischievously undercutting the noticeably abrupt happy ending where Dan and the now pregnant Valerie realise they've still been deeply in love all along. It says something about both Martin and the film that he manages to steal it completely with a few easy moves:

1. Walking into a pillar.
2. Falling over (twice).
3. Engaging in the following exchange with Deborah Kerr:
DEAN: I think I'll walk the dog.
DEBORAH: We don't have a dog.
DEAN: I'll find one.

It's the way he tells them. Despite his good work, *Marriage* marked a depressing finale to an on-screen partnership that began so well with *Some Came Running*. Martin never bothered to look at the end result, along with most of the paying public.

Realising they had an insultingly shoddy piece of merchandise on their hands, Warner opted to play it safe with *Marriage on the Rocks*, releasing the film off-peak on 16 September 1965. If the studio had hoped to avoid hostile press attention with this ruse, they scored a partial victory at best. Premiering in New York during a widespread newspaper strike, the film was initially covered by only two reviewers, both of whom did their best to give *Marriage* the reception it deserved. *New York Post* critic Archer Winsten rated the film 'well below the best Sinatra-Martin movie levels and almost out of sight of Deborah Kerr's best'. *New York Herald*

Marriage on the Rocks – Jim and Tracy. This is Nancy Sinatra's original nose.

Tribune writer Judith Crist struggled to find sufficient abusive adjectives, 'flat, insipid and watery' having to make do. Other than its general low quality, the only element in *Marriage* to attract much attention was a throwaway subplot featuring Tracy's Go Go dancer friend Lisa (Davey Davison). The product of a broken home, 23-year-old Lisa is in need of a father figure and hits on the newly divorced Dan as a likely candidate. Harbouring only platonic feelings for the young woman, Dan gives her a gentle brush-off, explaining that she's like another daughter to him. Having spotted the two of them dancing in Lisa's Cafe a Go Go cage (an environment both provocative and protective),

Valerie offers to be first with the wedding gifts: 'A crib for you and an oxygen tent for Dan.' This quip is remarkably similar to the various Sinatra-Farrow jokes doing the rounds at the time, most of which annoyed the star considerably. A strange multi-weaving of life and family-safe entertainment. If Sinatra had only cast Mia Farrow as Lisa, he could have had a major cult hit on his hands.

While most were content to write *Marriage* off as a spectacularly unamusing farce, there was stronger feeling against it south of the border. A mid-ranking Mexican government official disliked the film intensely, claiming that Sinatra had insulted the whole of Mexico with Cesar Romero's comic, amoral attorney. If the depiction of the instant marriage/divorce business wasn't bad enough, there were further outrages in the script, notably a less than complimentary Kerr-Sinatra exchange:

DEBORAH: You mustn't drink the water
 down here.
FRANK: The secret is not to come to this
 place at all.

These remarks seem thoughtless at worst, insensitive rather than deliberately malicious, yet the Mexican government would not accept a mere token apology and it took the combined efforts of Sinatra's attorney Louis Nizer and Academy of Motion Picture Arts and Sciences head Jack Valenti to straighten out the row. The star wisely opted to locate his next film in the Atlantic Ocean, where the locals were less sensitive.

ASSAULT ON A QUEEN 1966

Let's go to work.
Mark Brittain, modern-day pirate to the gentry

In early 1966, recently recruited Paramount executive Robert Evans checked out the studio's projected blockbuster releases for the year: *Promise Her Anything*, with Warren Beatty and Leslie Caron, *Is Paris Burning?*, an all-star wartime extravaganza, and *Assault on a Queen*. Less than impressed by what he saw, Evans felt particularly dubious about *Queen*'s commercial chances, correctly weighing it up as a stale 'B' property unwisely promoted to 'A' treatment with Sinatra's presence. Taken from a novel by *Body Snatchers* author Jack Finney, *Assault on a Queen* is a lacklustre nautical variation on *Ocean's 11*, this time with a real ocean but only six gang members. The storyline has possibilities, involving an attempt to rob the HMS Queen Mary using only a salvaged U-Boat and a dummy torpedo, yet the film misses even the most routine excitements, emerging as an incredibly stolid and solemn 'entertainment'. As with *Ocean*, the main characters are the usual bunch of assorted losers, including three World War II navy veterans, a war orphan, an ex-drunk and a smooth talking chancer with a fatal diamond fixation. Playing submarine lieutenant turned charter fisherman Mark Brittain, Sinatra delivers another by-the-numbers turn, dominating the screen but doing nothing with it. It's been suggested that Sinatra's various caper movies were really just childhood wish fulfilment fantasies; if so, he might have put a little more spirit into them.

Still on amicable terms with Paramount after *Come Blow Your Horn* and *For Those Who Think Young*, Sinatra agreed a three-way deal for *Assault on a Queen*, independent outfit Seven Arts coming on board as the third partner. While the star's team naturally included William Daniels, few would have expected him to retain the services of *Marriage on the Rocks* director Jack Donohue, Sinatra presumably placing friendship/subservience above talent on this occasion. Queen also marked Sinatra's only film collaboration with his producer friend William Goetz, a former Twentieth Century-Fox employee turned independent operator. Back in the early fifties, Goetz had briefly considered casting the out-of-favour Sinatra in a proposed film version of Georges Simenon's Mafia novella *The Brothers Rico* (see Appendix 2). Doubts over the downbeat ending quickly stalled the project, though Goetz eventually made the film in 1957, a modest production with Richard Conte as the lead. Re-established as a major Hollywood player by this time,

Sinatra didn't begrudge either Goetz or Conte the lost role, the latter joining his exclusive circle a few years later.

The job of adapting Finney's character-driven novel for the screen fell to Emmy Award-winning television talent Rod Serling, who'd recently scripted John Frankenheimer's political thriller *Seven Days in May* (1964). The Frankenheimer connection probably played at least a part in Sinatra's choice of writer, not that Serling delivered anything of comparable quality this time around. It's usually a bad sign when characters are required to articulate what should be self-evident, notably: 'We're digging ourselves a grave here. Each of us for his own particular reason.'

With Sinatra signed up for *Queen*, the Paramount executives felt no need to recruit big name co-stars. The bruised-glamour role of seductive war orphan Rosa Lucazi went to Italian actress Virna Lisi, whose only American movie to date was *How to Murder Your Wife* (1965), a patchy black comedy penned by George Axelrod. Anthony Franciosa got the part of Victor Rossiter, Brittain's rival in both leadership and love. Cast as former U-Boat captain Erich Lauffnauer, Swedish actor Alf Kjellin was an old MGM contract player, billed under the pseudonym 'Christopher Kent' for his Hollywood debut in Vincente Minnelli's *Madame Bovary* (1949). Richard Conte was the only *Ocean* gang member invited on board, back with Sinatra for the first time since the 1960 hit. Appearing 45 minutes into the film, his decorated then disgraced ex-submarine engineer Tony Moreno is a welcome sight. The most impressive new recruit was black actor Errol John, cast as Brittain's right-hand man Linc. Playing a former alcoholic rescued from the gutter by Mark, John suggests a sense of gratitude and loyalty without the uncomfortable kow-towing found in Sammy Davis Jnr's performances opposite Sinatra. While the tall, solidly built Linc doesn't look much like a recovering booze-hound, his healthy condition is doubtless a tribute to Brittain's nursing skills. Short on box-office names, this line-up at least ensured Sinatra's domination of the proceedings, though Franciosa

Assault on a Queen – Mark Brittain has his card game rudely interrupted.

requested and received special below-the-title billing on the advertising, his name in star-sized lettering after Conte, John and Kjellin.

A vital factor in getting *Assault on a Queen* under way was the co-operation of the real ship's owners, Cunard Steam Ship Company, and the US Coast Guard. There were few serious obstacles to this official seal of approval, as the final script presented both parties in a highly favourable light. The crew and officers of the Queen Mary are depicted as dedicated and caring professionals, placing the safety of their passengers above the gold and cash in the ship's vaults. When Rossiter assaults a female passenger for her diamond ring, a senior officer guns him down. The United States coastguard are portrayed in equally glowing terms, cruising to the rescue when they realise the liner is under siege. With only Brittain, Rosa and Linc left alive at the end, their submarine sunk and the loot abandoned, the film could certainly not be accused of glamorising

piracy or inciting imitation. Once all necessary permissions were obtained, *Queen* started shooting on 20 September 1965. Aside from some token location filming in Miami, Florida and Long Beach, California, the production was largely studio-based, leaving Sinatra little time to become restless. Jack Donohue celebrated his 57th birthday during the shoot, cast and crew presenting him with a suitably nautical cake.

Apart from a mildly arresting title sequence, involving a pencil line, a sea chart and a Queen of Hearts playing card (canny symbolism), *Queen* operates on a strictly television movie level, with matching cut-rate production values. William Daniels' sharp photography only serves to emphasise the film's studio-bound look, mixing the minimal location work with blatant back projection and fake boats. Supposedly an expert deep sea diver, Sinatra's character is required to spend prolonged periods underwater, slowing the film's already stumbling pace to a virtual standstill. Unable to find a convincing double for these sequences, the second unit crew settled for a noticeably younger, taller man with a more believable head of hair, occasional insert shots of Sinatra's face failing to disguise the substitution. This slipshod approach continued into post-production, Errol John handing Sinatra the same cup and saucer twice over in consecutive shots. In fairness, Donohue's direction of *Queen* marks a slight improvement over *Marriage on the Rocks*, though his surer sense of composition and camera movement is not matched by any quickening of pace. Briefly woken from his lethargy, Donohue does provide a shamelessly leering high angle shot of Virna Lisi's exposed legs, suggesting an unrealised potential for more voyeuristic material. Otherwise, there is little on offer other than ungripping scenes of treasure hunting, submarine raising, submarine restoration, and the climactic raid on the Queen Mary, all accompanied by Duke Ellington's jaunty but monotonous and utterly inappropriate score. The film's nicest touch is having Moreno and Rosa converse in Italian, conveying a sense of character far better than all the laboured past history exposition.

The minimal enjoyment to be found in *Queen* derives largely from its dialogue, only part of the effect intentional. Early on in the film, Brittain and Linc quarrel with their greedy marina landlord Trench (Val Avery), Brittain eventually throwing him into the bay.

LINCOLN: Can he swim?

BRITTAIN: We'll check the morning papers. Elsewhere, Serling's grasp of basic scriptwriting appears to have deserted him, aided and abetted by Virna Lisi's struggle with English, her pronunciation of 'Naples' sounding more like 'nipples'. Confessing her wildest dreams to Brittain, Rosa becomes positively lyrical: 'I want my life to be whipped cream and silk sheets', only 'silk' sounds like 'sick', which isn't an appealing image. Brittain can't resist this kind of talk, admitting to Linc: 'She's so deep in my gut we breathe together.' Eventually dumping the over-acting Rossiter for Brittain's more understated passion, Rosa has a heart-to-heart with the latter over their daring robbery plan:

ROSA: I didn't hear you say no.

BRITTAIN: That's because maybe you weren't listening. Come to think of it, I wasn't talking. *Queen* premiered on 27 July 1966, to no interest whatsoever. Paramount appear to have largely given up on the film before it even hit the theatres, employing such pathetic promo lines as 'They Stick Up the Queen Mary in Mid Atlantic.' Billed above the title with Sinatra, Verna Lisi's on-screen romance with the star figured in the advertising as much as the daring heist storyline: 'He's an I've-tried-everything-guy. She's an I'll-try-anything girl.' The love interest didn't sell any better than the robbery, audiences turned off by the lack of thrills, drama and poor quality special effects. The *Monthly Film Bulletin* verdict, 'Just about as enthralling as plastic boats in the bath', captured the general response all too well. Away in London for location shooting on *The Naked Runner*, Sinatra had good reason to feel anxious about his movie career. After two resounding flops in a row, the commercial momentum gained by *Von Ryan's Express* was grinding to a halt. He badly needed a hit, yet production on his spy thriller was not going well. Far from looking like a surefire box-office success, *Naked Runner* appeared in serious danger of not even being finished.

THE NAKED RUNNER 1967

Do it my way Sam, I'm warning you.
My way.
Martin Slattery, Her Majesty's less than
honourable Secret Service

Not to put too fine a point on it, *The Naked Runner* is an utterly useless film. Arguably no worse in real terms than *Marriage on the Rocks* or *Assault on a Queen*, it comes as far more of a disappointment thanks to the obvious amount of wasted talent involved. Intended as a determined bid to arrest the downward spiral of Sinatra's movie career, *Runner* ended up contributing to his freefall, pleasing neither audiences nor critics. Sinatra stars as mild-mannered businessman Sam Laker, a former army sharpshooter used as an unwitting pawn in a British intelligence plot to assassinate an enemy agent. What should have been a fast-paced, exciting, fashionably cynical game of cats and mice falls apart virtually from the first frame, doomed by an unworkable script, negligible characterisation, pointlessly tricksy handling and stiff-as-cardboard acting. Sinatra's fraught relationship with new wife Mia Farrow is often cited as a reason for the disastrous final product, yet *Naked Runner* could never have been much of a film. Even allowing for the various production troubles, it's an incredibly shoddy piece of work to emerge from a major studio.

Sinatra didn't need the miserable box-office returns from *Assault on a Queen* to remind him of his declining star appeal. By late 1965, he'd resolved to put more effort into his film career and looked to trusted aide Brad Dexter for suitable material. Dexter felt Sinatra had grown noticeably lazy both as an actor and an executive producer, selecting the projects that caused least disruption to his social life. Now Vice-President of Sinatra Enterprises in charge of production, Dexter found a script he thought would be ideal for the star, the cynical private eye thriller *Harper*, owned by independent producers Elliott Kastner and Jerry Gershwin. Based on the John Ross MacDonald novel *The Moving Target*, William Goldman's script was in essence a canny 1960s update of the old *film noir* genre, the more liberal climate of the times allowing for greater doses of explicit sex and violence. A long-time staple of television entertainment, the private eye genre had been out of fashion in Hollywood, studio executives feeling that audiences got more than enough of it on the small screen. Enthusiastic about the material, Sinatra was prepared to take a chance, proposing to make the film through Warner. Unfortunately the deal with Gershwin and Kastner fell through (see Appendix 2), the star having to wait another 14 years before working with the latter on *The First Deadly Sin*. Sinatra would shortly get a second stab at the genre with *Tony Rome*. For the time being, he agreed to go along with Brad Dexter's Plan B, a film version of Francis Clifford's downbeat espionage thriller *The Naked Runner*.

Financially speaking, the *Runner* project looked very good indeed. The deal gave Sinatra a $1 million fee up front, plus a generous share of the box-office gross. His films might be flopping but he could still negotiate the big star salaries. Dexter received a more modest $50,000 producer fee. Sinatra's astute choice of director for the film showed he'd learned at least a few things from the Jack Donohue experience. Recently acquainted with rising British star Michael Caine, Sinatra had been impressed by the latter's performance in *The Ipcress File* (1965), a low-key spy tale favouring modish 'realism' over James Bond-style pyrotechnics. Both Sinatra and Dexter wanted a similar approach for *Runner* and engaged *Ipcress* director Sidney J. Furie for their film. A Canadian talent from a television background, Furie's first Hollywood effort, the Marlon Brando western *The Appaloosa* (1966), proved traumatic during production and a failure on release. Doubtless hoping for a smoother collaboration with Sinatra, Furie little knew what he was getting into. Looking to duplicate his *Ipcress* style as much as possible, the director recruited the film's veteran cameraman Otto Heller, a Czech ex-patriate who'd been a director of photography since 1918. The script was entrusted to Furie's fellow Canadian Stanley Mann. Academy Award-nominated for *The Collector* (1965), Mann's talent appears to have deserted him shortly afterwards. Hurried rewrites aside, his script for *Runner* is an incompetent botch job. The mostly British supporting cast was headed by Peter Vaughan, with his sinister smile, and Derren Nesbitt, whose blond hair, piercing eyes and equally sinister protruding lower lip brought him plenty of Nazi-style villain roles.

Runner's London shoot commenced on 5 July 1966, its recently betrothed star relaxing after-hours at the local Playboy Club. While Sinatra proved amicable enough on set, his mind was fixed on more intimate matters. Less than two weeks into production, the star temporarily closed down the film while he flew to Las Vegas to marry Mia Farrow at The Sands Hotel on 19 July, William Goetz serving as best man. The star returned to London with Farrow around 25 July,

The Naked Runner – Sam Laker moves in for the kill.

intending to combine their honeymoon with his work on *Runner*. Despite regular weekend trips to Cap d'Antibes in the south of France, Sinatra soon got that old restless feeling, exacerbated by growing tension within the *Runner* camp. He knew that Brad Dexter disapproved of his wedding to Farrow, which didn't help their fledgling producer-star relationship at all. As with *Von Ryan's Express*, Sinatra wouldn't travel to locations by car, demanding a helicopter for all but the shortest journeys. Matters came to a head when a helicopter pilot hired to transport Sinatra and Dexter to a location 20 minutes from London became lost in the Thames fog. Arriving 45 minutes late to find Sidney Furie patiently waiting, the star declined to show a similar stoicism. Refusing all pleas to start work, Sinatra demanded that the entire London-based shoot be abandoned. *The*

Naked Runner production could be completed in the comfort of Palm Springs, the wildly differing locales and climates apparently not important. Feeling that months of hard work on the project were about to go up in smoke, Furie threw his own tantrum and abandoned the location, leaving cast and crew standing. Catching up with his fleeing director, Dexter calmed Furie down, eventually persuading him to return to work. Dexter then turned his attention to Sinatra, playing on both the commercial potential of the film and the serious financial losses to Sinatra Enterprises and Warner if it didn't get finished. With several hours of costly production time already wasted, the star finally agreed to resume filming, Furie managing to complete the last three days of the England shoot on schedule. Assuming that Dexter's version of events is more or less accurate, it's difficult to put a positive slant on Sinatra's behaviour. Any star who can provoke his director into walking off a film in tears needs at least a few tips on diplomacy and self-control. In fairness to Sinatra, the sensitive Furie had pulled a similar trick during the *Ipcress File* shoot in London, fleeing a Shepherd's Bush location by bus after an argument with producer Harry Saltzman.

Once the *Runner* production had moved on to Copenhagen, Sinatra appeared to mellow somewhat, his temperament perhaps improved by the chance to exercise a little superstar benevolence. A number of co-star Derren Nesbitt's scenes were originally scheduled for the Denmark shoot. Subsequent script revisions meant they could all be completed back in England, leaving the actor somewhat disappointed. Hearing about the incident, Sinatra arranged for Nesbitt and his family to be flown out to Copenhagen on the star's private plane, throwing in an extremely generous amount of krone to cover holiday expenses. With filming still running to schedule, Sinatra informed Dexter that he needed a weekend away in Los Angeles to perform at a rally for California's Democrat governor Edmund Brown, now running for a third term in office against Republican candidate Ronald Reagan. A fellow Brown supporter, Dexter had no problems with this, comfortably shooting around Sinatra for a few days. He then received a communication from Mickey Rudin, the star's lawyer, to the effect that Sinatra would not be returning to Copenhagen. His outstanding scenes could be filmed on a Los Angeles soundstage, much as he'd finished off the otherwise Spanish-shot *Pride and the Passion* a decade earlier. Now comes the strangest part of the story, at least as told by Brad Dexter. Instead of dispatching the existing *Runner* footage to Warner, as requested by Rudin, Dexter refused to follow Sinatra's orders. Citing the existing post-production contracts back in England, he and Furie chose to complete the film without its star. Reworking the script to minimise the number of essential Sinatra scenes left unshot, producer and director filmed the required material with a double, subsequently editing in close-ups of the star

taken from existing footage. When Rudin showed up in person to reiterate Sinatra's ultimatum, Dexter declined to comply, opting instead to deliver the finished film to Jack Warner in person two months later. Returning to Sinatra's office on the Warner lot, Dexter was unceremoniously fired from Sinatra Enterprises, the star refusing to discuss his dismissal personally. Still fine-tuning the final release print, Dexter requested that he at least be paid the outstanding $15,000 of his producer fee, money he never received. Questioned about the incident, Sinatra publicist Jim Mahoney argued that Dexter had brought his dismissal upon himself. Not only had the novice producer hijacked the film, he wouldn't even let Sinatra look at the rough cut. Whatever the truth of these various allegations, the net result was a film almost unreleasable.

Straying through the less appealing areas of London, Leipzig and Copenhagen, *The Naked Runner* makes the murky, treacherous world of global espionage look unbearably dull. The moody credit sequence where Peter Vaughan listens to classical music, his face in half-shadow, promises a level of competence the film simply doesn't deliver. Possibly distracted by behind-the-scenes strife, Furie's attempt to recapture the *Ipcress File* atmosphere flounders, despite a plethora of show-off camera flourishes. Deploying his full arsenal of isolating long shots, ominous low angles, looming close ups and off-kilter compositions, the director fails to create any sense of tension. As a succession of coffee pots, tea cups, bowler hats and briefcases dominate the Techniscope frame, the feeling persists that Furie is tarting up an empty package. His fondness for lingering on bold, if meaningless images also creates a rather static feel at times, as if the director couldn't bear to abandon a favourite set-up. Framing Sinatra's running figure through the handle of his guncase in the climactic sequence, Furie gives the impression of being fatally fixated on style over content. In the film's one reasonably effective scene, Laker is tormented by the mysterious Hartmann (Nesbitt), a British agent posing as an SS-nostalgic East German colonel. Driven out to a remote forest clearing, Laker is promised immediate execution, vomiting with fear even as Hartmann reveals his bluff. Certainly a screen first for Sinatra, if not a very pleasurable one.

Stanley Mann's script never strays into the realm of credibility. For starters, Sinatra isn't remotely believable as a designer of office furniture, even if his recent award-winning chair is orange. Similarly, Laker is supposed to be devoted to his young son Patrick, yet the token scenes with a child actor who looks nothing like Sinatra fail to create any sense of closeness, rendering the boy's subsequent disappearance just another by-the-numbers plot device. The film even fails to capitalise on its depressing atmosphere, the half-hearted attempt at a sense of post-war loss and regret falling flat. *Runner*'s cardinal sin is letting the audience in on the elaborate plot from the start, the overexplanatory script laboriously spelling out British Intelligence's every move. There is even a series of voiceovers mapping the step-by-step psychological manipulation of Laker. The puppet-on-a-string metaphor so effectively used in *Manchurian Candidate* is heavy-handed beyond belief here, Laker even stopping off at a Copenhagen marionette theatre to meet a contact. All this adds up to a film with no surprises or twists at all, Laker carrying out his mission almost to the letter, completely unaware that he is being used. The widely differing perspectives of character and spectator make it very difficult to empathise with Laker, already a somewhat remote figure. His panic over Patrick's faked kidnapping and murder is impossible to share, as is his subsequent decision to seek revenge on Hartmann. It's all just part of the game, Laker provoked into a murderous rage to ensure he'll carry out the assassination, shooting the desired target in the belief he's avenging the death of a loved one.

Given Brad Dexter's account of the *Runner* shoot,

the film's reputed emergency doctoring isn't quite as bad as expected. The post-production work is certainly intrusive at times, the heavy redubbing of dialogue rendering many scenes even flatter than they already were. Sinatra delivers his lines with bare professionalism and some of co-star Edward Fox's dialogue isn't even in sync with his lip movements. That said, only two brief scenes are obvious patchwork jobs, both occurring towards the end of the film as Laker deals with police officials, then customs officers. Placing the Sinatra stand-in with either his back to the camera or his head cut off by the frame, Furie keeps the action understandably brief. The borrowed Sinatra close-up footage appears to come from the same shot, Dexter and Furie obviously not spoiled for choice. Interestingly, the worst sequence in *Runner* was not the result of Sinatra's premature departure. The ending, filmed back in England, is absurdly rushed, Laker's British contact Slattery (Vaughan) blurting out an explanation to his unwitting political stooge as they flee the assassination scene. Laker doesn't even get an on-screen reunion with his son, supposedly safely stashed in Hartmann's waiting car. Leaving aside the discarded ethical questions involved in the whole business, the scene doesn't even make sense. Having recruited a civilian gunman rather than using known agents for the mission, why does the British secret service send two of its top men to retrieve Laker? The lingering impression is that no-one really cared anymore.

Released on 7 July 1967, *The Naked Runner* proved a sorry end to Sinatra's association with Warner, the intended follow up *Dirty Harry* scuppered by the star's ill-health (see Appendix 2). Switching his loyalties to Twentieth Century-Fox, Sinatra had thankfully got his act together with *Tony Rome* by the time the misbegotten *Runner* collapsed at the box-office.

14

Tough Guy
1967-1969

TONY ROME 1967

Nobody steals to do nice things.
Tony Rome, private detective with morals

There are certainly worse places than Miami Beach to resurrect a flagging film career. Hanging out in his de luxe motor cruiser, Sinatra found a worthy screen incarnation in ex-cop, compulsive gambler and alleged womaniser Anthony Rome, investigator for hire. A knowing retread of the cynical-yet-honourable Chandleresque loner, *Tony Rome* is a confident piece of work, Sinatra evidently comfortable in the kind of role favoured by friend and guiding light Humphrey Bogart. Beginning with a drunken rich girl in a seedy hotel room, the obligatory tangled-web plot involves a missing diamond pin, bigamy, blackmail, murder and a lot of *double entendre*. Rome tangles with a colourful assortment of self-made millionaires, predatory divorcees, retarded giants, drunken floozies, struck-off doctors, crooked jewellers, gay strippers, exasperated policemen and the usual junkies and whores. In between being roughed up by thugs and felt up by desirable women, Rome finds the time to solve a riddle or two, never losing his keen sense of wit. Aside from some dullish scenes with lacklustre *femme fatale* Jill St John, *Tony Rome* holds up well three decades on, following the expected paths with enough flair to conceal its shameless borrowings. Filmed at speed, with the usual assortment of Sinatra cronies inserted into the narrative, this is still top-flight entertainment, the kind of movie he should have been making back in the early 1960s instead of the misguided Clan films. Any star who casts his lawyer as a pawnbroker has to have some sense of humour.

Sinatra's return to the scene of his last box-office hit certainly made sense. Despite *Von Ryan's Express*'s fraught production, Twentieth Century-Fox received the star with more or less open arms, though none of the earlier film's major personnel were assigned to the new project. Producer Aaron Rosenberg knew a little about star temperament, having survived Marlon Brando's tantrums on *Mutiny on the Bounty* and *Morituri*. He certainly learned how to handle Sinatra, staying on board for both *The Detective* and *Lady in Cement*.

Tony Rome – Look but don't touch as Sinatra plays a private detective.

Tony Rome was derived from the novel *Miami Mayhem,* written by pulp-action specialist Marvin H. Albert. Screenwriter Richard L. Breen delivered a workmanlike blueprint, blending the standard private eye ingredients with a professional, if not overly inspired touch. There's even room for a little liberal comment on America's ingrained racism: 'Somebody'll squeeze something out of Tony the day Georgia elects a coloured governor.' It's funny because it's true.

Following Sinatra's decidedly mixed experiences with Mark Robson, Jack Donohue and Sidney J. Furie, Gordon Douglas was the natural choice for *Tony Rome*, the director well established at Fox after *Rio Conchos* and *In Like Flint* (1967). With Joseph Biroc, Billy May, Richard Conte and Jill St John recruited, Rosenberg and Sinatra were pretty much set to go. The supporting cast assembled for *Tony Rome* was suitably classy, headed by Gena Rowlands, Simon Oakland, Jeffrey Lynn and Lloyd Bochner. Given fewer scenes than Sinatra love-interest St John, Rowlands is a noticeably better actress. Bochner, cast here as a camp drug dealer, did well enough to earn a more substantial role in *The Detective*. *Tony Rome* also marked the last major screen appearance of Stanley Kubrick discovery Sue Lyon, whose post-*Lolita* career quickly fizzled out. Further down the cast, the film offered the charms of Tiffany Bolling, a nondescript television actress 'discovered' by Sinatra. Appearing with the star in two brief scenes, Bolling gets to snivel fairly convincingly as a put-upon nightclub waitress. Both St John and Bolling were rumoured to be ongoing Sinatra girlfriends, the star allegedly giving the latter a diamond-encrusted gold watch at the *Tony Rome* wrap party. Mickey Rudin aside, other non-actor Sinatra pals featured were ex-boxer Rocky Graziano - playing an ex-boxer - and former restaurant owner Mike Romanoff. Turning up on the Miami location for a short visit, Romanoff received both a bit role and a production assistant credit, the latter post netting him $750 a week. Hot from recording the title song for *You Only Live Twice* (1967), Nancy Sinatra got to perform similar labours on *Tony Rome*, reuniting with 'Boots...' composer Lee

Hazelwood. Their anthem isn't quite in the same class as the better known John Barry-Leslie Bricusse tune, despite such cool lyrics as 'Tony Rome will get 'em if you don't watch out'. That said, the song suits the film pretty well, its closing lines accompanied by Gordon Douglas' distinctive zoom-in on a bikini-clad rear as Sinatra purses his lips.

Setting up shop in Miami, Florida, *Tony Rome* started production on 3 April 1967. Obviously feeling that his time wouldn't be sufficiently filled, Sinatra accepted a simultaneous three-week singing engagement at the Fontainebleau hotel, which put paid to any early morning starts. Regarded by Rat Pack chronicler Richard Gehman as overdecorated and tasteless, the Fontainebleau seemed to suit Sinatra very well, the star making a return appearance during the *Lady in Cement* shoot the following year. His warm-up man for the show was comedian Shecky Greene, who got a small role in *Tony* as limping hood Catleg, a career criminal able to recite his own rights on arrest. The hotel also got a plug in the script, as divorcee St John's current residence. Scheduled for a 45-day shoot, the film wrapped in just 28 days, Rosenberg and Douglas well attuned to the demands of their star. As the producer explained at the time: 'He's a restless actor. We get everything lighted up before he arrives and do it immediately. We seldom have to take more than two takes, never more than four.' Mark Robson would have flinched but it worked on this occasion.

Compared to the glaring inadequacies of *The Naked Runner*, *Tony Rome* is Class A professionalism at its best, treating the conventionally lurid subject matter with both restraint and respect. Pacing the film with a sure hand, Gordon Douglas puts Sidney Furie's pseudo-artsy style to shame, his skill with composition, low angles, hand-held camera and tracking shots resulting in a highly fluid visual style. For all his self-professed lack of ambition, Douglas knew how to place actors on screen for maximum effect, a feature notably lacking in *Naked Runner*. In one largely inconsequential scene, Sinatra and St John conduct a conversation while lying on the floor of her hotel room,

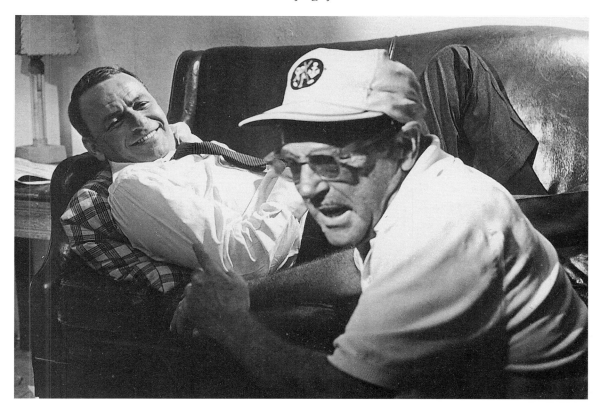

Tony Rome – Sinatra admires director Gordon Douglas' headgear.

their unusual positioning putting a useful spin on the mundane dialogue. True, Douglas also frames Sinatra and Conte either side of a foreground table lamp while they talk in long shot, but it's a minor lapse. Most of the jokes in the film are serviceable, carefully poised on the fine line between risqué and plain vulgar. A young couple's honeymoon antics on a neighbouring boat are accompanied by the strains of 'Something Here Inside Me'. About to be chloroformed by two hoods, Rome carefully watches one of them pour out the liquid onto a handkerchief before calling 'When'. Questioned by Rome about his useless son-in-law's possible infidelity, Simon Oakland's rugged construction boss is sceptical: 'I doubt it. He can barely farm his own land.' The film's most ingenious touch is to have the main culprit slowly dying off screen from a .45 bullet wound, the fatal injury incurred only half an hour into the action.

While Sinatra appears to have deliberately sought out a Bogart-style vehicle with *Tony Rome*, it's misleading to place too much emphasis on the connection. His emulation of Bogart exhibited itself far more in his life than his art. A proud member of Bogart's Rat Pack, Sinatra had formed a similar clique after his friend's death and dated Lauren Bacall, the press carrying reports of their impending marriage. A decade on, he would sing 'As Time Goes By' to Ingrid Bergman on Warner's old *Casablanca* set, fulfilling a long-standing wish for a fundraising television show. Tony Rome is very much Sinatra's own creation, his broadened, battered face displaying an easy charm and wry smile that owes little to Bogart's sharper, more aggressive style.

Starting off the film in a pale yellow sweater and nautical cap, Rome switches to a dark suit and hat once he is in serious Private Investigator mode. An unashamed dirty fighter, he threatens one opponent with a frying pan, kicks another in the shin and smashes a large vase into the head of a third. Harbouring few illusions about human nature, Rome is bemused by the devious antics of the estranged, secretive Kosterman family (Rowlands, Oakland and Lyon), politely declining Rita Kosterman's lucrative bribe to hide information from her husband: 'First Diana hires me. Then your husband hires me. Now you wanna hire me. If you had a bigger family I could retire.' Hardened to the brutalities that go with the territory, Rome is largely unfazed when he discovers the body of his crooked ex-partner under a desk during a phone conversation. The only jarring note to the character is the story behind his decision to quit the police force. A second generation cop, Rome could only stand back and watch as his straight-as-a-die policeman father was driven to suicide by the machinations of a corrupt local politician. Richard Conte's career policeman Santini represents the flip side to Rome, a devoted family man who's accepted the inherent flaws and injustices of the legal system. Aside from his aggressive lawn mowing, Santini seems pretty much at peace with himself. While there's a serious point to all this, it sits a little uneasily with the overall light-hearted tone. This is after all a private detective obliged to fend off a persistent old lady worried about her cat: 'You've got a pussy that smiles?'

Given its laudable lack of pretension or high ambition, *Tony Rome* hits few false notes. Gamely performing his own action scenes, the 51-year-old Sinatra is clearly unable to run very fast and he starts to deliver one line too early, obliged to pause while Simon Oakland says his piece. The film is also a little too nervously flip in its then-adventurous depiction of gay characters, hinting at executive timidity in the Fox front office. An unhappy butch/femme lesbian couple are given the sympathetic-yet-despairing treatment common to many late 60s/early 70s films, though the voyeuristic element is kept to a minimum. As the sobbing women embrace on their bed, the departing Rome switches the light out on them, reasoning it's for the best. Elsewhere, he beats up Lloyd Bochner's gay drug pusher Rood, ostensibly on the grounds of the man's evil trade rather than his sexuality. True, Rood had previously pulled a flick-knife on Rome and taunted a desperate client, yet

his 'punishment' seems excessive.

Released on 11 November 1967, *Tony Rome* finally broke Sinatra's dry run, audiences welcoming his overdue return to form. The perceived Bogart element backfired with some critics, who unfairly accused Sinatra of a pale imitation. Bosley Crowther felt the star had more or less let down the entire human race: 'It is provoking to see this acute and awesome figure turning up time and again in strangely tricky and trashy motion pictures that add nothing to the social edification and encouragement of man.' For the record, Crowther 'retired' from the *New York Times* shortly afterwards, his infamous attack on *Bonnie and Clyde* (1967) finally tipping the balance. It was left to Crowther's successor, Vincent Canby, to slag off *Lady in Cement*.

THE DETECTIVE 1968

This is Joe Leland's city - sick with violence...filled with prostitutes, junkies, perverts. The world of the detective... public hero. Full of private hells!
Publicity

It's what I do best. It's my life. And it's worth something.
Sergeant Joe Leland, NYPD's finest

A major, and mildly daring hit in its day, *The Detective* has rather faded from view over the years, often reduced to a footnote in the well documented Frank Sinatra-Mia Farrow split during the wildly over-schedule production of *Rosemary's Baby* (1968). Regarded as one of the first mainstream American films to exploit the new tolerance - and appetite - for graphic violence, sexual frankness and previously taboo subjects, it remains a striking achievement, featuring probably the last outstanding performance of Sinatra's career. The depiction of widespread police brutality and corruption is unrelentingly grim, contributing to the sombre, often oppressive atmosphere that permeates the film. Extremely well made and acted, *The Detective* falls just short of being a great film, its potency undercut by a slightly awkward narrative structure, one problematic main character and a rather underwhelming conclusion. The film is also weakened by an obvious queasiness in its supposedly sympathetic exploration of gay subculture. Whereas *Tony Rome*'s sorrowful depiction of marginal homosexual characters amounted to little more than a tasty throwaway, this attitude is central to *The Detective*, the story hinging on an intelligent, educated middle-class man driven to murderous rage by the torment of being gay. While the fair-minded Leland's 'live and let live' philosophy makes him an aggressive defender of all minorities, the feeling persists that even he would prefer to look the other way.

Had things proceeded smoothly at Twentieth Century-Fox, *The Detective* would probably have passed Sinatra by. The story begins in 1965 with aspiring movie mogul Robert Evans, a former Fox juvenile lead hoping to break back into films via his good friend David Brown, a producer at the studio. Constantly on the lookout for surefire film material, Evans had been greatly impressed by the manuscript for *The Detective*, a first effort from former policeman Roderick Thorp. Buying up the screen rights for $5,000, Evans offered to sell the book to Fox with himself attached as the film's producer. Initially reluctant to buy this non-negotiable package deal, the studio changed its mind when *The Detective* became a number one bestseller. Evans would produce the film, with Mark Robson directing and Abby Mann providing the script. An Academy Award-winner for *Judgement at Nuremberg*, Mann's impeccable liberal credentials lent *The Detective* an aura of respectability, offering an effective counter to charges of sensationalism.

The one thing missing from the deal was a star, which inevitably put the brakes on the project's momentum. Evans jumped ship to join Paramount Studios in 1966, handing David Brown all rights to *The Detective* as a parting gift. With the project going nowhere, Mark Robson decided to produce and direct *Valley of the Dolls* (1967) instead. Probably a wise decision, as he surely wouldn't have relished another close encounter with Frank Sinatra.

A rather more ambitious crime story than *Tony Rome*, *The Detective* drew on most of the same key personnel: Aaron Rosenberg, Gordon Douglas, Joseph Biroc, art director Jack Martin Smith, editor Robert Simpson, soundman David Dockendorf and co-star Lloyd Bochner. *Tony* composer Billy May stepped aside for Jerry Goldsmith, a more heavyweight Fox regular. The supporting cast line-up was exceptional, headed by Lee Remick, Ralph Meeker, Jack Klugman, Al Freeman Jnr, Tony Musante, Robert Duvall and Horace MacMahon. Playing Leland's troubled, pathologically promiscuous wife Karen, Remick had a strong track record in angst-ridden spouse roles, appearing in *The Long Hot Summer* (1958), *Anatomy of a Murder* and *Days of Wine and Roses* (1962). Best known as Mike Hammer in Robert Aldrich's *Kiss Me Deadly*, Meeker's sneaky, brutish screen persona earned him the part of Curran, one of Leland's corrupt colleagues. *The Detective*'s canniest piece of casting was MacMahon, playing Leland's affable but cowardly boss. Known to millions of television viewers as the senior cop in *The Naked City* (1959-62), MacMahon's portrayal of a gutless political stooge effectively subverted his old image as an honest, incorruptible lawman. Non-professional Sinatra buddies in the cast included stand-up comedian Pat Henry, playing a fellow plainclothes officer, 'bodyguard' Jilly Rizzo, briefly glimpsed as a bartender, and recently retired champion boxer Sugar Ray Robinson, capably impersonating a beat cop. For the pivotal, if secondary part of widow Norma MacIver, whose husband's mysterious suicide leads Leland to a major conspiracy plot, Sinatra had a very special piece of casting in mind: Mia Farrow.

Marriage on the Rocks bluff aside, the couple had previously announced that they didn't intend to co-star in any films, Farrow arguing that she had to advance her career independently of Sinatra. Nervous about acting with her husband, Farrow had reservations about appearing in *The Detective*, fearful she would disappoint Sinatra.

Unperturbed by the corruption element in the storyline, the New York Police Department co-operated fully with the production. Sinatra talked to real detectives as part of his research for the role and Gordon Douglas got to shoot a number of scenes in actual police stations. Filming commenced on 16 October 1967, making extensive use of New York locations. Unlike their characters, Sinatra and Lee Remick had a good professional relationship, the star praising his leading actress as a classy lady.

In retrospect, Mia Farrow's intended participation in *The Detective* appears as doomed as her marriage to Sinatra. Once Paramount had offered *Rosemary's Baby*, her supporting role in the Fox production inevitably became a secondary consideration, Farrow unable to resist the overtures of hot combo Robert Evans and Roman Polanski. Already committed to *The Detective*, Farrow was scheduled to start filming with Sinatra on 17 November. *Rosemary* wouldn't finish its 12-week production until 14 November, leaving barely any turnaround time. By the end of the first week, *Rosemary* was already an impressive seven days behind schedule. Contemptuous of Polanski's slow filming pace, Sinatra eventually lost patience, demanding that Farrow simply walk off *Rosemary* and join him for the *Detective* shoot. Alarmed, Robert Evans pointed out that the Screen Actors Guild would not permit Farrow to appear in *The Detective* if she broke her *Rosemary* contract. Evans finally won the argument, Farrow refusing to comply with Sinatra's wishes. Legend has it that Mickey Rudin turned up on the *Rosemary* set the next day, serving Farrow her divorce papers. Alternatively, Rudin was simply notifying Farrow of her formal dismissal from *The Detective* production, a legal requirement prior to replacing her with another actress. The role of Norma MacIver was cut down and handed out to Fox talent school graduate Jacqueline Bisset, a British starlet now making modest Hollywood inroads. Admired by many for her cool 'English Rose' looks, Bisset's acting in *The Detective* is adequate but unremarkable.

Somewhat unusually, *The Detective* has two distinct sections, suggesting that Thorp's novel did not readily lend itself to screen adaptation. The first segment intercuts Leland's investigation of a vicious gay murder and lengthy flashbacks to his unsuccessful relationship with Karen. Victim Teddy Leikman is from a powerful family, placing political pressure on the police to break the case fast. The investigation culminates in the successful capture and conviction of Felix Tesla (Musante), Leikman's disturbed roommate, and Leland is promoted to lieutenant. Unable to cope with his unfaithful wife's apparent nymphomania, Leland decides they should split up. Still drawn to Karen, he makes occasional sexual demands on her but won't respond to his ex-wife's plea for a reconciliation. In part two, Leland is approached by Norma MacIver, the young widow dissatisfied with the verdict on her husband's suicide. Ignoring warnings to back off, the increasingly suspicious policeman discovers that both he and his beloved department are entangled in a massive local government fraud. He also learns that the wrong man died for the Leikman murder, closet homosexual MacIver leaving a taped confession to the killing.

Filmed over a slightly longer schedule than *Tony Rome*, *The Detective* is film-making at its best. Douglas and Biroc use the New York locations very effectively, the vivid colours in marked contrast to *Tony*'s more easygoing visual style. Deploying his usual fluid camera, Gordon Douglas comes up with long, mobile takes to rival Vincente Minnelli's, following Leland around the murder scene as he stakes out the territory. Never a flamboyant film-maker, Douglas uses striking close-ups of Remick and Freeman, their eyes dominating the screen even when the script stumbles. When Leland goes to visit his estranged wife in her apartment, Douglas frames the policeman's approach to her door from the top of an elevator cage, the camera rising up with Leland, then watching him go, a mute witness to sad human folly. The director uses an even more extreme high angle for Tesla's execution scene, the camera looking straight down on the condemned man's walk to the electric chair. MacIver's suicide is staged as a dizzying point-of-view jump from a racetrack stadium roof, a good three years before Stanley Kubrick used a very similar shot in *A Clockwork Orange* (1971). When Leland learns that Tesla was not only demented but

The Detective – Leland brings in Felix Tesla (Tony Musante).

innocent, twin images of the man's electrocuted body appear either side of the policeman's head. Douglas even makes good use of back projection during the flashback sequences, giving the film an unreal, dreamlike feel as Leland's mind drifts away from the streets to his troubled professional and personal lives. On the soundtrack, Goldsmith's melancholy score is dominated by trumpet and electric guitar, enhancing the feel of a world turning very sour.

The more controversial elements in *The Detective* are still quite disturbing, working on a higher level than straightforward shock value. While Leland calmly discusses semen stains and a severed penis, the visual elements are more discrete, Leikman's mutilated genitalia carefully obscured by a strategic pot plant. One popular gay hangout is darkened lorry trailers down by the waterfront, offering a surreal image of the police unloading a truckful of homosexuals (presumably Thorp knew of what he wrote). Tesla's execution is quite harrowing, the wrongly convicted man strapped into the electric chair wearing a medieval-style leather mask. The climactic murder flashback is similarly gruesome for the time, MacIver repeatedly bashing Leikman's bloodied head with a heavy ashtray. *The Detective* is also strangely prescient in at least two respects. A 19-year-old junkie whore tells Leland she's being hassled by a cop called Callahan, while Captain Farrell (MacMahon) asks him to crack the Leikman case in 48 hours.

Where the film comes unstuck is in its drawn-out domestic subplot. Despite affecting performances from both Sinatra and Remick, the Leland-Karen odd couple relationship never quite rings true, becoming actively irritating during the latter stages of the film. A middle-class academic in regular therapy with LSD advocate Dr Wendell Roberts (Lloyd Bochner), Karen has no apparent connection to Leland's world, the self-sufficient cop taking a dim view of her psychoanalysis: 'People should try to work out their own problems.' The off-screen nymphomania is another non-starter, not helped by coyly framed shots of Remick's naked back, a standard movie tease before bare breasts became acceptable. While Sinatra's recent break-up with Farrow certainly gave him yet more first-hand experience of failed relationships, the marital storyline has nowhere much to go once Leland is aware of his wife's serial infidelity. Discussing Karen with the more easygoing Dr Roberts, Leland makes his - and the film's - position pretty clear: 'I'm not civilised enough to look the other way while my wife's screwing other men.' The detective's last-minute admission to Norma that he might try giving the marriage another try fails to counter the feeling that the film didn't really need Karen Leland in the first place.

Offering a strange kind of reactionary liberalism, Joe Leland is one of Sinatra's most ambivalent characters, a man who takes pride in his high moral standards yet allows himself to be used by those with no such scruples. Twenty years on the force, Leland's lonely figure is first glimpsed through an open doorway, clad in the standard dark overcoat and hat. Coming from a long line of cops, his career and family loyalties are intertwined, the man indistinguishable from the professional. A more uptight version of Tony Rome, Leland shows only flashes of the same mordant humour, his distinctive quiet chuckle

providing welcome relief from the general gloom. Preaching a gospel of honesty and tolerance, he does appear to be paying lip service to his ideals at times, David Shipman arguing that both hero and film flaunt concern without feeling it. Leland's attitude is more ambiguous than this, his personal integrity occasionally compromised in the name of professional loyalty. In one flashback, Leland attempts to explain to Karen why he can't break ranks over a police manslaughter cover-up, despite his fury at the officer involved. Whatever the offence, fellow cops must be protected to preserve the department's good name. With regard to the crucial homosexual element, it's reasonable to argue that both Leland and *The Detective* are pro sympathy and understanding for gays, as opposed to pro gay. When vicious bigot cop Nestor (Robert Duvall) punches a 'fag' around under the pretence of questioning him, Leland calls his fellow officer to one side and hits him hard in the stomach. Conversely, the interrogation scene captures Leland's approach at its most devious, concern masking ruthless ambition. Having let Curran and Nestor shout at Tesla for long enough, Leland tries the gentle touch, holding the suspect's hand and putting his arm around Tesla as he feeds him sufficient material for a confession. This is a hard-nosed professional at work, any feelings of sympathy for Tesla shunted aside in pursuit of a fast conviction and the promised promotion. Despite the slivers of compassion directed at Tesla, *The Detective* has nothing very positive to say about gay life: Leikman is a manipulative, self-centred hedonist, Tesla a gibbering psychotic wreck and MacIver a repressed, self-loathing killer.

On the other hand, few of Leland's fellow officers emerge with any great credit. New recruit Robbie Lockman (Freeman) displays the same ambition as Leland without the veneer of contempt for front office politics. Like previous black Sinatra sidekicks in *Ocean's 11*, *The Devil at 4 O'Clock*, *Robin and the 7 Hoods* and *Assault on a Queen*, Lockman attempts to follow his leader's example, though the colour barrier is never made an issue. This time around, Leland doesn't like what he sees. Inspired by footage of Nazi concentration camp atrocities, Lockman strips an elderly rape/murder suspect of his clothes before interrogating him, believing this will make the man more vulnerable. Reprimanded by Leland, Lockman advises him to think about his recent promotion. Leland knew that Tesla should never have been charged with first degree murder, but let justice take a back seat to his career prospects. As the unashamedly crooked Curran puts it: 'You think you're better than the rest of us. Wake up.' Leland's long-sustained image of righteousness begins to collapse after he discovers that members of the City Planning Commission are involved in a series of illegal land deals. Unable to fight high office corruption from within the police force, Leland turns in his badge rather than expose his department to big league city hall heat. This is a compromised moral victory at best, the detective walking away with more than his share of innocent blood.

Advertised as 'An adult look at a Police Detective', *The Detective* was released on 3 June 1968 to generally favourable reviews. The 'adult' content provoked no significant outcry, despite literally truckloads of active homosexuals, and the film made the year's box-office top 20. Released in Britain from 6 October, *The Detective* received an adults-only X-rating, the posters dominated by Sinatra swinging a foreshortened fist. The following month, *Lady in Cement* opened in the United States, Sinatra's final bow for Twentieth Century-Fox and his last box-office hit.

LADY IN CEMENT 1968

Rome works for money. That makes him easy to trust.
Waldo Gronsky, loveable thug

It's been said that whenever Frank Sinatra wanted guests at his Palm Springs home to retire for the evening, he would threaten to screen *Lady in Cement*. Generally written off as a hasty, uninspired follow-up to the more assured *Tony Rome*, the film deserves a better reputation. Shorter, faster and wittier than its

predecessor, *Lady* is the more enjoyable of Sinatra's two Rome ventures, despite some scrappy scripting and a noticeably rushed finale. While neither Sinatra nor co-star Raquel Welch appear to have had much time for the film, it's reasonable to argue that both were troubled by outside factors during its production, Sinatra depressed over his failed marriage, Welch frustrated at her perceived lack of good acting roles. Back in Miami Beach, with even more rust patches on his sports car, Anthony Rome finds himself involved in another complex murder case, the bodies piling up the further he progresses with his investigation. Even those who despise the overall film would have to admit it has an attention-grabbing scene-setter. Out on an underwater treasure hunt in Biscayne Bay, Rome chances upon the naked body of a young woman, her floating corpse weighed down by a large slab of concrete. A grim variation on Botticelli's Birth of Venus, it's a memorably tasteless image.

Derived from another Marvin H. Albert original, *Lady in Cement* reunited all the key *Tony Rome* personnel, Richard L. Breen undertaking the screen adaptation once more. Only part-way through the first draft, Breen died suddenly in late 1967, bringing preproduction to an abrupt halt. Albert agreed to finish off the screenplay himself, Jack Guss coming on board to fine-tune the result. The only other significant change-around was new composer Hugo Montenegro, Sinatra and Rosenberg perhaps feeling that Billy May's score for *Tony Rome* lacked impact. Montenegro's *Lady in Cement* score is a distinct improvement, an appropriately groovy blend of funk guitar, hip chorus, harmonica and harpsichord, slickly orchestrated by May.

If the supporting cast for *Lady in Cement* lacked some of *Tony Rome*'s thespian class, most of the sequel actors seemed more comfortable with the material than their predecessors. For the love interest part of wealthy drunk and murder suspect Kit Forrest, Fox selected underused contract player Raquel Welch, last seen as a sultry Mexican peasant in *Bandolero* (1968). Billed just below Welch on the credits, Richard Conte reprised his

Lady in Cement – Tony and Kit (Raquel Welch) in the 1968 follow-up to Tony Rome.

Lieutenant Santini role, while *Come Blow Your Horn* 'guest star' Dan Blocker agreed to play giant-sized ex-con Waldo Gronsky, a character clearly based on Moose Malloy in Raymond Chandler's *Farewell My Lovely*. The only other name actor in the film was former Mercury Theater player Martin Gabel, cast as retired gang boss Al Mungar. Opening for Sinatra during the star's simultaneous Fontainebleau stint, comedian Pat Henry also made a substantial contribution to the film. Sinatra's favourite warm-up man, Henry had proved himself a capable player in *The Detective* and was rewarded with a bigger part in *Lady in Cement*, the star casually handing him the script on a plane trip. Cast as easygoing cop Rubin, Rome's regular diving and gambling buddy, Henry even got to don drag. Jilly Rizzo and Joe E. Lewis were given walk-on parts, while

Mike Romanoff got his associate producer credit as before. Some of the casting was extremely last minute, the showy supporting role of club dancer and murder victim Maria Baretto left vacant well into the shoot. Sinatra saw fellow nightclub artiste Lainie Kazan performing at the Eden Roc Hotel, close to the Fontainebleau, and offered her the part there and then.

Writing at speed, Albert and Guss had a workable script cobbled together by the start of production on 26 February 1968. Rosenberg and Douglas followed their by-now standard practice of having each day's required sets prelit and Sinatra's moves mapped out in advance by his stand-in. The star's preferred noon-to-seven schedule was followed as Sinatra needed a little time each day to recover from his evening job at the Fontainebleau, where he performed every night from 3

March to 6 April. With very few delays, filming was completed in under six weeks. If Kitty Kelley's version of events is to be believed, Sinatra made the *Lady in Cement* shoot hell for cast and crew alike, taking out his grief and anger over Mia Farrow on anyone in sight. Refusing to film more than one take of most scenes, the star tore pages from the already slender script to speed up the production, treating Gordon Douglas as little more than an assistant. When Pat Henry blew three takes in a row, the star lost his temper and hit him. Filming her one big scene with Sinatra, Lainie Kazan was ordered not to lean so close to him. Presumably unhappy with the rewrites, the star cut down Jack Guss' hotel door with an axe. Contemptuous of the whole project, Sinatra left *Lady*'s post-production in the hands of 21-year-old production assistant Michael Viner.

Aside from the unlikely event of a major studio entrusting one of its big autumn releases to an inexperienced junior staff member, this image of Sinatra as a raging, broken-hearted monster seems a little extreme. While the star was certainly feeling depressed over his split from Mia Farrow the previous November, he appears to have remained reasonably stable. Coping with a very public break-up, the star earned nothing but praise from his colleagues.

Welch felt Sinatra handled the unending demands on his time with surprising grace: 'I never saw him anything but a gentleman.' Kazan informed set visitor Earl Wilson that her co-star was 'a very delicious man'. Despite an already substantial number of international credits, Welch felt nervous about working opposite Sinatra. Aware of this, the star kept out of sight while Gordon Douglas rehearsed her for their first big scene together. Worried that Welch's lack of confidence would show on screen, the director was reassured by Sinatra, who felt certain his co-star could deliver. For all her reservations about the end result, Welch enjoyed working on *Lady* with Sinatra, catching his show at the Fontainebleau after hours. Martin Gabel also benefited from Sinatra's generosity after a chance remark. Expressing admiration for the star's evening shoes, he received six pairs the following day.

Sinatra's one and only venture into the realm of sequels, *Lady in Cement* is quality entertainment, the star's Sid James-style dirty laugh setting the overall tone. A cheerfully trashy recycling of the standard genre ingredients, the film makes a virtue of its lack of ambition, delivering the goods with no pretensions to deep thematic content. Staged by former *Creature from the Black Lagoon* Ricou Browning, the opening underwater sequence shows what *Assault on a Queen* could have accomplished in better hands. Looking uncomfortable in wet black rubber, Sinatra is more effectively doubled this time around, the faster pace leaving audiences less time to dwell on the scene's more implausible elements. Accompanied by a vocal 'wah wah wah wah' on the soundtrack, Rome's first glimpse of the naked title character is mildly titillating in a necrophiliac kind of way. The camera lingers on the unbilled stuntwoman's breasts and floating halo of blonde hair, carefully placed seaweed obscuring her groin. Nonchalantly beating off an inquisitive shark, Rome feels this is no way to treat a lady: 'Dumping people in cement. That went out with violin cases.' Gordon Douglas handles the dry-land action sequences with his usual flair, offering a memorable scene where Gronsky smashes a policeman's head through his own squad car window, then beats the man repeatedly against the door. Framed for the murder of a gay club manager, Rome is forced to punch out old friend and arresting officer Santini, initiating a lengthy chase by car and foot around picturesque Miami. Naturally, the Fontainebleau gets featured in the sequence. Compared to the level of jokey violence, the nudity quota is very mild. Aside from the lady in cement herself, there's just a tactfully draped artist's model, whose increasingly strained pleas for a bathroom break quickly banish any sense of eroticism. Needless to say, Douglas zooms in on an exercising, white-clad rear, paying Raquel Welch a similar compliment in the film's final scene.

Aside from a throwaway quip about Vietnam draft-dodgers, there are few allusions to the real world in *Lady in Cement*, the script veering much more towards nostalgia. Along with the 1940s-style private eye

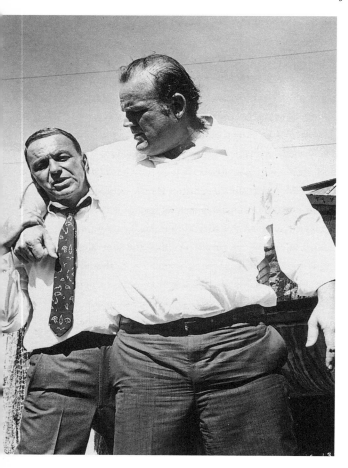

Lady in Cement – Tony and Gronsky (Dan Blocker).

camera. As with *Tony Rome*, there is a moderately dodgy element of homophobia, Rome baiting, then bashing camp club manager Danny Yale. The film lets Rome off the hook by having Yale threaten him first, but it's a very obvious cop-out device. Elsewhere, a female personal assistant with a horrendous mock-English accent sports a slightly masculine manner and a suspiciously short haircut.

More likeable than *Tony Rome* co-star Jill St John, Raquel Welch is similarly underwhelming in her role, unable to treat the flip dialogue with Sinatra's apparently effortless ease. First seen emerging from a swimming pool in a cleavage-enhancing bikini, Welch's performance is a little shaky, her lack of real acting experience showing through at times. That said, Kit Forrest is on the receiving end of some odd lines, notably Rome's unanswerable pronouncement: 'You'd look good in a paper napkin. But that wouldn't get me any answers.' In truth, Sinatra has far more screen chemistry with Lainie Kazan during their one scene together. Clad in a metallic mini-dress, dusky temptress Kazan milks her cut-out character for all it's worth, appearing very comfortable trading come-ons with Sinatra. The scenes with Sinatra and Dan Blocker are the strongest, Gordon Douglas employing strategic low angles to emphasise their greatly contrasting sizes. At one point Gronsky picks Rome up and sits him on a bar-top as if he were a small child, the private detective's legs dangling in the air. Shot in the foot with a .45 slug, Gronsky is forced to lean on Rome as they hurriedly depart from a crime scene, neither man overjoyed by the arrangement. Martin Gabel is also excellent value for money, the gruff, gravel-voiced Mungar perpetually exasperated by the constraints of a reformed character and a heart condition. Unamused by Rome's taunts over his gangster past, Mungar issues a less than subtle caution: 'I'd be careful with that mouth of yours. I could put my foot in it.' He also provides the film's one affecting moment, Mungar discovering that the son he raised on the straight and narrow is in fact a ruthless career criminal, using all the tricks from the old gangster handbook. Distressed and hurt, Mungar is

storyline and Gabel's old-time gangster, there's a curious series of *Guys and Dolls* references. Mungar's airhead young girlfriend sounds remarkably like Vivian Blaine, Rome and Kit attend a floating crap game at the local mortuary, and *Guys* actor B.S. Pully turns up as a strip-joint customer. Kit even gets to engage in a little Runyonesque banter with the crap dealer, Welch handling the quaint dialogue rather better than most of her 'normal' lines. Given Sinatra's less than happy time making the film back in 1955, it's strange he should want to pay homage. There's also an Ava Gardner in-joke, Rome remarking to Kit: 'I used to know a broad collected bullfighters.' Blocker's presence prompted a *Bonanza* in-joke, though Paramount declined to lend Fox actual footage from the show, obliging Gronsky to watch it with the television turned away from the sent upstairs to watch television while his only child plots murder, the sins of the father embraced by the son. Sinatra used Gabel again for his television movie *Contract on Cherry Street* (1977, see Appendix 3) and *The First Deadly Sin*.

Lady in Cement was the first Sinatra film to be slapped with a restrictive 'R' rating under the MPAA's new classification system, excluding all under-17s not accompanied by a parent or adult guardian. Given the generally knockabout level of violence, this seems a somewhat harsh decision, the brief flashes of bare breasts and buttocks presumably regarded as too hot for impressionable minds. Fox successfully appealed against the rating, winning a more box-office friendly 'PG' a short time later. Released on 20 November 1968, the film didn't enjoy the level of acclaim accorded to both *Tony Rome* and *The Detective*. Vincent Canby went straight for the throat: 'a perfect blending of materials and milieu...vulgarity and

sloppiness...consistently crude'. *Hollywood Reporter* critic John Mahoney begged to differ, declaring that the film was better than *Tony Rome*: 'It manages to have fun at its own expense rather than relying wholly on leering bad taste...the film has a fresher script, lighter hands playing, and the same sharp direction and cinematography.' Audiences tended towards Mahoney's view, *Lady in Cement* scoring a respectable box-office success. Sinatra's *Can Can* co-star Maurice Chevalier caught the film during its French release in early 1969. Impressed by Sinatra's enduring star power, Chevalier had strong reservations about his choice of material, dismissing *La Dame en Ciment* as sub-James Bond banality. A fan of both the performer and the man, the French star's dislike of Sinatra's 'phoney' heroics echoed a common sentiment. For a while it appeared that the star agreed. Sinatra would not be seen on screen again for two years.

15

Bowing Out

1970

DIRTY DINGUS MAGEE 1970

*Every time I take my pants off you come
at me with a gun*
Dingus Magee, $10 fugitive from justice

It seems some movie stars just never learn. Despite the poor reviews and meagre box-office generated by *Sergeants 3* and *4 for Texas*, Frank Sinatra clambered back onto his comedy saddle for the little remembered western spoof *Dirty Dingus Magee*, a film derided by its own creator. Nancy Sinatra suggests her father simply felt the need for a lightweight, 'fun' picture after the death of his own father Martin from emphysema in January 1969. No other explanation readily springs to mind, though Sinatra was perhaps swayed by director Burt Kennedy's recent success with the comedy western *Support Your Local Sheriff* (1968). Set around Yurkey's Hole, New Mexico circa 1870, the action starts when small-time outlaw Dingus Magee (Sinatra) robs old friend Hoke Birdsill (George Kennedy) of $400 while the latter is peeing behind Jackass Mail relay station. The resulting chain of events involves the irate Sheriff Birdsill, Indians, the cavalry, assorted whores, celebrity

bandit John Wesley Hardin (Jack Elam), an amorous schoolteacher (Lois Nettleton) and a brothel madam who also happens to be the local mayoress. Mildly funny at times, the film is more watchable than its reputation would suggest, yet makes the fatal error of treating the audience as ignored spectators chancing on a fun party rather than a howling mob demanding to be entertained. There are also a few too many 'bawdy' jokes about ass-breaking, cocks, hard-ons, horns, chests, moons and uprisings, a one-track line of sniggering humour that rapidly derails. Returning to a much-changed MGM after 12 years away, Sinatra found the once-mighty movie factory brought low, *Dirty Dingus Magee* reflecting all too well its fatal lack of insight into shifting audience tastes.

Forsaking his still impressive status as an executive industry player, Sinatra signed on for *Dingus* as a relatively humble star-for-hire. The driving force behind the film was director-producer Kennedy, whose extensive western credits included *Welcome to Hard Times* (1967) and *The War Wagon* (1967). Based on David Markson's novel *The Ballad of Dingus Magee*, the script for *Dingus* was the work of Tom Waldman, Frank Waldman and Joseph Heller. The Waldmans had co-written the Blake

Edwards-Peter Sellers farce *The Party* (1968). *Dingus* offers a similar blend of violent slapstick, 'zany' characters and crude sexual banter, rendering Heller's exact contribution difficult to determine. The title change came about partly to avoid confusion with *The Ballad of Cable Hogue* (1970), Sam Peckinpah's slightly less knockabout comedy western starring Jason Robards.

Most of the *Dingus* crew were old Burt Kennedy hands, including the director's regular cameraman Harry Stradling Jnr, whose father photographed Sinatra in *Guys and Dolls*. Of the cast, Kennedy had previously worked with Lois Nettleton on *Mail Order Bride* (1964), Jack Elam on *Support Your Local Sheriff* and George Kennedy on *The Good Guys and the Bad Guys* (1969). The showy part of whore-peddling mayoress Belle Knops went to stage actress Anne Jackson. The only familiar face for Sinatra was *Tender Trap* composer Jeff Alexander, who'd worked with Burt Kennedy on *Support Your Local Sheriff*.

Sinatra liked the *Dingus* project enough to forgo his usual $1 million fee, settling for a token payment up front and a larger percentage of the box-office gross. By 1970, MGM was in bad financial shape, occasional hit releases such as *Where Eagles Dare* (1968) failing to arrest its declining fortunes. New studio head James Aubrey had indiscriminately fired employees and slashed production schedules, rapidly transforming MGM into a no-go area for all but the most desperate or bloody-minded film-makers.

Against this less than comfortable backdrop, *Dingus* started filming on 24 February 1970, with location work in Tucson, Arizona. For all the strife generated in the MGM front office, the production proved a happy one, Sinatra treating cast and crew with courtesy. Anne Jackson was particularly taken with him, her enthusiasm tinged with nostalgia for the star's swooner-crooner days:

I was a stage-struck Bobby-socker when he was singing at the Paramount in New York City. I remained a tongue-tied fan of his...He was such a gifted singer - and then grew into a fine actor...I just remember having fun working with him. He's a very generous man... and has never outgrown his ability to beguile.

Burt Kennedy expressed similar sentiments: 'Frank was a pro... and I like him very much.'

Largely free from executive interference throughout the distant location shoot, *Dingus* didn't fare quite so well during post-production at MGM. While Burt Kennedy nobly bears all responsibility for *Dingus*' final form - 'I try not to blame others for my failures' - the release print runs just over 90 minutes, James Aubrey's prescribed length for comedies and westerns. There appear to have been disagreements over the film's score at least, with much of Jeff Alexander's original music discarded. The most obvious giveaway on *Dingus*'s credits is Mack David's theme song, sung by the Mike Curb Congregation. A protégé of Aubrey, singer-songwriter Curb featured on two other 1970 MGM releases, *Kelly's Heroes* and *Zabriskie Point*, his contribution to the latter protested by director Michelangelo Antonioni. The film also includes additional music by composer-arranger Billy Strange, who'd worked with Nancy Sinatra during the peak years of her singing career, most famously on the four million-selling 1966 hit 'Boots...' The compromised end result is disjointed and heavy-handed, distinguished only by some moody guitar-strumming.

In the event, all the coy sexual intrigue, slapstick violence and zero body-count add up to very little, the script's half-hearted digs at western cliches failing to hit home. A marginal improvement on Sinatra's earlier comic jaunts out west, *Dirty Dingus Magee* still feels like a lavish, self-indulgent fancy dress party to which the paying public weren't invited. In between the various chases and hold-ups, Indian girl Anna Hotwater (Michele Carey) falls for Dingus and wants to make 'bim bam'. 'Bim now, bam later' replies the pressed outlaw. Clad in an unlikely minidress, this devoted squaw appears not so much ingenuous as retarded. Like *Sergeants 3* and *4 for Texas*, the film fails to score even as the easygoing romp intended, the ramshackle narrative, faltering pace, unamusing 'comic' dialogue and

Dirty Dingus Magee – Dingus Magee takes a weight off Hoke Birdsill's (George Kennedy) mind.

overbroad acting rapidly taking toll. Stradling's location photography is easy on the eye, yet hardly makes up for Kennedy's erratic direction, some awkward editing, crude overdubbing and surprisingly shoddy process work. For the record, Anne Jackson, Jack Elam and George Kennedy are all quite likeable, suggesting characters who exist independently of the screenwriters' gags. Adorned with a dark wig, stolen Derby hat and pink longjohns, Sinatra looks cheerful enough but never gives the impression of being anything other than an actor having fun, his none-too-convincing stunt double taking care of the action highlights.

Released on 16 November 1970, *Dirty Dingus Magee* was a critical and commercial flop, no amount of Christmas goodwill sufficient to disguise its inadequacies. *Chicago Sun Times* critic Roger Ebert blamed *Dingus*' low quality largely on Sinatra, '...who's notorious for not really caring about his movies'.

Released overseas in early 1971, *Dingus* received a fairer, if still not terribly favourable hearing from British critics, hardened to innuendo-laden farce after nearly 13 years of *Carry On* films.

Having largely embarrassed himself once more in the Old West, Sinatra did not intend to watch his career slump back to its *Marriage on the Rocks* nadir. He planned to follow *Dirty Dingus* with *Dirty Harry*, in development with Warner since 1969. This downbeat, yet cathartic tale of an ageing cop stepping outside the law to hunt down a psycho killer offered a promising showcase, the kind of vehicle that now best suited his talents. Health problems intervened, forcing Sinatra to bow out from the project. Shortly afterwards, the star's movie career came to an abrupt halt. On 13 June 1971, just over six months after *Dingus*' release, Sinatra announced his retirement from the world of showbusiness.

16

Last Chances

1980

THE FIRST DEADLY SIN 1980

He's searching for a killer.
She's searching for a miracle.
...And time is running out.

Publicity

Weeks away from his much deserved retirement, a veteran New York policeman attempts to track down a psychotic murderer while his beloved wife wastes away in a hospital bed. Returning to *Detective* territory for his final starring role, Frank Sinatra's first film appearance in ten years was largely dismissed as a flop, a dreary, reactionary cop movie lacking any style or depth. Quickly fading from the public mind, the film served only as a desultory one-off coda to Sinatra's screen career, rather than the start of a major comeback. Loosely based on Lawrence Sanders' bestselling novel, *The First Deadly Sin* is undeniably flawed, largely by its relentlessly depressing atmosphere, yet the film is still a praiseworthy achievement, highlighted by Sinatra's dignified performance as Detective Sergeant Edward X. Delaney, of New York's 27th precinct. With failing eyesight and grey hair, Delaney is Sinatra's only screen portrayal of an elderly

man, his worn 64-year-old features lit without any attempt at flattery. The film also gives some indication of how *Dirty Harry* could have turned out with Sinatra in the lead, both storylines featuring a renegade lawman tearing through bureaucratic red tape in his obsessive pursuit of an insane killer. While *Sin* lacks the fast pace and dynamism of the Clint Eastwood-Don Siegel film, it is by no means a disappointment, the unhurried action and understated style befitting what is essentially a film of endings and farewells. The relationship between Sinatra and ailing screen wife Faye Dunaway forms the emotional centre of a story about loss, Delaney's stoical acceptance of his fading career contrasted with a bewildered inability to understand why modern science can do nothing for the woman he loves.

With *Dirty Dingus Magee* still haunting him and *Dirty Harry* now a frustrating might-have-been, Sinatra's film career remained dormant throughout the 1970s, a handful of possible film projects rapidly discarded (see Appendix 2).

Elsewhere on the Hollywood scene, a number of studios were showing keen interest in the work of crime writer Lawrence Sanders, whose 1973 novel *The First*

Deadly Sin proved a national bestseller. Smelling a surefire hit property, Columbia picked up the film rights and offered the project to Roman Polanski. A deal was made in January 1977, with Marlon Brando named as the first choice for Delaney. Following Polanski's arrest on a statutory rape charge, Columbia abruptly dropped *Sin* from their production schedules.

Left for dead after the Polanski scandal, the *First Deadly Sin* project lay dormant for nearly three years before producer Elliott Kastner got it rolling once again. Perhaps recalling Sinatra's enthusiasm for *Harper*, he approached the semi-retired star with the property. Sinatra liked what he saw and agreed to make *Sin* an Artanis co-production, undeterred by the lack of a big studio deal. Columbia had let its option on the book lapse, and *Sin* would be made in association with the independent Filmways company. Sinatra's involvement quickly made *Sin* a go-project once again, the three-way deal with Kastner and Filmways attracting a fair amount of media attention. According to Nancy Sinatra, her father was genuinely excited about his comeback, feeling he had a real chance to re-establish himself as a serious film performer. With Kastner and Sinatra serving as joint executive producers, the more hands-on supervisory work was handled by producers George Pappas and Mark Shanker. The director job went to Brian G. Hutton, who'd worked with Kastner on *Sol Madrid* (1968), *Where Eagles Dare* and *Zee & Co* (1972). Given an equal say over *Sin*'s personnel, Sinatra brought along *Contract on Cherry Street* cameraman Jack Priestley, whose film credits included the more frivolous murder mystery *No Way to Treat a Lady* (1968). The score was entrusted to long-time Sinatra collaborator Gordon Jenkins, who'd been arranging much of the star's recording and concert work since 1957.

Sin's high calibre supporting cast was led by seasoned character actors Martin Gabel, James Whitmore and Anthony Zerbe. The relatively unknown David Dukes was cast as white middle-class executive psycho Daniel Blank, while Brenda Vaccaro got the smaller part of housewife Monica Gilbert, recently widowed by Blank's murder spree. While her character is radically reduced from the book, Vaccaro provides a nice touch of weary stoicism in the face of grief. The memorable, if brief part of a sleazy apartment building doorman went to distinctive player Joe Spinell, usefully deployed in *The Godfather* (1972), *Taxi Driver* (1976) and *Big Wednesday* (1978).

Casting the crucial role of bed-ridden Barbara Delaney presented a few problems, offering little more than an extremely restrictive supporting part. Obtaining a star name for the role would raise the sketchy character's profile and give *Sin*'s commercial chances a boost, yet few major actresses would consider accepting such a glorified guest appearance. Fortunately, the producers got lucky with Faye Dunaway, still hot following her Academy Award win for *Network* (1976). A big admirer of Sinatra, Dunaway was available for the shooting dates and felt mildly intrigued over the challenge of acting in a confined space with little dialogue and even less movement. The ten days' work required paid a generous $750,000 and Dunaway accepted the role in early 1980.

Filming began on 10 March 1980, finishing around 20 May. The production made extensive use of actual New York locations, notably the Mother Cabrini Medical Center. The all-important hospital scenes were completed over two weeks at the start of the shoot, Dunaway working on her dialogue with long-time friend and mentor William Alfred, a respected playwright. Dunaway's husband, British photographer Terry O'Neill, had doubts over Sinatra's commitment to his comeback film, and stayed with her throughout the shoot in case she needed moral support. In the event, Dunaway found Sinatra to be a perfect gentleman, always friendly, respectful and a pleasure to work with on set. Accepting Barbara Delaney's minimal presence, Dunaway raised only one serious objection to the script during filming, feeling that it didn't sufficiently explore the poignancy of her character dying at Christmas time. Drawing on memories of a less than happy family Christmas nearly 30 years earlier, she suggested adding a line where Barbara asks Edward to put silver 'icicles' on their tree one strand at a time. It's a small detail, yet conveys some

The First Deadly Sin – Edward and Barbara Delaney (Faye Dunaway) coming to terms with retirement and ill health.

sense of a life outside the hospital sick ward.

Not the easiest nor most enjoyable film to watch, *The First Deadly Sin* is impressive film-making nevertheless. Ditching the book's political and psycho-sexual angles, Mann Rubin's script is generally sound and the sombre, cold visual style effectively emphasises New York's shadowy, threatening mean streets. Owing more than a slight debt to Bernard Herrmann, Gordon Jenkins' string-led score is suitably moody, alternately ominous and mournful. Brian Hutton's measured, unshowy direction also fits the overall tone well, making only occasional use of elaborate long takes, such as a dolly shot deployed in the first museum scene. The most visually striking sequence involves Delaney tailing Blank through a dimly lit building site, plastic sheeting billowing in the wind. As the predator-turned-prey

becomes increasingly panicked, the camera slowly tracks in on Delaney's motionless figure, the policeman's face impassive as he waits for Blank to make a move.

Largely confined to the background, the Christmas setting is used quite sparingly. Aside from Barbara's hospital predicament, the climactic shot of the second murder sequence is accompanied by the soulless recorded laughter of a mechanical Santa Claus. There's also a touch of religious imagery, notably the crucifix in Barbara's hospital room and the illuminated cross outside the Mount Pleasant Baptist Church, the setting for Blank's first murder. *Sin*'s most notable stylistic touch is its use of crosscutting for certain key scenes. During the opening sequence, the film cuts between an emergency operation on Barbara and the first killing, an effective, if not terribly subtle ironic juxtaposition of sharpened steel alternately preserving and destroying life. Curiously, the operation footage is by far the more graphic, the scalpel seen cutting into flesh, blood spurting onto the attending surgeons. By contrast, the ice hammer blows to the victim's head are largely obscured by shadow. The film later parallels Delaney working on the investigation, Barbara lying in bed and Blank preparing for another kill, then Barbara suffering a relapse and Blank prowling his apartment. A number of critics wrote this device off as an empty stylistic flourish, yet it does serve to draw Delaney's two worlds more tightly together until the fateful last night.

Aside from lacking some lighter moments to relieve the oppressive atmosphere and lend the overall gloom a little perspective, *The First Deadly Sin* hits no serious false notes. The predominance of the lethal ice hammer in the film's advertising was probably a mistake, as the characters take a long time to identify Blank's murder weapon, leaving the better-informed audience with the unfair impression that they're somewhat dim. In fact, Delaney's investigation seems efficient and methodical, pathologist James Whitmore explaining the nature of the head wounds and the shape of the probable implement involved. Crossing pickaxes and medieval-style weapons off his list, Delaney engages the help of museum curator Martin Gabel, who switches his attentions to modern tools and eventually tracks down the ice hammer at a sporting goods store.

The acting standard is generally strong, though Gabel stumbles over several of his lines, which suits his somewhat absent-minded character yet doesn't always sound like a deliberate touch (*Sin* was the 67-year-old actor's last film appearance). Spinell's doorman is a shameless, sharp-witted hustler, crawling to tenants for extra tips and taking a $100 bribe from Delaney while the latter makes an illegal search of Blank's apartment. David Dukes gives an edgy, discomforting performance as Blank, offering a credible portrayal of mind-shredding psychosis. While Dukes' killer can only generate a grudging pity, Faye Dunaway lends Barbara Delaney both sympathy and dignity, the terminally ill woman refusing to just curl up and die. Dunaway

regarded the part as 'undemanding', yet she contributes a genuinely touching performance, enhanced by such details as Barbara's weak, clutching hand when she wakes up disoriented in the night. *Sin* also features a split-second appearance from future superstar Bruce Willis, eight lean years away from his movie breakthrough in *Die Hard* (1988). During the scene where Delaney pursues Blank along shadowy New York streets, the policeman walks through a restaurant to avoid his quarry's eye. Just as Sinatra exits the building, Willis walks in with a date, his face partly shadowed by a cap.

Despite a slightly odd-looking toupee, Sinatra's performance in *The First Deadly Sin* is impressive, a touchingly low-key portrayal of a man faced with the realisation that his long planned happy retirement will probably never be. Delaney is first glimpsed at the Mount Pleasant murder scene, clad in the standard Detective garb of dark coat and hat. A few weeks away from handing in his badge with a clean record, Delaney is determined to pursue this last case with his usual professionalism, only to be frustrated by front-office indifference. Concerned only with crimes committed within the 27th precinct, his new captain doesn't want to know about a possible serial killer running amok all over New York City.

Delaney's confidence on the street is contrasted with his uneasiness in the hospital environment. Sinatra's sad-funny banter with Dunaway is effectively poignant, Delaney trying desperately hard to be easygoing and optimistic. Hoping to take Barbara's mind off her pain, he reads to her from a 'Honeybunch' book, one of her childhood favourites. Back at his lonely house, Delaney is reduced to a small figure lost in the shadows, a sad foretaste of his future life without Barbara. Unable to cope with his wife's losing battle, Delaney eventually snaps, violently turning on the doctor in charge.

The final section of the film sees Delaney effectively turn vigilante, resolved to either bring in Blank or execute him. The building site episode appears to badly rattle the normally impassive Blank, the snivelling killer curling up naked in his bathtub, then hiding in a cupboard like a naughty child. There are the genre-standard hints of a lonely and abused childhood: 'Please God, not the cellar... it's so cold and dark', but Blank lives up to his name far too effectively to generate real sympathy or understanding. Aware that Blank's social standing and connections will place him beyond the law's reach, Delaney shoots him in the head at point blank range, both men's faces distorted in reflections on surrounding objects. With Blank listed as just another wealthy robbery victim, Delaney can walk away, his career brought to a righteous, if highly illegal end. While this lone avenger climax is questionable to say the least, it carries no sense of the exhilaration or relief found in *Dirty Harry*'s riverside gun-down. Only one man lies dead but two lives have effectively ended. Back at the hospital, *Sin* reaches its sad coda, Barbara finally expiring while Delaney reads her another Honeybunch story. He carries on reading out loud for a little while, then breaks down and weeps, clutching Barbara's lifeless hand to his face. As the camera slowly pulls away from the couple, their images disappear into darkness, a fittingly moving last shot on which to end an outstanding career.

Filmways launched *The First Deadly Sin* with a charity premiere at Loew's State Theater, New York on 23 October 1980, the proceeds going to the Mother Cabrini Medical Center. Mediocre reviews were matched by indifferent box-office, audiences turned off by the depressing tone and ultra-downbeat ending.

Sunday Times critic Philip Oakes wouldn't even give the star credit for a decent performance: 'Sinatra's presence seems less like an acting job than a sullen endorsement of redneck authority.' Disappointed at *Sin*'s harsh treatment, Sinatra looked around in vain for another high-profile part, aware that his advancing years seriously limited the number of suitable leading roles available. There would be no more comebacks.

Frank Sinatra died of heart failure on May 14 1998 at the age of 82. Long retired from the world of film-making, he remained one of Hollywood's most respected figures, the old jibes against his big-screen achievements softened by time and at least a little re-evaluation. Speaking at the Cannes Film Festival, director Martin Scorsese paid tribute to Sinatra as a great actor, citing such career highs as *The Man With the Golden Arm* and *Some Came Running*. His funeral mass on May 20 was attended by old friends and co-stars Ernest Borgnine, Debbie Reynolds, Sophia Loren, Tony Curtis, Shirley MacLaine, Joey Bishop, Angie Dickinson, Henry Silva, Jill St John, Kirk Douglas, Tony Bennett, Faye Dunaway and Tom Selleck. Other showbusiness figures paying their respects included Robert Wagner, Jerry Lewis, Gregory Peck, Anthony Quinn, Jack Lemmon, Jack Nicholson, Liza Minnelli, Sidney Poitier and former wife Mia Farrow. While the deluge of media coverage inevitably focused on Sinatra's musical legacy, his movie career was not entirely neglected. Sinatra the film star may yet receive his due.

THE NIGHTCLUB & THE BIG MINSTREL ACT (1935).

Released under the collective title *Major Bowes' Amateur Theater of the Air*, these short films were made by Biograph Productions for distribution through RKO. Shot at the tiny Biograph Studios on Tremont Avenue, the Bronx, New York, both were produced and directed by John H. Auer, who completed them in a week. Paid $10 a day, Sinatra appears as a waiter in the first film - supposedly - and as one of the black-face chorus in the second, complete with comical spats, top hat, spotted shirt and matching bowtie. The star later regretted his participation in *The Big Minstrel Act*, which certainly went against his anti-racism principles. Premiered in October 1935 at New York's Radio City Music Hall, the films soon sank without trace.

LAS VEGAS NIGHTS (1941).

A minor Paramount comedy featuring Sinatra singing his number one hit 'I'll Never Smile Again' with the Tommy Dorsey Band, their sequence shot in October 1940. Paid the standard extra's rate of $15 a day, the unbilled Sinatra received some critical notice after the film's release on 24 March 1941, *Metronome* reviewer George Simon commenting: 'He sings prettily in an unphotogenic manner.'

SHIP AHOY (1942).

An MGM musical comedy starring tap dance queen Eleanor Powell. The Tommy Dorsey Band appear in white sailor suits, complete with spats, giving Sinatra an early taste of the outfit that would launch him into the movie big-time a few years later.

REVEILLE WITH BEVERLY (1943).

A highly successful $350,000 Columbia 'B' picture starring Ann Miller as an Armed Forces disc jockey introducing popular acts such as Duke Ellington, Count Basie, Bob Crosby and Freddie Slack. Clad in white tie and tails, Sinatra made his first screen appearance as a solo singer, performing Cole Porter's 'Night and Day' in a budget-price Busby Berkeley-style sequence featuring young women equipped with violins and pianos. Sinatra was paid a modest $1,000 fee for his three-minute slot, most of it eaten up by the cost of his trip from the east coast. Still struggling to establish himself on the New York nightclub circuit, he could barely afford the money, only accepting the film after a nationwide strike shut down all the recording studios. Originally released on 4 February 1943, with Sinatra seventh billed between The Radio Rogues and The Mills Brothers, *Beverly* was hurriedly reissued a short time later to cash in on the singer's new fame, Sinatra now headlining as the star attraction. One critic remarked: 'I'm convinced there has been nothing like him since goldfish eating', which may have been a compliment. The Sinatra connection boosted the film's final box-office take to $3 million.

TILL THE CLOUDS ROLL BY (1946).

Starring the ill-cast Robert Walker, MGM's typically anodyne biopic of Jerome Kern was a box-office smash, grossing $6.7 million in the United States. Seventh-billed Sinatra sings 'Ol' Man River' during the grand finale, surrounded by an all-white band. Clad in his white suit, standing atop a white dais, the star cuts an odd figure against the pink backdrop, his backcombed hair suspiciously dark. *Life* magazine voted Sinatra's cameo the worst moment in any 1946 Hollywood release, '...a high point in bad taste'.

MEET ME IN LAS VEGAS (1956).

Mediocre MGM musical from the Joe Pasternak stable, starring Dan Dailey as a professional gambler who hits a lucky streak when he teams up with dancer Cyd Charisse. Filmed partly at the Sands Hotel, the film features Sinatra as a slot machine player.

AROUND THE WORLD IN 80 DAYS (1956).

Mike Todd's epic period travelogue, designed to show off his new Todd-AO widescreen process, boasts 44 guest stars. Sinatra makes a non-speaking cameo appearance as a piano player in the western saloon scene with Marlene Dietrich and George Raft.

PEPE (1960).

George Sidney's mind-numbingly drab attempt to capitalise on Cantinflas' success in *Around the World in 80 Days*. Sinatra and his *Ocean's 11* cast are among the many stars encountered by loveable peasant Pepe as he searches for his horse in Hollywood.

THE ROAD TO HONG KONG (1962).

Ten years on from *The Road to Bali*, Bob Hope and Bing Crosby attempted to revive their *Road* series with this flat British-made production. Sinatra and Dean Martin turn up at the finale as spacemen.

THE LIST OF ADRIAN MESSENGER (1963).

John Huston's disguise-heavy mystery-caper movie offered audiences the chance to spot 'guest stars' Burt Lancaster, Tony Curtis, Robert Mitchum and Sinatra as they flitted across the action in heavy make-up. Supposedly appearing as a gypsy stableman, Sinatra was in fact doubled for the cameo, appearing only to rip off his lookalike mask at the climax, for which he was paid a tidy $75,000.

THE OSCAR (1966).

Sinatra's good singing buddy Tony Bennett took his one and only shot at an acting career in this notoriously dreadful Hollywood-exposé melodrama. Told as a series of flashbacks from the Academy Award ceremony where amoral star Stephen Boyd expects to pick up the Best Actor trophy, the film has an oh-so-surprising twist: the statuette goes to Frank Sinatra instead, the star loudly cheered by daughter Nancy. The idea of Sinatra winning a second Oscar at this stage in his career - the period of *Marriage on the Rocks* and *Assault on a Queen* - truly belonged in the realm of pulp fiction.

CAST A GIANT SHADOW (1966).

Produced by John Wayne's Batjac company, Melville Shavelson's ambitious biopic of Mickey Marcus, martyred hero of the 1947 Israeli-Arab war, made for an uneasy all-star epic. Sinatra appears in the brief role of an ill-equipped bomber pilot reduced to dropping soda syphons on the enemy.

Flying out to Israel on 24 June 1965, he worked on the film for a mere two days during the third week of production. Shavelson had offered to shoot Sinatra's scenes in Rome, only to find the star insisted on filming in Tel Aviv. It turned out he had a standing appointment to open the Francis Albert Sinatra Orphanage in Nazareth. Or possibly the Sinatra-financed Arab-Israeli Youth Centre. Or both.

CANNONBALL RUN II (1984).

A shoddy last bow for ex-Clan members Sinatra, Dean Martin, Sammy Davis Jnr and Shirley MacLaine. According to producer Albert Ruddy, Sinatra asked *Cannonball Run* star Dean Martin to include him in the sequel, hoping to recapture the fun of the Rat Pack escapades two decades earlier (for the record, Nancy Sinatra asserts that Davis asked her father to appear as a favour.) MacLaine claims that no-one bothered to look at the script prior to shooting, which figures. Turning up at the Tucson location in July 1983, Sinatra allegedly worked on the film for a mere four hours, appearing behind an office desk, then at the wheel of a sports car. With Jilly Rizzo at his side, the star reverts to his old *Higher and Higher* role as Himself, engaging in a witty exchange with star Burt Reynolds:

BURT: Mr Sinatra...
FRANK: You may call me Frank.
BURT (to sidekick Dom DeLuise): I can call him Frank.
FRANK: Not yet. I'll let you know when you can. Not exactly now, but I'll let you know.
BURT: What can I call you?
FRANK: Call me 'Sir'.

The original *Cannonball Run* made nearly $37 million at the American box-office. Warner were so unimpressed by the quality of *Cannonball II*, they opened the film in Japan six months before its US premiere in June 1984. The sequel flopped on its home turf, few turning up to witness Sinatra's last movie performance, such as it was, the slumming star delivering his lines with supreme indifference, The end credits roll over a series of out-takes taken from the film, Sinatra appearing amused rather than irritated when Dom DeLuise fumbles a line four times.

APPENDIX 2: NO-SHOWS: FILMS LOST, REJECTED AND CANCELLED

JUMBO (CIRCA 1946).

MGM producer Arthur Freed envisaged a screen version of the 1935 Rodgers and Hart Broadway show, starring Sinatra and original cast member Jimmy Durante.

JOHN LOVES MARY (1948).

Sinatra unsuccessfully campaigned for the second lead in Warner's film version of the Norman Krasna stage hit.

KNOCK ON ANY DOOR (1949).

Frustrated with his MGM career in early 1948, Sinatra hoped to erase the recent *Miracle of the Bells* humiliation with a more weighty dramatic performance opposite his old friend Humphrey Bogart in this courtroom drama. Now 32, he was regarded as both too old and insufficiently pretty to convince as moody slum kid Nick Romano.

THE BROTHERS RICO (CIRCA 1951).

Touting for work, Sinatra expressed a strong interest in playing the lead in William Goetz's proposed film version of the Georges Simenon story. Goetz liked the idea of casting Sinatra as a conscience-stricken Mob book-keeper, but didn't want to raise his hopes in case any bigger names showed interest.

ANDROCLES AND THE LION (1952).

RKO boss Howard Hughes must have been feeling either unusually benevolent or particularly sadistic when he agreed to let arch-enemy Sinatra test for the role of Androcles in this ill-conceived George Bernard Shaw adaptation.

ST LOUIS WOMAN (1953).

MGM's long-mooted teaming of Sinatra with Ava Gardner finally died away as the couple's relationship did likewise.

ON THE WATERFRONT (1954).

This Hoboken-set tale of union corruption would have made a perfect homecoming vehicle for Sinatra after his career resurrection in *From Here to Eternity*. Director Elia Kazan liked the idea, but producer Sam Spiegel had his

sights firmly set on the hotter Marlon Brando, only agreeing to Sinatra when United Artists offered a $500,000 deal. A verbal contract was made on 22 October 1953, paying the star $55,000 and one percent of the net profits. Once Brando was on board, Spiegel made a new $1 million deal with Columbia, attempting to appease the ousted Sinatra by offering him the key supporting role of Catholic priest Father Barry, only to discover that Kazan had already promised the part to Karl Malden. Sinatra sued Spiegel for $500,000 after *Waterfront*'s huge success, citing breach of contract. The matter was eventually settled out of court five years later.

PINK TIGHTS (1954).

Twentieth Century-Fox signed up Sinatra to co-star with contract player Marilyn Monroe in this musical remake of the 1943 Betty Grable vehicle *Coney Island*. Budgeted at $2.2 million, the Technicolor/Cinemascope production would be overseen by Sol C. Siegel, with songs by the newly reunited team of Jule Styne and Sammy Cahn. Unhappy with Fox, the script and her derisory fee, the overworked Monroe failed to show up for the first day of filming on 15 December 1953. Suspending their troublesome star, Fox briefly considered replacing her with Sheree North, then abandoned the project.

IT'S ALWAYS FAIR WEATHER (1955).

Gene Kelly hoped to revive his flagging career at MGM with a glorious Cinemascope sequel to *On the Town*, scripted by original writers Adolph Green and Betty Comden. The storyline depicted the ex-Navy buddies meeting up ten years on, only to find they no longer have anything in common. Sadly, Jules Munshin was unavailable and Sinatra had no pressing wish to climb back into his sailor suit.

MISTER ROBERTS (1955).

Sinatra was considered for the co-starring role of Ensign Pulver in Warner's film version of the Joshua Logan-Thomas Heggen stage hit. Director

John Ford insisted on Jack Lemmon, arguing that Sinatra was too old.

CAROUSEL (1956)

With *Pink Tights* a definite bust, Sinatra agreed to star as deceased carnival barker Billy Bigelow in Fox's de luxe film version of the Rodgers-Hammerstein stage hit. Signed up in the summer of 1955 for $150,000, the star underwent extensive wardrobe tests and recorded most of the required songs between 15-19 August. Already slightly uneasy about his casting as the big and burly Bigelow, Sinatra didn't relish the prospect of spending ten weeks far away from his Los Angeles base. Arriving in Booth Bay Harbor, Maine for the first day of location filming on 20 August, Sinatra discovered - allegedly for the first time - that Fox intended to shoot the film in both standard 35mm Cinemascope and their new Cinemascope '55 process. Informing the producers that he wasn't going to make two films for the price of one, Sinatra abandoned the location after a two day stand-off, his role hurriedly filled by Gordon MacRae. Outraged by this contract-breaking, Fox sued Sinatra for $1 million five days later, eventually settling for the more insidious punishment of *Can Can*. As *Carousel* was finally filmed only in the Cinemascope '55 format, the studio had a questionable case at best.

GUNFIGHT AT THE OK CORRAL (1957).

When original choice Humphrey Bogart proved unavailable, producer Hal Wallis considered offering the role of Doc Holliday to Sinatra before settling on Kirk Douglas.

PARIS BY NIGHT (1958).

Having wowed international audiences with the soft-core melodrama *And God Created Woman* (1957), French producer Raoul Levy hoped to team director Roger Vadim and star Brigitte Bardot with Sinatra for a musical follow-up, to be distributed by Columbia. The storyline would centre around a penniless expatriate American gambler who meets up with a sensational-looking girl during a cafe brawl and decides to make her a star. Harry Kurnitz was hired to write the script, which his friend Sinatra professed to like. Negotiating with Levy over 14

months in Las Vegas, Rome, London, Monaco and New York, Sinatra finally agreed to take the proffered role for $250,000 plus 40 percent of the profits as co-producer and an additional six percent as star. Once Levy had accepted these terms, Sinatra suddenly bowed out, unwilling to work on location in Paris for four months. He professed indifference to the missed opportunity, correctly guessing that American interest in Bardot would rapidly decline.

THE YOUNG LIONS (1958).

According to Martin & Lewis biographer Arthur Marx, Fox considered casting Sinatra as the combat-shy Broadway singing star eventually played by Dean Martin.

SOME LIKE IT HOT (1959).

United Artists originally wanted Bob Hope, Danny Kaye and Mitzi Gaynor for this cross-dressing romp, then settled on Sinatra, Tony Curtis and Marilyn Monroe. Despite his wariness over working with Sinatra, writer-director Billy Wilder went along with the casting. Sinatra read the script, showed some interest, then dropped out in favour of *A Hole in the Head*, making way for Jack Lemmon.

SAY ONE FOR ME (1959).

Bing Crosby donned clerical garb one last time in this misguided attempt to boost his faltering movie career. Unimpressed by the heartwarming story of a New York priest ministering to troubled showbiz folk, Sinatra declined the co-starring role of small-time heel Tony, who experiences a miraculous transformation under Father Bing's spiritual guidance.

MANOLETE (CIRCA 1959).

 Sammy Davis Jnr wanted Sinatra to star in a biopic of the famous Spanish bullfighter, recently gored to death in the arena. Fellow fight-fan Sinatra liked the outline written by Davis' friend Barnaby Conrad, but wouldn't make a film involving a sport unpopular with the American public.

ST PAUL (CIRCA 1959).

Frank Capra long dreamed of making a biopic about the Man from Damascus, originally with James Cagney as Saul/Paul. After working on *A Hole in the Head*, the somewhat deluded director

decided that Sinatra should play the part, an opinion not shared by any studio executives.

BROTHER BERTRAM (CIRCA 1959).

Another hopeless Frank Capra project, this comedy about a monk was rejected by both Sinatra and Elvis Presley.

THE JIMMY DURANTE STORY (1959).

Based on Gene Fowler's best-selling book, this authorised biopic of Sinatra's *It Happened in Brooklyn* co-star was announced as a Columbia release to be written and directed by Frank Capra. Sinatra, Bing Crosby and Dean Martin would co-star as Durante and his comedy partners Lou Clayton and Eddie Jackson, all three participating through their own production companies. Capra saw the dream deal rapidly fall apart as his stars demanded equal says in all aspects of the project, without a corresponding investment of capital. Once the director had bowed out, the film faded away.

LET'S MAKE LOVE (1960).

Sinatra, Fred Astaire and Jack Benny all agreed to make guest appearances in this Fox musical starring Marilyn Monroe and Yves Montand. An actors' strike during March and April 1960 caused their previous commitments to run over schedule, obliging all three performers to drop out. Fox cannily replaced them with Bing Crosby, Gene Kelly and Milton Berle.

EXODUS (1960).

Sinatra suggested to Spencer Tracy that Otto Preminger could cast them as the father and son in his Leon Uris adaptation. Tracy replied that he couldn't lose enough weight for Sinatra to carry him at the end.

POCKETFUL OF MIRACLES (1961).

Sinatra tentatively agreed to star as loveable gangster Dave the Dude in Frank Capra's glutinous, overblown remake of *Lady for a Day* (1934), bowing out after he took a closer look at the script.

THE EXECUTION OF PRIVATE SLOVIK (1960).

Sinatra was intrigued by the harrowing real-life World War II story of the only American soldier to be shot for desertion since the Civil War. The star bought the rights to William Bradford Huie's acclaimed book, intending to produce and direct an explicitly anti-war film version with Steve McQueen in the lead. His bold, if ill-considered decision to openly employ blacklisted talent Albert Maltz to write the script brought an immediate and unstoppable backlash. The *House I Live In* writer had been convicted of contempt of Congress in 1950, fleeing to Mexico after serving a year in prison. Once *New York Times* writer Murray Schumach broke the news on 21 March 1960, the right-wing press got into action, the *New York Daily Mirror* fuming: 'What kind of thinking motivates Frank Sinatra in hiring an unrepentant enemy of his country ...a hard revolutionist who has never done anything to remove himself from the communist camp?' Sinatra retaliated by taking out a full-page advert in *Variety*, defending his choice of Maltz. Had the fight been between just the star and his old critics, Sinatra might have weathered the storm. Inevitably, his Kennedy connection drew the presidential candidate into the fray, John Wayne commenting: 'I wonder how Sinatra's crony, Senator John Kennedy, feels about Sinatra hiring such a man?' Sinatra retaliated with: 'This type of partisan politics is hitting below the belt. I make movies. I do not ask the advice of Senator Kennedy on whom I should hire...' For all this bold stance, there was just too much ammunition aimed against the film. Outgoing Republican President Dwight Eisenhower was the Army General who'd ordered Slovik's death by firing squad, leading to further accusations of *Slovik* being blatant political propaganda against both Eisenhower and Vice-President Richard Nixon, Kennedy's opponent. Kennedy Patriarch Joseph Senior informed Sinatra that he would either drop Maltz or lose all Kennedy connections. Backing down, Sinatra issued a sufficiently humble public statement two weeks after his original announcement:

In view of the reaction of my family, my friends and the American public, I have instructed my attorneys to make a settlement with Albert Maltz and to inform him that he will not write the screenplay for The Execution of Private Slovik. I had thought that the major consideration was whether or not the resulting script would be in the best interests of the United States. But the American public has indicated it feels the morality of hiring Albert Maltz is the more crucial matter, and I will accept this majority opinion.

Paid his $75,000 fee in full, Albert Maltz quietly disappeared from the scene. Sinatra sold off the film rights to Huie's book, which was eventually dramatised as a television movie by Richard Levinson and William Link in 1970, with Martin Sheen starring as Slovik. There are a number of puzzling aspects to the incident. It seems unlikely that Sinatra really regarded Maltz as the only writer who could do justice to the *Slovik* story. In any case, Maltz could have worked uncredited, using the industry-standard cover of a pseudonym or 'front' name. Those unimpressed by Sinatra's liberal credentials have suggested that he simply wanted to emulate Otto Preminger, who'd recently hired blacklisted writer Dalton Trumbo to adapt *Exodus* for the screen. Trumbo was also associated with Kirk Douglas' production of *Spartacus* (1960), making him a less easy target than Maltz for Right-wing agitators. Moreover, neither *Exodus* nor *Spartacus* dealt with recent - and still controversial - American history. The star subsequently claimed that *Slovik* had been doomed anyway, as no bank would risk financing the sensitive project, with or without Maltz. Steve McQueen emerged from the debâcle unscathed, having already rejected the leading role in order to advance his career independently of Sinatra.

BORN YESTERDAY (1961).
Sinatra briefly toyed with the idea of starring in a musical remake of George Cukor's 1950 hit, with on-off girlfriend Marilyn Monroe in the Judy Holliday role. Monroe died during early negotiations for the film rights, killing the project.

THE GREAT TRAIN ROBBERY (CIRCA 1961).
One of several proposed Clan follow-ups to *Ocean's 11*, this comedy caper was another Peter Lawford project, intended to unite the Rat Pack with Marilyn Monroe. *Ocean* co-writer Harry Brown prepared a treatment, but never got as far as an actual script, Sinatra's exorbitant salary demands and Monroe's

death soon putting paid to the idea.

THE ACTOR (1962).
Clifford Odets agreed to adapt his own short story for MGM, only to find himself caught up in the studio's involved, ultimately futile negotiations with Sinatra over a major long-term deal (much like the one he would shortly make with Warner). MGM dropped the project, allowing Sinatra to acquire, then resell it to the studio along with himself as the star. Once the big deal fell through, Sinatra lost interest in *The Actor* completely.

A TREE GROWS IN BROOKLYN (CIRCA 1962).
Keen to find some use for his discarded *Pink Tights* score, Jule Styne approached Richard Zanuck with the idea for a musical remake of Fox's 1945 hit, starring Monroe and Sinatra. Zanuck liked the package and both stars were interested. After Monroe's death, the project was quietly dropped.

HOW THE WEST WAS WON (1963).
See Chapter 10.

LE MÉPRIS AKA CONTEMPT (1963).
Writer-director Jean Luc Godard wanted to reunite Sinatra with Kim Novak for his offbeat adaptation of the Alberto Moravia novel *A Ghost at Noon*. Novak would play an unhappily married film star, Sinatra a philistine producer who hires Fritz Lang to direct a peplum version of Homer's *Odyssey* at the Cinecitta studios. The roles went to Brigitte Bardot and Jack Palance.

WHAT A WAY TO GO! (1964).
Sinatra alumni Shirley MacLaine, Gene Kelly, Dean Martin, Betty Comden, Adolph Green, Nelson Riddle and Jule Styne all contributed to this Twentieth Century-Fox black comedy about a fabulously rich woman and her series of accident prone husbands. Intended first for Marilyn Monroe, then Elizabeth Taylor, the project began life in 1962 as *I Love Louisa*. Approached to play one of MacLaine's ill-fated spouses, Sinatra demanded what Daryl Zanuck considered an excessive fee of $200,000 for two weeks' work, his role going to the less expensive Robert Mitchum at MacLaine's suggestion.

MAROONED (CIRCA 1964).
Yet another Frank Capra loser, this

Columbia project about stranded astronauts was rejected by Sinatra and most other big Hollywood names.

SAY IT WITH MUSIC (1964).
Another of Arthur Freed's aborted MGM projects, this celebration of Irving Berlin's life and times would have reunited Sinatra with *Some Came Running* director Vincente Minnelli. MGM killed the project, despite interest from Julie Andrews, claiming that large-scale musicals were a thing of the past. A short time later, *The Sound of Music* premiered.

KING RAT (1965).
Columbia wanted a big-name star such as Sinatra for their film version of James Clavell's cynical World War II tale of allied soldiers in a Japanese POW camp. Writer-director Bryan Forbes fought for a younger actor, eventually settling on George Segal.

HARPER (1966).
This adaptation of John Ross MacDonald's novel *The Moving Target* looked a go-project for Sinatra until negotiations with Elliott Kastner and Jerry Gershwin stalled over their producers' fee. Mickey Rudin convinced Sinatra that Kastner and Gershwin didn't deserve to make $400,000 on the strength of his name.

A CLOCKWORK ORANGE (CIRCA 1965).
Having failed with the *Harper* project, Brad Dexter hoped to interest Sinatra in the film rights to Anthony Burgess' controversial cult novel. Thumbing through the book, the star claimed not to understand a word of it, quickly rejecting the novel as suitable film material. Judging by Stanley Kubrick's 1971 version, he was quite right.

IN COLD BLOOD (CIRCA 1966).
Otto Preminger wanted Sinatra to star as the investigating policeman in his proposed film version of Truman Capote's 'factional' true-crime bestseller. Discovering that the rights had already been sold to Richard Brooks, Preminger rowed with Capote's agent Irving Lazaar in a crowded Hollywood restaurant, receiving a scalp full of broken glass for his pains.

FUNNY GIRL (1968).
Sinatra was among the many names suggested for the role of Nick Arnstein opposite Barbra Streisand's Fanny Brice in Columbia's hit musical. Producer Ray Stark - Arnstein's real-life son-in-law - quickly vetoed the idea. Aside from his $750,000 price tag, Sinatra demanded top billing, an expanded role and four additional solo songs, none of which went down too well with Streisand.

THE ONLY GAME IN TOWN (1969).
Originally a flop Broadway play by Frank Gilroy, this glum tale of Las Vegas losers was inexplicably bought up by Fox for $600,000. Offered the role of musician-turned-gambler Joe Grady, Sinatra agreed to co-star opposite Elizabeth Taylor, both stars signing on in April 1968. *Game*'s start date was seriously delayed after Taylor underwent an emergency hysterectomy, obliging Sinatra to drop out for an engagement at Caesar's Palace in the real Las Vegas.

ON A CLEAR DAY YOU CAN SEE FOREVER (1970).
Having recklessly paid out $750,000 for the rights to this 1966 Broadway failure, Paramount turned it into a flop Barbra Streisand vehicle. Studio head Howard Koch attempted to interest his old employer Sinatra in the role of Streisand's French psychiatrist, Dr Marc Chabot, only to be given a polite 'no'.

DIRTY HARRY (1971).
Probably the most famous of Sinatra's non-appearances, this long-gestating project started life in the late 1960s as *Dead Right*, a screenplay by Harry J. and Rita M. Fink. Unhappy with the lead character's less savoury habits, first choice John Wayne passed on the film, which was rapidly snapped up by Warner for Sinatra. After three rewrites, *Dirty Harry* looked set to go under the direction of Irvin Kershner, only to be brought to an abrupt halt. Sinatra needed urgent surgery on his right hand to correct a bad case of Dupuytren's contracture, a shortening and distortion of muscle tissue in his palm and fingers that had bothered him for some time. Seeking a replacement star, Warner was turned down by Robert Mitchum, Paul Newman and Steve McQueen before Clint Eastwood said yes.

THE GODFATHER (1972).
No, really. Paramount offered their film version of the Mario Puzo novel to Otto Preminger, who decided that only Sinatra could do justice to the role of ageing family head Don Vito Corleone. Despite the director's generous offer to delete the supposedly Sinatra-based character Johnny Fontaine from the script, his *Golden Arm* star passed. Unwilling to make the film with any other actor, Preminger departed from the project.

HARRY AND TONTO (1974).
Writer-director Paul Mazursky concocted this one-man-and-his-cat road movie with James Cagney in mind. Cagney politely declined the role, as did Sinatra and Laurence Olivier. Fourth choice Art Carney won an Academy Award for his performance.

THE LITTLE PRINCE (1974).
Stanley Donen's flop musical fantasy reunited the songwriting team of Alan Jay Lerner and Frederick Loewe to no great effect. A Palm Springs neighbour of Sinatra, Loewe persuaded an initially doubtful Paramount to offer him the leading role of The Pilot. Intrigued by both the character and the $200,000 paycheque, Sinatra travelled to London for preliminary discussions in June 1972 before declining the part.

WINTER KILLS (1979).
Novelist Richard Condon wanted Sinatra to play the manipulative, Joseph Kennedy-inspired patriarch in this film version of his presidential assassination fantasy. The star quite liked writer-director William Richert's script, but rejected the role as too old for him.

THE VERDICT (1982).
After first choice Robert Redford turned down the role of Frank Galvin, a seedy, ambulance-chasing Boston lawyer, Dustin Hoffman, Roy Scheider, Cary Grant and Sinatra all asked to be considered, losing out to Paul Newman A few years after *The Verdict*, Sinatra was rumoured to be planning another film comeback, either in a drama about a psychiatrist or a biopic of columnist friend Walter Winchell.

LA CAGE AUX FOLLES (1986).

Aged 70, Sinatra had a sudden urge to co-star with Dudley Moore in a Hollywood remake of Edouard Molinaro's 1978 hit farce. Moore didn't see himself as an effeminate female impersonator and declined the honour. The idea of Sinatra playing an ageing gay nightclub owner is certainly intriguing.

THE GODFATHER PART III (1990)

Francis Coppola offered Sinatra the showy supporting role of a senior Mafia Don in the belated final instalment of his Corleone trilogy. Impressed by both director and script, Sinatra balked at the idea of a three-month shoot and passed. The part went to one-time *From Here to Eternity* contender Eli Wallach.

APPENDIX 3: MISCELLANEOUS: SINATRA SIDESHOWS

THE ALL-STAR BOND RALLY (1944).

A US Treasury film promoting the purchase of war bonds. Sinatra appears alongside Bing Crosby, Betty Grable and Harpo Marx, singing 'Saturday Night Is the Loneliest Night of the Week' with the Harry James Band.

THE ROAD TO VICTORY (1944).

A short propaganda film featuring Sinatra as himself.

THE HOUSE I LIVE IN (1945).

RKO. 10 minutes
Producers: Frank Ross, Mervyn LeRoy; director: Mervyn LeRoy; screenplay: Albert Maltz; musical director: Axel Stordahl; incidental score: Roy Webb; title song: Lewis Allen, Earl Robinson; editor: Philip Martin Jnr.
A short-and-sweet propaganda film devised by Sinatra and Mervyn LeRoy to promote religious and cultural tolerance in America. All the talents involved agreed to give their services free of charge, donating the profits to social work with adolescents. Likewise, RKO provided Sinatra with studio facilities *gratis* for the one-day shoot. The minimal story has Sinatra take time out from radio rehearsals to lecture a group of anti-Semitic boys on the evils of prejudice:

Look, fellas, religion makes no difference except maybe to a Nazi or somebody as stupid. Why, people all over the world worship God in many different ways. God created everybody. He didn't create one people better than another... This wonderful country is made up of a hundred different kinds of people and a hundred different ways of talking and a hundred different ways of going to church. But they're all American ways.

Sinatra then sings the title song, subtitled 'That's America to Me', sugaring the pill a little. Released on 11 September 1945, *The House I Live In* drew substantial praise. Sinatra, Ross and LeRoy were subsequently voted a special Academy Award, collected by the singer at the ceremony on 7 March 1946. A few years on, the film would be cited by Sinatra's enemies as conclusive proof of his Raving Red tendencies. He does smoke a cigarette, a clear incitement to juvenile delinquency. Looking both dated and naive five decades on, *House* retains a strong sense of integrity.

THREE COINS IN THE FOUNTAIN (1954).

Sinatra croons the Jule Styne-Sammy Cahn title song during the lengthy precredits sequence of this Fox production. His first stereo recording, 'Three Coins...' was released on the Capitol label in April 1953, proving a major hit and an Academy Award winner.

INVITATION TO MONTE CARLO (1958).

Sinatra makes a brief appearance in this British-produced travelogue short.

SINATRA IN ISRAEL (1962).

A documentary short.

FOR THOSE WHO THINK YOUNG (1964).

Described by Nick Tosches as 'a half-assed plug for Pepsi Cola', this witless college musical was made by Sinatra Enterprises for release through Paramount. Nancy Sinatra stars, alongside James Darren, Ellen Burstyn, George Raft and Claudia Martin, daughter of Dean. Mildly notable as the only Sinatra production not to feature Francis Albert himself. A man's got to draw the line somewhere.

THAT'S ENTERTAINMENT! (1974).

One of MGM's few box-office hits during the 1970s, this anthology of highlights from the studio's musical productions seems a little redundant in the age of instant video recall. Clad in mostly depressing seventies clothes and hairstyles, the onscreen 'hosts' include Frank Sinatra, Bing Crosby, Fred Astaire, Gene Kelly, Debbie Reynolds, Elizabeth Taylor, Peter Lawford, James Stewart, Mickey Rooney, Donald O'Connor and Liza Minnelli. Sinatra provides the opening off-screen narration, then stands in front of the old MGM studios, his dark suit matched by an even darker hairpiece. Delivering the banal script with professionalism rather than verve, he does a creditable job. The younger Sinatra is seen in lengthy excerpts from *It Happened in Brooklyn* ('The Song's Gotta Have Heart'), *Take Me Out to the Ball Game* (title song), *On the Town* ('New York, New York') and *High Society* ('Well, Did You Evah?') Footage from *Anchors Aweigh* features only Gene Kelly, Kathryn Grayson and Jerry Mouse.

THAT'S ENTERTAINMENT PART II (1976).

Director and co-host Gene Kelly narrates a brief segment devoted to Sinatra, with non-chronological excerpts from *Take Me Out to the Ball Game*, *The Tender Trap*, *Till the Clouds Roll By*, *Anchors Aweigh*, *It Happened in Brooklyn*, *High Society*, *Some Came Running*, *The Kissing Bandit*, *Never So Few* and *Meet Me in Las Vegas*. Nothing from *On the Town* or *Dirty Dingus Magee*. Few of the clips are properly identified, and some are so brief as to be largely pointless.

CONTRACT ON CHERRY STREET (1977).

150 minutes. Artanis/Columbia Television/NBC.
Executive producer: Renee Valente; producer: Hugh Benson; director: William A. Graham; screenplay: Edward Anhalt (based on the novel by Philip Rosenberg); photography: Jack Priestley; music: Jerry Goldsmith.
Cast: Frank Sinatra (Frank Hovannes), Harry Guardino (Ron Polito), Martin Balsam (Ernie Weinberg), Verna Bloom (Emily Hovannes), Martin Gabel, Henry Silva, Joe de Santis (Vin Seruto), Jay Black (Tommy Sinardes).
A tough New York cop avenges his partner's murder, driving mob scum from the city streets. After his mother Dolly was killed in a plane crash on 6 January 1977, Sinatra agreed to star in this adaptation of her favourite Mafia novel, despite a previous vow never to appear in a tv movie. Filmed on New York locations, *Cherry Street* started production on 21 June 1977, shooting slightly disrupted by a 24-hour power blackout over 13-14 July. Broadcast by NBC on 19 November 1977, the film received mixed reviews, though Sinatra's performance was generally praised.

Plans for a theatrical release overseas were abandoned, *Cherry Street* remaining unseen in Britain until its television premiere in 1988.

MAGNUM (1987).

Sinatra made a high-profile guest appearance on CBS's hit private 'tec series, cast as a retired policeman who joins forces with Tom Selleck to track down his granddaughter's killer. Filmed in early January 1987, the episode was broadcast on 25 February.

ENTERTAINING THE TROOPS (1989).

World War II documentary featuring glimpses of Sinatra in archive footage.

LISTEN UP: THE LIVES OF QUINCY JONES (1990).

Sinatra appears as one of the many interviewees in this extended homage.

SINATRA (1992).

Unknown Philip Casnoff stars as the Man himself in this authorised 250-minute telebiography, screened on the CBS network in November 1992. Executive-produced by Tina Sinatra, the film covers her father's life from 1920-1974. Marcia Gay Harden co-stars as Ava Gardner, Nina Siemaszko as Mia Farrow. The slightly better known supporting cast includes Olympia Dukakis, Gina Gershon, Rod Steiger, Jeff Corey and Jay Robinson.

THAT'S ENTERTAINMENT! III (1994).

This superior addition to MGM's compendiumn series includes an abbreviated version of *On The Town*'s title number and an extremely brief glimpse of the 'She Begged Me' dance sequence from *Anchors Aweigh*. Excerpts from *The Kissing Bandit* ('Dance of Fury') and *High Society* ('True Love') do not feature Sinatra.

FILMOGRAPHY

HIGHER AND HIGHER 1943

RKO 90 minutes
Producer: Tim Whelan; associate producer: George Arthur; director: Tim Whelan; screenplay: Jay Dratler, Ralph Spence (based on the musical by Gladys Hurlbut and Joshua Logan); additional dialogue: William Bowers, Howard Harris; photography: Robert De Grasse (black and white); art direction: Albert S. D'Agostino, Jack Okey; editing: Gene Milford; music director: Constantin Bakaleinikoff; orchestral arrangements: Gene Rose; musical arrangements for Frank Sinatra: Axel Stordahl; incidental score: Roy Webb; orchestrations: Maurice de Packh; vocal arrangements: Ken Darby; songs: music Jimmy McHugh, lyrics Harold Adamson; 'Disgustingly Rich': music Richard Rodgers, lyrics Lorenz Hart; choreography: Ernst Matray; sound: Jean L. Speak; assistant director: Clem Beauchamp.
Cast: Michele Morgan (Millie Picoux), Jack Haley (Mike O'Brien), Frank Sinatra ('Frank Sinatra'), Leon Errol (Drake), Marcy McGuire (Mickey), Victor Borge (Victor Fitzroy Victor), Dooley Wilson (Oscar), Barbara Hale (Katherine Keating).

STEP LIVELY 1944

RKO 88 minutes
Producer: Robert Fellows; director: Tim Whelan; screenplay: Warren Duff, Peter Milne (based on the play *Room Service* by John Murray and Allen Boretz); photography: Robert De Grasse (black and white); art direction: Albert S, D'Agostino, Carroll Clark; musical direction: Constantin Bakaleinikoff; orchestral arrangements: Gene Rose; musical arrangements for Frank Sinatra: Axel Stordahl; vocal arrangements: Ken Darby; songs: music Jule Styne, lyrics Sammy Cahn; choreography: Ernest Matray; sound: Jean L. Speak, James G. Stewart; assistant director: Clem Beauchamp.
Cast: Frank Sinatra (Glen Russell), George Murphy (Gordon Miller), Adolphe Menjou (Wagner), Gloria De Haven (Christine Marlowe), Walter Slezak (Joe Gribble), Eugene Pallette (Jenkins), Anne Jeffreys (Jean Abbot), Dorothy Malone (hotel switchboard operator, uncredited).

ANCHORS AWEIGH 1945

MGM 140 minutes

Producer: Joe Pasternak; director: George Sidney; screenplay: Isobel Lennart (based on the short story *You Can't Fool a Marine* by Natalie Marsin); photography: Robert Planck, Charles Boyle (Technicolor); art direction: Cedric Gibbons, Randall Duell; editing: Adrienne Fazan; music director: George Stoll; songs: music Jule Styne, lyrics Sammy Cahn; orchestrations: Axel Stordahl; Kathryn Grayson's vocal arrangements: Earl Brent; choreographer: Gene Kelly; assistant choreographer: Stanley Donen; sound: Douglas Shearer; costumes: Irene.

Cast: Frank Sinatra (Clarence Doolittle), Kathryn Grayson (Susan Abbott), Gene Kelly (Joseph Brady), Jose Iturbi (Himself), Dean Stockwell (Donald Martin), Pamela Britton (Girl from Brooklyn), Billy Gilbert (Cafe manager), Rags Ragland (Policeman), Henry O'Neill (Admiral Hammond), Edgar Kennedy (Police Captain); Grady Sutton (Bertram Kraler).

IT HAPPENED IN BROOKLYN 1947

MGM 103 minutes

Producer: Jack Cummings; director: Richard Whorf; screenplay: Isobel Lennart; photography: Robert Planck (black and white); art direction: Cedric Gibbons, Leonid Vasian; editing: Blanche Sewell; musical supervision and incidental score: Johnny Green; orchestrations: Ted Duncan; Frank Sinatra's vocal orchestrations: Axel Stordahl; piano solos: Andre Previn; songs: music Jule Styne, lyrics Sammy Cahn; choreography: Jack Donohue; sound: Douglas Shearer.

Cast: Frank Sinatra (Dannie Webson Miller), Kathryn Grayson (Anne Fielding), Peter Lawford (Jamie Shellgrove), Jimmy Durante (Nick Lombardi), Gloria Grahame (Nurse), Marcy McGuire (Rae Jakobi), Aubrey Mather (Digby John), Tamara Shayne (Mrs Kardos), Billy Roy (Leo Kardos).

THE KISSING BANDIT 1948

MGM 102 minutes

Producer: Joe Pasternak; director: Laslo Benedek; screenplay: Isobel Lennart, John Briard Harding; photography: Robert Surtees (Technicolor); art

direction: Cedric Gibbons, Randall Duell; editing: Adrienne Fazan; musical supervisor and conductor: George Stoll; musical arrangements: Leo Arnaud; incidental score: George Stoll, Albert Sendrey, Scott Bradley, Andre Previn; additional orchestrations: Axel Stordahl, Calvin Jackson, Conrad Salinger, Robert Van Eps, Paul Marquardt, Earl Brent; songs: Nacio Herb Brown, Edward Heyman, Earl Brent; dance director: Stanley Donen; additional choreography: Robert Alton; sound: Wilhelm W. Brockway; assistant director: Marvin Stuart.

Cast: Frank Sinatra (Ricardo), Kathryn Grayson (Teresa), J. Carrol Naish (Chico), Mildred Natwick (Isabella), Mikhail Rasumny (Don Jose), Billy Gilbert (General Torro), Sono Osato (Bianca), Clinton Sundberg (Colonel Gomez), Carleton Young (Count Belmonte), Edna Skinner (Juanita), Byron Foulger (Grandee), Ricardo Montalban, Ann Miller, Cyd Charisse (Dancers).

THE MIRACLE OF THE BELLS 1948

Jesse Lasky Productions/RKO 120 minutes

Producers: Jesse Lasky, Walter MacEwen; director: Irving Pichel; screenplay: Ben Hecht, Quentin Reynolds (based on the novel by Russell Janney); additional dialogue for Frank Sinatra: De Witt Bodeen; photography: Robert De Grasse (black and white); art direction: Albert S. D'Agostino, Ralph Berger; editing: Elmo Williams; music: Leigh Harline; song 'Ever Homeward': music Jule Styne, lyrics Sammy Cahn; sound: Philip N. Mitchell, Clem Portman; assistant director: Harry D'Arcy.

Cast: Fred MacMurray (Bill Dunnigan), Alida Valli (Olga Treskovna), Frank Sinatra (Father Paul), Lee J. Cobb (Marcus Harris), Harold Vermilyea (Nick Orloff), Charles Meredith (Father Spinsky), Philip Ahn (Ming Gow), Todd Jones (Jim Nolan), Veronica Pataky (Anna Klovna).

TAKE ME OUT TO THE BALL GAME 1949

MGM 93 minutes

Producer: Arthur Freed; directors: Busby Berkeley and Gene Kelly and Stanley Donen (uncredited); screenplay: Harry Tugend, George Wells; photography:

George Folsey (Technicolor); art direction: Cedric Gibbons, Daniel B. Cathcart; editing: Blanche Sewell; musical director: Adolph Deutsch; songs: music Roger Edens, lyrics Adolph Green, Betty Comden; title song: Jack Norworth and Albert Von Tilzer; vocal arrangements: Robert Tucker; choreography: Gene Kelly, Stanley Donen; sound: Douglas Shearer; women's costumes: Helen Rose; men's costumes: Valles.

Cast: Frank Sinatra (Dennis Ryan), Esther Williams (Katherine Catherine Higgins), Gene Kelly (Edward O'Brien), Betty Garrett (Shirley Delwyn), Edward Arnold (Joe Lorgan), Jules Munshin (Nat Goldberg), Richard Lane (Michael Gilhuly), Tom Dugan (Slappy Burke).

ON THE TOWN 1949

MGM 98 minutes

Producer: Arthur Freed; associate producer: Roger Edens; directors: Gene Kelly, Stanley Donen; screenplay: Adolph Green, Betty Comden (based on the Broadway musical by Leonard Bernstein, Adolph Green and Betty Comden); photography: Harold Rossen (Technicolor); art direction: Cedric Gibbons, Jack Martin Smith; editing: Ralph E. Winters; musical supervisor and conductor: Lennie Hayton; songs (original show): music Leonard Bernstein, lyrics Betty Comden, Adolph Green; additional songs: mus Roger Edens, lyrics Betty Comden, Adolph Green; orchestrations: Conrad Salinger, Robert Franklyn, Wally Heglin; vocal arrangements: Saul Chaplin; incidental score: Roger Edens, Saul Chaplin, Conrad Salinger; choreography: Gene Kelly, Stanley Donen; costumes: Helen Rose; sound: John A. Williams; assistant director: Jack Gertsman.

Cast: Gene Kelly (Gabey), Frank Sinatra (Chip), Betty Garrett (Brunhilde Esterhazy), Ann Miller (Claire Huddesen), Jules Munshin (Ozzie), Vera-Ellen (Ivy Smith), Florence Bates (Madame Dilyouska), Alice Pearce (Lucy Schmeeler), George Meader (Professor), Tom Dugan (Policeman), Bea Benedaret (Working girl), Hans Conreid (Francois, the Sambacabana headwaiter), Carol Haney (Dancer in green), Judy Holliday (voice of sailor's date).

DOUBLE DYNAMITE 1951
RKO 80 minutes
Producer: Irving Cummings Jr; director: Irving Cummings Sr; screenplay: Melville Shavelson (based on an original story by Leo Rosten; based on characters created by Manni Manheim); additional dialogue: Harry Crane; photography: Robert De Grasse (black and white); music: Leigh Harline; songs: music Jule Styne, lyrics Sammy Cahn.
Cast: Jane Russell (Mildred 'Mibs' Goodhug), Groucho Marx (Emile J. Keck), Frank Sinatra (Johnny Dalton), Don McGuire (Bob Pulsifer Jr), Howard Freeman (R.B. Pulsifer Sr), Nestor Paiva (Bookie).

MEET DANNY WILSON 1951
Universal-International 88 minutes
Producer: Leonard Goldstein; associate producer: Don McGuire; director: Joseph Pevney; screenplay and original story: Don McGuire; photography: Maury Gertsman (black and white); art direction: Bernard Herzbrun, Nathan Juran; editing: Virgil Vogel; musical direction: Joseph Gershenson; choreography: Harold Belfer; sound: Leslie I. Carey, Richard De Weese.
Cast: Frank Sinatra (Danny Wilson), Shelley Winters (Joy Carroll), Alex Nicol (Mike Ryan), Raymond Burr (Nick Driscoll), Tony Curtis, Jeff Chandler (themselves).

FROM HERE TO ETERNITY 1953
Columbia 118 minutes
Producer: Buddy Adler; director: Fred Zinnemann; screenplay: Daniel Taradash (based on the novel by James Jones); photography: Burnett Guffey (black and white); art direction: Cary O'Dell; editing: William Lyon; music: George Duning; musical director: Morris Stoloff; gowns: Jean Louis; sound: Lodge Cunningham; assistant director: Earl Bellamy.
Cast: Burt Lancaster (Sergeant Milton Warden), Montgomery Clift (Private Robert E. Lee Prewitt), Deborah Kerr (Karen Holmes), Frank Sinatra (Private Angelo Maggio), Donna Reed (Alma Burke -'Lurene'), Philip Ober (Captain Dana Holmes), Ernest Borgnine (Sergeant James R. 'Fatso' Judson).

SUDDENLY 1954
Libra/United Artists 76 minutes
Producer: Robert Bassler; director: Lewis Allen; screenplay: Richard Sale; photography: Charles G. Clarke (black and white); art direction: Frank Sylos; editing: John F. Schreyer; music: David Raksin; sound recording: Joseph Edmonson; sound editing: Delmore Harris; assistant director: Hal Klein.
Cast: Frank Sinatra (John Baron), Sterling Hayden (Sheriff Tod Shaw), James Gleason (Peter 'Pop' Benson), Nancy Gates (Ellen Benson), Kim Charney (Peter 'Pidge' Benson III), Paul Frees (Benny Conklin), Willis Bouchey (Dan Carney), Christopher Dark (Bart Wheeler), Paul Wexler (Deputy Slim Adams), James Lilburn (Jud Hobson).

YOUNG AT HEART 1954
Arwin/Warner 117 minutes
Producer: Henry Blanke; director: Gordon Douglas; original *Four Daughters* screenplay: Julius J. Epstein, Lenore Coffee (based on the novel *Sister Act* by Fannie Hurst); adaptation: Liam O'Brien; photography: Ted McCord and Charles Lang (uncredited) (Warnercolor/Technicolor print); art direction: John Beckman; editing: William Ziegler; musical direction: Ray Heindorff; songs: Cole Porter, George & Ira Gershwin, Harold Arlen, James Van Heusen, Johnny Mercer; sound: Leslie G. Hewitt, David Forrest.
Cast: Doris Day (Laurie Tuttle), Frank Sinatra (Barney Sloan), Gig Young (Alex Burke), Ethel Barrymore (Aunt Jessie), Dorothy Malone (Fran Tuttle), Robert Keith (Gregory Tuttle), Alan Hale Jnr (Bob Neary), Elizabeth Fraser (Amy Tuttle).

NOT AS A STRANGER 1955
Stanley Kramer Picture Corporation/United Artists 135 minutes
Producer: Stanley Kramer; director: Stanley Kramer; screenplay: Edward Anhalt, Edna Anhalt (based on the novel by Morton Thompson); photography: Franz Planer (black and white); production design: Rudolph Sternad; editing: Frederick Knudtson; music: George Antheil; costumes: Joe King; sound: Earl Snyder.
Cast: Olivia De Havilland (Kristina Hedvigson), Robert Mitchum (Lucas Marsh), Frank Sinatra (Alfred Boone),

Gloria Grahame (Harriet Lang), Broderick Crawford (Dr Aarons), Charles Bickford (Dr Runkleman), Myron McCormick (Dr Snider), Lon Chaney Jnr (Job Marsh), Jesse White (Ben Cosgrove), Harry Morgan (Oley), Lee Marvin (Brundage), Virginia Christine (Bruni), Whit Bissell (Dr Dietrich), Mae Clarke (Odelle).

GUYS AND DOLLS 1955
Goldwyn/MGM 150 minutes
Producer: Samuel Goldwyn; director: Joseph L. Mankiewicz; screenplay: Joseph L. Mankiewicz (based on the musical book by Jo Swerling and Abe Burrows); photography: Harry Stradling (Eastmancolor/Cinemascope); production design: Oliver Smith; art direction: Joseph Wright; editing: Daniel Mandell; orig music and lyrics: Frank Loesser; musical supervisor and conductor: Jay Blackton; incidental music: Cyril J. Mockridge; orchestrations: Skip Martin, Nelson Riddle, Alexander Courage, Al Sendrey; choreography: Michael Kidd; costumes: Irene Sharaff; sound: Fred Lau, Roger Heman, Vinton Vernon.
Cast: Marlon Brando (Sky Masterson), Jean Simmons (Miss Sarah Brown), Frank Sinatra (Nathan Detroit), Vivian Blaine (Miss Adelaide), Stubby Kaye (Nicely Nicely Johnson), Robert Keith (Lieutenant Brannigan), Veda Ann Borg (Laverne), B.S. Pully (Big Jule), Johnny Silver (Benny Southstreet), Sheldon Leonard (Harry the Horse), Regis Toomey (Arvide Abernathy).

THE TENDER TRAP 1955
MGM 111 minutes
Producer: Lawrence Weingarten; director: Charles Walters; screenplay: Julius J. Epstein (based on the play by Max Shulman and Robert Paul Smith); photography: Paul C. Vogel (Eastmancolor/Cinemascope); art direction: Cedric Gibbons, Arthur Lonergan; editing: John Dunning; music: Jeff Alexander; song '(Love Is) The Tender Trap': music James Van Heusen, lyrics Sammy Cahn; sound: Wesley C. Miller.
Cast: Frank Sinatra (Charlie Y. Reader), Debbie Reynolds (Julie Gillis), David Wayne (Joe McCall), Celeste Holm (Sylvia Crewes), Carolyn Jones (Helen), Lola Albright (Poppy), Jarma Lewis (Jessica Collins).

THE MAN WITH THE GOLDEN ARM 1955

Carlyle/United Artists 119 mins
Producer: Otto Preminger; director: Otto Preminger; screenplay: Walter Newman, Lewis Meltzer (based on the novel by Nelson Algren); photography: Sam Leavitt (black and white); art direction: Joseph Wright; sets: Darrell Silvera; editing: Louis R. Loeffler; music: Elmer Bernstein; orchestrations: Frederick Steiner; music editing: Leon Birnbaum; sound: Jack Solomon; costumes: Mary Ann Nyberg; titles: Saul Bass.

Cast: Frank Sinatra (Frankie Machine), Eleanor Parker (Sophia 'Zosh' Machine), Kim Novak (Molly), Arnold Stang (Sparrow), Darren McGavin (Louie), Robert Strauss (Schwiefka), John Conte (Drunky), Doró Merande (Vi), George E. Stone (Markette), George Mathews (Williams), Leonid Kinskey (Dominowski), Emile Meyer (Bednar), Shorty Rogers, Shelly Manne (Themselves).

JOHNNY CONCHO 1956

Kent Productions/United Artists 84 minutes
Producer: Frank Sinatra; associate producer: Henry Sanicola; director: Don McGuire; screenplay: David P. Harmon, Don McGuire (based on Harmon's story *The Man Who Owned the Town);* photography: William Mellor (black and white); music: Nelson Riddle; orchestrations: Arthur Morton.
Cast: Frank Sinatra (Johnny Concho), Keenan Wynn (Barney Clark), William Conrad (Tallman), Phyllis Kirk (Mary Dark), Wallace Ford (Albert Dark).

HIGH SOCIETY 1956

MGM 107 minutes
Producer: Sol C. Siegel; director: Charles Walters; screenplay: John Patrick (based on the play *The Philadelphia Story* by Philip Barry); photography: Paul C. Vogel (Technicolor/VistaVision); art direction: Cedric Gibbons, Hans Peters; editing: Ralph E. Winters; songs: Cole Porter; musical supervision: Johnny Green, Saul Chaplin; orchestrations: Conrad Salinger, Nelson Riddle; choreography: Charles Walters; sound: Wesley C. Miller; costumes: Helen Rose.
Cast: Bing Crosby (C.K. Dexter Haven), Grace Kelly (Tracy Lord), Frank Sinatra (Macauley 'Mike' Connor), Celeste Holm (Liz Imbrie), John Lund (George Kittredge), Louis Calhern (Uncle Willie), Sidney Blackmer (Seth Lord), Margalo Gillmore (Mrs Seth Lord), Lydia Reed (Carolyn Lord), Louis Armstrong and His Band (Themselves).

THE PRIDE AND THE PASSION 1957

Stanley Kramer Productions/United Artists 132 minutes
Producer: Stanley Kramer; director: Stanley Kramer; screenplay: Edward Anhalt, Edna Anhalt (based on the novel *The Gun* by C.S. Forester); photography: Franz Planer (Technicolor/VistaVision); production design: Rudolph Sternad; editing: Frederick Knudtson, Ellsworth Hoagland; music: George Antheil; costumes: Joe King; choreography: Paco Reynes; titles: Saul Bass.
Cast: Cary Grant (Captain Anthony Trumball), Frank Sinatra (Miguel), Sophia Loren (Juana), Theodore Bikel (General Jouvet), Jay Novello (Bellinger).

THE JOKER IS WILD 1957

AMBL Productions/Paramount 123/126 minutes
Executive producer: Charles Vidor; producer: Samuel J. Briskin; director: Charles Vidor; screenplay: Oscar Saul (based on the book by Art Cohn); photography: Daniel L. Fapp (black and white/VistaVision); music: Walter Scharf; orchestrations: Leo Shuken, Jack Hayes; song 'All the Way': music James Van Heusen, lyrics Sammy Cahn; song orchestrations: Nelson Riddle; speciality songs & parodies: Harry Harris; choreography: Josephine Earl.
Cast: Frank Sinatra (Joe E. Lewis), Mitzi Gaynor (Martha Stewart), Jeanne Crain (Letty Page), Eddie Albert (Austin Mack), Beverly Garland (Cassie Mack).

PAL JOEY 1957

Essex-Sidney/Columbia 109 minutes
Executive producer: George Sidney; producer: Fred Kohlmar; director: George Sidney; screenplay: Dorothy Kingsley (based on the musical book by John O'Hara); photography: Harold Lipstein (Technicolor); art direction: Walter Holscher; editing: Viola Lawrence, Jerome Thoms; songs: Richard Rodgers, Lorenz Hart; musical supervisor/conductor: Morris Stoloff; musical arranger: Nelson Riddle; orchestrations: Arthur Morton; choreography: Hermes Pan; costumes: Jean Louis; sound: Franklin Hansen.
Cast: Frank Sinatra (Joey Evans), Rita Hayworth (Vera Simpson [role sung by Jo Ann Greer]), Kim Novak (Linda English [role sung by Trudi Erwin]), Bobby Sherwood (Ned), Hank Henry (Mike Miggins).

KINGS GO FORTH 1958

Ross-Eton/United Artists 109 minutes
Producer: Frank Ross; director: Delmer Daves; screenplay: Merle Miller (based on the novel by Joe David Brown); photography: Daniel L. Fapp (black and white); art direction: Fernando Carrere; editing: William B. Murphy; music: Elmer Bernstein; sound recording: Francis J. Scheid; sound editing: Bert Schoenfeld.
Cast: Frank Sinatra (Lieutenant Sam Loggins), Tony Curtis (Sergeant Britt Harris), Natalie Wood (Monique Blair), Leora Dana (Mrs Blair), Karl Swenson (Colonel).

SOME CAME RUNNING 1958

MGM 136 minutes
Producer: Sol C. Siegel; director: Vincente Minnelli; screenplay: John Patrick, Arthur Sheekman (based on the novel by James Jones); photography: William H. Daniels (Metrocolor/Cinemascope); art direction: William A. Horning, Urie McCleary; editing: Adrienne Fazan; music: Elmer Bernstein; song 'To Love And Be Loved': music James Van Heusen, lyrics Sammy Cahn; sound: Franklin Milton; costumes: Walter Plunkett.
Cast: Frank Sinatra (David Hirsh), Dean Martin (Bama Dillert), Shirley MacLaine (Ginny Moorehead), Martha Hyer (Gwen French), Arthur Kennedy (Frank Hirsh), Nancy Gates (Edith Barclay), Leora Dana (Agnes Hirsh), Ned Weaver (Raymond), Larry Gates (Bob French), Betty Lou Keim (Dawn Hirsh).

A HOLE IN THE HEAD 1959

SinCap/United Artists 120 minutes
Producer: Frank Sinatra; director: Frank Capra; screenplay: Arnold Shulman and

Myles Connolly (uncredited) (based on the play by Arnold Shulman); photography: William H. Daniels (De Luxe/ Cinemascope); art direction: Eddie Imazu; editing: William Hornbeck; music: Nelson Riddle; songs: mus James Van Heusen, lyrics Sammy Cahn; sound: Fred Lau; costumes: Edith Head.
Cast: Frank Sinatra (Tony Manetta), Edward G. Robinson (Mario Manetta), Eleanor Parker (Eloise Rogers), Carolyn Jones (Shirl), Thelma Ritter (Sophie Manetta), Keenan Wynn (Jerry Marks), Eddie Hodges (Allie Manetta), Joi Lansing (Dorine), George DeWitt (Mendy), Jimmy Komack (Julius Manetta), Dub Taylor (Fred), Connie Sawyer (Miss Wexler), Benny Rubin (Mr Diamond), Ruby Dandridge (Sally), B.S. Pully (Hood).

NEVER SO FEW 1959
Canterbury/MGM 124 mins
Producer: Edmund Grainger; director: John Sturges; screenplay: Millard Kaufman (based on the novel by Tom T. Chamales); photography: William H. Daniels (Metrocolor/Cinemascope); art direction: Hans Peters, Addison Hehr; editing: Ferris Webster; music: Hugo Friedhofer; sound: Franklin Milton; assistant director: Robert Relyea.
Cast: Frank Sinatra (Captain Tom C. Reynolds), Gina Lollobrigida (Carla Vesari), Peter Lawford (Captain Grey Travis), Steve McQueen (Corporal Bill Ringa), Richard Johnson (Captain Danny De Mortimer), Paul Henreid (Nikko Regas), Brian Donlevy (General Sloan), Dean Jones (Sergeant Jim Norby), Charles Bronson (Sergeant John Danforth), Philip Ahn (Nautaung), Robert Bray (Colonel Fred Parkson), John Hoyt (Colonel Reed), Whit Bissell (Captain Olafson), Kipp Hamilton (Margaret Fitch).

CAN CAN 1960
Suffolk-Cummings/Twentieth Century-Fox 131 minutes
Producer: Jack Cummings; director: Walter Lang; screenplay: Dorothy Kingsley, Charles Lederer (based on the musical book by Abe Burrows); photography: William H. Daniels (De Luxe/Todd-AO); musical direction: Nelson Riddle; songs: Cole Porter; choreography: Hermes Pan.

Cast: Frank Sinatra (Francois Durnais), Shirley MacLaine (Simone Pistache), Maurice Chevalier (Judge), Louis Jourdan, Juliet Prowse, Marcel Dalio, Leon Belasco, Nestor Paiva.

OCEAN'S 11 1960
Dorchester/Warner 127 minutes
Producer: Lewis Milestone; director: Lewis Milestone; screenplay: Harry Brown, Charles Lederer (based on an original story by George Clayton Johnson and Jack Golden Russell); photography: William H. Daniels (Technicolor/Panavision); art direction: Nicolai Renisoff; editing: Philip W. Anderson; music: Nelson Riddle; songs: music James Van Heusen, lyrics Sammy Cahn; sound: M.A. Merrick; titles: Saul Bass.
Cast: Frank Sinatra (Danny Ocean), Dean Martin (Sam Harmon), Sammy Davis Jnr (Josh Howard), Peter Lawford (Jimmy Foster), Angie Dickinson (Bea Ocean), Richard Conte (Tony Bergdorf), Cesar Romero (Duke Santos), Patrice Wymore (Mrs Bergdorf), Joey Bishop ('Mushy' O'Connors), Akim Tamiroff (Spyros), Henry Silva (Roger Corneal), Red Norvo (himself), guest stars: Red Skelton, George Raft and Shirley MacLaine (uncredited).

THE DEVIL AT 4 O'CLOCK 1961
LeRoy/Kohlmar/Columbia 126 minutes
Executive producer: Mervyn LeRoy; producer: Fred Kohlmar; director: Mervyn LeRoy; screenplay: Liam O'Brien (based on the novel by Max Catto); photography: Joseph Biroc (Eastmancolor); art direction: John Beckman; editing: Charles Nelson; music: George Duning; sound: Josh Westmoreland; assistant directors: Carter De Haven Jnr, Floyd Joyer.
Cast: Spencer Tracy (Father Doonan), Frank Sinatra (Harry), Gregoire Aslan (Marcel), Bernie Hamilton (Charlie), Kerwin Mathews (Father Joseph Perreau), Jean-Pierre Aumont (Jacques), Barbara Luna (Camille), Marcel Dalio (Gaston), Alexander Scourby (Governor).

SERGEANTS 3 1961
Essex-Claude/United Artists 112 minutes
Executive producer: Howard W. Koch;

producer: Frank Sinatra; director: John Sturges; screenplay: W.R. Burnett; photography: Winton C. Hoch (Technicolor/Panavision); music: Billy May; second unit photography: Carl Guthrie.
Cast: Frank Sinatra (1st Sergeant Mike Merry), Dean Martin (Sergeant Chip Deal), Sammy Davis Jnr (Jonah Williams), Peter Lawford (Sergeant Larry Barrett), Joey Bishop (Sergeant Major Roger Boswell), Henry Silva (Mountain Hawk), Ruta Lee (Amelia Parent), Buddy Lester (Willie Sharpknife).

THE MANCHURIAN CANDIDATE 1962
MC/United Artists 126 minutes
Executive producer: Howard W. Koch; producers: John Frankenheimer, George Axelrod; director: John Frankenheimer; screenplay: George Axelrod (based on the novel by Richard Condon); photography: Lionel Lindon (black and white); art direction: Richard Sylbert; editing: Ferris Webster; music: David Amram; sound: Joe Edmondson; assistant director: Joseph Behm.
Cast: Frank Sinatra (Bennett Marco), Laurence Harvey (Raymond Shaw), Janet Leigh (Eugenie 'Rosie'), Angela Lansbury (Mrs Iselin), Henry Silva (Chunjin), James Gregory (Senator John Iselin), Leslie Parrish (Jocie Jordon), John McGiver (Senator Thomas Jordon), Khigh Dhiegh (Yen Lo), James Edwards (Corporal Melvin), Douglas Henderson (Colonel), Albert Paulsen (Zilkov), Barry Kelley (Secretary of Defence), Lloyd Corrigan (Holborn Gaines), Reggie Nalder (Dimitri), Whit Bissell (Officer).

COME BLOW YOUR HORN 1963
Essex-Tandem/Paramount 112 minutes
Executive producer: Howard W. Koch; producers: Bud Yorkin, Norman Lear; director: Bud Yorkin; screenplay: Norman Lear (based on the play by Neil Simon); photography: William H. Daniels (Technicolor/Panavision); art direction: Hal Pereira, Roland Anderson; editing: Frank F. Keller; music: Nelson Riddle; song 'Come Blow Your Horn': music James Van Heusen, lyrics Sammy Cahn; sound: John Carter, John Wilkinson; costumes: Edith Head.
Cast: Frank Sinatra (Alan Baker), Tony Bill (Buddy Baker), Lee J. Cobb (Harry

Baker), Molly Picon (Mrs Baker), Barbara Rush (Connie), Jill St John (Peggy Dawn), Dan Blocker (Eckman), Phyllis McGuire (Mrs Eckman).

4 FOR TEXAS 1963
SAM Company/Warner 124 minutes (premiere version)/115 minutes (standard version).
Executive producer: Howard W. Koch; producer: Robert Aldrich; associate producer: Walter Blake; director: Robert Aldrich; screenplay: Robert Aldrich, Teddi Sherman; photography: Ernest Laszlo, Joseph Biroc (uncredited) (Technicolor); art direction: William Glasgow; editing: Michael Luciano; music: Nelson Riddle; sound: Jack Solomon; second unit director: Oscar Rudolph; second unit photography: Joseph Biroc, Burnett Guffey, Carl Guthrie.
Cast: Frank Sinatra (Zachariah Thomas), Dean Martin (Joseph Jarrett), Anita Ekberg (Elya Carlson), Ursula Andress (Maxine Richter), Charles Bronson (Matson), Victor Buono (Harvey Burden), Edric Connor (Prince George), Nick Dennis (Angel), Richard Jaeckel (Mancini), Mike Mazurki (Chad), Wesley Addy (Trowbridge), Jack Elam (Dobie), Marjorie Bennett (Miss Emmaline), Jesslyn Fax (Widow), Allison Ames (Maid), The Three Stooges (themselves), Arthur Godfrey (himself, whoever he was).

ROBIN AND THE 7 HOODS 1964
PC/Warner 123 minutes
Executive producer: Howard W. Koch; producer: Frank Sinatra; associate producer: William H. Daniels; director: Gordon Douglas; screenplay: David Schwartz; photography: William H. Daniels (Technicolor/Panavision); art direction: LeRoy Deane; editing: Sam O'Steen; music: Nelson Riddle; songs: music James Van Heusen, lyrics Sammy Cahn; choreography: Jack Baker; sound: Everett Hughes, Vinton Vernon.
Cast: Frank Sinatra (Robbo), Dean Martin (Little John), Sammy Davis Jnr (Will), Peter Falk (Guy Gisborne), Barbara Rush (Marian), Victor Buono (Sheriff Potts), Bing Crosby (Allen A. Dale), Allen Jenkins (Vermin Witowsky), Hank Henry (Six Seconds), Phil Crosby (Hood), Edward G. Robinson (Big Jim, uncredited).

NONE BUT THE BRAVE 1965
Tokyo Eiga Co. Limited/Toho Film/Artanis/Warner 105 minutes
Executive producer: Howard W. Koch; producers: Frank Sinatra, Kikumaru Okuda; associate producer: William H. Daniels; director: Frank Sinatra; screenplay: John Twist, Katsuya Susaki (based on a story by Kikumaru Okuda); photography: Harold Lipstein (Technicolor/Panavision); art direction: LeRoy Deane; editing: Sam O'Steen; dialogue coaches: Thom Conroy, Satoshi Nakamura; music: John Williams; musical supervisor and conductor: Morris Stoloff; sound: Stanley Jones; assistant directors: David Salven, Mitsushige Tsurushima; technical advisor: Kazuo Inoue; interpreter: Masao Mera; special effects: Eiji Tsuburaya.
Cast: Frank Sinatra (Chief Pharmacist's Mate Francis Maloney), Clint Walker (Captain Dennis Bourke), Tommy Sands (Second Lieutenant Blair), Brad Dexter (Sergeant Bleeker), Tony Bill (Air Crewman Keller), Tatsuya Mihashi (Lieutenant Kuroki), Takeshi Kato (Sergeant Tamura), Sammy Jackson (Corporal Craddock), Christopher Dark (Private Searcy), Phil Crosby (Private Magee), Richard Bakalyan (Corporal Ruffino), Richard Sinatra (Private Roth).

VON RYAN'S EXPRESS 1965
Twentieth Century-Fox 117 minutes
Executive producer: Mark Robson; producer: Saul David; director: Mark Robson; screenplay: Wendell Mayes, Joseph Landon (based on the novel by David Westheimer); photography: William H. Daniels (De Luxe/Cinemascope); art direction: Jack Martin Smith, Hilyard Brown; editing: Dorothy Spencer; music: Jerry Goldsmith; orchestrations: Arthur Morton; sound: Carlton W. Faulkner, Elmer Raguse; second unit director: William Kaplan; second unit photography: Harold Lipstein.
Cast: Frank Sinatra (Colonel Joseph L. Ryan), Trevor Howard (Major Eric Fincham), Sergio Fantoni (Oriani), Raffaella Carra (Mariella), Brad Dexter (Sgt Bostick), John Leyton (Lieutenant Ord), Edward Mulhare (Captain Costanzo), Michael Goodliffe (Captain Stein), Wolfgang Preiss (Major Von Klementz), Adolfo Celi (Major Battaglia), James Brolin (Private Ames),

Richard Bakalyan (Giannini).

MARRIAGE ON THE ROCKS 1965
A-C/Sinatra Enterprises/Warner 109 minutes
Producer: William H. Daniels; director: Jack Donohue; screenplay: Cy Howard; photography: William H. Daniels (Technicolor/ Panavision); art direction: LeRoy Deane; editing: Sam O'Steen; dialogue supervision: Thom Conroy; music: Nelson Riddle; sound: Francis E. Stahl.
Cast: Frank Sinatra (Daniel Edwards), Deborah Kerr (Valerie Edwards), Dean Martin (Ernie Brewer), Cesar Romero (Miguel Santos), Hermione Baddeley (Jeannie MacPherson), Tony Bill (Jim Blake), John McGiver (Shad Nathan), Nancy Sinatra (Tracy Edwards), Davey Davison (Lisa), Joi Lansing (Lola), DeForest Kelley (Mr Turner), Michel Petit (David Edwards), Trini Lopez (himself).

ASSAULT ON A QUEEN 1966
Sinatra Enterprises/Seven Arts/Paramount 106 minutes
Producer: William Goetz; associate producer: William H. Daniels; director: Jack Donohue; screenplay: Rod Serling (based on the novel by Jack Finney); photography: William H. Daniels (Technicolor/Panavision); art direction: Paul Groesse; editing: Archie Marshek; dialogue coach: Thom Conroy; music: Duke Ellington; sound: Stanley Jones, Charles Grenzbach; second unit director: Robert D. Webb.
Cast: Frank Sinatra (Mark Brittain), Virna Lisi (Rosa Lucazi), Anthony Franciosa (Victor Rossiter), Richard Conte (Tony Moreno), Alf Kjellin (Erich Lauffnauer), Errol John (Langley Lincoln), Muir Matheson (Queen Mary Captain), Reginald Denny (Master-at-Arms), Val Avery (Trench).

THE NAKED RUNNER 1967
Sinatra Enterprises/Artanis/Warner 104 minutes
Executive producer: Frank Sinatra; producer: Brad Dexter; director: Sidney J. Furie; screenplay: Stanley Mann (based on the novel by Francis Clifford); photography: Otto Heller (Technicolor/Techniscope); art direction: Peter Proud; editing: Barrie Vince; music: Harry Sukman; sound: Maurice Askew,

Peter Greves.
Cast: Frank Sinatra (Sam Laker), Peter Vaughan (Martin Slattery), Derren Nesbitt (Colonel Hartmann), Nadia Gray (Karen Gesavius), Toby Robins (Patrick Laker), Edward Fox (Ritchie Jackson).

TONY ROME 1967

Arcola-Millfield/Twentieth Century-Fox 110 minutes
Producer: Aaron Rosenberg; director: Gordon Douglas; screenplay: Richard L. Breen (based on the novel *Miami Mayhem* by Marvin H. Albert); photography: Joseph Biroc (De Luxe/Panavision); art direction: Jack Martin Smith, James Roth; editing: Robert Simpson; music Billy May; title song: Lee Hazelwood, sung by Nancy Sinatra; sound: Howard Warren, David Dockendorf.
Cast: Frank Sinatra (Tony Rome), Jill St John (Ann Archer), Richard Conte (Lieutenant Dave Santini), Gena Rowlands (Rita Kosterman), Simon Oakland (Rudolph Kosterman), Jeffrey Lynn (Adam Boyd), Lloyd Bochner (Rood), Sue Lyon (Diana Kosterman Pines), Rocky Graziano (Packy), Shecky Greene (Catleg), Mike Romanoff (Motel clerk), Mickey Rudin (Pawnbroker), Tiffany Bolling (Waitress).

THE DETECTIVE 1968

Arcola-Millfield/Twentieth Century-Fox 114 minutes
Producer: Aaron Rosenberg; director: Gordon Douglas; screenplay: Abby Mann (based on the novel by Roderick Thorp); photography: Joseph Biroc (De Luxe/Panavision); art direction: Jack Martin Smith, William Creber; editing: Robert Simpson; music: Jerry Goldsmith; sound: Harry M. Lundgren, David Dockendorf.
Cast: Frank Sinatra (Sergeant Joe Leland), Lee Remick (Karen Leland),

Ralph Meeker (Curran), Jack Klugman (Dave Schoenstein), Lloyd Bochner (Dr Wendell Roberts), William Windom (Colin MacIver), Tony Musante (Felix Tesla), Al Freeman Jnr (Robbie Lockman), Horace MacMahon (Captain Tom Farrell), Robert Duvall (Nestor), Pat Henry (Mercidis), Jacqueline Bisset (Norma MacIver), Tom Atkins (Harmon), Sugar Ray Robinson (Kelly), Jilly Rizzo (bartender).

LADY IN CEMENT 1968

Arcola-Millfield/Twentieth Century-Fox 93 minutes
Producer: Aaron Rosenberg; associate producer: Mike Romanoff; director: Gordon Douglas; screenplay: Marvin H. Albert, Jack Guss and Richard L. Breen (uncredited) (based on the novel by Marvin H. Albert); photography: Joseph Biroc (De Luxe/Panavision); art direction: LeRoy Deane; editing: Robert Simpson; music: Hugo Montenegro; musical arranger: Billy May; sound: Howard Warren, David Dockendorf; underwater sequence staged by Ricou Browning.
Cast: Frank Sinatra (Tony Rome), Raquel Welch (Kit Forrest), Dan Blocker (Waldo Gronsky), Richard Conte (Lieutenant Dave Santini), Martin Gabel (Al Mungar), Lainie Kazan (Maria Baretto), Pat Henry (Rubin), Steve Peck (Paul Mungar), Frank Raiter (Danny Yale), B.S. Pully (strip club customer), Joe E. Lewis (massage parlour customer), Jilly Rizzo (man in gents).

DIRTY DINGUS MAGEE 1970

MGM 91 minutes
Producer: Burt Kennedy; associate producer: Richard E. Lyons; director: Burt Kennedy; screenplay: Tom Waldman, Frank Waldman, Joseph Heller (based on the novel *The Ballad of Dingus Magee* by David Markson); photography: Harry Stradling Jnr

(Metrocolor/Panavision); art direction: George W. Davis, J. McMillan Johnson; editing: William B. Gulick; music: Jeff Alexander; additional music: Billy Strange; title song: Mack David, sung by The Mike Curb Congregation; sound: Hal Watkins, Bruce Wright; costumes: Yvonne Wood; stunt co-ordinator: Jerry Gatlin
Cast: Frank Sinatra (Dingus Magee), George Kennedy (Hoke Birdsill), Ann Jackson (Belle Knops), Lois Nettleton (Prudence Frost), Jack Elam (John Wesley Hardin), Michele Carey (Anna Hotwater), Paul Fix (Chief Crazy Blanket), John Dehner (General George), Henry Jones (Preacher), Harry Carey Jnr. (Charles Stewart).

THE FIRST DEADLY SIN 1980

Artanis/Cinema Seven/First Deadly Sin Company/Filmways 112 minutes
Executive producers: Elliott Kastner, Frank Sinatra; producers: George Pappas, Mark Shanker; director: Brian G. Hutton; screenplay: Mann Rubin (based on the novel by Lawrence Sanders); photography: Jack Priestley (TVC color/Movielab); production design: Woody Mackintosh; editing: Eric Albertson; music: Gordon Jenkins; costumes: Gary Jones; Faye Dunaway's costumes: Theoni V. Aldridge; associate producer/unit production manager: Fred Caruso; sound: Ron Kalish, Sandy Tung, John Bolz, Peter Ilardi.
Cast: Frank Sinatra (Sergeant Edward X. Delaney), Faye Dunaway (Barbara Delaney), David Dukes (Daniel Blank), James Whitmore (Dr Sanford Ferguson), Brenda Vaccaro (Monica Gilbert), Martin Gabel (Christopher Langley), Anthony Zerbe (Captain Broughton), George Coe (Dr Bernardi), Joe Spinell (Charles Lipsky), Anna Navarro (Sonny Jordeen), Fred Fuster (delivery man), Jeffrey De Munn (Sergeant Corelli), Bruce Willis (uncredited extra).

Arnold, Edwin T. and Miller Jnr, Eugene L. *The Films and Career of Robert Aldrich*. University of Texas Press (Knoxville) 1986.

Ashman, Chuck & Trescott, Pamela. *Cary Grant. An intimate portrait of a Hollywood Legend*. Star/W.H. Allen (London) 1988.

Aumont, Jean-Pierre. *Sun and Shadow*. W.W. Norton & Company Inc (New York) 1977.

Baker, Carroll. *Baby Doll. An Autobiography*. W.H. Allen (London) 1984.

Base, Ron. *Starring Roles. How Movie Stardom in Hollywood Is Won and Lost*. Little, Brown and Company (London) 1994.

Berg, A. Scott. *Goldwyn*. Sphere Books (London) 1990.

Bergan, Ronald. *A master of reel-politic*. Gordon Douglas obituary. *The Guardian*. 23 October 1993. *The United Artists Story*. Octopus (London) 1986. *Wordsmith of film*: Dorothy Kingsley obituary. *The Guardian*. 9 October 1997.

Bergman, Ingrid and Burgess, Alan. *Ingrid Bergman My Story*. Sphere (London) 1981.

Bogart, Stephen with Provost, Gary. *Bogart. In Search of My Father*. Sidgwick & Jackson (London) 1995.

Bosworth, Patricia. *Montgomery Clift. A Biography*. Harcourt Brace Jovanovich (London) 1978.

Braun, Eric. *Deborah Kerr*. W.H. Allen (London) 1977. *Doris Day*. Orion (London) 1994.

Bret, David. *Maurice Chevalier. Up On Top of a Rainbow*. Robson Books (London) 1992.

Britt, Stan. *Frank Sinatra. A Celebration*. Hamlyn (London) 1995.

Brown, Peter Harry. *Kim Novak: Reluctant Goddess*. St Martin's Press (New York) 1986.

Bryce, Allan. *Pure Goldsmith. The Dark Side*. Issue 71. 1998.

Brynner, Rock. *Yul. The Man Who Would Be King*. Collins (London) 1989.

Cahn, Sammy. *I Should Care. The Sammy Cahn Story*. W.H. Allen (London) 1975.

Caine, Michael. *What's It All About?*

An Autobiography. Turtle Bay Books (New York) 1992.

Capra, Frank. *The Name Above the Title. An Autobiography*. Macmillan (New York) 1971.

Carey, Gary. *All the Stars in Heaven. The Story of Louis B. Mayer and M.G.M*. Robson Books (London) 1982. *Marlon Brando. The Only Contender*. Robson Books (London) 1985.

Casper, Joseph Andrew. *Stanley Donen*. Scarecrow Press (Metuchen, New Jersey) 1983.

Chandler, Charlotte. *Hello, I must be going. Groucho and his friends*. Abacus (London) 1995.

Chevalier, Maurice. *I Remember It Well* (trans Cornelia Higginson). W.H. Allen (London) 1971.

Clarke, Gerald. *Capote. A Biography*. Cardinal/Sphere Books (London) 1989.

Connor, Jim. *Ann Miller. Tops in Taps. An Authorized Pictorial History*. Franklin Watts (London) 1981.

Cross, Robin. *The Big Book of B Movies*. Muller (London) 1981.

Curtis, Tony and Paris, Barry. *The Autobiography*. Mandarin (London) 1995.

Daniell, John. *Ava Gardner*. W.H. Allen (London) 1982.

Davidson, Bill. *Spencer Tracy. Tragic Idol*. Sidgwick & Jackson (London) 1987.

Davis, Richard. *Dirty Dingus Magee* review. *Films and Filming*. February 1971. Volume 17 Number 5.

Davis Jnr, Sammy. *Hollywood in a Suitcase*. Granada (London) 1980.

Davis Jnr, Sammy with Boyar, Jane and Boyar, Burt. *Why Me?* Michael Joseph (London) 1989. *Yes I Can*. Cassell (London) 1965.

Day, Doris and Hotchner, A.E. *Doris Day. Her Own Story*. W.H. Allen (London) 1976.

Douglas-Home, Robin. *Sinatra*. Michael Joseph (London) 1962.

Downing, David. *Robert Mitchum*. W.H. Allen (London) 1985.

Dunaway, Faye with Sharkey, Betsy. *Looking for Gatsby. My Life*. HarperCollins (London) 1995.

Eames, John Douglas & Bergan, Ronald. *The M.G.M. Story*. Hamlyn (London) 1993.

Eells, George. *Robert Mitchum. A*

Biography. Robson Books (London) 1984.

Evans, Robert. *The Kid Stays in the Picture*. HarperCollins (London) 1995.

Farrow, Mia. *What Falls Away. A Memoir*. Doubleday (London) 1997.

Fisher, John. *Call Them Irreplaceable*. Elm Tree Books/Hamish Hamilton (London) 1976.

Fishgall, Gary. *Against Type. The Biography of Burt Lancaster*. Scribner/Simon & Schuster (New York) 1995.

Forbes, Bryan. *A Divided Life*. Heinemann (London) 1992.

Fordin, Hugh. *MGM's Greatest Musicals. The Arthur Freed Unit*. Da Capo Press (New York) 1996.

Fowler, Gene. *Schnozzola. The Story of Jimmy Durante*. Hammond, Hammond & Co Ltd (London) 1952.

Freedland, Michael. *Dino. The Dean Martin Story*. W.H. Allen (London) 1984. *Shirley MacLaine*. W.H. Allen (London) 1986.

Frischauer, Willi. *Behind the Scenes of Otto Preminger*. Michael Joseph (London) 1973.

Fuller, Graham. *An American in Paradise*. Gene Kelly interview. *Projections 4* (ed John Boorman, Tom Luddy, David Thomson & Walter Donohue). Faber and Faber (London) 1995.

Gansberg, Alan L. *Little Caesar. A Biography of Edward G. Robinson*. New English Library (London) 1983.

Gardner, Ava. *Ava. My Story*. Bantam Press (London) 1990.

Gehman, Richard. *Sinatra and his Rat Pack*. Mayflower (London) 1961.

Geist, Kenneth L. *Pictures Will Talk. The Life and Films of Joseph L. Mankiewicz*. Scribners (New York) 1978.

Grobel, Lawrence. *The Hustons*. Bloomsbury (London) 1990.

Haining, Peter. *Raquel Welch. Sex Symbol to Superstar*. W.H. Allen (London) 1984.

Harbinson, W.A. *Bronson! A biographical portrait*. W.H. Allen (London) 1976.

Harris, Warren G. *Natalie & R.J. Hollywood's Star-Crossed Lovers*. Sphere (London) 1988.

Hay, Peter. *Movie Anecdotes*. Oxford

University Press (Oxford) 1990.

Hecht, Ben. *A Child of the Century.* Simon and Schuster (New York) 1954.

Hickey, Des and Smith, Gus. *The Prince. The Public and Private Life of Laurence Harvey.* Leslie Frewin (London) 1975.

Higham, Charles. *Brando. The Unauthorized Biography.* Sidgwick & Jackson (London) 1987.

Higham, Charles & Moseley, Roy. *Cary Grant. The Lonely Heart.* New English Library (London) 1989.

Hirschhorn, Clive. *Gene Kelly. A Biography.* W.H. Allen (London) 1984.

Holden, Anthony. *The Oscars. The Secret History of Hollywood's Academy Awards.* Little, Brown and Company (London) 1993.

Hotchner, A.E. *Sophia. Living and Loving. Her Own Story.* Michael Joseph (London) 1979.

Howe, Rupert. *Pack Life. Neon.* August 1997.

Howlett, John. *Frank Sinatra.* Plexus (London) 1980.

Hunter, Allan. *Faye Dunaway.* W.H. Allen (London) 1986.

Hyer Wallis, Martha. *Finding My Way. A Hollywood Memoir.* HarperCollins (New York) 1990.

Jewell, Richard B. with Harbin, Vernon. *The RKO Story.* Octopus (London) 1982.

Kanin, Garson. *Tracy and Hepburn. An Intimate Memoir.* Angus & Robertson (London) 1972.

Karney, Robyn (ed). *Chronicle of the Cinema. 100 Years of the Movies.* Dorling Kindersley (London) 1995.

Katz, Ephraim. *The Macmillan International Film Encyclopedia* (New Edition). Pan Macmillan Ltd (London) 1994.

Kelley, Kitty. *His Way. The Unauthorized Biography of Frank Sinatra.* Bantam Press (London) 1986.

Knight, Vivienne. *Trevor Howard. A Gentleman and a Player. The Authorised Biography.* Sphere (London) 1988.

Kobal, John. *Rita Hayworth. The Time, the Place and the Woman.* W.H. Allen (London) 1977.

LaGuardia, Robert. *Montgomery Clift. A Biography.* W.H. Allen (London) 1977.

Lasky, Jesse L. with Weldon, Don. *I Blow My Own Horn.* Victor Gollancz Ltd (London) 1957.

Leaming, Barbara. *If this was Happiness. A Biography of Rita Hayworth.* Weidenfeld and Nicolson (London) 1989.

Leigh, Janet. *There Really Was a Hollywood.* John Curley & Associates, Inc (South Yarmouth, Massachusetts) 1984.

LeRoy, Mervyn as told to Kleiner, Dick. *Mervyn LeRoy: Take One.* W.H. Allen (London) 1974.

Levy, Emanuel. *George Cukor: Master of Elegance.* William Morrow and Company, Inc (New York) 1994.

MacLaine, Shirley. *Dance While You Can.* Bantam Books (London) 1991. *My Lucky Stars. A Hollywood Memoir.* Bantam (London) 1995.

Maltin, Leonard (ed). *Leonard Maltin's Movie and Video Guide.* Signet (London) 1985.

Manso, Peter. *Brando.* Weidenfeld and Nicolson (London) 1994.

Marill, Alvin H. *The Complete Films of Edward G. Robinson.* Citadel (New York) 1990.

Marx, Arthur. *Everybody Loves Somebody Sometime. The Story of Dean Martin and Jerry Lewis.* W.H. Allen (London) 1975.

Marx, Groucho. *The Groucho Letters.* Sphere (London) 1969.

McBride, Joseph. *Frank Capra. The Catastrophe of Success.* Faber and Faber (London) 1992.

McClelland, Doug. *Eleanor Parker: Woman of a Thousand Faces.* Scarecrow Press (Metuchen, New Jersey & London) 1989.

McCoy, Malachy. *Steve McQueen.* Robert Hale & Company (London) 1974.

Medved, Harry and Medved, Michael. *The Fifty Worst Movies of All Time.* Angus & Robertson (London) 1979. *The Golden Turkey Awards.* Angus & Robertson (London) 1980. *The Hollywood Hall of Shame.* Angus & Robertson (London) 1984.

Menjou, Adolphe. *It Took Nine Tailors.* Sampson Low, Marston & Co Ltd (London) 1950.

Miller, Ann with Browning, Norma Lee. *Miller's High Life.* Doubleday (New York) 1972.

Minnelli, Vincente with Arce, Hector. *I remember it well.* Angus and Robertson (London) 1975.

Mitchell, Glenn. *The Marx Brothers Encyclopedia.* Batsford (London) 1996.

Mitchum, John. *Them Ornery Mitchum Boys. The Adventures of Robert and John Mitchum.* Creatures at Large Press (Pacifica) 1989.

Montalban, Ricardo with Thomas, Bob. *Reflections. A Life in Two Worlds.* Doubleday (New York) 1980.

Mordden, Ethan. *Medium Cool. The Movies of the 1960s.* Alfred A. Knopf (New York) 1990.

Murphy, George with Lasky, Victor. *Say...Didn't You Used to be George Murphy?* Bartholomew House Ltd (US) 1970.

Nelson, Nancy. *Cary Grant.* Headline (London) 1992.

Nolan, William F. *McQueen.* Arthur Barker Limited (London) 1984.

Norman, Barry. *The Film Greats.* Hodder and Stoughton/BBC (London) 1985. *The Movie Greats.* Hodder and Stoughton/BBC (London) 1981. *Talking Pictures. The Story of Hollywood.* Arrow (London) 1991.

Parker, John. *Polanski.* Victor Gollancz (London) 1993.

Pasternak, Joe as told to Chandler, David. *Easy the Hard Way.* W.H. Allen (London) 1956.

Peary, Danny. *Guide for the Film Fanatic.* Fireside/Simon & Schuster (New York) 1986.

Phelps, Guy. *Film Censorship.* Victor Gollancz (London) 1975.

Polanski, Roman. *Roman by Polanski.* Heinemann (London) 1984.

Powell, Dilys. *The Golden Screen. Fifty Years of Films* (ed George Perry). Headline (London) 1990.

Pratley, Gerald. *The Cinema of John Frankenheimer.* A.S. Barnes (New York) 1969.

Preminger, Otto. *Preminger. An Autobiography.* Doubleday (New York) 1977.

Quinlan, David. *The Illustrated Guide to Film Directors.* Batsford (London) 1983.

Reynolds, Debbie & Columbia, David Patrick. *Debbie. My Life.* Sidgwick & Jackson (London) 1989.

Riva, Maria. *Marlene Dietrich. By Her Daughter.* Bloomsbury (London) 1992.

Robinson, Edward G. with Spigelgass, Leonard. *All My Yesterdays.* W.H. Allen (London) 1974.

Robinson, Jeffrey. *Bardot. Two Lives.* Simon & Schuster (London) 1994.

Rockwell, John. *Sinatra. An American*

Classic. Elm Tree Books (London) 1984.

Romney, Jonathan. *Framespotting: Beyond Contempt: the tale of Bardot's bum*. The Guardian. 12 September 1996.

Rosen, Marjorie. *Popcorn Venus. Women, Movies & The American Dream*. Peter Owen (London) 1975.

Rubin, Sam and Taylor, Richard. *Mia Farrow*. Robson Books (London) 1990.

Russell, Jane. *An Autobiography*. Sidgwick & Jackson (London) 1986.

Ryan, Paul. *Marlon Brando. A Portrait*. Plexus (London) 1991.

Sanders, Lawrence. *The First Deadly Sin*. New English Library (London) 1987.

Scherle, Victor and Turner Levy, William. *The Complete Films of Frank Capra*. Citadel (New York) 1992.

Seaton Lawford, Patricia with Schwarz, Ted. *Peter Lawford. Hollywood, The Kennedys, The Rat Pack and The Whole Damn Thing*. Sidgwick & Jackson (London) 1988.

Shaw, Arnold. *Sinatra. Retreat of the Romantic. A Biography*. W.H. Allen (London) 1968.

Shepherd, Don and Slatzer, Robert F. *Bing Crosby. The Hollow Man*. W.H. Allen (London) 1981.

Shipman, David. *The Great Movie Stars. 2: The International Years*. Macdonald (London) 1989.
    Marlon Brando. Sphere (London) 1989.
    The Story of Cinema. Volume Two. Hodder and Stoughton (London) 1984.

Sinatra, Nancy. *Frank Sinatra. An American Legend*. Virgin (London) 1995.
    Frank Sinatra, My Father. Hodder and Stoughton (London) 1985.

Sinclair, Andrew. Spiegel. *The Man Behind the Pictures*. Weidenfeld & Nicolson (London) 1987.

Spada, James. *Grace. The Secret Lives of a Princess*. Sidgwick & Jackson (London) 1987.
    Peter Lawford. The Man Who Kept the Secrets. Bantam Press (London) 1991.
    Streisand. The Intimate Biography. Little, Brown and Company (London) 1995.

Spiegel, Penina. *Steve McQueen. The Story of a Bad Boy in Hollywood*. Fontana/Collins (Glasgow) 1987.

Spoto, Donald. *Dietrich*. Bantam Press (London) 1992.
    Marilyn Monroe: The Biography. Chatto & Windus (London) 1993.
    Stanley Kramer Film Maker. Samuel French (Hollywood) 1990.

Summers, Anthony. Goddess. *The Secret Lives of Marilyn Monroe*. Warner Books (London) 1992.

Sweeting, Adam. *The daddy of all legends*. The Guardian. 13 November 1995.

Swindell, Larry. *Spencer Tracy. A Biography*. W.H. Allen (London) 1970.

Taylor, Theodore. *Jule. The Story of Composer Jule Styne*. Random House (New York) 1979.

Terrill, Marshall. *Steve McQueen. Portrait of an American Rebel*. Plexus (London) 1995.

Thomas, Bob. *King Cohn. The Life and Times of Harry Cohn*. Barrie and Rockliff (London) 1967.

Thomas, Tony and Solomon, Aubrey. *The Films of Twentieth Century Fox. A Pictorial History*. Citadel Press (New Jersey) 1980.

Thompson, Charles. *Bing. The authorized biography*. W.H. Allen (London) 1975.

Thompson, Douglas. *Dudley Moore. On the couch*. Little, Brown and Company (London) 1996.

Tosches, Nick. *Dino. Living High in the Dirty Business of Dreams*. Secker & Warberg (London) 1992.

Vermilye, Jerry. *The Films of Charles Bronson*. Citadel Press (Secaucus, New Jersey) 1980.

Viertel, Peter. *Dangerous Friends. Hemingway, Huston and others*. Viking (London) 1992.

Vonnegut, Kurt. *Slaughterhouse 5*. Triad Granada (London) 1979.

Vosburgh, Dick. Gordon Douglas obituary. *The Independent*. 6 October 1993.

Walker, Alexander. *Elizabeth*. Weidenfeld & Nicolson (London) 1990.

Walker, John (ed). *Halliwell's Film Guide* (9th edition). HarperCollins (London) 1993.
    Halliwell's Filmgoer's Companion (10th edition). HarperCollins (London) 1993.

Wayne, Jane Ellen. *The Life and Loves of Grace Kelly*. Robson Books (London) 1991.

Wayne, Pilar with Thorleifson, Alex. *John Wayne. My Life with the Duke*. New English Library (London) 1988.

Wilson, Earl. *Sinatra*. W.H. Allen (London) 1976.

Windeler, Robert. *Burt Lancaster*. W.H. Allen (London) 1984.

Winters, Shelley. *Shelley. Also Known As Shirley*. Granada (London) 1981.

Zec, Donald. *Sophia*. George Prior Publishers (London) 1976.

Zinnemann, Fred. *An Autobiography*. Bloomsbury (London) 1992.

TITLES
(film unless otherwise stated)